A

First and foremost, all thanks and praise to the most high, God Almighty, for blessing me with the heart of a storyteller and for giving me vision and a purpose to write this novel.

To my children, JaCari Tatterian and Ashton Isaiah, there will never be enough words in the dictionary to explain the depths of my love for you two. I love you both with every single beat of my heart and every single breath that I take. Everything that I do is directly motivated by my desire to be the best mother and role model that I can be for you. I love you so much!

For the people who have always been there for me, who have cheered me on through so many endeavors, who have given me unconditional love and support throughout my various journeys in life…thank you so much from the bottom of my heart. Robin, Candi, Taleece, Jamelle, Latasha, David aka Trick, Tye, Anthony aka Soundz, O.C., Candice, Candis, Griff, Vic, and my sister Lashonda.

To the family and friends that I wasn't able to mention know that I love you all and appreciate you as well. Don't charge it to my heart!

Special shout out to not only my mother Darlene for being an awesome grandma to my children, but also to my mother-in-law Wilma Jean and the rest of my in-laws for not only always stepping up to the plate and being there for my daughter, but for always stepping up and treating my son as he was your family as well when the parental side of his family chose to abandon him. Y'all are definitely the real MVP's!

To one of the inspirations for this novel, Trebion: You will always be my person.

Last although certainly not least, I would like to dedicate reaching this goal to my grandmother Bettye J. Wesley and my husband LaQuinpas A. Austin…I love you both and I hope I make you proud!

Rest in peace!

<u>*Preface*</u>

Alicia Dawson stood in her downstairs half bathroom, hands gripping the sides of the sink and staring at her reflection in the mirror. A million thoughts ran through her head as she waited patiently for an answer that will either ease her mind or send her into a frenzy. A part of her was scared to know, yet another part of her just had to know. She closed her eyes and took a deep breath. *May as well just do it and get it over with.* She thought to herself. She pulled down her pajama pants and grabbed the Styrofoam cup from the sink then squatted over the toilet and begin to urinate into the cup. Once the cup was half full she placed it carefully on the paper towels on top of the sink then finished urinating in the toilet. After wiping, washing her hands, and fixing her pajamas she removed the pregnancy test from box then dipped the test end into the cup with her urine and held it there for 10 seconds as the box directed. Once the ten seconds were up, she immediately replaced the cap and laid the test on the paper towels. She flushed the urine down the toilet, threw away the cup, and washed her hands again. Then she closed the lid on the toilet, sat down, and waited. Nervousness trembled through her body as she waited for what seemed like an hour but only one minute had passed. Her mind started to think back to everything that had gone on in her life over the past 7 months, and she began to reminisce about the first time she laid eyes on her boyfriend Cameron.

Chapter 1

It was a cold and wet December morning in Killeen, Texas and Alicia waited anxiously for the commentator to announce that the buses carrying the Army soldiers returning from the year-long deployment in Iraq were about to arrive. She was so nervous yet excited because today would be the first time she would meet her online friend in person. Alicia met Cameron Thompson through a mutual friend, who was the boyfriend of one of her friends, in the middle of November while he was on his first deployment. From the first conversation they immediately hit off, finding that they had much in common including both having birthdays on the same day. Alicia was born on February 15, 1984 and Cameron on February 15, 1983. They had similar taste in television, movies, music, and even somewhat similar personality. Both were playful and silly and loved to laugh and both were homebodies. Cameron, a Specialist in the Army, had so far seemed like the perfect complement to her, a home health attendant/nurse aide. She didn't want to like him too much before actually spending time with him, but she had a feeling that he was going to be a good guy for her. They had a one-time situation the previous week stemming from a phone call from his soon to be ex-wife. Cameron had initially told Alicia that he was already divorced, fearing that if she knew he was still married she wouldn't want to be involved with him. He was right, she wasn't about breaking up marriages; besides she figured if he cheats with you he will cheat on you. She received a phone call from his soon to be ex-wife, Danielle Cousins, claiming that he was a liar and cheater and that they were still married and very much together. Alicia immediately confronted Cameron about what Danielle had told her. At first he tried to deny it but then he decided to tell the truth. That he was in fact still legally married to her but that he had filed for divorce in August, before Alicia had ever even known he existed. Alicia was skeptical about that. If he had filed for divorce then why not just tell her that instead of lying about it. He'd told her that he had started to like her a lot and that he really believed she wouldn't talk to him anymore if she knew he was still legally married. At first she didn't know whether to believe him but Danielle kept calling her and texting her, and every time she talked to her lies came to light a little more. She claimed he told her he was filing for divorce but that she had never received the papers so she thought he changed his mind like he always did. Cameron asked Alicia to be at his the homecoming ceremony when he returned from deployment to prove to her that he and Danielle were really over. His parents were going to be there and he wouldn't allow Danielle to come. Danielle didn't realize it but all the while she was trying to convince Alicia that Cameron was no good and that they were still together, all she really did was further push Alicia to believe what Cameron said to be true. The last conversation she had with Danielle turned out be the straw that broke the camel's back.

"Well I'm not saying that you are lying, but if you guys are still together and not getting a divorce then why do you live in North Carolina. And why are you not coming to be with your husband when he arrives from Iraq?" Alicia asked Danielle.

Danielle's voice dripped with annoyance as she responded, "I came to North Carolina right before he left for Iraq because we were having problems. But we have been doing good since he has been there. We even spent the whole two weeks together when he came home for his r and r back in April."

"Okay, so why are you not coming to his ceremony if y'all have been doing so good?"

"Because he told me not to come. I want to come. Me and our daughter were going to come but he said no."

"That makes no sense. That doesn't even sound right. Again, obviously he has told me a lie by saying that y'all were already divorced, but it seems odd to me that you wouldn't come to your husband's welcome home from Iraq ceremony especially if y'all are still very much together and doing so well." Alicia responded.

Danielle began yelling, "Look, I really don't care what you think.

We are still married and you dumb for trying to be with a married man. And you aint even the only person that he been talking to since he been over there anyway. And if he filed divorce papers as he say he did then where are they at? You must not know about the military because you can't even file for a divorce while you are in Iraq. I used to be in the army boo. But it's all good cause I'm calling his company commander and watch how much trouble I get him into when I tell them he is cheating."

Alicia was a little upset now. She didn't like how she was being spoken to when she never once raised her voice and had been very respectful. But now she had to speak up. "Look Danielle, first of all I don't appreciate your tone of voice, I didn't disrespect you so you were way out of line. Secondly, I was born into the Army life and you must not know about the military sweetie because you can indeed file for a divorce while you're in Iraq, as a matter of fact, you can actually get the divorce while there. I know this because my sister got a divorce while she was deployed." Since Danielle didn't respond, she kept talking.

"You say I'm dumb for talking to him because he was talking to other females while he was there but remember I just started talking to him a month ago so whoever he talked to before me has nothing to do with me. Also if you know he was talking to other females, and he wants me to be at his welcome ceremony and not you, wouldn't that make you the dumb one? You dug yourself into the ground because I was believing what you were saying until you started showing your true colors. If you hadn't kept calling and bothering me, you wouldn't have kept talking and the truth wouldn't have slipped your mouth. So please don't call me anymore and you have a great day."

Alicia hung up the phone and immediately after she received a text from Danielle calling her all kinds of curses and threatening her. After talking to her older sister Ralonda and another friend, Alicia decided she would still talk to Cameron and come to his ceremony but keep an eye for him, just in case. Yes Danielle was clearly lying about a lot things, including being in the army (she was only in the army for 3 weeks; she didn't even make it half way through basic training) and obviously if she would go through all that trouble to keep him then he must be something worth keeping...Right? The thoughts of that didn't last long because before Alicia knew it the buses with the soldiers were pulling up. *This is it.* She thought to herself, then went to the field to wait for them to exit the bus.

Chapter 2

Alicia lay cuddled up with Cameron in her bed watching Wanted, a DVD starring Angelina Jolie. It was Saturday night and they had just come from the home of his friend and music buddy Michael Fowler. Alicia had hoped that she would get to meet his wife Benita, but she wasn't home when she got there. Cameron had only been back in Killeen for 3 days but he and Alicia had been spending as much time together as possible. When he got back on Thursday he met her at the ceremony and introduced her to his parents. After the ceremony, he and his parents spent the day together shopping and getting settled while Alicia went to work. Later that evening he came over to Alicia's house and they just relaxed at her house talking, laughing, and getting to know each other face to face. She was surprised at how relaxed and comfortable they were with each other. On Friday they talked on the phone and texted throughout the day but weren't able to get together. Alicia had some business to take care of in Dallas after she got off work and by the time she made it back it was pretty late and she had to be to work in the morning, it was her weekend to see clients. He made sure that he called before she went to bed though.

"Hey beautiful, how did your day end?" Cameron said into the phone as soon as Alicia answered.

She smiled then answered, "Well since I'm talking to you it's going to end on a good note."

"I like that answer." he said with a laugh. "I wish we could've spend some time together today. My parents are leaving to go back home to Georgia first thing in the morning, so right now we are just hanging at out the hotel talking."

"Aww well tell them I hope they have a safe trip. I have to work tomorrow. A couple of hours in the morning and then go back in for a couple more hours in the evening." she said to him.

There was a quick silence before he spoke, "does that mean I won't get to see you again tomorrow?"

"Well we can get together after my first shift, then again after my second."

They finalized the plans and said goodnight.

When Saturday arrived Alicia was up bright and early. After brushing her teeth, showering quickly, and pulling her loosely curled shoulder length hair into a ponytail she threw on her royal blue scrubs and white Nike Air Force Ones'. Since she never really ate a big breakfast before work she grabbed a strawberry pop tart and a bottle of water and headed out of the door. After locking up her two bedroom townhouse apartment on Kylie Circle off of Fort Hood Street, she hopped into her black Nissan Altima and headed to Copperas Cove. Once she got to her client's home she let herself in and got to work. First she went into the bedroom to wake Ms. Mary up. This woman reminded her of her great grandmother. She had this deep red caramel complexion, big sad looking eyes, and she wore glasses. She was dealing with Alzheimer's disease and could no longer care for herself. Some days she was a sweet as sugar, and some days she was so defiant and stubborn. Nonetheless, Alicia enjoyed working with her and could even count on a laugh or two. After waking Ms. Mary, she went into the kitchen to get her medicine. Since Ms. Mary couldn't swallow her pills, Alicia would crush them up and put them into her oatmeal. After feeding, she would bathe her, dress her, comb her hair then help her with rang of motion exercises. Once she'd gotten her situated in her favorite recliner in the living room she would make and even bigger breakfast of pancakes and eggs in which Ms. Mary would feed herself while Alicia made her bed, cleaned up her kitchen, vacuum the floor, and take out the trash.

After she had finished with Ms. Mary, Alicia did her timesheet and headed home. She called Cameron to let him know that was going home to shower and change and that she would be at his barrack's room to pick him in about an hour since he didn't have a car yet. After showering Alicia dressed in a pair of black skinny jeans, a purple turtleneck, and black knee boots with a fur trim. She wore her hair down and flowing in the back and the top half pulled back with a clip. She applied lip gloss and finished her ensemble by adding a pair of black dangle earrings and a black breast length necklace. Once she was finished she stood in her bathroom admiring herself. Alicia was not a gorgeous woman but she was indeed very cute. She had a cocoa brown complexion, big brown almond shaped eyes, full lips, and a small gap in between her two front teeth which gave her a perfectly imperfect smile that could melt anyone's heart. Or at least thats what she'd heard on a few occasions. She had a full figure and curves in all the right places and was what black men considered thick. Satisfied with her appearance she grabbed her purse and keys and took off to Fort Hood to pick up Cameron from his barracks.

She called when she was pulling into the parking lot and he came bounding down the stairs. He wore a red button up long sleeve shirt, with black jeans, and black boots. His fresh line up and haircut looked good against his dark brown skin. He had dark brown eyes set underneath long, thick, and beautiful eyelashes. He had a beautiful, big, bright smile and such a youthful look. Though he was 26 years old he didn't look a day over 18. Though he was about 5'11 and only weighed about 150 pounds, he was still very attractive to Alicia. He hopped into her car and gave her a hug and peck on the cheek.

"You look really nice." he said after looking her over. "You're beautiful."

Alicia blushed. "Thank you. You're looking good too."

They had went everywhere that day. To the mall, Guitar Center, Ross Department store, and even Walmart! Alicia loved the way Cameron held her hand as they shopped and the way he looked into her eyes while they chatted about everything and nothing. It felt as if they had been together for years. So easy flowing and natural. After grabbing a quick bite to eat they headed back to his barracks to drop him off before she headed back home to change for her second shift at work. Michael had met them in the parking lot so that Cameron could ride with him back to his house so that they could work on some music. Cameron and Alicia agreed that she would come over to Michael's once she got off and that they would spend the rest of the night together. After gathering his things out of her car and putting them into Michael's, Cameron pulled Alicia to him to hug her. He wrapped his arms around her waist as her arms went around his neck and they enjoyed a long, warm embrace. When they pulled back he smiled at her while looking into her eyes. "Can I have a kiss?" he asked.

She smiled and leaned in for a sweet, simple smooch on the lips.

They said goodbye and headed their separate ways. After Alicia finished her second shift she went home, showered and changed into black tights with a red t-shirt and black flip-flops. This is what she called her relaxed, in home clothes. Once she got to Michael's house she officially met Michael and another music buddy name Polk. They were just finishing up the editing on a song which they let her hear. Alicia was shocked at how professional sounding it was. They really had talent. She sat next to Cameron as they played some more songs for her. He held and caressed her hand while she laid her head on his shoulder. He placed sweet little kisses on her cheeks and forehead. Alicia felt like she was on cloud nine. And now here they were laying in her bed cuddled up watching a movie. All she knew at that moment was that if she had not been on her monthly cycle she would have definitely wanted to make love to him. Everything felt perfect at that very moment as she drifted off to sleep wrapped in his arms.

Chapter 3

The weekend had passed and Alicia was still floating on cloud nine even though she hated Mondays. All day at work she kept daydreaming about her weekend with Cameron. They vibed together so well and even though it had literally only been a weekend it felt as if they had been together forever. She had never been so comfortable around a man so fast or felt such an instant connection. She couldn't wait until later to arrive because she had yet another date with Cameron tonight. They were going to dinner and she was more than excited to be spending more time with him.

After working until three, Alicia had headed home, cleaned up her place a little bit then laid down for a quick nap. She was awakened by the ringing of her cell phone. She struggled to sit up and reached for her phone.

"Hello?" she said groggily into the phone without even looking at the caller id display.

The other end was silent. She waited a moment before speaking again. "Hellooo?" she asked again. This time she heard heavy breathing followed by low, calm voice that simply said, "Dumb witch." then the caller hung up. Alicia was taken aback. She looked at the call log and saw that it was from a private caller. She knew that it was Danielle playing on her phone again. *I wish she would grow up.* Alicia thought to herself as she glanced at the clock on her nightstand. She hadn't realized that she had been asleep for so long. She was supposed to pick Cameron up at 7and it was already 6:15. She rushed out of bed and into her closet to find something casual yet cute to put on as she called Cameron.

"Hello?"

She smiled at the sound of his voice. "Hey Cam. What are you up to?"

"What's up babe? I just got out of the shower, getting dressed." he said.

"Okay. Well I slept a little longer than I meant to so I'll be there at about 7:30 instead of 7. Okay?" she said and waited for his response.

"Okay that's cool. I'll be ready when you get here." he responded.

After hanging up she took a quick shower and dressed in a pair of indigo skinny jeans with a magenta short sleeved fitted tee. She wore her hair down and flowing around her face with loose curls and brown wooden dangle earrings with two matching bracelets on her right arm. After applying a coat of lip gloss she headed to her closet once again for shoes. It had been a pretty warm day even though it was the middle of December so she opted for a pair of brown thong sandals. After giving herself a once over in the mirror, she was satisfied and headed out the door.

It was five minutes to 8 when she pulled into the parking lot of Cameron's barracks. She had texted him when she left her townhouse to let him know she was on her way. Once he was in the car he gave her a kiss and the headed down highway 190 to her favorite restaurant Cheddar's Casual Cafe.

"So how was your day babe?" Cameron asked looking at Alicia as she turned down the radio.

"It was a typical Monday. For some reason I never like Mondays." she said as giggled. "What about your day?" she asked while giving him a smile.

"Well it was alright for the most part. You know since we just got back we don't really do nothing at work. We go in just to be accounted for then we leave."

"Yeah I know, must be nice." she teased.

"It is but it won't last long." he said with a smile. "I missed you today though. Hate it when I can't be around you. Wish I would've been able to see you earlier today. Man people just be pushing my buttons and I know just being around you would've made me feel so much better."

Alicia glanced at him. "What happened?"

"Man, Danielle had some dude calling me talking some BS." he said.

"Really? Well what did he say?" Alicia asked with concern.

Cameron placed a hand on hers. "Just talking stupid. Kept calling me talking bout 'Yea Danielle got some good stuff between her legs, I know you miss it.' Just dumb stuff. He said I must be real dumb for letting her go."

Alicia sat quietly listening to him, nodding her head as he talked.

"I told that fool that I'm the one who filed for divorce and that she still want to be with me but I don't want her. I'm not even thinking about that girl. I told him that my girlfriend I got now is badder than Danielle and any female he could ever get." he looked at her again, "And I mean that too. You are like the whole package. You're beautiful, sexy, and smart. You are a very good person and very sweet. I don't know how I ended up with someone like Danielle." he finished. Alicia smiled at the compliments he had given her. "Well. I just say don't let all that bother you. Be the bigger person. You don't need to go back and forth with them." she said supportively.

He smiled and relaxed just as they pulled into the parking lot of the restaurant. As she reached to open her door to get out of the car her phone rang. Seeing the name on the display she debated on if she should answer or not. It was a guy that had been pursuing her for months but she had been dodging him and his calls simply because she didn't want to hurt his feelings but he clearly wasn't getting the hint. She looked up and noticed that Cameron was waiting for her, she didn't want to look like she was being suspect so she answered the phone.

"Hello?"

"Alicia? Hey it's Pierre." the Haitian accent spoke through the phone. "Girl I thought you said you would call me when you got back from Dallas on Friday."

Alicia didn't want to be mean but she didn't want to lead him on either. After she began talking to Cameron she had basically decided that she wouldn't keep dating any of the guys that she'd been talking to before she met him. She felt in her gut that they were going to be so great together so she didn't want to be playing the field. Besides, she wasn't the type to have a man and others on the side, it just wasn't in her to be a player. She cut off all romantic relationships but remained friends with a couple. Alicia decided to just be honest with Pierre without being rude.

"Sorry about that. It was late when I got back and I was really tired." she said as she walked up to the entrance hand in hand with Cameron.

"Okay Alicia, tell me something. Am I wasting my time with you?" he asked sounding a little upset.

"Honestly, yes you are." she stated. After a long silence she heard the signal that her call had ended. He hung up on her. *Well that was rude but at least he won't keep bugging me.* She thought to herself as the hostess informed them that it would be at least a 45 minute wait to be seated. They were both starving so Alicia suggested that they go to her next favorite place hoping that it wouldn't be a long wait there too. Ten minutes later they were walking into Plucker's Wing Bar. Cameron had never been here before so he was excited to see how it was. They got a table and after placing their drink orders they looked over the menu.

"Well I already know what I'm going to get." Alicia said. "I get the same thing every time."

She helped Cameron decide on his meal just as the waitress came out with his sweet tea, her lemonade, and an order of chips and queso.

"This place has the best lemonade in the world. I love it."

Alicia ordered the 10 wing meal with medium hot wing sauce and a side order of mac and cheese while Cameron ordered the same only with barbecue sauce instead of medium wing sauce, he didn't like spicy food. They talked and held hands and laughed and kissed a few times while they ate the appetizer and waited for the meals to arrive. Alicia loved how affectionate he always was with her and the fact he seemed to love having her on his arm. After eating and talking for a few more minutes they headed back to Alicia's place. It was almost 10 and Alicia had to work in the morning but she didn't want to just go to sleep so they decided to watch a movie as they cuddled up in bed. Alicia was a little sleepy but she was determined to stay up and at least finish the movie. She dozed off a couple of times but forced herself awake when had to go to the bathroom.

When she came back into the bedroom she looked at Cameron

laying in her bed, looking so comfy and so at home. It was almost as if that's where he belonged. She climbed back in bed beside him and snuggled up to him with her head on his chest. He wrapped his arms around her and kissed her forehead. Then her cheek. She lifted her head to look into eyes. He kissed her softly on her lips. That one soft, sweet kiss turned into a slew of kisses then into a deep passionate, soul stirring kiss. Before long their hands were exploring each other's body and removing clothes. Cameron sat up on his knees in front of Alicia and removed her shirt and bra. He made a trail of kisses from her neck, down her chest, and to her belly. She took off his shirt and pulled him back down to her for another kiss. Soon her panties and his boxers were laying at the foot of her bed and she was spreading her legs as he slipped himself inside of her. He moaned as he pushed deeper inside her warmth while she pushed her hips back at him. They rocked in harmony, each enjoying the moment of being tangled in the other's arms. Cameron began to move faster. One hand gripped Alicia's thigh while the other held onto the bed for dear life. And in a matter of minutes he exploded inside of her, releasing all of his juices. He lay on top of her, breathing hard and sweating. Alicia just lay there waiting for him to catch his breath. *Okay, not what I expected.* She thought to herself. *Maybe he was just nervous. After all, it's been a while since he's had sex. I'm sure next time will be better.* After he finally rolled off of her she got up and headed to the bathroom. Once she finished peeing, she washed her hands then grabbed a washcloth from the closet and soaked it with warm water and soap. She washed herself up then soaked the towel again. Cameron jerked and sat up alarmed when he felt the warm towel on his manhood. Once he realized it was Alicia cleaning him, he relaxed. They lay back in bed with Alicia's head on his chest and his arms wrapped around her. He kissed her forehead and before long sleep came for both of them.

Chapter 4

Alicia and Cameron were both laying on the couch watching TV. It was a rare Monday that they both were off due to a holiday. It had been only a month since they had first laid eyes on each other but it sure felt like an eternity and Alicia was already falling in love. The lovebirds were not only living together now, but they spent majority of their free time together and it seemed as though they were a match made in heaven. Cameron always made sure that she knew how much he liked being with her. He always told her how beautiful she was, they went out on plenty of dates, he showered her with lots of affection, and whenever they were away from each other they constantly sent text messages back and forth. They had become so close so that not only did they share everything and talk to each other about everything, but Alicia had even gotten on a song with him once when they were at home playing around. After he had come back from his leave they went to Shreveport, La for an overnight trip to visit her mom and see her little brother for his birthday. He had just come back from a 10 day leave in Georgia only 3 days ago and she couldn't believe how much she had missed him. Even though they saw each other every day on Skype and talked on the phone constantly, it still didn't compare to him being there in person. They had hoped that his divorce would be finalized while he was there but when they went to court Danielle had told the judge that she didn't receive the paperwork. The judge granted her time to get prepared and moved the divorce proceedings back to May. Cameron was so crushed that as soon as he left the courtroom he called Alicia and told her the news. She could hear him sniffling and felt bad that she wasn't able to be there to comfort him. He wanted the divorce so badly but now he had to wait another four months. Also, with him being in the army they had to keep the fact that they were a couple from reaching his company commander or he would be in huge trouble since he was still legally married.

So here they were on this cool January morning living as if it were only the two of them in the world. Alicia decided to make a quick breakfast this morning so that she could relax and get back to watching a marathon of The Game on BET. It was their favorite show. She scrambled up some eggs and smoked sausage then put them on top of toast with grape jelly. She added cheese then put the other piece of toast on top. She put one sandwich on a plate for her and one on a plate for Cameron. After pouring two glasses of orange juice and grabbing napkins she balanced the breakfast on a serving tray and headed back to the living room where she and Cameron were watching TV. Cameron told her thank you and immediately began scarfing down the food. Alicia laughed to herself, she had gotten used to the barbaric way that he ate. The phone rang and the TV displayed that it was Georgia number calling, thinking that it was a telemarketer or wrong number they didn't answer. A few minutes later the same number called again. They let it ring again. Alicia went upstairs to get a pair of socks to put on and as she was headed back out her cell phone began to ring. By the time she made it back to it she had missed the call. When she looked at the caller id she was surprised to see that her friend Jay had called 4 times. Then she realized that the number that had been calling the house phone was him also. *What is going on?* She thought to herself. Jay had never called back to back like this before. They used to talk for a quick minute but their relationship never went past that friend stage. There just wasn't any chemistry between them but they did remain friends. Just then she got a text message.

Hey. Call me ASAP. It's important. It was from Jay.

Curious to know what was going on, she hurried and called him back.

"What's up Jay? Everything ok?" she asked sitting down on her bed.

"I don't think so." he responded. "I have some info for you that I think you really would want to hear."

Alicia was getting nervous. "Info about what?"

"You're dating a guy named Cameron right?"

"Yeah."

"He is like going through a divorce and has a daughter right? Is from Georgia and just got back from Iraq like a month ago?" he asked her.

Now Alicia was really wondering what was up. "Yes...Jay tell me what's going on?"

"Is he there? I got some things to tell you."

"Yes he is here. What do you have to tell me?" panic was starting to overtake her emotions.

"Well apparently he is supposed to be talking to my home girl. Can you get away to meet me somewhere and I will fill you in on everything."

Alicia and Jay made plans to meet up at the Mickey's convenience store on Old FM 440 in 15 minutes. It wouldn't take her that long to get there but she couldn't wait to leave. She had to know what was going on. She threw on a pair of sneakers and didn't bother changing out of her pajamas and t shirt. When she went downstairs she grabbed her car keys and purse and headed towards the door.

"Babe I'll be right back. Gotta go see about a friend real quick." she said to Cameron.

Cameron looked up from his laptop, "Is everything ok baby?" he asked.

Alicia smiled as sweetly as she could. "Yes, everything is fine. She just needs me real quick. I shouldn't be long."

Alicia pulled into the parking lot of Mickey's and backed in. She sat patiently waiting for Jay to arrive and less than two minutes later she saw his black Impala pulling up. He parked next to her Altima, got out of his car, and got into hers.

"So what's up Jay? Tell me what's going on." she said.

"Well I don't really know where to start." he said looking at her sympathetically.

He was starting to get on her nerves. "Man Jay just tell me what you know, dang."

"Ok well, my home girl Denise said she has been talking to your boyfriend and that he came to see her at a hotel in your car the other night." He said.

Alicia's heart dropped. "Are you sure Jay?"

"Yes, she described all the Tinkerbell decor in your car and the

Louisiana logo on the back window as well as these pics on your dashboard." he waited for her to respond and when she didn't, he continued. "She said that they hung out and kissed and he told her that the car he was driving was his homeboy's wife's car."

"I know what night she is talking about. It was just Saturday when we got back from visiting my family in Shreveport. He was going to do music at Michael's house but his car wouldn't start so I let him take mine." Alicia was beyond pissed. After talking to Jay a few minutes longer she learned more info. Denise had figured out who Alicia was from Facebook. She saw the car on different pics and put it all together. Then she noticed that they were both friends with Jay so she contacted him to get to her. Jay had also told her that Denise said she was going to send her a message on Facebook as well. He said that he would forward the conversation that he had with Denise on yahoo messenger to Alicia too. When Jay had told Alicia everything that he knew, she went home. She had a plan.

When she walked into the door Cameron was still sitting on the couch on his laptop. He looked up at her and smiled, "Hey babe. Everything cool?" he asked her.

She forced a smile, "Yeah everything is good." she said as she sat on the other couch with her laptop and logged onto Facebook. Sure enough there was a message waiting for her from Denise Nixon. It didn't say much only that she wanted to talk to her. Alicia got her phone number and stored it in her cell phone. She would call her later. Alicia decided that she wouldn't mention anything to Cameron just yet. She knew that he would just lie about it like men always do. No she had a better idea. Alicia got up and went into the kitchen and looked through the fridge and cabinets. She came back out and grabbed her purse and keys again.

"I'm going to run to the store real quick. I want something but I don't want anything we got." she told Cameron.

"Okay babe." he said and kissed her cheek.

Once Alicia was in her car she called Denise.

"Hi Denise this is Alicia."

"Hi."

"Um will you tell me what's going on with you and Cameron? Jay told me a little already."

"Well Cam and I started talking online while he was deployed. Then in like November we stopped. But then we started up again when he got back. We talked on yahoo messenger while he was in Georgia. And when he got back we talked on the phone like two or three times. I asked him if he had a girlfriend he said no and that he lived with his homeboy in Harker Heights." Denise said. "The day he got back from Georgia we were supposed to go out to eat but he didn't show up. He wasn't answering when I called so I sent him a message on Tagged."

Alicia thought back to the day that he got back. She remembered sitting next to him while he was checking his messages on tagged. She remembered seeing that message that Denise sent. It said *you could've told me you weren't coming. I had gotten dressed and everything. If you didn't want to talk to me you could've just told me that.* When Alicia asked him what she meant he acted like he didn't have a clue what she was talking about. Alicia was suspicious but she didn't have proof of anything. She had actually forgotten all about it.

"So y'all made plans to go on a date and he didn't show up?" Alicia said. "Ok well tell me what else happened and tell me about the night he came to see you in my car."

Denise complied. "Well, I know we were supposed to get together this past weekend but he said his wife was going to be in town and that she was crazy and he didn't want to have all that drama going on so we couldn't get together. We text a little bit this past weekend. On Saturday night he said he was going to be doing music with his homeboy. I asked if he was going to come see me. I got a hotel room cause I live with a friend of mine because I'm going through a divorce too and I didn't want him to come over there and my ex possibly show up."

Alicia was getting more upset by the minute. On the drive back from

Shreveport Cameron did text a few times but he said he was texting Michael cause he was wondering how long before he would be at his house. She should have asked to see the phone.

"So when he came to the hotel what happened?" Alicia asked.

"He came to the hotel and we sat and talked for about ten minutes. Then he said he needed to put some gas in the car and he was hungry so we went to put gas in the car and went to Sonic's."

Alicia remembered him texting her that night while she was in bed asleep saying that he was finishing up this song and then getting gas and would be on his way home.

Alicia cut her off, "Did he pay for it?"

"No, I paid for us." she said

"Ok, go ahead."

"Then we went back to the hotel and ate and talked some more. We kissed and he left."

"What do you mean you kissed? What kind of kiss?" Alicia asked her trying to control her temper.

"It was just a quick peck on the lips. I kissed him but he didn't move or anything." Denise said. "I just want to know why he had to lie. I thought he was different."

Alicia was mad but also a little skeptical at the same time. If he kept dodging her and not answering her texts or calls then why would she think he was different?

"I want all of us to talk together, in person. I'll come pick you up. Are you cool with that?" Alicia asked her.

She gave Alicia directions to her house and ten minutes later Denise was riding in the backseat of Alicia's car to her house. Denise kept talking. She said if she had known he had a girlfriend she wouldn't have talked to him. But then in the same breath she said she figured that he had a girlfriend and was living with her. Alicia made a mental note of that. They pulled up to Alicia's townhouse and saw Cameron standing outside talking on the phone and smoking a black and mild. Alicia was glad that her back windows were 5 percent tint so nobody could see through them. He had no clue that Denise was in there or that anything was even wrong.

"Stay here." Alicia said to Denise. "I'm going to tell him I have bags in the car." she said then got out and walked toward the front door of her townhouse.

"Cam can you get the bags out of the backseat for me please?" she said to him as she walked past him into the house. He nodded his head and began to put out the cigar. She went into the living room and grabbed his car keys then put them in her pocket. He was going to stay here and explain everything. As she walked back outside she saw him walking to the backdoor on the driver's side. He opened it but didn't look in the car. Alicia guessed that he hadn't saw Denise since she was on the other side so she walked over and opened the other door. Denise got out and once Cameron saw her and realized what was going on he spoke into the phone, "Ma I gotta call you back." He walked around the car looking like he had seen a ghost. He was busted and he couldn't deny it.

Chapter 5

Cameron stood there mouth wide open, looking guilty has he ran a hand over his head. He looked down at the ground, still in shock. Alicia folded her arms over her chest.

"Who is this Cam?" she asked him nodding in her head towards Denise.

"Um, my friend." he said nervously.

"Oh, I'm just your friend?" Denise said to him.

He looked at her, "Yeah."

Alicia stepped up closer to him. "Your friend, huh? The same friend you went to a hotel to see and had all up in my car when you were supposed to be at Michael's house?"

"I did go to Michael's house." he said quickly.

Alicia shot him a hard glance.
"Cam, you just gonna lie like that?!" Denise yelled.

"I did go to Michael's house. But yes, I hung out with Denise too."

Denise was getting ready to start going off and causing a scene so Alicia quickly interjected. "Look, let's take this inside, I don't need my neighbors all up in my business." she said as she led the trio into her townhouse. Once inside, she took a deep breath and sat on one end of the brick red microfiber couch. Denise sat on the other end and Cameron sat on the matching loveseat.

"What I want to know right now is why and how you ended up in a hotel room with Denise." Alicia said calmly as she looked at Cameron.

He blew out a long breath before speaking. "Honestly, I only went cause I didn't want to hurt her feelings. She been asking to see me and hang out with me and I been basically doing and saying anything I could to not do it."

Alicia looked at Denise then back at Cameron. "Why were you even talking to her like that in the first place when you are in a whole relationship?"

"She said she wanted friends. I didn't realize that she wanted more than a friendship until she kept calling and texting me. I didn't really think it was that big of a deal."

Denise spoke up. "You never said nothing about just being friends. All the stuff we talked about, you knew what I've been through with my husband and other men. If you didn't want to talk to me you could've just said so. You didn't have to lie."

"It's not like it was really anything going on though. You only saw me and hung out with me that one time and we've only talked for like three days." he said nonchalantly.

Alicia was getting annoyed with him. "If you thought that all she wanted was to be friends, and if you only wanted to be friends with her then why didn't you tell her you have a girlfriend? Why did you tell her you lived with your homeboy in Harker Heights?"

"I didn't tell her that. She asked what I had been up to and I told her i was at my homeboy house in Harker Heights. And she never even asked if I had a girlfriend."

"I did ask you if you had a girlfriend and you told me no. And hell you told me about your wife." she exclaimed.

Alicia was seething but she maintained a calm demeanor. "Whether she asked or not, if you claim that you only wanted to be friends with her then why would you tell her about Danielle but not your girlfriend?"

"I don't know it just didn't come up." was his lame reason.

"Now what is this that y'all kissed?" Alicia asked.

Cameron blurted, "She kissed me. I didn't kiss her back."

Alicia looked at Denise. "Yea I kissed him but he didn't push me back or nothing he just stood there. But yes, both times I kissed him."

"Both times?!" Alicia shrieked. "You kissed twice? What kind of kissing?"

"It was just a peck. And I didn't know she was going to do that."

Again Alicia looked at Denise. Again Denise spoke, "He didn't know and they were both just quick pecks on the lips. The first time I did was when we were sitting on the bed watching TV and the second was when he was at the door about to leave."

Alicia was about tired of this convo already. She was about to ask Cameron a question when she remembered the convo between Jay and Denise that he had forwarded her. She turned to face Denise.

"I have a question for you, you already suspected he had a girlfriend and you knew that you were in my car. Why did you still want to hang with him and why did you still kiss him? Even more so why were you still calling and texting him?"

"I didn't know for sure that he had girlfriend, after a while I just had a funny feeling. He said that your car was his homeboy's wife's car so I didn't really think about it." Denise stated.

Alicia knew she was lying because in the messages she sent to Jay she said that she thought the car he came to see her in was his girlfriend's, then she put lmao (laughing my ass off) right behind it. She told Jay she wanted revenge for him trying to play her but here she sat in Alicia's face trying to play an innocent role, not knowing that Alicia had their convo saved on her laptop. Alicia didn't feel the need to clue her in or to make this a long conversation.

"Yeah. Ok." Alicia stated plainly. "Cam do you want to talk to Denise? You want something with her?"

Cameron looked at Alicia like she was stupid. "No, I don't. I want to be with you." he said to Alicia then sat up and looked at Denise. "Look I'm sorry if you think I led you on in any way and I'm sorry that you're feelings are hurt but I really don't know what else there is to say to you." he said to her.

Alicia felt kind of bad but at the same she had a gut feeling that Denise knew about her the whole time. "Denise you have anything else you want to say before I take you back home?"

Denise wiped away some tears then sat, with her back straight and her hands resting on her legs balled into fists. "All I want to know is why you did this. I really liked you and cared about you. You were so wrong for this. That's all I have to say." she said finally.

Cameron resisted the urge to roll his eyes but tried to speak with sincerity. "I told you I'm sorry. I don't know what you want me to say. We talked for like two days. It's not that serious. But I do apologize to you Alicia. I was out of line."

Alicia just looked at him, ignoring his apology. She stood up and grabbed her keys from the table directing Denise to get up as well. Alicia walked over to Cameron and leaned in front of him. "I'll be back in a few. We are going to finish our talk later. Now give me a kiss."

Cameron looked confused. She was a little too calm and cool right now. He didn't know what was going on but he placed a kiss on her lips anyway.

Alicia glanced over at Denise as she drove her home. She didn't trust this girl, she could just sense that she was shady. Nonetheless, she decided to be cordial. Hell she wasn't going to see the chick again anyway.

"You ok?" Alicia asked her.

Denise sniffled then wiped her nose. "Yeah. I just can't believe he played me like that. I thought he was different." The ladies rode silently for a few seconds the Denise broke the silence. "So what are you going to do?" she asked Alicia.

"About what?"

"About Cameron. Are you still going to stay with him?"

Alicia eyed her suspiciously. "Well I don't really know yet. This is a lot to digest. Except for this incident we actually have a really good relationship. I have to think this over." She glanced at her again, "what would you do?"

"I would break up with him. He is foul for this whole mess. It was totally disrespectful for him to have me in your car. Plus, he lied." she said.

Alicia couldn't help but feel like her "advice" was purely from a biased view point. She could tell that Denise still liked Cameron and probably would date him if he wanted her. They made small talk for the remainder of the drive back to Denise's apartment. Once she pulled up the parking space, Alicia wished Denise good luck and told her that she appreciated her help. Denise apologized again and told her she hoped that she makes a good decision about Cameron.

Alicia drove away shaking her head at the whole scenario.

Alicia made it back to her townhome and before she even got a chance to put the car in park he cell phone started to ring. She groaned when she looked at display showing a private caller. She didn't know whether to answer or not. Danielle always called private and she wasn't in the mood for her games but her sister often called from Iraq and it showed up as a private call as well. She decided to answer and immediately regretted it.

"I just wanted to let you know that Cameron is playing you. He went to see another female in your car at a hotel the other night." Danielle spoke into the phone as soon as Alicia said hello. "He called me and asked me to call the girl and tell her to stop calling him. I told you he was a liar and cheat. I know all about it." she gloated.

Alicia rolled her eyes. "Danielle I already know about this. I've already talked to the girl and to Cam. There's no need for you to be calling me."

"Well I was just trying to let you know what was going on. You think y'all so perfect but look at what he did. I told you."

She wasn't about to sit and listen to this girl or argue with her. "Okay well thanks for calling. Have a good day." she said then hung up the phone without waiting for a reply. She pulled Cameron's keys out of her pockets and tossed them in her glove compartment. She walked into the house to find Cameron sitting on the couch on his computer. She rolled her eyes at him then walked upstairs without saying anything to him. She sat on her bed staring at the wall. Not really knowing what to feel she let her mind just run free. A few minutes later she heard him coming up the stairs.

"Babe, I'm really sorry about all this. I swear I didn't mean to hurt you. I know it was disrespectful and I know I was wrong but I was trying not to hurt her feelings. When I realized she wanted to be more than friends I tried to figure out a way to get myself out of the situation."

Alicia just looked at him for what seemed like forever. "If that's really the case then why didn't you just tell her you had a girlfriend?

If you were really trying to get out of the situation."

"She didn't ask me if I had a girl." he replied

"She shouldn't have had to ask you." she snapped. "The moment you knew she wanted more than a friendship you should have let her know. If you were really trying to get out the situation that sounds like the smartest and easiest way to get out of it."

He sat down beside her, "You're right. I just made a bad call. But i promise i was not into that girl, I just didn't want to hurt her feelings. I'm so sorry."

"Are you sorry about calling Danielle and telling her our business too? Why would you tell her about Denise?"

"Because I figured that since she knew I was married that I could use Danielle as a way to get out of the situation." he replied.

Alicia scrunched up her face. "How in the hell does that even make sense in your mind?"

"I thought that since Denise had been blowing me up and begging me to come see her that if I just stopped by and hung with her for a few minutes that she would be satisfied and I could just ignore her calls and texts once I left. But after that she called and texted even more. Like she was really blowing me up. So I knew I had to find another way to get her to stop calling me" he explained.

She wanted to slap him. "And again you didn't think to tell her you were spoken for."

He dropped his head. "I know I should have but I wasn't thinking that at the time. I didn't want you to find out and mess up what we have so I asked Danielle to call her and tell her to stop calling me. I knew that Danielle could get her to stop."

"That's really stupid. Did you believe Danielle wasn't going to call me and tell me? You know she hates me and she wants us to break up."

"I didn't think about that either. I just wanted her to leave me alone.

I didn't really think Danielle would call you." he turned to face her and looked into her eyes. "Babe, I don't know what else to say except I'm sorry. I made very bad decisions and I never meant to hurt you."

Alicia forced back tears. She hadn't cried through this whole situation and she wasn't about to do it now. The look in his eyes told her that he truly was sorry and she wanted to forgive him right then and there and be happy again but she couldn't. How could she trust him again after this? How could she be comfortable with him again after this? She needed some time to think. She got up and walked downstairs and poured herself a glass of grape juice. Sipping it she walked to the couch and sat down. Her cell phone buzzed alerting her of an instant message form her sister, Ralonda. She wanted her to go get her Yukon Denali out of her storage unit because she would be home for two weeks on escort duty tomorrow. Alicia had completely forgotten about that.

Cameron came down the stairs. "Have you seen my keys?"

"Where are you going?"

"Nowhere, I just don't know what I did with them."

"I have them." she said flatly.

"Oh. Ok." he said.

"I need you to come with me to get my sister's truck out of the storage unit."

"When?"

"Now."

They hopped into Alicia's car and headed to Red Barn Storage. After opening the unit and hooking up the jumper cables they sat in her car and waited.

"You ok babe?" Cameron asked her.

"I don't know. I don't how to feel right now."

"Do you think this is something that you can forgive me for? Will we be able to work this out?" he asked with pleading eyes.

"I told you before that I wouldn't leave you over a kiss. And I meant that." she paused. "But I also have to know that I can trust you."

"Babe you can trust me. I just made a mistake."

"I have to just sort out my feelings. I'm not leaving you but I need to think."

He nodded his head. "That's fair enough." He got out of the car and went over to the other side and grabbed her hand to pull her out of her car and into his arms for a hug. He wrapped his arms around her waist and squeezed her tightly and held her for what felt like an eternity. Finally he broke the embrace.

"I'm going to stand over here and smoke my black and mild. We should be ready to go by the time I'm done."

Alicia nodded and then went to sit back in the car. She saw something light up in the seat next to her and noticed that it was Cameron's cell phone. He had a text message from Denise.

Hey. Can you call me?

Alicia was mad. She knew that girl was full of crap. Another message from her came in.

I guess u still with your girl.

That was it. Alicia was seething now. She had already known that Denise was still liking Cameron, it was evident in how she tried to convince her to break up with him on the ride taking her home. She didn't expect her to be so disrespectful and still trying to talk to him knowing that he was spoken for. Now Alicia knew that her claim that she had no idea Cameron had a girlfriend was complete BS. She didn't care if he had one or not because she wanted him. Alicia picked up her own cell and sent a text to Denise.

Is there some reason you are still contacting Cameron?

Denise responded in a matter of seconds. *I'm sorry. I just want to talk to him.*

Talk about what? Y'all don't have anything to talk about. He already told you what the deal was and is. Alicia typed. Just as she pressed the send button Cameron's phone got another text from Denise. *I really want to see you. If you can get away then stop by. You know where I'm at.* This chick has some nerve!

Denise texted Alicia's phone still trying to seem innocent. *I just want to know why that's all.*

Alicia responded. *First of all he already told you all you need to know. And secondly, you just asked him to come to your hotel room. There is no reason for you to be still contacting my man. You know he has a girlfriend so there is nothing for y'all to talk about.*

After that she didn't send anymore messages. Cameron finished smoking and unhooked the jumper cables. He climbed into the driver's seat of Alicia Altima as she got into her sister's Denali. Once they made it home she showered and put on boy shorts and a tank top then remembered she still had his keys. She went and retrieved them from her car. She hadn't said much to him since they had arrived home although he was trying to make small talk. She needed time to get her thoughts together and she didn't want to start crying so she opted not to say anything to him or even look at him. After having an apple she decided to go to her room. Usually he stayed up a little later than she did but tonight when she got in bed to go to sleep he was behind her five minutes later. Not sure if it would be a good idea to cuddle with her like he usually did, he just lay in bed as close to her as he could get without making her uncomfortable. Praying that she could really get over this mess, Alicia closed her eyes and tried to force sleep.

Chapter 6

It had been a little less than two weeks since Alicia had found out about the Denise situation. The day after she found out about it her sister Ralonda had gotten in from Iraq. She was happy that her sister was here for two weeks but she decided not to tell her about what happened. Since that night Alicia had barely said two words to Cameron and could barely even look him in the face. She still did her usual things: cooking, cleaning, laundry but she wouldn't kiss him, cuddle with him, have sex with him, or go anywhere with him. Most of the time if he was in one area of the townhouse then she would go to another. If she was bored and wanted to get out she would go hang out with her friends or her sister instead doing something with him. He gave her space and the time she needed to get her feelings together. It was Friday and her sister would be leaving on Monday to go back to Iraq. She wasn't ready for her to leave yet but she knew that she had no choice. She hated not having her sister around though.

Cameron had convinced Alicia to go out on date with him this evening in hopes that they could possibly have a start at getting back like they were before the Denise incident. She wasn't sure if it would help any but she figured it couldn't hurt. She had just gotten out of the shower and put lotion on her body with Victoria's Secret Pure Seduction scented lotion. She put on a black sheer thong and matching strapless bra. Then she slipped into a long flowing black and red maxi dress that tied around the neck with black thong sandals. It was a pretty warm day considering that they were in the middle of January so she assumed the night wouldn't be too cool. She let her hair hang on her shoulders in big bouncy curls and put on a pair of black dangle earrings and black bracelet. After applying lip gloss to her luscious lips she stepped back and glanced at herself in the mirror. Cameron loved seeing her in this dress and with her hair flowing like this. She told herself that tonight she would make a real effort to get their relationship back on track. She wasn't going to let any negativity or doubts or anything else keep her from having a good time. She owed it to herself and to her relationship.

Alicia walked down the stairs where Cameron was waiting on the couch watching TV. He immediately stood and smiled when he saw her.

"Babe you look beautiful." he told her.

She smiled as she grabbed her purse and cell phone.

They hopped in his car and headed to Copperas Cove. Once at the movie theater they waited in line to buy tickets for the horror movie Legion but the seven o'clock show was sold out Cameron got tickets for the nine o'clock show. They decided to go have dinner at one of their favorite places Plucker's Wing Bar.

They were finally seated at a small table after waiting for ten minutes. So far the night was going good for them. They were holding hands and laughing again and really enjoying each other's company like they used to do before. Alicia had to admit it felt good to be with him again. They ordered their usual meals and when they arrived they dug right in, feeding each other and sampling the other's food. While talking about nothing in particular Alicia's cell phone began to ring. Looking at the caller id she saw that is was a number she didn't know.

"Hello?" Alicia said into the phone then sipped her lemonade.

"Um can I talk to Cam?" the voice on the other end said.

Alicia rolled her eyes. *Here we go again with the phone games.* She thought to herself. "He is busy right now." she said to the young sounding female.

There was a quiet pause and a little noise in the background before the girl spoke again. "Well can you tell him that I'm three weeks pregnant by him?"

Alicia almost laughed. "Yes, I will be sure to tell him"

"Ok. Bye." the girl said.

Alicia put her phone down and continued eating her mac and cheese. She looked at Cameron and smiled. "Some girl just asked me to tell you that she is three weeks pregnant by you." she said laughing.

"Wow. You do know what's going on right?" he said slightly amused.

She nodded. She wasn't dumb. She knew that Danielle had gotten someone to call and say that to mess up not only their evening but also their relationship. Since she knew about the Denise situation she thought it would cause more trouble by doing that. Danielle was the dumb one. She should've got some one older sounding to do it and besides that how would this random girl just happen to get my number. Yep. She was definitely not the sharpest tool in the shed.

They finished eating and Cameron payed the bill. They walked to his car in a warm embrace still in a great mood. After making it back to the movie theater and only being able to find seats in the front row they sat down and got comfortable and chatted 'til the previews began to play. Cameron sat on her right side holding and kissing her hand. They stole sweet kisses as they watched the movie. Before the movie was even halfway over Alicia began to get sleepy. They were extremely happy once the movie was over, they both agreed it was a terrible movie and so did many of the others in the theater with them. As they drove home still happy and in good spirits Alicia felt that she had totally forgiven him and that things were back to normal. Tonight was the first night they had kissed or held hands or even held a conversation in weeks and she was happy that she had decided to come out with him. And so was he.

When they got home Alicia changed into her short thin strapped night gown and Cameron stripped down to his t-shirt and boxers. They got in bed and Alicia lay in his arms with her head on his chest as he stroked the side of her face.

"Babe, I really missed you these past couple of weeks." he said looking into her eyes. "I missed us and the way we used to be."

Alicia smiled and she could see the sincerity and feel the warmth of his words. "I missed you too babe. I guess we really needed this night out to start rebuilding us."

"Yes we did. I just want to say again that I'm sorry for messing us up in the first place. I missed you so much." He said as he kissed her.

Alicia reached up and caressed his face as their kiss got deep and more passionate. He parted her lips with his tongue and she captured it in her own mouth and began to gently suck it. They kissed for what seemed like forever pulling back only to look into each other's eyes. He lay her on her back and lifted her nightgown up and over her head throwing it to the floor. He gazed at her naked body as she pulled off his shirt. He climbed on top of her and kissed her again. She rubbed his back grinded her hips underneath him. He was ready for work. He began to place a trail of kisses down her neck leading to her breast. He continued down her belly and to her thighs, placing sweet little kisses on her inner thighs. Then he lay on his stomach, and with her legs on his shoulders he dove in. Kissing her sweet spot slowly and sensually. She placed her hands on the back of his head and rolled her hips to his rhythm. She moaned and he moaned. He enjoyed going down on her, loved that he could give her such pleasure. He got more into it, speeding up and sucking on her most sensitive spot. She loved it. "Oh babe. Ohhhh." she moaned as she was on the verge of orgasm. He knew just what to do to take her there. He sucked faster as she rolled her hips faster, moving against his tongue. A few seconds later she was clenching the sheets and moaning loudly as her juices spilled out and he drank every bit of it. Legs shaking she pulled him up to her and kissed him deeply. Alicia pushed him on his back onto the bed and rolled on top of him. Hovering on her knees over him she kissed him. Then she flicked his earlobe with her tongue. She then used her tongue to make circles on neck as she traveled down his body. She lightly teased his nipples with her tongue as she used her hand to massage his swollen manhood. He always loved when she did that. She slid down his body then took his manhood in her warm mouth. She slid her mouth up and down using her hand to give extra satisfaction. She knew how to please her man and she knew that he couldn't get enough. "Dang babe. Oh my goodness." was all he could manage to say. She knew he was close letting go so she stopped and straddled him. Cameron positioned himself and slowly eased her down. Once he was in she began to roll her hips as he met her stroke beneath her. They moved together in a harmony that only they could create together. Gripping each other tight, moaning, and experiencing a pleasure that no one else could give. As they moved deeper and faster he moaned loudly and gripped her waist while they stared into each other's eyes as he exploded inside of her. They lay there, sweaty and breathing hard as his manhood sat inside of her. After a few minutes Alicia got up and went to the bathroom. After peeing and using a soapy washcloth to wash up, she lathered up the washcloth again and went to wash Cameron up as well. Afterwards she dropped the towel in the laundry basket and climbed back into bed. Cameron pulled her into his arms and kissed her lips. "Goodnight babe." he said to her right before drifting off to sleep. *Oh, I love this man.* She thought to herself as she fell asleep too.

Chapter 7

Alicia woke up early on Sunday morning excited and wanting to go praise God. It was Valentine's Day so after she went church she was going to spend the day with Cameron. She was also excited because both of their birthdays were tomorrow, even though she had to work in the morning they were still going to do a small celebration.

After showering and getting dressed in black dress pant and a red blouse, Alicia pulled her hair into low ponytail and applied her lip gloss. She slip on a pair of black ballerina flats and gave herself a once over in the mirror. Cameron was still in bed asleep so she kissed his lips and told him she would be back soon. It was only 830 and she was hoping she could find a church with a 9 am service. After driving around for about 30 minutes and no luck she decided to head back home. When she got home Cameron was already up and had just gotten out of the shower. He was downstairs watching TV as he finished dressing.

She smiled at him as she closed the front door. "Happy Valentine's Day babe."

He kissed her lips and smiled back. "Happy Valentine's Day baby. How was church?"

"I didn't go. I couldn't find the one I was looking for so I just came back home." She looked him up and down as she delighted in seeing how handsome he was looking even though he was dressed very casual in blue jeans, a tall white tee, and white air force ones. He was definitely a compliment to her looks with his dark brown skin and pretty eyes. He also had the most amazing set of long thick beautiful eyelashes that match perfectly with his deep brown eyes.

Alicia went upstairs to get more casual for their date and get his gifts out of her hiding spot in the closet while he finished putting on his watch, necklace, and Curve cologne. Once she made it up upstairs she smiled as she rounded the corner and saw her gifts from him strategically placed on her bed for her. She walked over to the gifts and smiled again. He bought her a huge pink teddy bear holding a heart in his hands, an even bigger white stuffed bunny with hearts on its ears, a heart shaped box of chocolates, and beautiful promise ring with a star shaped stone in the center of it. She was surprised that he even got her rings size correct. She opened the card and read words that warmed her heart.

I'm glad I have you to hold my hand

To share my thoughts and understand

I'm glad I have you to share my dreams

To share my laughter and other things

For all you are and all you do

I'm so glad that I have you

Love Cam

Alicia wiped away tears as she read the card. Although he hasn't yet told her that he loved her at that very moment she knew he did. She gathered her composure then changed into a pair of jeans and a white and pink fitted tee and then slipped on her white and pink air force ones. She grabbed her bag of gifts for Cameron and headed downstairs, with her ring on her finger. She walked up to him and hugged him then kissed him on his lips and told him thank you. Then she handed him the bag of gifts she bought.

"Babe, I didn't think you were gonna get me anything. Valentine's Day is really about the woman." he said laughing.

"Well to me it's about both of us and how we feel about each other." she handed him a huge card and he cracked up laughing.

"Where did you find such a big ole card girl?" he said teasingly.

She laughed, "Don't worry about all that babe, I got connections."

He sat down and began digging in the big gift bag pulling out different gifts. First he pulled out a blue striped Ralph Lauren Chaps polo shirt, then a yellow one exactly like it. Next he pulled out a bottle of Gucci cologne and cute little stuffed bulldog with a heart attached to it. He smiled, then read the giant card.

Babe I'm happy to be spending our first Valentine's Day together. Although we have only been together for a little less than 3 months, I really care for you and I feel as if we've been together our whole life. Though we have had our ups and downs I'm proud to be your woman. Love, Alicia.

He walked up to her and wrapped his arms her waist. Dipping his head, he kissed her tenderly on the lips. "I feel the same way baby. Thank you so much. I love my gifts." he said to her. After taking a few pictures together they headed out for lunch at Cheddar's Casual Cafe.

Once there they were seated at booth on the back wall of the restaurant. They ordered a sweet tea for Cameron and a lemonade for Alicia and chips and queso as their appetizer. When the waitress came back to take their meal orders Alicia noticed that the young lady seemed to be paying more attention to Cameron than to her. She kept smiling hard at him and trying to hold a conversation with him as if Alicia wasn't even sitting there. She shook her head and laughed, she wasn't getting a good tip today.

"So what are you going to have today? I can make suggestions if you'd like." the petite caramel colored waitress said to Cameron as she smiled all up in his face.

"Um thanks but I already know what i want. I get the same thing every time." he said to her completely unaware that she was flirting with him.

He is too freaking friendly. And he never notices anything. Alicia thought to herself. She leaned back in her seat and laughed to herself. It's a good thing she has a lot of confidence and is very secure with herself otherwise this would have bothered her. Instead it made her feel good to know that her man was a good catch.

"I'm gonna have the full rack of ribs with fries and broccoli and cheese casserole." Cameron was saying to the waitress when Alicia finally snapped out of her own thoughts. The waitress wrote it down and finally acknowledged Alicia.

"You ready to order?" she said to Alicia without the same vibrant demeanor she shared with Cameron,

Alicia didn't get upset, she simply smiled at her. "I will have the grilled chicken pasta please without the vegetables." The waitress wrote it down then gathered the menus.

"Okay I'll put these in and your meals will be out shortly." she said before turning to Cameron with a smile and saying, "If you need anything at all before then please just let me know." Cameron nodded and she walked away.

"Can you believe that chick?" Alicia asked as she let out a laugh.

Cameron had a blank look on his face. "What?" he said.

"You didn't notice how she was flirting with you like I'm not even sitting here?"

"That girl was not flirting with me. She was just doing her job and trying to get a good tip." he said laughing.

"No she was flirting and was all up in your face and not even paying me no mind. Watch how she act when she come back." she said to him.

When the waitress came back with their food she placed their plates on the table in front of them. The stood close to Cameron and put a hand on his shoulder. "You look like you need some more tea. I'll refill it for you." she said leaning over him to grab his glass. She left the table with his glass.

"You see that? She didn't even bother to refill mine!" Alicia said incredulously.

Cameron laughed, "Ok, I see what you mean now."

"Yeah you thought I was just imagining it" she said laughing. "You see how she was touching all on your arm? She won't be getting a good tip."

"That's funny. You pay attention to everything babe." he said smiling at her.

"Darn right I do."

When they finished eating Cameron paid the bill and asked Alicia how much of a tip he should give the waitress.

"Give her two dollars." Alicia said. "I ought to write her a note so that in the future she make sure to give the woman more attention. That's who determines the tip." she laughed at her own joke.

They drove to Condor Park off of Veteran's Memorial Blvd and walked to the pond where the ducks were. They cuddled on the bench and watched the ducks swim and walk around the park. It was a beautiful day and Alicia wished it could last forever. She loved being with Cameron and he made her feel so special and loved. They stayed at the park for about an hour before deciding to go to the Red Box to rent some movies to watch while lying in the bed that evening. After picking 3 movies they headed home.

Once they got home Alicia took a quick shower and changed into her pajamas. Her cycle just went off yesterday so they weren't going to be making love tonight. She liked to wait at least a day after it went off just to be sure. They lay cuddled up in bed watching movies and eating ice cream. She loved these moments that they shared. Before long they were both in a deep sleep.

The next morning Cameron got up to go pt. After he brushed his teeth and put on his PT uniform he kissed Alicia on her lips, like he did every morning that he left before she got out of bed. She woke up an hour later. After showering and brushing her teeth she dressed in her royal blue scrubs, white air force ones, and pulled her back into a ponytail. She grabbed a pop tart and a bottle of water then grabbed her purse, work bag, and keys and headed out the door. It was 730 and as she walked to her car Cameron pulled into the parking lot. He got out and walked toward her. Grabbing her work bag and putting it in her car for her he kissed her lips.

"Happy Birthday baby." he said to her smiling.

"And happy birthday to you babe." she said smiling back.

"What do you want to do today when you get off?" he asked her. "I don't have to go back to work today."

"Well I get off at 2 so let's just go eat some pizza and browse the mall or something. Nothing big. I got your gifts in my car so you can't see them 'til I get home."

"Ok well that works out good because you can pick out your gift when we go to the mall. You want to eat CiCi's Pizza?"

Alicia smiled and kissed him before getting into her car. "Yes that will be good. I gotta go babe before I'm late." they said goodbye and she drove away.

After work, eating, and shopping at the mall. They returned home and Alicia gave him his gifts. New floor mats for his car, cleaner for his rims, Georgia Bulldogs clip on car air freshener, toothbrush, hat, car decal, and keychain. He loved all the Georgia Bulldogs stuff. He bought her a pair of grey, black, and green air force ones. She loved sneakers, especially odd colored ones. She had a closet full of them. The day had been nice and their relationship was good again. Aside from the occasional phone call from Danielle, things were as good as ever.

A few days later Alicia and Cameron were hanging out at the house watching movies and decided to order some pizza. Alicia went to pick the pizzas up from Dominoes and as she sat waiting in the lobby for the order to be ready she received a text from Danielle.

Alicia since u think your relationship with Cam is so perfect I'm bout to forward the texts he's been sending me today.

Alicia rolled her eyes she was not in the mood for her games tonight.

It's bad enough that Cameron had been previously telling Danielle our personal business, she thought that he had stopped after she confronted him about it.

FWD: I miss you so much. I want us to be a family again. You and Kennedy mean the world to me.

Danielle sent that message followed by another one.

FWD: I'm just with her for now because you're not here. I don't care that you are pregnant for Ronald. I still love you.

Alicia was getting a little upset, she didn't believe that he was really saying these things but at the same time, was he? Another message.

Fwd: I'm so sorry for what I've done but we can fix this. I love you Danielle.

Alicia don't tell him I'm sending the messages that he is sending me. I told you he was foul.

Alicia didn't even bother to respond. She got the pizzas then went home. Cameron had just gotten out of the shower and was still in the bathroom. Alicia knocked on the bathroom door then walked in. He was standing with a towel wrapped around his waist plucking hairs from his face and chin. She noticed that he had his phone in the bathroom with him. She eyed him suspiciously.

"Can I see your phone please?" she asked him.

He looked puzzled. "Uh. Ok." he said handing the phone to her.

She went to his text messages and sure enough he and Danielle had been texting each other but the texts Danielle sent to Alicia were manipulated and reworded.

Danielle it's over between me and you. I love Kennedy with all my heart but I don't want to be with you.

That was the real first message he sent to her.

Alicia is a good woman and a good person. I really care about her and it's not right that you keep doing stuff to try and break us up. You're pregnant by Ronald so you should try and make things work with him.

That was message number two.

I'm sorry about all the things that happened between us and I'm sorry that you still feel hurt but we are done. Please accept that.

That was the real third message.

"I knew it!" Alicia exclaimed. She handed Cameron's phone back to him.

He was still looking puzzled. "What's going on?"

Alicia pulled out her cell phone and showed him what Danielle had done.

"Wow. She is really trippin." he said.

"I know. I had a feeling she was lying but I had to make sure."

"I understand." he said. Alicia left the bathroom breathing a sigh of relief as Cameron finished grooming himself. After they ate they headed to bed, they were moving into a bigger place tomorrow so they needed to get some rest.

Chapter 8

It was the end of the first week in March and they were finally settled and comfy in the new two story duplex on Opal rd. They loved this place a lot better because even though it was a two bedroom and one and half bathroom just like the townhouse, this one had way more extra space. It had a huge high ceiling living room with fireplace, a separate dining room, a bigger kitchen, a garage, a huge fenced backyard, and separate vanity and sink in the master bedroom. She didn't feel so closed in anymore. Now Cameron could use the garage to work on his music and he wouldn't be disturbing her or the neighbors.

Alicia and Cameron had decided to spend this beautiful March Saturday shopping at the mall and spending quality time together. He dressed in a red polo shirts with black jeans and his red Georgia hat that Alicia had bought him for his birthday. Alicia wore a pair of brown tights and a mustard yellow blouse with matching thong sandal with rhinestones. Cameron kept wandering off to take pics of himself while they were in the stores and Alicia was too busy trying to find some cute clothes in the clearance racks to care. After, paying for her items they stopped at Sonic's Drive In to get burgers and cokes for dinner then headed home.

After eating Cameron went into the garage to do some music while Alicia watched TV in the living room. An hour later her phone began to ring. She answered without looking at the caller id.

"Hello?" no response.

"Hellooo?" she said again and still got nothing. She was just about to hang up when she heard two female voices talking on the line. One of the female voices was Danielle and she guessed the other was one of her friends. She was about to hang up but something told her to just listen for a while. Danielle tried to make it seem as if she was unaware that she had called Alicia but she knew that purposely called and was pretending like she didn't know. Danielle played so many childish games that Alicia was starting figure her out a little bit.

"Girl she so stupid and believe everything he say to her." Danielle said to her friend. "When she not around he be talking on the phone with me and texting me."

The other female voice responded. "For real girl? What she look like anyway?"

Danielle laughed. "Girl that dog face chick is ugly. She a cheeseburger away from being fat and she got big bug eyes." She said with venom dripping in her voice. "She's stupid cause he be on skype with me all the time just dogging her out."

Alicia was getting agitated. She made sure that her phone was muted so that Danielle couldn't hear then she went into the garage and motioned for Cameron to come and listen.

He followed her into the living room and remained standing as Alicia took a seat on the couch. "What's going on?" he whispered to her. She placed a finger over her lips to hush him up.

"Yeah girl, he be on skype with me looking at my titties and talking so bad about her. He showed me his thing and everything. She stupid. He be telling me he love me and he can't wait to get back to Georgia so we can be together again." Danielle told her friend.

Cameron was rubbing his head and pacing back and forth across the living room floor. "Oh my goodness. Why would she say that?" he said to no one in particular. Alicia just looked at him. They listened to the call for just a few more minutes and Alicia hung up the phone.

"Cameron, I want to trust you. Is there any truth in anything that she said?" Alicia asked him.

Cameron stopped pacing and walked over to her. "No babe. Nothing she saying is true. I just get on skype and see Kennedy and that's it. I don't be looking at that girl. I promise she's lying." he said to her.

"Just so we are clear, you are telling me that you never looked at her naked on Skype, you don't tell her you love her and want to be with her and you don't be dogging me out to her?" Alicia said as she looked at him through narrowed eyes.

"Babe that's exactly what I'm telling you. I wouldn't do that."

"Ok." Alicia said. She wanted to trust him so badly but she had this nagging doubt in her mind. Something was pulling at her gut. She pushed everything out of her mind and headed upstairs to bed.

Two days had passed since the phone call from Danielle but Alicia couldn't shake the feeling that what she said might have some truth to it. She tried to push it from her mind but the harder she tried the more it weighed down her. She left work early today because her client was going over to her daughters' home to spend the day with her family. When she got home she saw that Cameron hadn't made it home from PT yet. She put her things down on the couch and stood there debating whether or not she should go check his laptop. After only a few seconds she headed into the garage and sat down at his desk. She was glad that he had left his laptop up and running so that she didn't have to guess his password. She began browsing not knowing exactly what to look for. After a few minutes and a few folders she came across the folder that he kept his pornos in. She laughed out loud. He loved his porn. Just as she was about to go to another folder something caught her eye. She read the title of the file and her heartbeat instantly quickened. This couldn't really be what she thought it was. Her hand trembled as she clicked on the file. Her heart dropped as she watched the clip and reality set in.

Chapter 9

Alicia watched in disgust as a video played with Danielle dancing her bra and panties to some slow song in the background. She was smiling and making a goofy face, "Hey baby, I just wanted to make you something to show you how much I love you." Danielle said into the camera. "I miss you and I love you. Muah! Aarrgghh!" she said and then laughed and began dancing again.

Alicia closed that file which was titled *Danielle Slow Grind* and clicked on another file titled *Danielle Poppin.* In this video she was on the floor with her back facing the camera, popping her butt like a nasty stripper. The third video was titled *Danielle Towel,* I'm sure you can guess what that one was about. She was in a towel then dropped it to reveal a naked body. Alicia wanted to throw up. Danielle's body was disgusting. She was a pretty slim person but she had belly pouch with stretch marks and wrinkled looking skin. She had no curves, and no booty and she was in serious need of lotion. Alicia was so upset and so hurt but she wouldn't let tears escape her eyes. She thought that maybe these were the videos that Danielle sent to him while he was in Iraq when they were working on their marriage. He told her about them. Maybe he just forgot that they were still on his computer. She tried to calm herself down. She looked at the dates that the files were last accessed and she got angry all over again. February 22, 2010. Tears began to fall. He looked at them less than three weeks ago.

How could he do this to me? How could he be so foul? She thought to herself. Alicia grabbed her cell phone.

"What's up babe?" Cameron answered.

"Where are you?" she asked him.

"I'm on my way home from pt. You ok?"

She tried to hide the anger in her voice. "Yes. Just hurry and get home please. I want to talk to you about something."

"Ok, I will be there in a few minutes." They hung up.

Five minutes later she heard Cameron's key in the front door. She was in the garage with the door open, still sitting at his computer. When she heard him walking toward the garage she pressed play on the video file of Danielle dancing in the towel, then turned to the face the door and waited for him to walk in.

A look of shock was on Cameron's face as he realized what Alicia was watching. She leaned back in the chair. "What is this Cam?" she asked trying to remain calm.

"Babe, that's old. I told you she sent me those while I was still in Iraq." he told her.

She leaned forward. "Yeah you told me she sent you those in Iraq but that doesn't explain why they are still on your computer."

"I honestly forgot that those videos were still on my computer." he said looking at her with pleading eyes.

Alicia felt her temper growing. "You're such a liar dude. If you so called forgot they were on here then why does it say you accessed them on February 22?"

He immediately began explaining. "I didn't actually watch them." he said to her. Once he noticed the, oh please, look on Alicia's face he continued explaining. "I was looking for a certain porno and I had to go through all my videos to find so as I clicked on each file I just named them so that I wouldn't have to do it again."

Alicia snorted. "You must think I'm some kind of fool. That excuse don't even make sense." she told him. "If you didn't watch them why would you need to name them?"

"So that I wouldn't make a mistake and click on them in the future. I'm not attracted to Danielle at all so why would I watch those videos?"

"If you didn't watch them how did you know what to name each one? She sent you those videos over a year ago." Alicia challenged him.

"As soon as I heard the music I knew what she was doing in them. I remembered from when she sent them." he said still trying to convince her of his innocent mistake.

"Whatever Cam. You claim to never remember anything about anything but you amazingly remembered what she was doing in the videos without watching them? And not to mention, if you didn't want the videos then why didn't you just delete them instead of naming them?" she said angrily.

"I don't know, I guess I just didn't think about that." he told her.

Alicia was livid. She began going through his computer again and came across a bunch of pictures of Danielle, from their sessions on Skype. She jumped up and ran up in Cameron's face. "What the fuck is this Cam?!" she said pointing to his computer. "All this time you tried to make me believe that she was lying about you looking at her naked on Skype and here is the proof!" She could no longer hold the tears back, this had become too much. She felt like such a fool. Everything Danielle had said on the phone that day was true. There were pics of her with no shirt on, no bra on, with thongs, naked, and with a towel. Alicia was disgusted again.

"Alicia that's not what you thinking." he said to her.

"How is this not what I'm thinking? It's right here in my face!" she yelled at him and pushed him hard in his chest.

"Look don't put your hands on me. I know you mad but you don't need to put your hands on me" he told her.

"Fuck that, you are so foul!" she cried.

He was still trying to explain the pics to her. "I was not looking at her. I didn't even realize she sent those pics while we were on skype cause I was playing my video games while we were on so I wasn't even paying attention. I saw that it said file sending but I didn't know what it was. So she would say something to me and catch my attention so I just hit save on all the pictures without even looking at them."

Alicia wasn't buying what he was saying. She wanted to believe him so bad but the proof was right in her face. "I can't believe you would disrespect me so bad in my own house. All this time I would be upstairs in bed waiting on you to finish doing your music or playing your video games. Trusting that you were only on Skype to see your daughter but this is what you've been doing all along."

Cameron walked up to her trying to hug her. She pulled back. "Babe I swear to you, it's not what you thinking. I have to play the game with Danielle in order to see my daughter. If she tells me love me, yes I say it back but I don't mean it. I just want to be in my daughter's life. Please babe. I'm sorry." Alicia just turned and walked upstairs. She didn't want to hear his lies and excuse anymore.

A few weeks had passed since Alicia had found out about Cameron's dirt. She had forgiven him yet again, but she was starting to become very paranoid and suspicious about the things he was doing. His car had broken down and was getting fixed so they were sharing her car. Odd things just seemed to keep happening. When they were at home she would sit in the garage reading her book while he did music. It seemed like every time she would be around him Danielle was either calling or texting him. He sent her pics simply because she asked for them. He swore up and down that they never really talked much it was just a coincidence that she would call or text while they were with each other because she didn't anything or time. Although Alicia had now had passwords to all of his email and social networking accounts she still didn't have the same trust that she once had. She had saw him on Skype one day trying to see Kennedy and instead Danielle was sitting in the camera just staring at him.

"If Skype is supposed to only be for you to see your daughter, why isn't she even on the camera?" Alicia asked him.

"I don't know. Danielle said she was sleep." Cameron answered.

"So why the hell don't you tell her to get her monkey ass off then?" she was irritated.

Cameron sighed. "I told her we don't need to speak unless it's about my daughter but she was looking all sad and she just asked if she could just watch me doing my music. She said she would be quiet she just wanted to watch me."

Alicia had heard it all. This was beginning to be too much for her to deal with. Cameron had better man up and start making some changes ASAP or they were going to be over.

Chapter 10

Alicia and Cameron were getting along so much better ever since Cameron had put his foot down and set boundaries with Danielle. He wouldn't speak with her unless it was pertaining to his daughter, he no longer got on Skype with her if Kennedy wasn't awake and on the camera. They spent more time together whether it was in the garage working on his music, or going out to eat or to the movies, or just cuddling up in bed playing the super text twist word game on his phone together. Things were finally starting to feel right between them again. They made love almost every day and truly it actually felt as though they were living the life of a happily married couple. They had made a song together and everything. Alicia wasn't a rapper but she once did a rap to a beat that Cameron made while she was frustrated about something Danielle was doing. He encouraged her to use that anger and just right a quick rhyme to release it. She had never rapped before and the fact that it was something they did together was exciting for both of them. As it turned out, she was actually good at rapping. When he played the song back to her she was amazed that that was her.

Bitch you going crazy for a nigga that don't want you.

Always talking shit but what the fuck you really wanna do?

Silly ass trick wanna walk a day in my shoes

I'm a boss bitch and I get any man that I choose

You aint on my level so there is no competition

All this swag I'm packing I know that you really wishin

That you had my life and all this diva intuition

Independent bitch on a independent mission.

That was her whole song. Though it wasn't much she was shocked at how even Michael and Polk thought she had skills. She hated doing all that cursing but at the time she wrote the song she was angry and that was how she felt. After that she and Cameron did a song together. It was a song called Call Me Up, basically it said some very sexual things in it. Michael loved that one too. He really though Alicia had potential, but to her it was just all in fun. The day was drawing near that Cameron was going to be stationed in Fort Stewart, GA and Alicia really didn't want him to go. They pushed the thought of being apart out of their minds and just focused on the time they had left together. They made the most of it. They spent so much time together and had so much fun. Cameron would do some of the silliest stuff just to see a smile on her face. He would strip butt naked and walk around the room with his manhood stuck between his legs. Or he would pretend to be a feminine man talking to me, he even did all the hand and neck movements and changed his voice. He did so much that would have Alicia cracking up. They would be lying in bed watching a movie and he would just lick her face for no reason. This always disgusted Alicia but she laughed because he would run when she tried to hit him for doing that. Neither of them were ready for the distance of this move. He didn't want to go back to GA. Yes his parents and sister were there and so was Kennedy, but he had only re-enlisted to go there because Danielle wanted to be close to home and they were married at the time they made the decision. He regretted it. He tried seeing if he could get out of it but it was cemented in stone. He had to go.

The day had finally come that both dreaded. April 25, 2010. His dad had flown down to Killeen to help Cameron make the 18 hour drive back to Ga. Alicia had to go to work that day too. It was her weekend rotation. After her first shift, she came home and made him breakfast like she had done every day for the past 4 months. She was determined not to cry today. It wasn't the end of them. They just would have live to apart for a little while. She kept telling herself that in an effort to keep her tears from falling. After they had breakfast they made love and then lay in the bed holding each other as if there were no tomorrow. Cameron had to make it to the airport in an hour to get his dad and get on the road.

"I really don't want to leave you babe." Cameron said to Alicia.

Alicia smiled. "I know you don't but you don't have a choice."

"You will be coming to visit me soon though right?" he asked her

"You know I am."

"I'm really going to miss you." he said and kissed her lips.

Chapter 11

When Alicia got home from work and walked into the apartment that she once shared with Cameron, tears began to form in her eyes. She stood in the living room and stared at a picture of the two of them kissing. She missed him so much already. It felt weird coming home to an empty house. No one to cook for, nobody to clean up behind. She had gotten so used to having him there that now the house just seemed too big for her. She went upstairs, stripped naked and took a long hot shower. After putting on her pajamas she turned on her cd player and lay down. Cameron had made two songs about for her to express the way he felt about her. One when they first started dating and one after they had been together for a couple months. She loved them and so did her friends and family as well as his parents. He really had talent and Alicia felt like every word in those songs were how he truly felt deep down inside. Tears began to fall as she lay there listening to the words of the songs and thinking about him.

The way she walks....the way that she's walking

The way she talks...the way that she's talking

The way she moves....the way that she moves

It's all in her attitude....it's something about her

Something about her....it's something about her

Something about her....it's something about her

Something about her.....it's something about her.

She loved Michael's singing on this song. He and Cameron both really had talent but Cameron couldn't sing to save his life. He was however great at producing beats and all the songs he made about her showcased his rapping ability. Michael on the other hand was a jack of all trades when it came to music. He sings, raps, produces, and does the artwork for his albums and mixtapes as well his videos for the songs. Alicia began to cry again when she heard Cameron's verse start.

It's all you baby!

It must be something about you that makes me look twice.

You got that perfect shape and you always look nice.

You the reason me and my nigga got this hook right.

You shut the competition down like Suge Knight.

Could it be your smile or better yet be your swag.

I gotta stop and get a flash every time you pass.

With yo lil sexy ass. Shawty I gotta ask,

What a nigga gotta do to be up in yo class.

I'm a grown man and you say that you Ms. independent

So come back from them lames and get with something that's different.

And when you need to talk I can be the one to listen

You the star in my sky so baby let's go lifted.

Alicia smiled at the last line in the song. It was their little personal saying for each other. He called her Star when they first started talking and his parents and family called him Skyler since was a child. One day they were talking and she made a joke about calling him Sky and they came up with she is the Star in his Sky. So for almost every song he made for her he would put that in it somewhere if he could. She really loved this man and hoped that even with the distance their relationship would still grow and stay intact.

The next song began to play and she recalled that he had made this song for her while he was at home in Ga on leave.

She's the Star in my sky. Without her in my life, I know I could never fly

Baby feel my love, never let it die. She so classy and I can tell you why.

She so classy, so classy. So classy, so classy.

The way she talk, the things she do. She make me want to act a fool.

Alicia loved this song too but it made her laugh because he had to use auto tune to in order to sing the hook. She rolled over in her bed and saw that the clock said 10:30 pm. It was getting late, and even though she had heard from Cameron periodically throughout the day, she hadn't talked to him since before she left work. She picked up the phone to call him.

"Hello" he answered on the second ring.

"Hey babe how is the drive going?" she asked him.

"It's alright. We are about to stop at a hotel and get back on the road in the morning. It's been a long drive."

"Oh okay." she said. "You make sure to get as much sleep as possible and keep me updated tomorrow."

"You know I will. I miss you babe." he said sounding sincere.

Alicia smiled, "I miss you too. Goodnight." and with that she hung up and lay down to sleep her first night without Cameron cuddled up beside her.

Chapter 12

Almost 24 hours had passed since Alicia had last talked to Cameron. She had called his cell phone several times but each time it went to voicemail. She checked his Facebook profile to see if he had posted anything and saw that he hadn't. She was beginning to worry that something had happened to him. He was supposed to call her once he made it to Georgia. She looked at the clock and saw that it was 10:07 pm. She tried calling him again and this time it didn't go to voicemail.

She heard slow music playing in the background, followed by a woman's voice saying, "Stop babe." then the female giggled and answered his phone.

"Hello?" she said.

Alicia hung up, confused. She thought that maybe she accidentally called the wrong number so she tried again. Again the same female answered.

"Alicia what do you want?" It was Danielle.

Alicia looked at the phone with a blank stare before putting it back up to her ear and speaking. "Where is Cam?" she asked.

"He said he doesn't want to talk to you. He is laying here next to me in the bed." when Alicia didn't respond she kept talking. "He is here now and we are going to be together so stop calling him. Now you are going to see what it's been like for me while he was in Texas with you." after a devilish laugh she hung up the phone.

Alicia sat there for a minute, her heart pounding and her mind going a mile a minute. Something wasn't right. She called his parent's house number. She'd had the number since he the time he went home on leave and called her from there. He was going to be living with his parents for a while. After dialing the number his mom picked up on the second ring.

"Hello?" Brenda Carter said into the phone.

"Hi Ms. Brenda." Alicia spoke. "I'm sorry to be calling so late but Cam was supposed to call me when he made it there and I haven't heard from him yet. I'm getting a little worried."

"Oh, Alicia. He is here. He just made it about 15 minutes ago. His phone was dead when he came in so he put it on the charger. He is in the front with Kennedy and his sister and Dad." Ms. Brenda informed her.

Alicia was still a little confused. "I just called his phone a few minutes ago and Danielle answered it. She said he was lying next to her in bed and that he didn't want to talk to me."

"What?!" Ms. Brenda said. "That girl is a mess. I see now she must have taken his phone off the counter in the kitchen when she left because it was up there charging and it's not now. He hasn't even been in the room yet. We have all been up in the front with Kennedy."

"Oh, wow! She had me really nervous. I can't believe she would do that. Well I won't hold you up, I know you want to get back to the family. Can you please tell Cameron to call me before he goes to bed?"

"Yes I sure will. Talk to you later." Ms. Brenda said.

About 20 minutes later Cameron called. "Hey babe I'm sorry I didn't call when I made it but my phone was dead and then Danielle stole it off the counter while it was charging and she still has it."

"It's ok. You had me worried." Alicia said happy to be hearing from her man.

"I miss you so much babe. I'm so happy that I get to see my daughter but I don't want to be here. I want to be with you in Texas. I miss you already." he told her

"I miss you too babe. I had a rough night last night sleeping without you. I can't wait 'til our visit." After talking on the phone for another ten minutes they said goodnight and went to sleep.

Chapter 13

A week had passed since Cameron left for Georgia and although Alicia talked on the phone with him every day and they Skyped often it was still hard being away from him. They were already making plans for her to come visit in June. She would purchase her own plane ticket and he would pay for her hotel and food. She was so excited about seeing her man again and felt like June wasn't coming fast enough.

Alicia had just gotten off the phone with Cameron and was getting ready to lay down and go to sleep when she received a text message from Danielle.

I am not in the mood for her stuff tonight. Alicia thought as she grabbed her phone and read the messages.

Just thought you would like to know that Cameron is already down here cheating on you. He is talking to some girl named Jaslyn that he met at the gas station. He be going over to her house way in Jesup and everything. I told you he was foul.

Alicia didn't bother responding back to her. She was tired of this already. She lay down to go sleep and tried not to think about anything negative.

Her phone rang waking her up out of her sleep. "Hello?" she

answered groggily.

"I just wanted to call and let you know that my divorce has been finalized." Cameron said to her.

Alicia sat up quickly, beaming from ear to ear. This was the news she had been waiting to hear. "Babe, I'm so happy to hear that!"

"That's not all I called to tell you though." he said to her. "Even though we are divorced now, I realized that I am still in love with Danielle and I want to try to make things work with her and be with her again."

Tears began pouring down Alicia's face as she tried to register the news. "But why?!" She wailed. "After all she has done to you and how she tried to use Kennedy against you. Why would you just walk away from us like that?"

Just then she heard Danielle on the phone. "I told you he didn't want you. Stop calling and leave us alone so we can put our family back together." and with that she hung up the phone. Alicia lay in her bed tears falling one after the other, drenching her pillow. She couldn't understand why all of a sudden he decided to be with Danielle again. Her heart hurt so badly and she thought she was on the verge of a having a panic attack. And then... her alarm went off. She popped up out of bed frantically then calmed down once she realized it was only a dream.

Chapter 14

Alicia was sitting at work taking a break while her client was asleep. She was thinking about the dream she had last night. For some reason it shook her to the core. Today was the day that Cameron and Danielle would be going back to court to get their divorce finalized and to establish child support and custody for Kennedy. Just as Alicia was thinking of calling Cameron her phone rang. It was Cameron.

"Hello?" she answered.

"Good morning babe. How are you?" Cameron asked her.

"I'm doing pretty good for the most part. How about you?"

"I'm great! So ready to get this thing out of the way. In a couple hours I'm going to be rid of Danielle and I can see my daughter without having to kiss her butt." he said sounding relieved and excited at the same time.

Alicia smiled when she thought about how happy he sounded. Her smile faded when she thought about the dream she had the previous the night. She told Cameron all about it.

"Wow babe, that's crazy!" he said. "Well you don't have to worry about that because it won't ever happen. I don't want to be with her." he said to reassure her.

They talked a bit more then got off the phone so that he could get ready for court and she could get back to work. He promised to call her after the hearing and let her know what happened.

Alicia had gotten off work at 4pm and headed home. After eating leftover pizza and taking a shower she realized she still hadn't heard from Cameron so she decided to send him a text.

Hey babe. How did everything go today? I been waiting to hear from you.

After about 5 minutes he responded. *It went okay. I got the divorce.*

Alicia wondered why he seemed so distant with her. *Are you ok?*

Yep. I'm fine. I gotta talk to Danielle about visitation because they didn't put it in the divorce decree. I'm gone hit you up in a little bit.

She responded back to him. *Okay just make sure you call me.*

He didn't respond after that. Alicia got this weird feeling in the pit of her stomach. She couldn't help but think about that dream she'd had. When he hadn't called or sent a text message she called him. The phone rang but he didn't answer. She waited a few minutes and then called again. And again. And again. No answer. She was getting nervous and she wondered what was going on. She sent him a text message. ***Is everything ok? I'm still waiting to hear from you.***

Yeah, I'm good. I'm with my mom talking about some things. I'll call you in about an hour. Was Cameron's response.

When he didn't call or text after two hours had passed she picked up the phone and called his mom.

"Hi Ms. Brenda, this is Alicia." she said when she heard her answer the phone. "I was just wondering if Cam is still with you. HE was supposed to call be back an hour ago but I still haven't heard from him."

Ms. Brenda responded, "Alicia I haven't seen or talked to Cameron since I left him at the courthouse. I told him to go talk to Danielle about visitation for Kennedy because they didn't put it in the decree, the judge said for them to work it out amongst themselves."

Alicia was upset. Why would he just lie to her like that? "Oh. He told me he was with you still."

"I haven't seen him since about 2 o'clock. Let me call him and see where he is."

"Okay. Thank you Ms. Brenda." Alicia hung up the phone. Now she was even more confused and worried than before. He had lied to her about where he was. He was really with Danielle. But why? And more importantly, why lie about it?

She text him again. ***Cameron what's going on?***

He texted back. ***I don't want to talk to you right now.***

Alicia was taken aback. ***What? Why?***

He didn't respond so she called him.

"Hello?" he said into the phone.

"What's going on Cam? Why don't you want to talk to me?"

"Cause I don't. Well I can't. I'm kinda busy trying to get something taken care of right now." he told her.

Alicia was getting upset but she tried to control her anger. It didn't make it any better that she heard Danielle in the background making all sorts of negative comments. "Cameron what is going on? I hear Danielle in the background and I know you haven't been with your mom since y'all left the courthouse."

"It's just some stuff going on right now. I had to talk to Danielle about visitation."

"It doesn't take 7 hours to talk about visitation. What's really going on Cam? Please stop lying to me" she pleaded with him.

Just then she heard him and Danielle talking to each other, next, Danielle got on the phone.

"Alicia he doesn't want to be with you. Since he has been here we've been a couple. We've been on dates to the movies, shooting pool, out to eat. All of that. Those texts that you got and he said I stole his phone wasn't true. He would give me his phone to prove to me that y'all were done. He just didn't want to hurt your feelings."

Alicia was fuming. She heard what Danielle was saying but she wanted to hear it from Cameron's mouth. "Well put him on the phone and let him tell me that." she said.

Cameron came back to the phone. "What's up man?" he said as he sighed heavily.

"Cameron is what she said true?" Alicia asked him thinking back to the time he had gone to the movies to see Nightmare on Elm Street. He had told her that he went with his friend and his wife but Alicia had a funny feeling about that. He didn't answer when she called but he called back like 30 minutes later and was talking in a hushed tone saying that he was still in the movies and would call when he got out which ended up being 4 hours later.

"Alicia I am so sorry. We did get our divorce today but I realized that I'm still in love with Danielle and that I want to work things out with her."

Alicia felt like someone punched her in the stomach. Tears began to flow and she hoped she was dreaming again. She pinched herself but it only confirmed that she was indeed wide awake and the man she loved just told her he was going back to his ex-wife.

Chapter 15

Alicia sat on her couch holding a picture that she and Cameron took on New Year's Eve while they waited for him to board his plane at the airport. They were cuddling and kissing and you could see the love between them even that early in their relationship. Tears continued flowing as she flung the picture across the room, watching it crash into the wall and shatter on the floor. She picked up the phone and waited for Ms. Brenda to pick up.

"Hi Ms. Brenda." Alicia said into the phone. "I really hate to call and bother you and to pull you into our drama but I was just wondering if you could just give me some answers."

"Answers about what?" she asked.

Alicia told her about what had just taken place and the conversation she had with Cameron and Danielle.

There was a long pause before Ms. Brenda. "You have got to be kidding me." She said angrily. "He told you out of his own mouth that he was still in love with Danielle and that they are still going to be together even though they are divorced now?"

"Yes." Alicia said still sobbing softly.

"Oh I don't even believe this shit." Ms. Brenda said. "Alicia let me tell you something, that's not going to happen. That girl will never be my daughter-in-law." she said angrily.

"I thought you knew about it because he said he talked to you earlier today after court. She said that they had been going out on dates and spending family time together and everything." Alicia began crying again at the thought of them being together. "You remember the night I called you looking for him he was telling me that he was Walmart and that Danielle left Kennedy in the car and jumped out to talk to him so he was basically corned because he didn't want to leave Kennedy sitting in the car and Danielle was blocking his way to leave. But Danielle said they had gone to Kmart in Jesup together and he was lying about the whole situation. Ms. Brenda I just don't know what to believe any more about anything." she cried into the phone.

"Alicia stop crying. I'm going to find out what's going on and I'm going to talk to him and his father and figure this out. It's going to be okay so stop crying. Like I said, that girl is not my daughter-in-law." she said before they hung up the phone.

Not even five minutes after Alicia spoke to Cameron's mom, he called.

"Hello?" Alicia said barely above a whisper.

"Babe, I'm so sorry. I don't even know where to begin. Danielle knew what she was doing, babe. I can't believe that she wou-" Cameron said before the phone hung up.

What just happened? Alicia thought. She tried calling back but it went straight to voicemail. She tried 3 more times but every time it went straight to voicemail. She put the phone down and began to cry until she fell asleep. When she woke up it was 10:23 pm. She grabbed the phone and tried to call Cameron again even though she was an hour behind Georgia time.

"Yea." he answered.

"Hey what's going on? You hung up earlier." she said, her voice still sounding groggy.

"My battery died. But it don't really matter cause the damage has been done." he said with an attitude. Alicia was confused.

"What do you mean?" she asked him.

He let out an annoyed sigh." You called my parents and told them what happened before you even let me explain the situation, and now because of you I gotta move out. I don't have anywhere to go and if I go to the barrack's they going to take my bah and I have to pay Danielle 600 dollars a month for child support so now I'm going to be broke." he said.

"What do you mean I didn't let you explain the situation? What was there to explain? You said you didn't want me and you were still in love with her and was going to be with her. You basically said y'all been dating and had already made plans to be together after y'all got divorced before the divorce was even finalized. I called numerous times to see if you were really serious and you weren't answering so please tell me where I was wrong at?" she said raising her voice.

He got angry. "Don't none of that even matter. You're feelings are just hurt but I'm about to be kicked out because of you. It's none of my parent's business what I do but you got me kicked out."

"No, you got yourself kicked out by being devious. Your mom is mad because she paid all that money to get you the divorce that you begged and cried for but then you say you're still in love with Danielle and want to be with her. Y'all should have just stayed married." she spat at him.

"Well if you wouldn't have called them then they wouldn't have known about that. And for your information that is why I was calling you back before my phone died. I don't love Danielle and I don't want to be with her. I still have to play her in order to see Kennedy because they didn't put it in the divorce decree. I need to be in my daughter's life and I will do whatever I have to do to be in it. I hate Danielle and the only way to be in my daughter's life is to play her and make her think I want to be with her but none of that matters now." he said.

"Well if that's true then why didn't you just tell me that instead of blindsiding me?"

"Alicia as much as we talked and as much as I confide in you, you should have already known that I didn't really mean what I was saying to you. You should have known my feelings for you." He told her.

"But how would I know after hearing you say that stuff? And not to mention the fact that you been going out on dates with her and God knows what else." she screamed.

"Babe listen to me, we were not going out on dates like you thought we were. We only went to the movies and to shoot pool that one time and that's only cause she asked me if she could come along. All of that was the same night. But it doesn't matter now. What's done is done. I hope you have a good life." he said then hung up the phone.

Alicia sat confused yet again with tears rolling down her face.

Chapter 16

It had been a week since Alicia had spoken to Cameron. She missed him so much. She wondered what he was doing and was he missing her too. She had been an emotional wreck since the night of their last conversation. She didn't have an appetite, she was always crying or trying to keep herself from crying, she didn't want to go anywhere or do anything. All she did was go to work, come home, and lay in bed. As she lay in her bed after work this day she decided to call him.

"Hello?" he answered on the first ring.

Alicia took a deep breath before speaking. "Hey Cam." she said softly trying to hold in the tears.

"Hey. How you doing Alicia?" he asked.

"Not too bad. Was just calling to see how you're doing."

Cameron paused, then spoke. "Well I'm not too bad. Been thinking about you though. I'm sorry for how I reacted the other day. It wasn't your fault that things got out of hand. I didn't get kicked out though."

Alicia smiled for the first time in a week. "Well I guess that's good for you then." she said then spoke again. "So what about you and Danielle?"

"What about it? I told you I was just playing her to see my daughter and that's the true. I don't want to be with her, I never did. Right now the only person I keep thinking about is you. I made a song for you too."

"You made another song for me? When?" Alicia asked suddenly feel the love between them again.

"I'm going to email it to right now then get on skype so that I can see please."

"Ok." Alicia said then hung up and plugged in her laptop. She checked her email and downloaded the song he sent then she played it. She began to cry as she listened to the words of the song,

Baby can we just work it out. All we gotta do is work it out.

We don't have to go and scream and shout, I know we can work it out.

Aye hold up shawty slow ya roll let's talk for a minute

I know we going through a lot but I can't see us ending.

See I aint perfect but at least I know I can admit it

And I don't mean no harm when I don't want you in my business.

We aint done yet so I don't see why we should finish

And we can work out anything if we take the time to listen

You getting mad at me cause you think I don't pay attention

Sometimes I just forget a lot of things that you would mention

I know that we can make it through the weather

We got each other back so I know we can make it better

You my baby girl, you like my queen

The way you are with me is like love in a dream

Why would I let it go don't even let it grow

I rather keep you by my side and just let it flow

We gotta take our time and not the other route

See all I'm trying to say is baby we can work it out

Baby can we just work it out, all we gotta do is work it out

We don't have to go and scream and shout, I know we can work it out

I know that I done made mistakes but I still try

We go through it all and every time you still cry

But then you feel why

But that will never change the fact that you still my girl so we will fly

Don't even worry bout it, it's all gone be ok

See problems gone come but we gone find a way

It aint a lot of things that I can really say

But you always on my mind each every day

You hear your friends talking but they just saying stuff

They got the details but they don't know enough

How can anybody judge not knowing us?

In my mind I can only see us going up

Forget her its only me and you

Even though she got my baby what we got right here is true

Tell me what you want that's what I will do

And we can work it out cause girl it's only for you aye!

Alicia sat with tears slowly rolling down her face. She was so moved by the outpouring of his emotions. She never realized how much he truly loved her until that moment. Cameron watched her on Skype as she wiped the tears from her eyes then began smiling at him. He missed her so much and he missed waking up to her every day. He loved everything about her. Her smile, he silliness, and even though she was a 26 year old woman she still had this innocence about her.

"Babe, I think it's time to start planning for your visit down here. I miss you." he told her.

"I miss you too. I was thinking maybe the middle of June is a good time to come. I can buy my ticket on June first. You will have to pay for my hotel and food though." she said and smiled at him.

"You know I got you babe. I just can't wait to get you here with me. In 3 weeks I will have my baby by my side."

Chapter 17

Alicia smiled as she booked her flight online for her trip to Georgia on the 16th of June. She was so excited, only two weeks and she would see Cameron again. After that whole divorce fiasco she and Cameron had started communicating better and the past couple of weeks they hadn't argued or anything. She was feeling secure in her relationship again and just knew that they were going to continue being happy. She remember that Cameron had asked her to let him know when she booked her flight so she picked up her cell and sent him a text message.

All set babe!

A few minutes later her cell vibrated with a text message from him.

What's all set babe?

Alicia frowned then responded. *Duh, I booked my flight to Georgia like we talked about.*

Another incoming text. *Oh that's right. Good babe. When are you coming?*

June 16 through the 20. You will have to pick me up from the airport at 6pm.

She didn't hear anything else back from him so she went upstairs and took a shower. After putting on her night clothes she decided to check her Facebook page. After logging on and reading her emails and checking her notifications she went to look at Cameron's profile just see what he had posted. As soon as his page loaded she saw a posting on his page from a young pregnant girl named Teanna. She tagged him in her post saying "missing Cameron Thompson" Alicia shook her head in disbelief. It had to be some kind of mistake. She went to the girl's page and was further shocked at all the post she made about Cameron. She had post saying she was on a date with him, post about being on the phone with him, post about him making her feel beautiful, post that he wanted to be with her and her unborn child. Alicia was fuming. She picked up the phone and called Cameron. He didn't answer. So she called again and again until he did.

"Babe what's up?" he said sounding concerned.

Alicia began to yell into the phone, "Don't babe me! Who the hell is Teanna Wilson?"

"Teanna?" he asked.

"Yes, Teanna. And don't even try to play dumb because I already know you know her."

"I don't know her like that. She is just a friend. I went to school with her brother so that's how I know her." he said.

Alicia rolled her eyes, "Well if that's all it is then why is she posting on your fb wall that she is missing you?"

"What? I didn't know she did that."

"That's all you got to say? You didn't know she did it? You've been creeping with this ugly pregnant chick and that's all you got to say?" she spat.

"Whoa babe. I haven't been creeping with nobody! Why would you say that?" he said

"Well if you haven't then why has she been posting everything y'all been doing on her page? Lying ass! I can't believe you got me going through this mess again!" she didn't care that she was yelling because she was pissed off.

Cameron began getting defensive. "Babe I don't know why she would be putting that stuff on there. Aint nothing going on with that girl. If you don't believe me then ask her, she will tell you the truth."

"I already did ask her and she got an attitude with me talking bout ask him what it is and she don't fight over no niggas and all this other BS. That's how I know. Now you better start talking."

"Babe I don't know what's going on with that but i promise I aint messing with that girl. She is pregnant, she is ugly, and she is only 18. I just be being nice that's all. She like me but I didn't want to hurt her feelings. That's all it is."

"Whatever Cam. I don't believe that at all. If that's not what it is then you need to put that little girl in her place." Alicia demanded. "You better delete that comment off your page, and tell that girl to leave you alone and stop posting stuff about you or me and you are going to have a huge problem."

"I'll take care of it babe. I promise, just let me handle it ok."

Alicia hung up still fuming and in disbelief over all this. She hoped it was only what he said it was. She wanted to believe him but his past lies, actions, and misdeeds were making seriously doubt him.

Besides that, her gut feeling was telling her something. She went to bed trying to ease the thoughts that threatened to keep her up. Tomorrow was a new day, she wouldn't let this get to her. Cameron was her man and he had better get his stuff together soon.

Chapter 18

Alicia was so excited because tomorrow she would be boarding the plane to go see her man. The past couple of weeks had been very testy for her. Not only did she and Cameron continuously argue but she had to also deal with Danielle calling every time they got into trying to convince her that Cameron was no good and that Alicia would be better off without him. Danielle called her and let her hear the conversation she had with Ms. Brenda about him having Jaslyn in their house while she was out of town. Danielle said that Jaslyn told her she spent the night with him and even described how the house looked. Alicia didn't know if Ms. Brenda believed her or not, heck she wasn't even sure if she believed him or not because Danielle had a history of being as big a liar as Cameron. Like the time she told Cameron and his parents that her boyfriend, and father of the baby she is pregnant with, forced her to have sex with him and she only did it because she didn't have anywhere else to go and her and Kennedy needed a place to live. The truth was, she had been with this guy for over a year and she got pregnant by him and was mad that Cameron hadn't allowed her to come see him when he got back from Iraq because she was going to trick him into sleeping with her and say that it was his baby because she was only 3 weeks pregnant when he came back. Alicia just didn't know. This Jaslyn story could be true and could not be true. Cameron was adamant that she was just a friend he knew back in the day through other friends. Then there was also the Teanna girl that they kept arguing about. Cameron had obviously still not put her in her place because not only was she still posting stuff about him she began posting stuff about Alicia as well. She called her ugly, said she was supposed to be a grown woman but acting like a child, said she was crazy and that's why Cameron don't want her. She had gotten fed up. She would never understand why the chick on the side always got mad at the main chick when they didn't do anything wrong. It always puzzled her. But after fighting so much with Cameron and hearing all this stuff that Danielle was telling her not only about what Cameron was doing but also all the negative stuff she said Cameron was saying about her she decided not to let anything get to her. She would be down there with him and would see what's up on her own.

Danielle had actually called Alicia last week being super nice to her. When Cameron first got to Georgia Danielle kept saying that they had sex. First she said it was multiple times then she said only a couple times. Cameron swore on Kennedy's life that he did not have sex with Danielle. Alicia hoped not but couldn't be so sure. He said he had to play her to make her think that he loved her so that she would let him see his daughter but he never had sex with her or even kissed her but he would hug her and let her kiss him on the cheek. Danielle had decided to move back to North Carolina with her boyfriend Ronald and have the baby there, she finally realized that Cameron was not going to leave Alicia. Before she left, Cameron made sure that he went down to the courthouse and got joint custody for their daughter. He legally can get her every summer and every holiday and birthday on even number years as well as every other weekend. So when Alicia goes down there to visit him, they are driving to NC to get Kennedy.

When Danielle called Alicia, she was skeptical about picking up the phone. She called 3 times before Alicia finally gave in.

"Yes Danielle?" she said without saying hello.

Danielle sighed, "Look Alicia, I'm not calling to start any drama or anything I just wanted to tell you that I'm sorry for all the things I've done to you and said about you, you didn't deserve any of it. I was hurt and upset and I was taking it out on the wrong person."

Alicia was shocked. She couldn't believe that Danielle was actually apologizing and sounding sincere.

When Alicia didn't respond Danielle continued. "I know you probably don't believe me but that's understandable. I also wanted to tell you that Cameron really does care about you. He told me that you are a great girl and that he wants to make things work with you. He said he doesn't want to hurt you anymore than he already has. That's all I wanted to tell you."

Alicia didn't know what to say so she just said thank you and they hung up. That was last week and she hadn't heard from Danielle since then except when she called earlier that day to say that Teanna was more than just a friend to Cameron. Alicia and Cameron had gotten into it so bad that he called her and Danielle both on 3way and cursed them both out. He told them both that he didn't want to keep going through all the drama and that Danielle had better not ever call him again unless it has to do with his daughter and that he didn't want Alicia to come down if she was going to argue about Teanna the whole time. He sent her the money for her plane ticket and told her not to come. After he hung up Alicia decided right then that it was over between them. She couldn't understand how he could be the one doing wrong but then want to go off on her when she has been nothing but good to him. She wasn't going to kiss his ass. He called not even an hour later and apologized for what he said and how he behaved. He told her that he missed her like crazy and he hoped she would still come to visit. She said she would, so tonight she went to bed early so that she could be up and at work early and then back home to get to the airport on time.

Chapter 19

Alicia was so excited as she boarded the plane at Killeen regional airport. In just a few hours she would be in the arms of the man she loved. He called her that morning to make sure of the time that her flight would get in. H said that he would probably be a little late because they had some kind late formation at work. She wasn't really paying attention to what he was saying though.

After a one hour layover at the Atlanta airport she was finally walking out of the gate at the Savannah airport. She had just spoken to Cameron who said he was on his way. Knowing he had to drive from Hinesville which was about an hour away, she went to the pizza hut and got some wings and a drink while she waited. Fifteen minutes later he called and said he was coming up the escalator, she told him where she was and no sooner than the hung up the phone he was heading her way with a huge smile on his face. She stood and began packing up her food and gathering her purse. He walked over to her and hugged her then gave her a quick peck on the lips. He picked up her travel bag and stepped aside so that she could lead the way out the door. He smiled at her. "Babe you look good. But you look smaller, have you been eating?" he teased her.

Alicia laughed, "Cam stop it. I eat." They put her bags in his car and settled in as he made the drive back to Hinesville. They made small talk but something just didn't feel right about their vibe to Alicia. Like he was hiding something from her. She pushed the negative thoughts from her mind and decided to just enjoy her time here. They went to her hotel first so that she could check in and leave her bags. Then they went to his parents' house so that she could meet them in person finally and he could pack his ACU's, his PT clothes, his pajamas, and some toiletries since he was going to be staying with her in her hotel.

When they arrived at his parent's house he introduced them and Alicia went into Ms. Brenda's office to talk with her and Mr. Eric while Cameron packed up his things.

"So how long are you going to be visiting for?" Ms. Brenda asked her.

"I'm leaving on Sunday." she replied.

"OH ok. Well we are going out of town on Friday morning and won't be back until Monday but you can stay here. You can sleep in Cameron's room and he can sleep in the guest room."

Cameron yelled out from his bedroom, "Nah Ma she already got a hotel room."

Ms. Brenda replied, "Oh ok. I want you to make sure you come by the house tomorrow so we can talk some more. My son always talks about you and he says that you are a good girl. You're so different from that ex-wife of his and that's what he needs." she said laughing. "I have a standing appointment every Thursday to get my hair and nails done so I will be home after 8 tomorrow night but make sure my son brings you back over to see us ok."

"Yes ma'am I will."

After chatting for a few more minutes she and Cameron left to get something eat and then head back to the hotel room.

Chapter 20

Once they made it back to Alicia's hotel room, they ate and then Alicia decided to shower and put on her pajamas since it was getting kind of late and Cameron had to get up early in the morning. Her hair was down in big spiral curls around her face just like Cameron liked it so she pulled it back into a ponytail and tied her head scarf around it. Then she took off her brown plaid baby doll dress that stopped just below her round backside and threw it on the bathroom floor. She removed her bra and panties the put on her shower cap and hopped into the shower. She let the warm water massage her skin as she lathered her towel and began to clean her body. First her neck, then her arms and underarms, then her back and shoulders, next she did her stomach and under her breast, then down to her legs and back up to her vagina and her butt as well as between her butt cheeks, last she cleaned her feet then rinsed the soap from her body and got out. She grabbed a towel, dried off thoroughly and then walked out of the bathroom completely naked. She sat on the bed and began to lotion her body. She felt Cameron's eyes on her but every time she looked over at him he hurriedly turned his eyes away as if he was looking at something else. She continued applying lotion as she spoke to him. "Babe you may want to go ahead and shower. It's getting late."

Cameron stood up, gathering his pajamas bottoms and his toiletry bag. "I was just about to babe." he said then headed in the bathroom smiling.

While Cameron showered Alicia put on her blue plaid boy short pajama bottoms and matching white tank top camisole with blue lace. She sat in the bed and watched TV until Cameron was done showering which only took about 3 three minutes. He got in the bed and Alicia turned off the TV.

"Alright, we got to get to sleep. No sexing tonight cause I got to get up early." Cameron said and then smiled at Alicia.

"Who said anything about sexing? I'm good." she laughed then lay down on the other side of the bed and pulled the covers up.

Not even 30 seconds later Cameron was pulling her arm. "Come her babe. I want to hold you." he said wrapping his arms around her body as she lay her head on his scrawny chest. "This feel so good lying next to you again babe. I really missed this and you." he said kissing her forehead.

Alicia smiled then relaxed as he Cameron rubbed his hand up and down her back so gently. He looked down at her then smiled. "Can I have a kiss?" he asked.

Alicia tilted her head to kiss him. She only intended to give him a sweet little peck but before long they were kissing deeply and passionately as their tongues explored each other's lips and mouths. Alicia caressed his face as he massaged her back. His hands traveled from her face to her back to her butt to her legs then back up again. He rolled her completely onto her back and spread her legs so that he could climb on top of her. He lifted her shirt and pulled her breast out of her bra gently sucking each one. He kissed her neck then began to remove her bottoms right before removing his own. He positioned himself to enter her then he went in as deep as he could. They began grinding against each other as they kissed ravenously. Grabbing and rubbing each other anyplace they could, Alicia rolled her hips underneath him matching each stroke he delivered. He pulled out then dove face first into her chocolate center. He ate her womanhood like he hadn't eaten in years. He missed the way she tasted and he loved the way she moaned when he gave her oral pleasure. He did that until her juices began to pour all over his face and into his mouth. He elevated her butt then slurped up every drop. he came back up and wiped his mouth with his hand then guided his member back inside of her and rocked her until he climaxed and collapsed out of breathe. He kissed her mouth then rolled off of her, grabbing her and pulling her close to him. They cuddled and the last thing she heard was him saying he missed her before they drifted off to sleep.

Alicia felt hands roaming her body and grinding against her butt. She opened her eyes and the clock said 2:07 am. Cameron was aroused and he obviously wanted another round. Alicia backed her butt up against his groin and began to grind back against him. He cupped her breast in his hand and kissed her neck. She turned her head to kiss him back and then rolled over onto her stomach without a word, and spread her legs and put an arch in her back for him to enter her easily. He did so and round two lasted about twenty minutes then they were off to sleep again, until the alarm went off.

Chapter 21

Alicia woke up the next morning to Cameron leaning over the bed kissing her cheek. She looked into his smiling face as she stretched and pulled the covers back to get out of the bed. It was Thursday which meant Cameron had sergeant time training so he was fully dressed in his ACU's.

"Are you already ready to go?" Alicia asked him as she walked into the bathroom to pee. After cleaning herself up from the previous night's lovemaking, she washed her hands then went back into the other room and slipped on her pajama bottoms and flip flops.

"Yes babe. I hate to wake you up so early but I won't be able to bring my car back to you 'til lunch and I don't know what time we will get released for lunch today and I don't want you sitting in here bored all day." he told her as he walked to the door with her right behind him.

"I don't really know what I'm supposed to do though. I've never been here before."

Cameron held the door open for Alicia to go out before he exited the room. "Well babe since we've been talking about you possibly moving here, why don't you go check out some apartments?"

Alicia smiled. She didn't think he was really serious about her moving down there when they had spoken about it before so hearing him mention it again made her happy.

"Ok babe. I'll do that."

Once they pulled into the parking lot of his designated unit Cameron stopped right in front of the walk way without parking lot. He put the car in park and began gathering the things he needed from his car.

"Babe let me see your phone please." Alicia said to him. He handed it to her and put the code in to unlock it.

She immediately opened his Facebook account and saw that the comment Teanna left about missing him was still on his page. She was mad. He told her he deleted it but all he really did was hide the comment so that she couldn't see it from her page. Just as she was about to go off on him she regained her composure and remembered they were in front of his workplace. She didn't want to start drama in front of his NCO's. So instead she went to Teanna's page and posted a comment as Cameron.

Look Teanna, I'm not trying to hurt your feelings or nuttin but you need to stop posting stuff on my page and stop posting stuff about me on yours. That's not cool. You starting trouble between me and my girl with this BS.

When Cameron finished getting all his gear out of his trunk he got back into the car to get his phone.

"Look babe." Alicia said showing him what she posted on Teanna's page.

Cameron looked at his phone before putting it into his pocket. "Babe I don't care about that. I'll call you in a bit okay?" he said as he got out of the car.

Alicia got out and walked around to the driver's side. As she got into the driver's seat she heard a few of Cameron's friends yelling to him across the parking lot.

"Damn T that's you?" one of them said pointing toward Alicia.

Another one yelled out, "Dawg she is baaad!"

Alicia laughed as she watched Cameron smile and his chest swell up with pride and ego at the fact that his friends saw he had a beautiful girlfriend. He leaned into the car and kissed her before saying goodbye.

Chapter 22

After dropping Cameron off at work Alicia went back to her hotel room where she showered and dressed. She drove around Hinesville looking at different apartments and just observing her scenery. She was supposed to pick Cameron up when he called for lunch so she tried to just stay out as long as possible. She decided to check Facebook on her phone and when she did she was beyond upset. On Teanna's page she saw a post on her wall that made her want to drive to Cameron and slap him in the face.

I ain't got time for the dumb chicks that wanna be playing today. So u hack into his fb account and post that BS on my wall Danielle or Alicia whichever one of you did it. I would have believed it too had Cameron not called me personally this morning and tell me that one of y'all hacked into his account. Nice try loser but it didn't work! Lmao at you dummy!

Alicia was furious! Why would he go and call her and tell her that nonsense? She drove back to his unit to pick him from work and as soon as he got into the car she let him have it.

"Why in the hell would call that girl and tell her that i hacked into your account and posted that message?" she yelled at him.

Cameron tried looking confused but it didn't work. "What are you talking about babe?"

"Don't play with me cam, you know exactly what I'm talking about!" she said angrily. "She posting stuff on her page that you called her this morning after I left."

"Oh, well I just didn't want to hurt her feelings. My mom and grandma are on my fb page, I didn't want them thinking that I'm that type of person. You posted some mean stuff on her page." he said

Alicia was in disbelief. "You're kidding right? How in the hell did anything I posted come off as mean? And you claim you aint talking to her or whatever then why did you call to smooth it over? She deleted you and was done with you so why go and tell her you didn't know I did that when I told you this morning that I was doing it?"

"Babe I'm asking you to just let me handle the situation. I'm trying to let her down easy, she is young."

After arguing for what seemed like an eternity and him even trying to blame Danielle for Teanna posting that stuff, Alicia gave up talking about it she was tired and she was done. She had decided then and there to just make the best of the rest of her trip and when she got back home decided if she wanted to continue in this relationship with Cameron.

Later that night they went to visit his parents and then went to see Killers at the movies. Although Alicia was confused and her heart was hurting, she still had a good time with Cameron. They hugged and kissed and cuddled while watching the movie and laughed like they used to when they first got together. They went back to Alicia's hotel room, showered and made love for the rest of the night. They were so spent after arguing all day and making love all night that Cameron fell asleep still inside of her and woke up in the middle of night and made love again. Friday was a bad day too. They argued the whole day and it had gotten so bad that they weren't even speaking. Once again Alicia had to be the bigger person and push her pride aside even though she was right about the arguments. Cameron had been on the phone with his cousin in Atlanta telling him that she was ruining the trip because she kept arguing and questioning him about Teanna whom he says nothing is going on. Besides all the obvious signs, Alicia felt it in her gut that it was more than what he said. But none the less she was tired of arguing and she just let it go. After they got into another argument at Cameron's friend's house while he was cutting hair Alicia left walking down the street and to the park. Cameron called to see where she was and when she told him he drove there and picked her up. The argued again on the drive back to the hotel room and by the time they got into the room, they were both silent and mad. Alicia decided to be the adult and she went into the bathroom to take shower. After turning on the water she went back into the room completely naked.

"Are you coming in with me?" she asked trying to make at least a little bit of peace.

Cameron looked up from his laptop and half smiled. She saw his manhood stand at attention through his pants. "Do you want me to?" he asked her.

"If I didn't want you to I wouldn't have asked." she said to him.

"Well in that case, yes I'm coming in too." he stood and led her by the hand into the bathroom. He undressed and they both got in, Alicia stood under the water and Cameron stood behind her.

He grabbed a washcloth and the soap and lathered it up, then gently cleansed her body from head to toe. Once she rinsed the soap off the switched places and she washed him. He rinsed then turned to face her. He grabbed her face in his hand and kissed her gently.

"I'm sorry baby." he said softly. "I don't want to keep fighting."

Alicia kissed him back and they got lost in the love that the two of them shared. He began to allow his hands to roam over her wet body as he kissed her neck and then licked and sucked her nipples. She turned around to face the wall then propped one foot up on the tub and spread her legs. He bent down a bit then entered her from behind. He stroked slow and gently but ever so deep. Soon the sounds of moans escaped their mouths and before long both had reached their climax. They washed up again and then exited the shower. The next morning they got up bright and early for the drive to North Carolina to pick up his daughter Kennedy.

Chapter 23

The drive to North Carolina was wonderful. Alicia was determined not to argue at all that day because tomorrow she would be heading back to Texas. During the 5 hour drive the two lovers talked about everything they could think of. Cameron told Alicia how much he wished he was still living in Texas with her and how he believed in his heart that no matter what they go through, he knew one day she would be his wife and give birth to his child. He told her that even though Danielle was his wife he never wanted to marry her. He just was in love with idea that someone wanted to marry him and have a family with him so when she suggested they get married he agreed. He said that was the worst mistake he ever made. He went on to tell Alicia that she was the best woman he had ever had and that he was happy she was a part of his life.

"Babe you have no idea how I feel about you. Listen to this song. Every time I hear it I think about you." he said as he turned up the volume to a song by Chamillionaire.

When I look back at my life

I realize, realize somethin aint right

I'm missing yooooou, oh in myyyyy life

Alicia laughed, "You're silly babe."

"But I'm serious. You have everything that I could ever want in a woman. I know I do and have done some dumb stuff but I never want to hurt you." he said sincerely.

Alicia smiled. For the rest of the drive they laughed and talked and made plans for when he would visit her in Texas. A song by Nicki Minaj came on the radio and Alicia smiled. "I love this song." she said to Cameron. She began to sing along with it.

Baby ima only tell you this once you the illest

(babadaba ooo) and for ya lovin ima die hard like Bruce Willis

(babadaba ooo) you got spark, you you got spunk you got something all the girls want

You're like a candy store and I'm a toddler you got me wantin' more and more, more of your love your love

Then Cameron joined in singing the back ground vocals. They both started laughing. It was starting to feel like they could get back on track after all. Alicia decided to just wait a little bit to see where they could go.

When they arrived at Danielle and Ronald's apartment Alicia observed the scenery as Cameron parked down the street out of view and waited for the police escort to come and mediate the exchange of Kennedy. Cameron's parents advised him to have the police come out because they believed that when Danielle saw Alicia she might try to start trouble. No one knew just how right they were.

Once Cameron spotted the police officer pulling up to Danielle's apartment he drove up to the patrol and got out to greet him. Alicia stayed in the car but it was so hot out and Cameron's air wasn't working properly. She hoped it wouldn't take long because his leather seats were starting to make her sweat a little. Cameron and the officer walked up to the door, knocked, then waited patiently for an answer. After knocking a second time Danielle came to the door. Words were exchanged and Alicia could tell that Danielle was upset that Cameron had the officer with him. Danielle went back into the house, Alicia assumed to get Kennedy and her bags. Alicia was so hot and it had already been ten minutes of waiting in the car. She got out and stood next to his car to get some air. When Danielle came back out and saw Alicia standing there she immediately went into a rage.

"Hell no she ain't here!" she said yelled. "I'm not letting Kennedy go with you. Forget that!"

"Ma'am" the officer interjected, "He has legal documents stating that he gets this child today and she is to remain with him for the rest of the summer. If you don't allow him to have his child he can report you and you will go to jail for failure to obey a court order."

Danielle wasn't having it. "I know what the court order says but I have a restraining order against her. She is not allowed to be anywhere near me or my child." she told the officer in hopes that she would keep Alicia and Cameron from getting here.

"Man that's a lie Danielle! You are so foul." Cameron said to her.

The officer spoke up, "Ma'am do you have the actual restraining order so that I make take a look at it?"

"Hold on a minute, the papers are inside." she said then disappeared into the house again. This time when she came back out she brought Kennedy and her bags along with her. She was frowned up and Alicia just looked at her with disgust. Here she was 7 months pregnant by another man and was still upset that Cameron was with Alicia. She looked tore up too. She was wearing a black sundress with a black du-rag tied around her head and some worn out flip flops. She was tall and slim, except for her huge pregnant belly. Alicia had finally seen Danielle in person and she was just as bad looking in person as she was on her pictures. Now she could understand why Danielle always tried to talk bad about her. Alicia was very pretty with big brown almond shaped eyes, full and luscious lips, and a beautiful dark brown skin tone. The icing on the cake was her baby making hips, thick thighs, and round back side which she showed slightly in her long flowing maxi dress.

as Cameron, Ronald, Danielle, and the officer all walked toward Cameron's car with him holding an almost two year Kennedy in his arms Danielle began talking noise to Cameron but directing it at Alicia.

"You better not let her touch my baby's hair." she said as she handed him Kennedy's bags. "Cause since she wear weave, that means she's bald headed and don't know how to comb hair."

Alicia was about to get into the car but turned around when she heard Danielle talking. Just as Alicia was about to say something back to Danielle, Cameron cut her off. "Babe don't say nothing just get in the car right now."

That was all Danielle needed to begin going off. "Oh what trick you got something to say?!" she said to Alicia. "Say something bitch. Act bad!" she yelled as she began walking toward her.

"Alicia get in the car right now!" Cameron said as he started walking toward the car.

Alicia really wanted to slap the taste out of Danielle's mouth but decided against it for two reasons. She was pregnant and there was a police officer standing right there. "You a big miserable giraffe." Alicia said to Danielle as she got into the car and locked the door so that she wouldn't have to put her hands on a pregnant woman. "You still mad that Cameron don't want you? Does Ronald know how you still be blowing up his phone and acting a fool over another man?" Alicia teased her. "Get your life together boo, I don't entertain drama. You're pathetic."

Danielle went ballistic! "Forget you trick! Ronald knows everything so don't worry bout what I got. Get your scary ass out the car and watch I fuck you up bitch!" Danielle began trying to open the door. When she saw it was locked she began knocking on the window still irate and cursing at the top of her lungs. "You will see me again bitch and I'm gonna beat yo ass." she said then made a gun with her fingers, pointed at Alicia, and pulled the fake trigger.

Alicia smiled at her then gave her the finger and said "Oh God bless you and have a wonderful day Danielle."

Cameron fastened Kennedy into the car seat and placed her bags on the seat next to her. He wasn't shocked at all by Danielle's behavior, he knew that's what she would do. He was shocked that not only did Ronald not try to stop Danielle from fighting even though she was carrying his baby, but also the officer didn't do a single thing to keep Danielle from trying to attack Alicia nor did he do anything when Danielle threatened to shoot her.

Cameron and Alicia rode back to Georgia talking about what just took place and in the midst of multiple texts to his phone from Danielle still trying to keep up trouble and back to back private phone calls to Alicia's phone. When Alicia picked up one time it was Danielle screaming on the other end of the phone still threatening her and cursing at her so Alicia just hung up in her face and didn't answer anymore. Cameron not only got calls from Danielle, he also got a call from her Grandmother cursing him out, calling him a bitch, and talking noise about Alicia saying she was a hoe and that both of them are going to get their asses beat. Alicia was convinced that Danielle and her family was just crazy.

Chapter 24

Once they made it back to Hinesville Alicia and Cameron went to his parents' house so that they could see Kennedy and he could get more clothes for the night. They hung out with his parents for a couple of hours then got some food and headed back to the hotel with Kennedy in tow. After eating, showering, and bathing Kennedy they all lay down in bed and drifted off to sleep. Alicia woke up in the middle of the night. Her mind was racing and she couldn't get back to sleep. She kept thinking about going home tomorrow and it dawned on her that even though today was a good day she and Cameron still had the issue with Teanna that hadn't been resolved yet and she didn't trust him as much anymore like she used to. How could they make a relationship work when he keeps doing things to make her question if she should even be with him? She was saddened at the thought that tomorrow might be the last time they are together. she was feeling confused and she didn't know what to do so she got out of bed, went to the chair on the other side of the room and sat quietly while she cried for hours 'til there wasn't a tear left.

The next morning they showered dressed and checked out of the room. They decided to have breakfast at an IHOP in Savannah since she would be flying out from that airport there. The drive was a pretty quiet one except for Kennedy in the back seat singing every song that came on the radio and playing with Alicia's hand.

"Babe you ok?" Cameron asked Alicia.

She nodded her head.

"You sure? You haven't really said much since last night. Is there anything bothering you?" he asked her.

"No, I'm fine." she said turning her head to look out the window before tears fell. Once they arrived at IHOP they were seated and given menus. As they looked over and decided what they wanted the waitress came over making small talk.

"Oh my goodness this little girl is so pretty." she said to Alicia who was holding Kennedy in her lap. "Are you her auntie?" She asked

Alicia.

Alicia looked at her dumbfounded. "The auntie?"

The waitress smiled mischievously.

Cameron interjected, "No she isn't the auntie she is the stepmother. That's my daughter."

The waitress faked a smile, "Oh I'm sorry I thought you were brother and sister."

"It's cool. We ready to order though." Cameron said pleasantly.

After placing the orders the waitress took the menus and sashayed away.

"Ain't that bout nothing." Alicia said annoyed at the waitress.

Cameron talked while they ate but Alicia barely said two words. Her mind was all over the place. Cameron asked her what was wrong and she burst into tears right there in IHOP.

"Babe what's wrong? Why are you crying?" he asked with concern in his voice.

She couldn't tell him why she was crying because she really didn't even know. She just sat there silently with tears streaming down her face trying to control her emotions.

"Oh are you okay?" the waitress asked her.

Cameron answered for her. "Yes she is fine. Just having a rough day that's all." he said rubbing her hand softly. Alicia continued to cry quietly.

"Babe for real why are you crying like this? You ain't pregnant already are you?" he said then laughed.

Finally Alicia laughed too. "No stupid." she said to him. "I'll be fine. I'm just emotional I guess."

After eating they went to a park in downtown Savannah where they sat on the grass by a pond and water fountain. They played with Kennedy and talked and tried to enjoy themselves before her flight that departed in less than three hours. They made it to the airport an hour and half before her departure. The sat in the waiting area until thirty minutes before boarding call. When it was time to go Alicia asked one of the really nice airport guards if Cameron and Kennedy could at least walk down to the security check with her but he regretfully told her it wasn't allowed. So they had to say their goodbyes right then and there. That was something Alicia wasn't ready for. She began to cry again. Cameron sat Kennedy on a bench next to them then pulled Alicia into his arms, holding her as close as he could for as long as he could. He hugged her while he wiped her tears away and kissed both of her eyes, her nose, her cheeks, and her lips. "It's ok babe." he said into her ear.

The guard looked like he wanted to hug her too. "You deploying soon or something son?" he asked Cameron.

"No sir, she is just really emotional because she is going back home today." he responded.

He turned back to Alicia. "Baby stop crying okay? We are going to be okay. Everything will work out fine." he said trying to comfort her. "I want you to text and call me when you get to the next airport and as soon as you make it to Killeen, ok?"

Alicia nodded. She couldn't speak any words because once she boarded the plane she didn't know what was going to happen between them. It broke her heart to think it might be the end. What were they going to do with no trust and 1100 miles between them?

Cameron hugged Alicia again and gave her one last long kiss. Then Kennedy kissed her cheek and hugged her. Cameron stood holding Kennedy and watching Alicia until he could no longer see her. As Alicia settled into her seat on the plane, she reached for her phone to power it off and received a text from Cameron.

I miss you so much already. I wish you didn't have to go. Make sure you call me as soon as you can. I miss you babe.

Alicia smiled and tried to fight back tears but they rolled down her cheek anyway. She was so emotional today. She sent him text, *I miss you too babe and I will call as soon as I land in the ATL. Happy Father's Day btw. Ttyl.* Then she powered off her phone and settled in.

Chapter 25

Four weeks had passed since Alicia had gone to visit Cameron in Georgia. They were still together but things had been up and down ever since she got back. He was still lying to her about Teanna so she contacted Teanna again and convinced her to be on the phone during a 3way with Cameron. Teanna agreed but opted not to say anything or let him know she was on the phone. She thought that Alicia was just some crazy ex-girlfriend who wouldn't let go and this would prove that she wasn't. Although Teanna said she had never kissed, had sex with, or been intimate with Cameron, Alicia still didn't like Cameron allowing the girl to hang around him or post all the stuff about him which she was still doing. Teanna and Alicia had spoken on the phone prior to bringing Cameron in on the call.

"What I want to know is how you could possibly think he is your man?" Alicia asked her.

"What do you mean how could I think that?" Teanna said with an attitude. "Let's see," she said with a sarcastic laugh. "We talk on the phone, we hang out, he always ask about me and my baby, he talks to me about a lot of stuff like his goals and all that, I went to the hospital when his daughter had to go to the ER for her fever...do i need to go on?" she said starkly. "He even said he wanted me to move in with him when he got his own place in September."

Alicia began to laugh. "Little girl you are funny." she said to her. "That's what makes you think he is your man?" Alicia laughed again even harder. "You have been so called talking to him for over a month and you haven't so much as even held his hand or kissed him. Y'all didn't go on any dates, the only time you ever saw him was when you would invite yourself to go hang out with him and his friends while they played pool, in which you drove yourself."

"So? I don't have ride in his car boo I have my own car." she said it like Alicia was walking or something and that ticked Alicia off.

"Not only that sweetie. But if he is your man how could I have come down there to visit him for 5 days and 4 nights and you not talk to him during lunch or after 5pm and didn't see him at all? That's your man though right? How is he your man and you have never been to where he rest his head or even met his parents? I was driving around Hinesville in his car while I was there. I was out and about on dates with him while I was there honey. His parents know about me baby, we have an actual relationship. If you're his girl why did I go to North Carolina with him to get his daughter instead of you?"

Teanna was mad now. "That don't mean nothing. I don't have to go pick up his daughter with him and I have met his mom for your information." she said.

Alicia sighed," girl stop lying no you haven't met his mom. Ms. Brenda knows he is with me and his whole family likes me there is no way they would meet some random chick he brought home and there is no way he would bring you home boo. She don't know nothing about you so cut it out."

"Well just go ahead and call him on the three way then. Show me that y'all are together."

They got him on the phone and just as Alicia said he denied almost everything. He said he never told her he wanted her to move i with him. He said he didn't like her and he don't know why she think he do, he only let her come to play pool to be nice but he didn't really want her there. So much stuff he said but he took Alicia by surprise when he said that he told Teanna he was single because he and Alicia never confirmed that they were back together. She cursed him out because he didn't care about confirmation when was going down on her or spilling his seeds inside of her. He didn't care about confirmation when he was professing his feelings for her. That day was a long day of arguing followed by other days of arguing because Teanna was still trying to cause more trouble between them. She kept commenting on his pics and posting stuff about him. Finally Alicia made him delete her and he then decided to not answer any of her calls or texts even though she contacted his friends begging them to get Cameron to talk to her again. Alicia was happy that he finally put her in her place and got some sense. He had messed up the trust in their relationship which caused them to argue so much but after he stopped talking to Teanna, Alicia felt as if he was trying to regain her trust little by little.

Chapter 26

Alicia stood in her downstairs half bathroom, hands gripping the sides of the sink and staring at her reflection in the mirror. A million thoughts ran through her head as she waited patiently for an answer that will either ease her mind or send her into a frenzy. A part of her was scared to know, yet another part of her just had to know. She closed her eyes and took a deep breath. *May as well just do it and get it over with.* She thought to herself. She pulled down her pajama pants and grabbed the Styrofoam cup from the sink then squatted over the toilet and begin to urinate into the cup. Once the cup was half full she placed it carefully on the paper towels on top of the sink then finished urinating in the toilet. After wiping, washing her hands, and fixing her pajamas she removed the pregnancy test from box then dipped the test end into the cup with her urine and held it there for 10 seconds as the box directed. Once the ten seconds were up, she immediately replaced the cap and laid the test on the paper towels. She flushed the urine down the toilet, threw away the cup, and washed her hands again. Then she closed the lid on the toilet, sat down, and waited. Nervousness trembled through her body as she waited for what seemed like an hour but only one minute had passed. Finally three minutes were up. Alicia picked up the stick and her mouth dropped as she read the result. She was pregnant. She closed her eyes then opened then again. The results were still the same. She didn't know whether to cry from sadness or tears of joy. Her only emotion was shock, and her only word was "wow".

They had sex almost every day for five months straight and then she goes to visit for 5 days and comes back pregnant. This was crazy. She sat there for about an hour in a daze. What should she do? She called her best friend Carol and told her the news. Carol was excited because she was due to have twins in less than a month and she was excited for her friend pregnant as well. After talking to Carol she sent a text to her mother and her sister letting them know the news and all they could both say was the same thing she said, "Wow!" She had one more very important person to tell about this discovery. She picked up the phone and called Cameron.

"Hey, are you busy? Because we need to talk." she said to him.

She heard him sigh into the phone. "Babe I don't feel like arguing about Teanna or answering questions I've already answered. She is irrelevant and I don't even talk to the girl." He said.

Alicia let a groan. "Oh Cam, right now Teanna and asking questions is the least of my concern. I'm pregnant."

Chapter 27

Silence filled the other end of the phone for what seemed like forever. "Girl stop playing. Are you for real?" Cameron asked Alicia.

"Why would I play about something like this?" she irritation dripping in her voice.

Cameron let out a small chuckle. "Wow. That's crazy." he said before pausing. "You sure about this?'

"Yes I'm sure." she said.

"Well you know I'm going to be there for you, right?" Cameron said with sincerity.

Alicia smiled. She knew Cameron wanted another baby because he barely ever got to see his daughter. "Yes, I know."

They talked for a few minutes, deciding that they really needed to address the issues in their relationship and come up with a plan of action for their future but they would have to wait to talk 'til later when he was off work. They decided to chat on Skype later that evening.

Later that night as Alicia was chatting on Skype with Cameron she noticed he looked a little down. He said he was happy about the baby but still she knew something else was bothering him.

"What's wrong?" she asked him.

He just shook his head before responding. "It's just real messed up the way my mom talks to me sometimes."

"What happened?" she asked him.

"Well I told my parents that you are pregnant and my mom just started going in on me telling me how I'm so stupid and why would I get you pregnant and I'm the dumbest person in the world. She just went off on me big time. She said I messed your life up." he said looking as if he was about to cry.

Alicia felt really bad for him. She didn't think it was right for his mother to say those things. He didn't do it by himself, he didn't wear a condom but she didn't make him wear one either. Not anytime they were together so she was just as stupid as he was.

"Well don't even worry about all that. Just think about this new beginning.
And the fact that you will have a child whose life you will be able to be in more than just during the summer." she gave him a reassuring smile.

"Yeah and I will get to see all of this baby's first moments. First words, crawling. First steps, first teeth, first everything. I'm excited babe. We are going to have a baby!" he said with a huge smile on his face.

Alicia laughed and rubbed her belly even though she wouldn't be showing for a very long time. "So what do you want to have?" she asked him.

"I don't know. I'll be happy as long as the baby is healthy but I kinda want another girl." then he thought before speaking. "But I really want a boy too. Someone to take my name and play sports and video games with."

"Well I want a boy. I am praying for it." she said crossing her fingers. "You think if it's a boy you would want him to be a junior?"

"Nah. I don't believe in that. He is his own person with his own identity so I think he should have his own name."

They talked for a little while longer but Alicia began to dose off.

"Babe, I'm going to let you go to sleep. I will call you in the morning okay." Cameron said to her.

She smiled at him and said goodnight, then turned off her laptop and snuggled under her cover ready for sleep. Her cell phone chimed indicating a text message. She reached on her nightstand and grabbed her phone and saw a text from Cameron.

I am sooooooo happy that u r having my baby. Words can't even explain how I feel right now. I really miss u and I can't wait to see you again. Goodnight.

And with a smile on her face and love in her heart, Alicia lay down and dosed off.

Chapter 28

Alicia and Cameron had been doing a lot of talking ever since she found out she was pregnant. They seemed to argue a lot less and get along better even though they still argued about Teanna and Danielle occasionally. Danielle would text her being friendly and cordial but Alicia suspected it was all another game that she was playing because all she ever talked about was the baby and asked if Alicia would move to Georgia. Alicia had been dealing with Danielle long enough to know she was only friendly when she was up to no good so she kept the conversation at a minimum and barely gave her any info about what she was planning. Teanna wasn't as big a problem anymore. Cameron had deleted her off of his page once she began to become increasing disrespectful towards Alicia and stirring up more drama. He had told Alicia that he even stopped answering her calls and responding to her texts so she had begun messaging his friends asking if they knew why he wouldn't talk to her. Alicia and Cameron had decided that they wanted to make the relationship work and try to be a family so because Cameron was stationed there at Fort Stewart they decided the best thing was for Alicia to move there. She was nervous yet excited at the same time. She didn't like being away from her family and friends plus she would have to find another job, and apartment since Cameron was still living with his parents. Cameron told her that his mother was mad at him at first for getting her pregnant but that she was now happy and hoping for a grandson. He said she was looking forward to Alicia moving down there and that Alicia might even be able to go with them on their annual family weekend trip to a timeshare in Orlando on Labor Day weekend. They had only 4 weeks 'til she was set to move so Cameron was looking for a place for Alicia there in Georgia.

After weeks of apartment searching and job searching and planning and packing her things and putting her furniture in storage, Alicia was all set to make the 18 hour drive from Killeen, Texas to Hinesville, Georgia. She got up early and after saying goodbye to her family she got on the road towards her future. Cameron had found her a small 2 bedroom mobile home in Allenhurst about 5 minutes away from his parents who lived in Walthourville. Alicia had only seen a couple of pictures of it that Cameron had sent her and it was not up to par compared to how she is used to living but she figured it wasn't all that bad and besides she didn't plan on living in that mobile home for long anyway. As she drove the 18 hours Cameron, her mother, and her sister would call her periodically to check on her and make sure everything was ok. She pulled over once in Alabama to get a room and take a 3 hour nap before she was up and on the road again. Finally at about 830 on Tuesday morning she had made it. She called Cameron to let him know she was there and he made plans to meet up with her as soon as he was released for lunch. She busied herself until then by going to get the keys to her place, getting a P.O. box, having her electricity turned on and getting a hotel room to stay in for the night since she didn't have anything to sleep on yet. Cameron met her at the KFC on Oglethorpe highway at lunch and when he saw her with her pregnancy glow and barely noticeable pudge he was overcome with joy. She had worn her hair in long cornrow braids with a yellow fitted t-shirt and blue jeans shorts. She smiled as he wrapped her in a warm embrace and kissed her lips.

"I missed you babe." he said to her as he looked into her eyes and placed a hand on her belly. "How was the drive? How are you feeling?" he asked her.

She placed her hand on top of his. "I'm ok. Glad I made it safely." she said to him. He just smiled and simply said, "Me too." They stood there for a while both with a hand on her stomach neither saying a word just marveling at the notion of a baby with half of both them was inside of her. They finally went over to his car and sat inside while they ate. As they finished eating, Alicia dropped a potato wedge on the floor of his car. She reached down to pick it up but brushed something under the seat by accident. She wondered what it was so she got out of the car and reached her hand under the seat but accidentally pushed it back further. She climbed out of the car and went to open the back door to try and get whatever it was. Cameron looked at her curiously. "Babe what are you doing?"

"I accidentally pushed something under your seat and I'm trying to get it." She said as she knelt down on the ground and reached her hand under it. Just as she heard Cameron walking around to the back door saying "Babe don't worry about it." she finally grabbed whatever was under the seat. And to her surprise it was two boxes of condoms. One was a 3 pack but all were still there and the box wasn't even open. The other box however, was a 12 pack and 3 were missing. Alicia's heart dropped as she stood up with the boxes in her hand and turned to face Cameron with tears forming in her eyes. He stared with his mouth hanging open. She had been there less than 4 hours and already she felt that she had made a huge mistake.

"What the hell is this Cameron?!" she yelled at him, holding the boxes in the air.

Cameron began rubbing his head. "Babe it's not even what you think. My mom gave me those."

Alicia wanted to slap him. "You expect me to believe your mom gave you two boxes of condoms? Really Cam?"

"Yes because it's the truth. She gave me one box and Tara gave me the other one." he said.

"And why in the ell would your mom and best friend that you claim has been trying to sleep with you, give you boxes of condoms?"

Alicia folded her arms across her chest waiting for his answer, knowing it was about stupid.

He took a deep breath. "They gave them to me when I told them you were pregnant. They said because I don't need nomore babies after this one." He thought that answer was enough to end the conversation but he was wrong.

"That's stupid on so many levels first of all. And why would Tara give you this box of opened condoms with 3 of them missing? Tell me that."

"I don't know but that's how she gave them to me. Maybe she used the three that are missing."

Alicia almost lost her temper but she reeled it back in. "Do you know how stupid you sound right now?" she spat nastily at him. "Tara has been married for ten years, why in the hell would she need condoms dumb ass?!"

"I don't know, I guess for the same reason that she has been trying to have sex with me."

Alicia narrowed her eyes at him. She couldn't believe this. The day she moves 1100 miles away from her comfort zone to start a new life with this man that she loved, this is what happened. She wanted so badly to believe him but in heart she knew the truth.

"Babe please let's not start things out like this. This is supposed to be our new beginning. We out here in this parking lot cursing and arguing I'm all in uniform, come on babe. It's not what you think. Just let it go please." he said looking into her eyes.

Even though she felt like he was full of crap she decided to just let it go. She was going to give him a new start. She didn't believe he was faithful to her while she was in Texas but she was here now so she would forgive him once again and try to make the best of it now that she was there.

Chapter 29

After the argument in the parking lot at KFC Alicia was left to think things through on her own. She wanted so badly to believe Cameron but in her heart she knew he had been unfaithful and his excuse as to why he had the condoms was complete bs. She needed someone to talk to. She decided to check into a hotel in Hinesville since the army lodging hotel she had stayed at on post during her visit was booked up. She checked into the Econolodge and after showering and changing into sweats and t-shirt she went out the door to go to Walmart. Cameron was at work and they hadn't spoken to each other since the fight earlier during lunch. She wanted to call him but she didn't feel like she had done anything wrong so quickly she pushed the thought out of her mind. She decided to call her best friend. Cookie Hendson had her best friend since they were both being carried in their mothers' uterus. Cookie was always there for Alicia and never once judged her or made her feel stupid for any choice she'd ever made and she had made many bad choices throughout her life.

"What's up girl? How you like it so far?" Cookie spoke into the phone without saying hello. Immediately Alicia began to cry, right in the middle of Walmart. She couldn't stop the tears from falling. She was homesick, she missed her friends and family and her heart was hurting so badly. "Alicia?!" Cookie screamed into the phone. "What's wrong? What happened?"

Alicia began to tell her about what took place earlier that day, pausing every two minutes to let out some more tears. Cookie listened as Alicia sobbed and recounted the day she had already had.

"I just don't know what to do Cookie. I came all the way down here and gave up everything to be with him and this is what I get." Alicia sobbed quietly.

"Alicia he could be telling the truth about the condoms. I doubt that he is but hey you know that was before you got down there. If you think you can forgive him them do so and just try to move on from it" Cookie said, trying to console her best friend. "And if you feel like you want to leave that's okay too. Nobody is going to judge you or think anything bad about you if you do. You live and learn and you do what's right and what's best for you."

Alicia talked to Cookie for about twenty more minutes before getting off the phone. She purchased a drink and some snacks for the night before heading out of Walmart.

She was feeling a little better after talking to her best friend and she decided that she would give Cameron another chance and stay there in Georgia. After today they wouldn't mention it again. She called Ms. Brenda to let her she made it safely and to see if she could stop by to see them tomorrow. Alicia was smiling from ear to ear when Ms. Brenda picked up the phone but her smile soon faded when Ms. Brenda informed her that she had no idea Alicia was moving down there.

"Oh my goodness. I wish you would have talked to me first before you had given up everything and moved down here. We had no idea you were moving here." she told Alicia.

"I thought you all knew. Cameron said he told y'all and that y'all said it was a good idea too." Alicia felt so stupid.

"No we did not. He didn't tell us anything about it. If he had we would have tried to convince you not to come. Oh my goodness. So let me ask you this, whose idea was it?"

Alicia fought back tears. "It was both of our ideas. He said you all knew about me moving here and that you said I might even be able to come to y'all family get together Labor Day weekend in

Orlando."

"I just don't know why he would lie like that."

"Ms. Brenda can I ask you a question?"

"Yes go ahead."

"Did you give Cameron some condoms?" Alicia asked dreading what she already knew the answer was.

"No I did not. I wouldn't do that." she said.

Alicia's heart dropped yet again. She felt like the wind had been knocked out of her. Today was just getting worse and worse. She talked with Ms. Brenda for a little while longer agreeing to come by and see her the next day. Ms. Brenda had also said she was going to talk to Cameron and his father which meant Cameron was about get a lecture.

Later that evening once Cameron was off of work and he talked to his parents he called Alicia, very angry that his parents had gone off on him for the two of them deciding on Alicia moving down there. He said they called him stupid and told him he was going to ruin her life. Alicia didn't understand why they thought he was going to ruin her life or why Cameron was so mad at her when he was the one who should've been a man and told them the truth. They argued for about fifteen minutes and Alicia couldn't take it anymore so she hung up on him. She was exhausted after a long day of driving, running errands, arguing, and crying. All she wanted to do was go to bed and try again tomorrow. Just as she was drifting off to sleep her phone rang. It was Cameron.

"Hello?" she said barely audible.

"Were you sleep?" he asked her, no trace of anger in his voice.

"I was about to be." she responded.

"I'm going to come stay with you in your hotel room tonight. You shouldn't be alone on your first night here."

Alicia was happy that he decided to come but she wondered if his parents made him do it. He arrived ten minutes later with his pajamas on and his backpack with is PT clothes in it. They didn't exchange any words at all. He lay down in the bed next her, pulled her into his arms and they went to sleep.

Alicia was elated today. After 3 weeks of job searching and worrying about her little bit of savings being gone, Alicia had finally gotten hired at a home health agency. Even though it was only part time, she was still happy because a part time job was better than no job at all. She had even enrolled in Savannah Technical College and started taking the first 3 classes on her road to a nursing degree. Things were going really well between her and Cameron lately even after the condom incident. She forgave him and had not mentioned it since then. Cameron helped pay for her schoolbooks along with her mom and older sister Ralonda chipping in as well. He called and texted her throughout the day just to let her know she was on his mind and he missed her. They went to lunch together every day and the love between them began to grow stronger and stronger. He even cleaned up her mess when she vomited on the floor one day at her place. He stayed over almost every night and he was constantly rubbing her belly and telling her how beautiful she was. He would tell complete strangers out in public that she was pregnant and he was so excited about the baby. She was showing a bit now so it made her happy to know that everything was going well. This weekend was his family's trip to Orlando but she wasn't able to go because she had to work. He called her five times a day while he was there and constantly told her how much he loved her. On one occasion she overheard him speaking with his Aunt Alphie when she asked him who he was on the phone with his reply was, "I'm talking to Alicia. I really love this girl." His Aunt then got on the phone and told Alicia that she couldn't wait to finally meet her and welcome to the family. Alicia was overcome with joy knowing that not only did he love her, his whole entire family did as well. She couldn't wait for the weekend to be over because she missed him soooo much.

Chapter 30

It had been almost two months since Labor Day weekend and Cameron and Alicia had been doing better than ever. They continued to spend quality time together and growing closer. Alicia was enjoying her job and school and was getting more excited as the time came near to find out the sex of the baby. Cameron was staying over her place at least three times a week. They were going out on dates to the movies, out to eat, spending time at his parent's house, she went to a Halloween function with him that his unit was holding at work. They even had a picnic in the park. Everything seemed to be going so good until she began getting texts from Danielle again. Danielle would text her and say that Cameron was always calling her and dogging Alicia out. She said he told her that he wasn't attracted to her because she had gained weight and that he couldn't even bring himself to have sex with her anymore. She said he had also said that he wished she hadn't moved down there and that he really didn't want to be with her. Alicia tried to act like what Danielle said didn't bother her but deep down it cut her to the core because she wondered if Danielle were telling the truth. She started noticing things changing between her and Cameron but every time she would try to talk to him about what she was feeling he would start an argument. He said that she always nagged him about everything and that she should stop worrying about Danielle so much. Danielle had also told her that her friend saw him in Walmart with a Latino girl and that he told her that he wished he was with his ex-girlfriend Tina instead of Alicia. Alicia had begun to get a little insecure because Cameron wasn't telling her she was beautiful anymore. He wasn't spending time with her anymore. He wasn't sending ten text messages a day telling her he loved her and was thinking about her like he used to do. Heck he barely even came over to check on her anymore. She was confused, she didn't do anything wrong so why was he suddenly distancing himself from her? That is the thought Alicia had been thinking as she drove to Walmart. It was a beautiful Sunday afternoon and Cameron had just left Alicia's place. He said he was going home to his parents' house to get his things ready for work the next day. Alicia was bored so she decided to get out of the house. She walked around Walmart just browsing for about 45 minutes. After she purchased some snacks and t shirt she headed out through the garden center exit and proceeded to the crosswalk in the parking lot to her car. Before she made it to the middle of the crosswalk a silver Honda turned into the street and hit Alicia on her left side cause her feet to come from under her and she landed on her back. Alicia screamed and cried loudly. She couldn't believe she had just been hit by a car. All she could think about was if her baby was ok. *My baby! Please God let my baby be ok!* That's what Alicia kept repeating until she heard voices talking to her trying to get her attention.

Chapter 31

A lady in a SUV jumped out of her car and ran to Alicia's side as well as a man walking across the street and the driver of the Honda. They helped her to move to the sidewalk and sat her down on the curb. The woman called 911 as she rubbed Alicia's back and the man was asking her if she was ok.

"I don't know if I'm okay or not." Alicia cried. "I'm five months pregnant." The man had a look of worry on his face as he asked Alicia for her cell phone to call her husband. Luckily another bystander had gathered all of Alicia's things out of the middle of the street for her. Alicia sat crying and rocking and rocking her body as she cradled her stomach praying that her baby would be ok. She would've been embarrassed at all the nosy people walking by looking at her as she cried loudly but right now they didn't matter only the well-being of her unborn child. Alicia called Cameron's cell phone and waited as he answered after the second ring.

"Hello?" he said into the phone.

Alicia began crying even harder than before as she tried to tell him what had happened. "Cam! I, I g-ot hit by a a a ccar!" she cried so much that she was incoherent.

"Babe calm down. I can't understand you. Why are you crying? What happened?" Cameron didn't sound all that concerned, he sounded more irritated that she was calling him crying like that.

The man waiting with her took the cell from her hands and sat down beside her. "Hey man, I'm here at Walmart with your wife and she was just hit by a car as she was going across the parking lot. I think you may want to get down here pretty quick." the man listened to whatever Cameron was saying before he spoke again. "Yes the ambulance has been called and she is doing ok so far but she is really scared and worried for the baby." another pause before speaking. "Ok, I'll tell her."

After hanging up the phone the stranger turned to Alicia and handed the phone to her.

"Don't worry he is on his way, you and your baby are going to be fine."

Alicia was escorted into an ambulance just as Cameron pulled into the parking lot, he couldn't get through so he left the car running and hopped out and ran to the ambulance where Alicia was at.

He looked concerned and as if he nervous as well. "Babe are you ok?" he said as he climbed and hugged her. Alicia cried some more as she nodded her head. He searched her face to be sure she was really ok then he wiped her tears away and kissed her forehead. He lay a hand on her belly and told her that everything was going to be okay. Since they would need a ride home from the hospital he decided to follow the ambulance in his car. Once they got there they were seen right away and escorted up to labor and delivery to check on the baby. The nurses reassured her that the baby was fine and that she had nothing to worry about. They told her that her body is like a cocoon for the baby and that it is designed to protect her baby. They did an ultrasound just to be a hundred percent sure and unfortunately weren't able to see the sex of the baby so Alicia had to wait 'til tomorrow when she had her prenatal appointment. She was so relieved that she and the baby would be ok. But her happiness was short lived when Cameron opted to go home after dropping her off at Walmart to get her car instead of coming home with her. She felt like she had such a trying day that he should've been there to comfort her. But she didn't want to argue, they had been doing too much of that lately so she just went home and showered then got into bed. The next morning she had an early appointment and she was excited because today was the day she learned the sex of her baby. She hadn't gotten much sleep the night before because she was sore from the accident and her mom, sister, cousin, and best friend kept calling her all night to check on her and make sure she was ok. She loved that they cared so much about her even though felt like Cameron really didn't anymore. She was beginning to think the things Danielle had told her were true. He hadn't even bothered to call her this morning to see if she was ok or make it to the appointment this morning. She was there alone again. She received a text from Ms. Brenda saying that she hoped she was feeling ok and she was excited to know what she was having. The nurse called her name and after taking her vital signs and weight she was escorted to the exam room where she would have the ultrasound done. The moment of truth had finally come she knew the sex of her baby. After leaving the office she sat in her car and looked at the ultrasound pics in amazement. She pulled out her cell phone and begin typing.

Ok everybody ready?! She sent the message to everyone in her phone.

*It's....*she sent that message.

*A....*she sent that message then waited five minutes. Her mom and sister and even Ms. Brenda were all texting her saying stop playing and tell them. She giggled knowing she had them on the edge of their seats because everyone was hoping for the same thing. Finally she sent the last text message...*BOY!!!!!!*

Soon after her phone was flooded with texts from everyone expressing their joy at bringing a boy into the family since both her family and Cameron's family was mostly girls.

Chapter 32

Cameron and Alicia were overjoyed knowing that would be having a boy. They had already started trying to come up with baby names. Cameron's family wanted the baby to be a junior but Alicia and Cameron opted not to do that. They wanted him to have a combination of their names so they decided to give him Cameron's middle name. They couldn't agree on a first name though. Julian,

Caden, Xay, and Julius but no one agreed on any of them. They were both just so joyful and overwhelmed about having a boy that they postponed trying to figure out a name so that they could just bask in the happiness. But the happiness was short lived. Cameron began to become distant towards Alicia as she got further along in the pregnancy. He stopped sending the *I was just thinking about you* and *just wanted you to know i love you* texts that he used to send five and six times a day. He stopped taking her to lunch every other day like used to do. He stopped staying overnight with her and spending time with her. He barely called to check on her. He would barely answer his phone or respond to her texts. He would say and do things that he knew would cause an argument just so that he would have a reason not to be around. They stopped having sex and every time she would try to talk to him about what she was feeling he would turn it around on her and make her feel like she was nagging him and had no reason to feel as she did. Things were getting really bad between them and Alicia just didn't know what to do. Her pregnancy had caused her to gain a lot of weight too. Her face, hands, legs, and feet were swollen and her back was always hurting. She couldn't sleep and she was so homesick and lonely. She had made one friend there but that wasn't enough for her. She needed the love and presence of her family. But mainly, she needed the love and support of Cameron but he was nowhere to be found. He had basically deserted her when she needed him the most. He would call or come by maybe once a week but for the most part she was there all alone. She was sleeping on an air mattress in a rundown trailer while he was in a king sized bed in his parents' house and he didn't even care. She cried almost every day, trying to continue working and going to school even though she was miserable and alone. As if all of that wasn't bad enough, Danielle began to call and text her again and tell her all these things that Cameron had been saying about her. Danielle said that Cameron told her that Alicia looked so different now tht she was pregnant that he was no longer attracted to her. He told her that he didn't want to go to any of Alicia's doctor's appointments so he lied and said his NCO wouldn't let him come. He told her that he wished Alicia had never moved down there and that he didn't love her and he wished he would've never gotten her pregnant. Danielle also knew about everything they argued about and everything bad going on between them. Alicia was already devastated because although she was denying it she knew in her heart that Danielle was telling the truth because there was no way she could know all this stuff unless he told her. When Alicia confronted Cameron about it he flipped the script and started arguing with her. He said she should know better than to believe anything that Danielle says. He got angry and told her that if she wanted to believe Danielle then he didn't care. Alicia was torn between what she knew in the back of her mind and what she felt for Cameron.

It seemed as though things for Alicia was going even more downhill. Every time she looked up she was finding out something else Cameron was doing or saying. She found a half-naked picture of Danielle in his phone. When she saw it, she threw the phone at him. "Why do you have a half-naked picture of her in your phone?!" she yelled at him. Cameron tried to look surprised that the picture in was there but Alicia wasn't buying it.

"Man that's an old picture that i forgot was in there. Chill out." he said to her.

"No the hell it's not Cam. That's the same hairstyle, mirror, and bathroom of the pics you showed me the other day that you said she sent to you saying that she look way better than me. I'm not stupid. You sure as hell didn't mind letting me know that she sent the other pics but this one you forgot to mention."

"I told you I don't know why she sent those pictures to me. She is so unattractive to me. Like eww I don't see anything appealing about her." he said.

Alicia was getting enraged because he was trying to act like she was stupid. "Then why the hell did you keep that picture then?"

"I told you I didn't know it was in there. I thought i deleted them all but I must have accidentally saved that one."

"You must think I'm some kind of fool. You deleted all the other ones but somehow the half-naked one was saved. You know what screw you Cameron you may as well go back and be with that trick." and with that Alicia stormed off.

About an hour after that Cameron called to apologize still sticking to his story that he didn't know it was in there. He told her that he called and went off on Danielle for sending those pictures and all Danielle did was laugh. Alicia wasn't buying his story still but she was already depressed and stressing and she just didn't have it in her to argue anymore. She lay down on the used king sized bed that Cameron's parents had gotten her the previous week to sleep on. She was very thankful that his parents cared about her because they were the only reason she had a nice bed to sleep on instead of that flat air mattress. She could've called her family and gotten money for a bed but she didn't want them to know how bad things were for her down there. She was embarrassed that she gave up her nice home, a good job, and stability to move to Georgia to be with him. He didn't do anything to help her. She was struggling to pay her bills, didn't have any furniture except the bed his parents gave her and the TV she came with because all of her furniture was in storage in Texas. Sometimes she barely had enough gas to get to where she had to go. She barely had food and she was never able to go out and do anything because she barely had any money. She had never lived like this before and she was ashamed that Cameron wasn't helping her with anything at all. She couldn't understand how he was being this way after all she had done to help him. Allowing him to live in her house, drive her car when his was messed up, cooking, cleaning, great sex, helped him with his music, motivated him to excel in his career, forgave him time and time again after all the crap he did. She made him look good. When they were in Texas he was way more of a man. Even though he was doing his dirt behind her back he made sure he came home every night, he made sure his portion of the bills were paid, he took her out all the time, they had fun together, he even paid for to get her tooth pulled without her even asking him to. He wasn't the same man that he was before, or is this who he really is but he was playing a role before.

Alicia lay in bed thinking of how things used to be with them and how far they had fallen from that. She wondered what went wrong. She opened her laptop and logged on to Cameron's Facebook account. Because of their trust issues he had given her the password to prove that he wasn't doing anything wrong. She would go and check it periodically just to see what he was doing. He would get friend request and she noticed two things. The first thing was that one of the request was from Jaslyn. She was the girl that Danielle had told her he was seeing when Alicia was still in Texas. She accepted the request for him. Then she saw a request from a young looking Puerto Rican girl named Maria Gomez. She noticed that the girl had sent the request a few weeks ago yet even though he had been on and accepted other request he didn't accept hers. Alicia made a mental note of that then logged off without accepting the request. Something wasn't right but she was too tired to think about it, besides, she had to get up and get dressed to go over to Cameron's parents' house for Thanksgiving dinner.

Chapter 33

Alicia arrived at The Carter's home a little after noon on Thanksgiving Day. The food was already prepared but their guest hadn't shown up yet except for Ms. Palmer who lived next door. Ms. Brenda wasn't even dressed yet. Alicia was used to being at there house so when she got there she spoke to everyone then went into the movie room. Mr. Eric was in there watching something on the projector screen.

"Hey Alicia. How are you doing?" he asked her like he always did.

"I'm ok Mr. Eric. Thanks for having me over today."

"You know yo are always welcome over here. How's my grandson doing in there? How does the pregnancy have you feeling?" he asked like he knew something was wrong.

Alicia sighed and broke down in tears. "The pregnancy is fine but I'm miserable."

Mr. Eric looked concerned. "Well what's wrong?"

Alicia shook her head. "I just don't understand it. I left my life behind to come here and be neglected and left to live in these horrible conditions by myself." she said between sobs. "I go to my appointments by myself, I am by myself almost every day. He doesn't rub my belly anymore, he doesn't check on me, and he doesn't spend time with me" Her voice was barely above a whisper but Mr. Eric heard every word. He even noticed that Cameron, whom they affectionately called Skylar, hadn't even come in to say hello to Alicia.

"It's going to be okay Alicia. Don't cry. We talk to Skylar all the time, he knows what he's supposed to do but you can't allow him to treat you like this." he said in a fatherly tone. "Skylar still needs to grow up and he has his priorities all messed up. You're going to be okay, just don't let him keep you feeling sad."

They talked a little bit more before he left and Cameron came in.

He smiled at her and sat down next to her. "Hey babe."

"Hey" she said between sniffles.

"What's wrong?"

"Nothing" she said.

"Then why are you crying?" he asked.

"Because I'm tired of this." she said.

"Tired of what?" he asked like he was oblivious to how he treats her.

"Being neglected and treated like crap. You out doing I don't know what. Acting like I don't even mean anything to you. I'm so tired of this."

He sat up and looked at her. "How am I neglecting you and treating you like crap?" he asked incredulously.

"You have got to be kidding." she said. "You never spend time with me. You always got an excuse for why you're never around anymore. You always talking to Danielle and telling her all our business and talking bad about me. You don't help me with anything when you know this is not how I am used to living. You eating out all the time, sleeping in a nice house, getting to watch your cable and use the internet and do just whatever you want while I'm at home by myself all the time watching to same DVDs over and over again rubbing my own belly. Going to doctor appointments by myself. No friends no family no nothing. I left everything to be with you and you keep mistreating me." Alicia was sobbing heavily now. Her hormones were so out of whack but she was hurting inside.

"Why you gotta be like that with me?" he asked her.

Alicia got angry, "Be like what? You're treating me wrong."

Cameron began to get loud. "You need to grow the hell up and stop crying and acting like a little girl because everything doesn't go your way. You don't know what the hell I got going on. You just assume you know everything. Sorry everybody can't be perfect like you." he spat.

Alicia wasn't surprised that he reacted this way. This is what he always does when he knows he is wrong. She didn't even argue anymore. She simply looked at him, grabbed her bag, and got up to walk out. She heard him call her name but she kept going. She ran into Ms. Brenda as she was going through the kitchen.

"Sorry Ms. Brenda but I have to go. Thank you for inviting me over. I don't want to ruin y'all day." She said as she continued toward the door.

"You didn't even eat. Do you want to take a plate home? What's wrong? What happened?" Ms. Brenda asked.

"I just need to go. And no thank you." and with that she left. She burst into tears as soon as she got into her car. This was the worst Thanksgiving ever. She went and ate a peanut butter and jelly sandwich. Cameron was calling and texting her trying to apologize and asking her to come back over. She simply responded with "no" then turned her phone off and cried herself to sleep.

Chapter 34

It was almost Christmas time and Alicia was in class to take her last final before the semester was over. She was so relieved because she was having a hard time focusing on her studies. She had to quit working her part time job because her pregnancy had her in a lot of pain and it was hard to tend to her patients in her state. She was a little over 6 months pregnant and she was huge. She looked like she was carrying twins. As she sat there trying to focus on the exam she began thinking about Cameron and how he still had not changed or made an effort to do right by her. In fact he was getting worse. They had a Christmas party at work and he didn't even ask her if she wanted to go. She had gotten behind on her light bill and when his parents told him as a man he should help her pay it he got angry with her. She didn't understand why giving her 90 dollars was so much to him when he didn't have any bills to pay and he splurged on stupid stuff. Why didn't he want to help her? She tried concentrating on her exam but in addition to all of these thoughts she began feeling weird. The room started spinning and she began feeling really hot and flushed. She was jittery and her heart began racing. She was becoming a little nervous because she didn't know what was going on. She thought maybe she needed some water so she got up from her seat to inform her instructor but before she even made it to his desk she began stumbling and before she realized it she was falling face first to the ground. Luckily one of her classmates was within arms-reach and she kept her from hitting the floor too hard. Alicia lay there not knowing what was going on. Her class mates crowded around her trying to fan her and make sure she was ok. The dean and paramedics were called. They looked up her emergency contact information and called Cameron.

Alicia lay there on the floor trying to regain her composure while speaking to an instructor from the nursing department who was tending to her until paramedics arrived. She was a little shaken up and scared because she didn't know what was going on with her. The paramedics told her that she was fine and that they could transport her to the hospital but they didn't think it was necessary. She opted to stay and finish her testing. As she sat at a table sipping water and composing herself, Cameron walked in. He didn't really looked very concerned but he came over and kneeled down in front her and held her hand.

"Are you ok? What happened?" he asked. Alicia told him what happened. He asked her if she was sure she wanted to stay and she told him yes. He told her that if she started feeling bad again then call him and he will come back and drive her to the hospital. He went back to work and she went on the finish her exams.

The days passed on an Alicia and Cameron were still in a kind of dark place in their fragile relationship. It was Christmas day and Alicia was at home by herself spending it eating sliced ham, mac and cheese, green beans, and a roll. That was all she could afford to have for Christmas dinner after buying gifts for family members. Cameron nor his parents invited her over for Christmas even though they had a house full of people celebrating the day with them including Cameron's daughter Kennedy. He had come over to Alicia's house with Kennedy to bring her gift and they only stayed for about an hour. Although his gift to her was very thoughtful and something that she loved (3 books that she hadn't read autographed by the author), she was very hurt and ashamed even that he didn't even spend the holiday with her nor did he bring her a plate of food from his parent's celebration or invite her to come. Once again she was sitting there in her tiny two bedroom trailer, sad and lonely. And once again all she could do was cry.

New Year's rolled around and she was in a little bit of a better spirit than she was on Christmas. She and Cameron had driven together to take Kennedy back home to North Carolina to Danielle. They didn't fight or argue with each other even though they did have a little bit of an issue with Danielle once they got there. Cameron made plans to bring in the new year with Alicia at home, just the two of them and she was very happy about that. But of course like always with him that happiness was short lived. He was already 3 hours later than the time he said he'd be there and to make matters worse he was out with his friends and putting her on the back burner. When they were on the phone she could have sworn she heard female voices in the background but he swore that it wasn't like that. That Pippen's girlfriend was there and she was the voice in the background. Alicia sat up for hours, well past midnight waiting for him to get there and he never showed despite numerous texts promising that he would be there soon. She just couldn't understand how someone who claimed to lover her so much could just keep doing these things to her not only while she was pregnant with his child but also when she was many states away from her family and friends and had absolutely nobody there but him. Of course this was yet another holiday that she spent crying herself to sleep. Damn hormones!

Chapter 35

Alicia opened the letter that she had just received from the mail and began jumping up and down and thanking God. Finally, the settlement check from her accident had arrived and incidentally he income tax check had also been deposited into her account. She was so happy and relieved because she didn't know how she was going to make it much longer with her bills piling up and Cameron not helping and complaining about his own so called bills. She breathed a breath of relieve and left to go deposit the check into her account. She now had a little less than eight thousand dollars. She decided to get caught up on her bills and pay off some other debts that were haunting her since she had been in Georgia. She felt so relieved that she was able to do that and still have money left over to finally buy furniture for her living room and to get her car fixed, not to mention buying stuff for the baby which is what she and Cameron planned to do this upcoming weekend. It was the first week of February and the baby was due to be delivered via C-section on March 11. Alicia looked like she was overdue because of how big she was. Cameron and Alicia drove to Jesup so that they could go to K-Mart to buy stuff for the baby. Well technically Cameron only drove her there because he didn't spend anything during that shopping trip, only she did. Alicia's mother bought a swing for the baby and some clothes, her sister Ralonda bought the convertible playpen/changing table/sleeper, and Cameron's mother bought the infant carrier and stroller. They also received lots of baby clothes from Alicia's Aunt as well. Today at Kmart Alicia just wanted to get a bouncer, a memory book, and some blankets. As they were heading to check out line Cameron's phone began to ring and he answered it.

"Hello? What's up?" he said into the phone and waited for a reply. It didn't take long for Alicia to figure out that it was Danielle on the other end. She expected it to be a brief conversation and hoped Cameron would tell her that he would call her back later since they were spending time shopping for the baby and she wasn't calling for anything important, only to have a general conversation. When he didn't do that but instead kept talking Alicia began to get an attitude.

"Um is the conversation between y'all really that important?" she asked him.

"Nah she just wanted to talk." he said.

"Okay well I feel like you're being kinda rude right now." Alicia said nicely.

He rolled his eyes. "How am I being rude?"

"Because we are here trying to shop for our baby and not only are you taking away from it by having an insignificant conversation that can wait 'til later, but you're having a whole conversation as if I'm not here." she explained.

"So I'm not supposed to have a conversation with her? You always tripping about something. She wanted to talk it's not a big damn deal." he said getting angry.

"Oh and I supposed the conversation couldn't wait for another hour after we got back to Hinesville when you run off and leave me as soon as we get back?" she said to him her voice almost a yell. "You are supposed to be here focusing on me and our baby for one damn day and you can't even do that. Like how hard is it to say hey I'm being rude I'll call you back later." they began arguing and Alicia really just wasn't in the mood for it so she simply said her peace and didn't speak to him for the rest of the shopping venture. Once at home she unpacked all of the things she'd bought and began assembling everything...by herself. She had the playpen, swing, and bouncer put together in no time and she did it without the help of Cameron. *I don't know what his problem is.* She thought to herself.

They hadn't talked much over the next week, she was trying to not stress too much given that she seemed to spend a lot of time going to the ER during this pregnancy. She didn't want to cause unnecessary stress on the baby so when she spoke to her sister Ralonda about being lonely and having no friends there, Ralonda decided to give her nice weekend getaway in Savannah as sort of a Pre-Valentines/Birthday gift. She was excited to get away from Hinesville and all the tears and just have a weekend to focus on herself and relax a little. Ralonda booked Alicia a room at the Wyndham hotel and Alicia was very pleased with the accommodations. She spent the weekend shopping, dining, and sight-seeing. She loathed going back to Hinesville that Sunday when the trip was over. The night before the end of her trip she had been texting Cameron. He tried to act like he felt bad that she went to Savannah without him but Alicia believed that he was actually happy that she did so that he could do whatever he was doing without her being close. Their birthdays were next week and Cameron had already gotten his gift from Alicia. Since he liked watches and bracelets and things of that nature she got him a black and silver chain link bracelet. He said that he had already gotten her gift and that it was such a great gift that she was sure to love it. She got excited because he had also said that he had gotten her a great Valentine's Day gift too.

Valentine's Day had finally made it and Alicia was excited to be spending the holiday with Cameron. She missed the way they used to be without all the arguing. He texted her about four different times and said that he was in his way over with her gift but as the hours passed, he never showed up. Alicia was not only heartbroken but she was livid! She went to bed the same as the other holidays. The next morning she woke up to a bunch of text messages and Facebook posts from friends and family wishing her a happy birthday. She felt the love of the people whom she loved the most. She looked at Cameron's page and noticed that he had been online and posted about God blessing him to see another year yet even by the time 3 pm rolled around he still had not called, text, or come by to wish Alicia a happy birthday. She was fed up and without even thinking about it she changed her relationship status to single.

Ms. Brenda had called Alicia to come over and talk with her so she was heading over to The Carter's home. When she got there

Cameron was in his room and he didn't even come out to say hi to her.

"Hey Alicia." Ms. Brenda said.

"Hi." she replied as she sat down in the room Ms. Brenda used as an office.

"Why did you change your relationship status?"

"Because your son is no good and I'm tired of him treating me like crap."

"What did he do?" she asked

"Well besides what he does everyday, he had me waiting on him yesterday to come spend Valentine's Day with me and bring my gift but he didn't even show up and then on top of that he didn't even say happy birthday to me today. In fact he hasn't said anything at all to me. Not even an apology." Alicia's voice began to crack as she teared up. "I'm just so tired of being treated like nothing when I don't deserve it at all."

"I can't even believe him." Ms. Brenda said. "I thought he was with you yesterday, he said he was going to your house." she paused. "So he didn't spend Valentine's day with you?" she asked.

"I didn't see him at all yesterday." Alicia cried.

As if right on cue Cameron walked in. "What's up yo?"

Alicia just looked at him like he was stupid.

"So you single now huh?" he asked her.

She still didn't say a word.

"Okay I guess that's what's up then." he said trying to sound like he cared.

Alicia went off. "Don't try to act like you care dude! You keep standing me up, don't want to do anything for me and then have the nerve to not even get me anything for Valentine's day after you lied and said you already had my gift. Then can't even say happy birthday to me but you can be all on Facebook? You are so sorry!"

"Man I'm sorry yo. I said I already your gift because I knew what I was going to get you but I waited 'til the last minute and when I went to get it, it was sold out so I didn't come yesterday because I felt bad about not having anything to give you." he said sounding like he just pulled that lie out of his butt.

"Whatever Cameron. You are so full of it." Alicia sneered and walked out of the door.

Alicia heard a key in the door and she automatically knew it was Cameron since he was the only person she had given a key to. He walked in carrying a Walmart bag and handed it to her.

"Happy birthday." he said smiling.

Alicia opened the bag and pulled out her gifts. She tried to keep from frowning. He bought her a Valentine's Day nightgown that looked about 3 sizes too big and a Valentine's Day pajama pants set that was also too big.

"Thanks." she said unenthusiastically. She wished he would have just not gotten her anything instead of this crap that he clearly got off of the after Valentine's Day clearance rack. No thought put into it at all. And he probably just went and bought it. She just shook her head and laid the bag on the couch. He sensed that she wasn't happy with that at all so he offered to help do some chores around the house. The only thing she need done was the trash to be taken out and the leaves to be raked in the yard or her landlord would charge her 60 dollars if it wasn't done by Sunday. Cameron kept saying he was going to rake them up but no matter how many times she reminded him he never came through. Her neighbor offered to do it for 40 dollars and Cameron said he would pay him to do but he claim to never have any money. She hope that he would get it done tomorrow. Cameron snapped her out of her thoughts by informing her that he was about to leave and he grabbed the trash and headed out the door.

It was Saturday morning and Alicia was tired and sore but she needed to get out of bed and call Cameron to see if he was going to come rake the yard. After calling him five times and texting him 8 within two hours with no response she figured she would have to get out there and do it herself because she didn't have 40 dollars to pay her neighbor. As she was eating breakfast her neighbor came and knocked on her door.

She opened the door and stood in the doorway to talk to him. "Good morning Mr. John. How are you?" she asked politely.

"I'm pretty good but I just wanted to come over and let you know that your boyfriend threw a bag of trash of behind your trailer and the animals done got a hold to it and spread it all over your yard."

Alicia's mouthed dropped. "Are you serious?"

"Yes I am. I saw him with my own two eyes go back there and toss it back there." he said shaking his head.

"Okay. Thanks Mr. John. I'll get it up." Alicia said and closed the door.

She was so mad she could scream. It's bad enough that she has to go out here and rake up some leaves at 8 and half months pregnant but to have to clean up this trash that he threw out there for no reason was the icing on the cake. She was furious. All he had to do was take a ten second walk down to the dumpsters and put the trash in it but he couldn't even do that! If he didn't want to take the trash he should have just left it in her kitchen and she would've taken it to the dumpster herself. But instead she has even more work to do now. She bundled up and put on some boots and gloves and went to her yard. First she picked up all the trash which took about 30 minutes then she grabbed her rake and some trash bags and begin raking up the leaves. After about an hour and a half he body begin to hurt but she refused to quit because if she did she would never get done in time and she still had more than half the yard left to go. As she raked she looked up and saw Mr. John walking over with his rake and without any words spoken to her he began raking up the leaves on the other side of her yard. She smiled at him as a way to thank you since she couldn't speak due to a combination of being extremely tired, out of breath, and in tears. She was so grateful that he came to help that she couldn't stop crying. Then she cried even more because of the realization that Cameron didn't care about her or her well-being. He just continuously treated her bad and left her out dry.

Chapter 36

Over the next week Alicia busied herself with reading books and getting prepared for the birth of her baby. Even though her C-section was scheduled for another 4 weeks away, she wanted to have her hospital bags packed and ready to go just in case. She was also kind of nervous, yet excited because her dad, whom she hadn't seen in about twenty years, was coming from Alabama tomorrow to see her. He was bringing her older brother that she'd only just met back when she first moved to Hinesville as well as her younger brother whom she had pictures of but had never seen in person. She didn't know what it was going to be like and although she had a little bit of anger towards her father she was determined for this to be a good visit. I t was around 4 in the afternoon and she was relaxing on the couch feeling a bit bored so she decided to play games on Facebook. She figured she would just check Cameron's page and see if there was anything new going on. When she logged on she noticed that again he had accepted some friend requests but still hadn't accepted the request from Maria. Alicia was about to log off but something told her to just accept the request. She did so and then went to look at Maria's page. Her eyes widened and her heart began to beat fast and hard. She could not believe what she was seeing. Many status updates dating all the way back to the beginning of October. And most of them were about Cameron. She saw one that Maria posted talking about how she couldn't believe that Cameron was ten years older than she is but it didn't matter to her because she could handle it. Then another about her stomach hurting and Cameron taking her to the hospital. There was one about Cameron trying to get stationed in Germany and her planning to go with him. She got even angrier when she saw the one saying that she had been upset that she couldn't go see him perform at Revolutions nightclub because she wasn't old enough to get in being that she is only 17 years old. Alicia was livid. More proof of him playing her like a fool. She knew that no matter how he would try to deny it that he and Maria had been talking because some of this stuff she would only know from talking to him. Alicia slammed her laptop down, grabbed her keys, and took off towards his parents' house. Luckily they only live three minutes way because she was driving so crazy she might not have made it too far.

She rang the doorbell and Mr. Eric opened the door and stepped back to let her in.

"Hey Alicia. How are you doing?" he asked the same question every time he saw her. Alicia thought he was such a nice person.

"I'm not too good at the moment Mr. Eric. I need to speak to Cameron please." she asked her voice barely above a whisper.

Cameron walked out into the front room and told her to come back to his room to talk. He tried to close the door but Alicia wouldn't let him. She took a seat at his computer desk while he sat on the bed.

"What's up?" he asked her as he picked at the hairs on his chin and neck.

Alicia looked at him for a minute before she spoke. "Who is Maria?"

He tried to look impassive but Alicia didn't miss the panic that flashed in his eyes.

"She is just a young girl that I know through her dad. Basically nobody." he said casually.

"Mmm." Alicia said then turned to his computer and logged onto his Facebook page then went to Maria's page. She turned back around to face him. "Well these posts on her page sure doesn't seem like she's a 'nobody' to you."

Cameron walked over to the computer and read some of the post. "Wow I had no idea she was posting all this stuff." he looked at Alicia. "I don't know why she is putting that stuff on there."

Alicia got instantly pissed. "What the hell do you mean that you don't know why she posting this stuff?" she said to him. "She posting it because you been messing with her all this damn time and don't try to lie either."

"I'm not messing with her. I swear I'm not. I only know her because I know her dad and he does music."

Alicia rolled her eyes. "That is some serious BS. If all it was is that you only know her from that then why is she talking like you are her man? Why is she saying she is going to Germany with you? Why was talking about your performance and all that other stuff she said about you?"

Cameron hesitated for a second. "Man it's not like that. I guess she just took me being nice to her in the wrong way. Why are you always just assuming that everything you see is the real truth?"

Alicia lost it then. "Don't try to play me like I'm some little dumb girl that don't know that you are lying and are full of crap. She is 17 years old! You are 27. She hasn't even graduated high school! She has no car, no job, no place to call her own, and to top it off she is sloppy looking and way bigger than me and I'm 8 months pregnant! Are you that nasty and low class? Like really? What could you possibly do with her? You say you're not attracted to me anymore because I gained weight carrying your baby but you talking to her. You supposedly too busy to help me or be concerned about me or do things for me that you can't even call or text to check on me but you have time to be doing God knows what with this little girl!" Alicia was screaming at the top of lungs and crying by now. She was so angry and so embarrassed.

"Look I told you it's not like that with her. She is a little girl to me. And even if we were dating you broke up with me remember?"

Alicia was ticking like a time bomb by now. "So what?! We weren't broken up when you started talking to her way back in October so you don't even have a valid point. And regardless of that you are still wrong for treating me like crap while you're out here taking up with other females anyway. You are so sorry and I would say I wish I'd never met you but then I wouldn't be pregnant with my son." She turned to walk out of the room and he followed her. They stood in the kitchen arguing for about ten minutes before his parents decided to mediate the conversation.

"Cameron you are wrong on so many levels." Ms. Brenda said to him. "Even if this little Maria girl hadn't come into the picture you still have not been doing what you're supposed to do as a man when it comes to how you've been treating Alicia."

Cameron went off then. "Well I'll tell you what, since everyone has so much to say about me and our situation then you can take your ass back to Texas." he said to Alicia. "I got 5,000 dollars in my savings account I will give it all to you so you can go home and leave me alone. Call me when my baby is born. You can bounce." he said angrily and tried to walk into the bedroom. Ms. Brenda stopped him and backed him against the wall. "Now I don't know who you think you are or who you think you are talking to but as long as you are in my house you will not talk to her or disrespect her like that ever again. Do you hear me?" she said to him.

He was angry so he began yelling in Ms. Brenda "Y'all sitting up here jumping down my throat but nah man forget that she can bounce. I don't care. She can go tonight." he said before his dad came walking into the kitchen and getting up in his face.

"Boy you think you so hard and grown but if you ever get up in your mother's face like that again or talk to her like I will beat you down to the ground. You better back up and get your sense back." Mr. Eric said to Cameron.

Cameron backed up and leaned against the stove.

Ms. Brenda sat down at the table and started in on him again. "I don't know how you call yourself a man. What kind of man has a woman move 1100 miles away from her family and friends and job and nice home to come to a place where she doesn't know anybody, lives in a run-down trailer, and can barely make ends meet? Then to top it off you don't even live there with her. You didn't help her get furniture. You don't want to help her financially. You're never there with her and to top it all off you continuously disrespect her and treat her bad." she looked at him. "How can you think that it's okay to tell the woman who is 8 months pregnant with your son, my grandson, to drive 18 hours by herself back to Texas? Do you not have any concern for her or your baby?"

Cameron looked down at the ground as Alicia sat there quietly crying. "Ma I didn't mean that but I'm just, I don't know. Things changed and feelings change." he said.

Alicia finally spoke. "Well if so much has changed why did you keep begging me to stay every time I said I was going to go back home? I could've have gone back to Texas months ago without all this crying and suffering if you felt like this isn't what you want. You played me and been playing me all along. Everything you do or have done is all for your own selfish pleasure or gain. You used me in Texas. All I've done for you and this is how you do me?" Alicia said with tears streaming down her face.

That must have struck a nerve because just like Cameron was angry again. He kept walking up too close in her face. Ashley would tell him to move but he insisted on being in her face yelling and arguing. "Stop acting like a little girl because things don't go your way all the time. You supposed to be grown well act like it. People fall out of love all the time it's not the end of the world. Grow the hell up and stop acting like a little ass kid!"

Before Alicia knew what was happening she had punched Cameron in his jaw and continued punching him in the face, chest, stomach, head, and anywhere else she could land a punch in at. She fought him so violently that he ended up cowering in the corner trying to cover his head from her hard blows.

She didn't want to fight him, especially not while pregnant with their son but he had just pushed her past her breaking point and she was tired of it. Mr. Eric and Ms. Brenda let her fight him for a few minutes before Mr. Eric finally pulled her off. He checked to make sure she was okay as she stood in the front yard crying and trying to gain her composure before driving home. Even out in the front yard she could still hear Cameron yelling and cursing like a lunatic. She was just so tired and depressed and it was all because of a little boy who tried to pretend to be a man. She went home and contacted Maria. She had to talk to her for some reason she didn't know why. She contacted her on Facebook and at first Maria was getting smart with and trying to crazy to her. She said that she didn't why Alicia needed to talk to her and that she trusts Cameron completely so she doesn't have an issue with him coming to her house to see his baby because she knows that is the only thing he will go over there for.

Alicia was going to go off on her but then she realized that she is young and that is what young stupid girls do. She didn't the real deal between Cameron and Alicia but Alicia was definitely prepared to tell her. Once Alicia let her know that she was more than just his "baby mama" and that she wasn't trying fight Maria agreed to talk to her on the phone and to Alicia's surprise she was actually nicer.

Maria had told Alicia that Cameron had said that he and Alicia were on a break and that he considered Maria to be his girlfriend. He said that even told Alicia that Maria was his girlfriend. Alicia was shocked at that because he never mentioned one word about Maria ever. Maria told her that although she thought she was Cameron's girlfriend they had never kissed, or held hands, or even gone out anywhere together. She said that she had only seen about 3 times since they started talking in October and only one of those times they were alone. She had never even been in his car or to his house. Alicia found it odd that she would still consider him her boyfriend with only having seen him 3 times in 5 months. At the end of the conversation they agreed to meet up at Maria's house the next day when Cameron came to pick Alicia up to go buy the bassinet for the baby.

The next day Alicia had met Cameron at Walmart early. She and Maria had been texting each other and the plan to meet up was still a go. Alicia wanted Cameron to pick her up and they ride to Walmart together but he was very insistent on them just meeting up there which struck as odd. He has never done that before especially since it would have been smarter and easier since they lived really close to each other. She didn't dwell on it long though. Once she got there she headed straight for the baby section. Cameron arrived about ten minutes after her and joined her in the baby section.

"What's up yo? What are we supposed to be getting out here again?" he asked Alicia as they stood in the aisle.

She really didn't even want to be around him so she kept the conversation to a minimum. "Bassinet and other things."

"Oh ok." he said to her. "Well I had just wanted to say that I'm sorry about the fight and the things that I said to you. I didn't mean I was just mad cause you were trying to come at me like I would really mess with that little ass girl."

"Well it doesn't matter cause you still lied about her and you are still dead wrong. I talked to her yesterday." she looked at him awaiting his response.

"Talked to her about what?"

"About what y'all had going on." she told him everything that they had talked about but she found it odd that basically everything Maria had said last night after the initial attitude on Facebook was almost exactly what Cameron had said about the situation before hand. It was starting to make sense to her now.

"So if y'all claim that nothing went on between y'all and you only saw her three times then why would she think and why would you tell her that she is your girlfriend?" Alicia folded her arms.

Cameron shifted his eyes around the store before answering. "She took it the wrong way. I wasn't saying it like she is my girlfriend I was just joking like aww look at little my girlfriend like she is a kid to me." he looked like he was lying and that explanation was dumb as hell to Alicia.

"Yeah right Cam! You really expect me to believe that? If that's the case y'all never talked or been around each other like that but she knew about you wanting to go to Germany and she knew you had a performance at Revolutions when I didn't even know." Alicia said.

"Man everybody knows that. That stuff ain't no deep conversation type stuff. That's general knowledge. It wasn't even like that."

Alicia's voice began to crack as she spoke to him without realizing that she was raising her voice in the store. It all finally clicked in her head at that moment. The reason why Cameron didn't want to ride to Walmart together but meet up instead....Maria had told him the plan after they talked last night. And obviously Cameron told Maria to say that they werent talking in that way and that they had never done anything. It was clear. Maria had an attitude when Alicia first contacted her on Facebook and she didn't really want to talk to Alicia but then all of a sudden an hour later she was ready to talk and she was nice about it and her story corroborated with Cameron's. The jig was up. They clearly thought Alicia was stupid.

"So that's how you going to do me Cameron?" with tears threatening to stream down her face she stood firm looking him straight in the eye. "All I've gone through with you, as much as I have been there for, as much as I've done for you and put up with from you still can't be a man and tell me the truth?" her voice was steadily rising. "I'm so damn pissed right now cause you are really trying to play me like I'm stupid like I don't see what's really going. Like do you hate me or something? Why do you do me the way you do? That's all I want to know." she said loudly not caring who heard their conversation.

Cameron looked around the store wildly, embarrassed even. He walked closer to her and tried to pull her to him but she stepped back from his grasp. "Alicia please calm down. Stop that. Don't do that please. Not here."

Alicia continued to let the tears fall from her face but she had no words left for him. She simply pushed the basket in silence gathering up onesies, bottles, bibs, blankets, towels, socks, pacifiers, lotions, baby washes, and everything else the baby would need. The only time she said anything to him was tell him which bassinette to put into the cart and to inform him that although she was paying half of the miscellaneous items they are getting that he was going to pay for the bassinette by himself. She was ready to get out of the store and go home. *The hell with him and all his lies. I'm so done.* She thought to herself. After paying for their things Cameron walked her to the car and loaded it. She drove off without even saying goodbye.

Alicia's dad and brothers had gotten there a little after she got home from Walmart. They went out to eat and then hung around her trailer just talking. Her dad was a little concerned because she was feeling a little pain in her pelvic area and back and she could barely walk up the stairs to her trailer or get in and out of her car. She wasn't too worried because she had just had a doctor's appointment and the doctor said everything was fine. Her dad and brothers left that evening to go back to their hotel room but came right back about thirty minutes later because they didn't feel comfortable leaving her by herself. They knew that Cameron didn't live with her and she had told them about the fight they had so Cameron was afraid to come around them. He was such a coward. She didn't want them to do anything to him and they weren't going to do anything to him. She could handle herself. That Sunday after her dad and brothers left to go back home to Alabama, Alicia was feeling extremely tired and a little down. She decided to get some laundry done and tidying up the house a bit even though she was still hurting a little. She didn't get to fold her clean laundry because she was sleepy so she lay down to take a quick nap. She woke up about an hour later because she was uncomfortable. She went and got a drink of water then went back to the couch to lay down but as she put her legs up on the couch she felt a warm gush in between her legs that made her bolt upright. She stood up and felt frozen to the spot she was standing in with her feet spread apart looking down at a flood of fluid flowing from her vagina to the floor. It seemed to have gone on forever and didn't look as though it was going to stop anytime soon so she walked as quickly as she could to the bathroom and squatted over the toilet. It was still flowing steadily. After about two minutes it slowed down so she took that opportunity to get her phone to call Cameron. She called three times in a row and got no answer. She called his parents' cell phones and house phone as well but got no answer. She called Cameron again still no answer so she sent him a text message letting him know that her water broke and that she was going into labor. Then she jumped in the shower.

Chapter 37

As soon as she got out of the shower Alicia checked her phone to see if Cameron had called her back. He hadn't so she told herself that if she couldn't reach him by the time she put her clothes on then she would just drive herself to the hospital. As luck would have it he called just as she was trying to put on her shoes.

"I been sleep Alicia I just got your messages. Are you ok?" he asked her.

She rolled her eyes, trying to control her irritation. "Yes I'm fine. Can you please just hurry up and get here. My water broke like twenty minutes ago."

Within five minutes he was walking through her front door, grabbing her overnight bag, and ushering her towards the car. They had to put a towel between her legs and on the seat of the car because she still had some fluids coming out. When she got into his car she was once again angry because she noticed he had no gas.

"Your gas light is on!" she said to him.

He looked at her as he put the car in drive. "It's cool man, we will make it to the hospital."

"Um no, I'm not trying to take that chance. We need to stop at a gas station or hell we could take my car."

"No" he told her as he drove down the street. "We will make it."

Alicia was in too much discomfort to argue about it so she said a quick prayer that they made it to the hospital with no issues. As Cameron drove, Alicia called her doctor and informed them that her water had broken and she was on her way to the hospital. Everything was ready for her when she arrived. Cameron had wheeled her to labor and delivery in a wheelchair and informed them that she was not only in labor three weeks early but also two weeks earlier than her planned C-section. Within 30 minutes of arriving at the hospital Alicia was prepped for surgery and was laying on the operating room table staring up into the ceiling as Cameron held her hand while they delivered her 7 pound 14 ounces baby boy whom they named Alton Jeremiah Thompson.

Alicia had experienced an allergic reaction to one of the drugs during her C-section so they gave her Benadryl which caused her to become woozy and fall asleep. The last thing she remembered was the doctor holding her son up so that she could see him before taking him to get cleaned up. Then as they rolled her back to her recovery room Cameron told her he was going home to shower and get his stuff for pt in the morning and that he would be back shortly. When Alicia woke up hours later Cameron was asleep on the sofa chair next to her bed. She felt a sense of tranquility now that her son had finally made his way into the world. She hoped that this would make things between herself and Cam a little better where they could at least tolerate being around each other and maybe begin to build a friendship. Those feelings didn't last long. The next day when Cameron came to the hospital from work they barely said two words to each other. They both cooed over their baby boy and took turns feeding and holding him. Cameron changed him every time his diaper was dirty while Alicia just looked on with love. They weren't really talking to each other but at least they weren't arguing either. That was short lived when Danielle began calling Cameron and instead of him telling her that he will talk to her later, he stayed on the phone with her for an hour despite Alicia asking him to stop being disrespectful.

"How am I being disrespectful by talking to her?" he asked angrily. "She is my baby mama too."

"I could understand if y'all were talking about Kennedy but y'all aren't. She called less than 24 hours after we just had our baby while I'm still in this hospital and you're supposed to be bonding with your son. She is taking attention away from us that we haven't gotten damn near the whole time I was pregnant! I mean really, how could you not see where I would be upset?" Alicia said to him.

Of course Cameron didn't agree with her about that so the conversation turned into a huge argument inside her hospital room. When his parent came to visit Cameron told them why they were arguing and the Carters sided with Alicia causing Cameron to be even angrier.

"Alright fine I will just say forget it and tell her next time she call I can't talk to her since everybody say it's so disrespectful. I'm tired of this."

Alicia looked at him in disgust. "Shit, you and me both." Then she lay her son on her chest and stared at him with pride.

Chapter 38

Alicia was discharged from the hospital a few days later, but she wasn't feeling as happy she thought she should be. When she arrived home with Alton, all she wanted to do was cry. She looked around her tiny living space. Laundry was still in the basket waiting to be folded. The towels that she used to catch the fluids when he water broke were still in the same spot on the living room. The trash needed to be taken out. There were dishes in the sink, and there was a stale odor in the air. She immediately got upset just looking at the place. Cameron said that he would come to clean up before she brought the baby home but he clearly hadn't even been here at all. Over the next few weeks Alicia struggled with the baby almost completely on her own. With no family in the state of Georgia and no friends, she had to rely heavily on Cameron and his family. Unfortunately though, Cameron was a huge liar and wasn't dependable at all. He was supposed to be able to have ten days of leave to stay at home and help Alicia with the baby. He was at the house with her for two days then claimed that his commanding officer wouldn't allow him to do that because they were not married. Alicia thought it was a lie but she didn't have proof. She figured that even if he couldn't take those days off that he would still come straight there after work and actually be around and help out in some kind of way. That didn't happen either. He barely came to spend time with his son except for a few nights where he stayed over to help out with him. Alicia had a C-Section so she wasn't supposed to do much lifting and moving around for at least a month after giving birth. Every time she sat down or tried to get up she would feel the sharp pain in her lower abdomen where the doctors cut her. She was barely able to walk without feeling the pain so she just dragged her feet slowly as she was hunched over to keep her movement at a minimum. She cried all the time, barely got any sleep, and was physically and emotionally drained. Cameron just seemed so oblivious to Alicia's struggles, even after she told him that she thought she was experiencing "baby blues". Mrs. Brenda and Mr. Eric came over a few times to see their grandson and offered to keep him at their home sometimes whenever Alicia was ready to let him be out of the house. Alicia felt as if she would never be back to normal but as the weeks passed, and she was able to get help from Cameron and his parents, she slowly started settling into motherhood. She adored her baby boy and couldn't imagine life without him.

Within the two months since having their son, Cameron and Alicia seemed to be getting along much better. He started pulling his weight with Alton and he even began spending more quality time with Alicia. They were beginning to get back into a good space. Cameron had told her that he was going to drive down to Atlanta with an old childhood friend to see WrestleMania live. Alicia told him that it wouldn't be a good idea to drive his car down there. She thought it might get stolen but he felt like it would be ok. Alicia disagreed but she decided to keep her thoughts to herself so that she wouldn't cause any tension between them when they were doing so well now. The day after Cameron went to Atlanta he called Alicia.

"Man guess what! You won't believe this!" he exclaimed into the phone when she answered.

"What?" she said as she was sitting on the couch feeding Alton a bottle of formula.

Cameron sighed deeply into the phone before saying, "My car got stolen last night."

Alicia didn't respond.

"Did you hear what I said?" he asked her.

"Yes, I heard you. Did you file a report and how are you getting back home?" she asked.

Cameron sounded like he was trying not to cry. "Yes I did and I guess I have to rent a car. I don't really have the money for that though."

Alicia shook her head and thought to herself. *How does he not have the money for it? Why would you go on a trip with no money? And where is his money going because he really isn't giving me anything for his son.* "Well do you need me to let you borrow some money to get home?" she asked him.

"Nah, I'll be good. Martez dad is going to rent the car for me and I will pay him back on payday."

Alicia just said okay and told him to drive safe. He was getting on her nerves, but she felt like his karma may finally have started to catch up to him.

Chapter 39

Cameron had finally made it back to Hinesville after his car had been stolen and he had to figure out how he was going to a new one. His insurance company wouldn't cover it because he only had liability coverage which Alicia thought was pretty stupid. His credit was bad and he had a car repo on his report already. Cameron came to Alicia for help as usual because his parents told him that it was his own fault that he was in the predicament that he was in. They sat down to evaluate his income and bills, and to see what the best route would be.

"Alright", Alicia said to him. "I just realized that I have never even asked you before, but how much do you make?"

"Well I get roughly about two thousand dollars on both the first and the fifteenth." He said to her without any thought.

Alicia cocked her eyebrow at him but said nothing.

"Why you looking like that?" he asked.

"No reason. Okay what are your bills looking like?" she picked up a pen and notepad to write down all the bills that she just knew he had.

"Well I have to pay my parents $200 a month to live with them. I have to pay Danielle $687 a month for Kennedy. My car insurance was $80 every month. My cell phone bill is about $100." He was just rattling off his tiny list, not even realizing that Alicia was getting angry. He glanced up and saw the look on her face and quickly tried to add in extra stuff. "Oh but you know you gotta add in gas for my car, maintenance for it, and money for me to eat all month long." He said thinking that would be a sufficient amount of bills. He was wrong. Alicia blew up.

"You mean to fucking tell me that you make damn near four thousand dollars a month and your bills only add up to a little over $1,060 a month?!" she yelled at him. "Is that what you're telling me?" she asked.

Cameron tried to explain, "No it's more than that if you add in the gas for the car and my food. I can't eat the food at my parent's house they said I have to feed myself and I don't know how to cook so I eat out every day." He said as if that made it sound better to her.

Alicia was still going off. "I don't care about that. It still doesn't add up to anywhere near $4,000 a month. All this time you've been complaining that you're so broke, that you couldn't even help me by putting $90 on a light bill for me, that me and my family had to buy damn near all of Alton's baby items while you barely contributed anything at all, that I compromised with you to only pay $150 a month in child support for him and allowed you to divide between your checks and you don't do anything extra other than little bit. But you've had money this whole got damn time!" she was fuming at this point. Alicia thought she had been doing the right thing by taking his alleged financial situation into consideration and not just constantly bugging him to help out. She was pissed because all this time she would notice that he would get new electronics and gadgets and jewelry but it never registered in her mind that he was lying about his finances. She wanted to just beat his face in but she refrained from touching him. She just simply turned to him and screamed at the top of her lungs, "GET YOUR ASS OUT OF MY HOUSE RIGHT NOW!" Then she picked up her son and went into the bed room and closed the door.

Cameron left quietly and locked the door behind him. Alicia was livid, she just didn't understand how he could be so conniving. About a week had passed since the argument about Cameron's finances and Alicia hadn't really talked to him much. He had come by a couple times to pick up Alton and take him over to his parents' house but there wasn't speaking between the two of them. Alicia had heard on the radio that comedian Rickey Smiley was doing a show in Savannah and she really wanted to go. She had seen him do a live show with singer Fantasia a few years ago in Shreveport, Louisiana and had really enjoyed herself. She didn't have any friends here though so really had no one to go with. She didn't want to ask him but she decided to have Cameron with her just so that she didn't have to go alone. He agreed and she bought the tickets and he agreed to pay for dinner in Savannah.

The night of the show Alicia dressed comfortably in some brown leggings and gold button up blouse with brown thong sandals. She still had a lot of baby weight on her but she looked damn good tonight. After dropping the baby off to Cameron's parents, he hopped in the driver's seat of Alicia's car and they headed off on the 45 minute drive to Savannah. They barely said a word to each other on the whole drive there and Alicia hoped that once they were seated the show would start immediately. The mood was definitely different after the show. Alicia assumed that being able to laugh together broke the ice between them and made them more able to have fun and not be so tense for the rest of the night. They ate at a little soul food restaurant that they found on Google. Cameron barely had enough money to pay the bill for it. Just seeing that made Alicia go back to being distant towards him.

Chapter 40

It was the beginning of August and four months had passed since the Rickey Smiley with Cameron. Alton was almost six months old now and he was crawling and getting into everything imaginable. Alicia was amazed at how fast he was growing up and how much of a joy he was in her life. He started having respiratory problems when he was around five months old so Alicia was constantly taking him to his pediatrician for nebulizer treatments until they gave her a machine for him to keep at home and use as needed. Other than that he was thriving. Alicia was gearing up to move into a bigger place this month. A two story townhouse apartment in a little town about 20 minutes away from Hinesville. She was going to move back to Texas with her family because she felt like she wasn't getting the support she needed there from Cameron. The past four months had been a very trying for her. She had found out that everything Danielle said over a year ago about the girl Jaslyn and Cameron was all true. Jaslyn had personally called Alicia and told her everything from her own mouth. They even called Cameron on three-way but of course he suspected that it was a set up so he denied everything, but Alicia knew that Jaslyn was telling the truth. Cameron's best friend Tara had come down to visit her family for the summer while her husband Walt was away on deployment. She had been asking for Cameron and Alicia to bring the baby to see her. Cameron kept making excuses why he couldn't see Tara or only saw her once or twice. Alicia had gone to Jacksonville, Florida for the Fourth of July just to get out of Hinesville. She left Alton with Cameron and his family while she took the two hour trip by herself. Cameron had called and said that Tara invited him and their son to the celebration on the army base. She was fine with him taking their son. Even though Alicia and Cameron had been constantly arguing she wouldn't keep him from being in his son's life. Alicia had gotten a message from Maria saying that she was with Cameron and Alton at the celebration, spending time together. Alicia was furious. She hoped that Cameron wouldn't be that disrespectful to have her child around that little skank. She tried calling him but he didn't answer. She called again and still got no answer. Alicia sent a message to his friend Tara asking if she was with him. Tara said she hadn't seen him since earlier. This was a new low even for him. After she got home, Cameron came by to drop off their son. Alicia told him about the message and asked why he lied about spending the day with Tara. He tried to say that he was with Tara but Alicia cut him off and told him that Tara had said differently. He then said well he wasn't really Tara for very long and that he tried not to be around much because she had been trying to have sex with him since she had come down there. Alicia couldn't believe that he would try to throw his so-called best friend under the bus just to cover his tracks. They argued so much within those four months not only because he was a liar but also because he barely did anything for his son and he rarely spent any time with him. Alicia tried to be patient but she decided that it was best for her to move back to Texas. When she told Cameron about her decision he begged her to stay. He told her that he would be better and that he would help out more. He promised to start the telling the truth and to stop all the fighting. Alicia wasn't trying to hear any of that. She felt like he had been saying the same things for a year now. He saw that she didn't believe him so he told her that his parents would be heartbroken if she took their only grandson away. Alicia couldn't really afford to move anyway and she didn't want to ask her family so she decided to just stick it out for a little while longer. Cameron had purchased an old beat up Monte Carlo that Alicia had driven him to go get. It was so bad that he only had it for a couple weeks before he decided to get rid of it. Alicia helped him find a "buy here, pay here" car dealership that only used income for approval and not credit. He traded the Monte Carlo in for a used Ford Explorer, but now he had a car note. Surprisingly he had used his new SUV to help Alicia move some of her stuff to her new place in Ludowici.

All that had happened over the four months had Alicia feeling like she was just over trying to be with him or having any type of relationship with him except for co-parenting. She decided she would stay in Georgia until she came up with a plan for her future. It seemed as if once Cameron noticed that Alicia was no longer trying to make the relationship work he started putting forth an effort. They had decided to go dinner at Alicia's favorite wing place and then to the drive-in to see a movie. The night was going well, they were laughing and talking and just enjoying each other's company. Somehow Jaslyn got brought up into the conversation and it went downhill from there. They argued and then didn't say another word to each other for the rest of the night even though Cameron still stayed over that night. They didn't talk for a week and he again he barely came to see his son. When he would come to get him he would just grab him up and take him, without any conversation between Alicia and Cameron. Weeks have passed and now Cameron suddenly decides to start trying to spend time with Alicia and Alton. This came as a shock to Alicia because he always claimed to be so busy. Too busy for his own son even. Nevertheless, he began coming over more. They would play cards, joke on each other, and play with their son together. Alicia wasn't trying to get back into a relationship with him but she appreciated the fact that it seemed as though they were at least building a friendship now. He kissed her on two different occasions but both times it felt very awkward and forced. She didn't know how to take it. With Cameron coming around more and acting as if he wanted to try and salvage the relationship, Alicia felt confused and unsure of what to do next. The feelings of confusion didn't last very long though because she made a shocking discovery. October had come and Alicia had been feeling as if Cameron was trying get back together lately since he started to take her out on dates again and began spending more time with her and Alton. She didn't really want to get back into a relationship with him, though, she felt that he wasn't capable of being honest and that he was a manipulator. She decided to check some things out to see if he was still up to his same old shenanigans. She grabbed her laptop and logged into Facebook. First she went and looked at his page. Nothing out of the ordinary. No comments or posts from random females or any females that he had dealt with in the past. No new female friends. *Okay, so far so good,* Alicia thought to herself. Next she looked at the pages of Teanna, Jaslyn, and Danielle. *No mentions of him or any posts about him on any of their pages. Okay cool. One more thing,* she thought. The last page she went to look at was Maria's. At first everything looked normal. She posted about things she was doing with her family and posted pictures of herself, the usual stuff. As Alicia scrolled further down she started posts about being in love and her talking about her fiancée. She didn't put a name on it but Alicia had a bad feeling about it. She kept scrolling but was frozen stiff by a post that Maria made in the middle of August. Alicia couldn't believe her eyes. She thought she had to be seeing things, because there was no way that she was looking at this post correctly. She was trembling as she picked up her cell phone and called Cameron. He didn't answer the first time, so she called again, and again until he finally did.

Chapter 41

"What's up yo?" Cameron said into the phone after Alicia finally got a hold of him. She tried to remain calm as she began to speak. "Do you have something that you would like to tell me Cam?" she asked as her voice trembled.

He paused, "About what Alicia?"

"Just anything that you feel you may want to get off of your chest." She said. "Anything that you want to be honest about."

He paused again, "Um, noooo. Should I?"

Alicia played it cool. She gathered her thoughts quickly. "So tell me something, have you seen or spoken to Maria since you claimed that you let her know that she took things the wrong way with you and that whole situation?"

"Nah I haven't." he said nonchalantly.

"Mmmm…then why has she been posting on her page that she's been seeing you and spending time with you and all that?" She asked the question to give him an opportunity to tell her the truth before she put him on blast for what she called for.

Cameron sighed into the phone. "Man I don't know why she would post that stuff cause I haven't seen or spoken to her in months except for one time when I ran into her at the store. And even then we only said 'hey' and I asked her how she been. Then I left."

Alicia knew he was lying, she could tell in his tone. She decided to drop the bomb then. "So if that was the only time you saw her, why the fuck is she posting on her Facebook page that she is pregnant by you and that y'all are engaged?"

Cameron acted like he was shocked by the revelation. "What?! Why would she say some shit like that?"

"You tell me why she would say some shit like that Cam? Apparently that's your fiancée!"

"Yo Alicia I swear I don't know why she saying that. I never did nothing with that girl and I haven't seen her since that one time at the store." He said trying to make her believe him. "I put that on my kids."

Alicia laughed coldly. "Don't put nothing on my son!" she screamed into the phone. "If this shit isn't true then you need to put her in her place and stop allowing this bullshit to continue. Although, I am certain that there is some truth to some things that she is posting. I'm just not sure of how much. Either way, you better fix it." She told them and then hung up the phone.

Over the next few weeks Cameron had started regressing back to his old habits. He stopped coming around as much, barely seeing his son. The only time he would pick Alton up is when his parents wanted to see him. She was back to having no support there and once again she thought about moving sooner rather than later. She didn't really see the point in staying there anymore when Cameron wasn't even trying to be active in Alton's life like he should. She had amended their agreement on child support no longer only accepting $150 a month when he clearly was more that capable of providing more, as he should. So they agreed on $300 a month, to be split into two payments on the 1st and the 15th. That was her way of getting her child at least a little bit of what he deserves but still compromising with Cameron.

Alicia was back in Texas for a few days to attend her sister Ralonda's wedding. Cameron had taken them to the airport but hadn't even attempted to check on them to see if they had made it safely. She called him. "What's up?" he said into the phone.

"What are you doing?" she asked him.

"Um, nothing really at the moment, about to do some music in a little bit."

"Oh ok, well yeah we made it safely. Thanks for asking." She said sarcastically.

"My bad I was gonna call you in a little bit to see if y'all did." He lied.

Alicia just shook her head. "Yeah, ok." She said. "Just don't forget to get us from the airport on Sunday, please."

"I got you babe." He said to her.

Alicia cringed at him calling her babe. "Bye." She said, and hung up before he could respond. She figured she wouldn't hear from him for the remainder of her trip so she decided to take the time to enjoy her family and let them fall in love with her son since it was most of their first times seeing him in person. When she arrived at the airport in Savannah, Cameron was there waiting for them. He tried to give her a hug but she really didn't want him to touch her. He then went to Alton and kissed his cheeks while he sat in his stroller. Alicia felt that was a fake gesture because he hadn't bothered to check on him the entire time they were gone. On the car ride back to Hinesville there was minimal conversation between them. He tried to strike up a casual conversation but Alicia was tired and quite frankly she was just over the whole situation at this point. As he drove she sat there contemplating and finally made up her mind once and for all to move away from Georgia. It was the beginning of November and she planned to be gone by the end of the month. She talked to her mother and her sister and decided to go to Tennessee with her mother and her mother's husband and her younger brother. She was hoping that there would be some great opportunities there and it was closer to Georgia then Texas so maybe Cameron would get his act together and attempt to be in his son's life a little more.

Alicia had told Cameron and his parents about her decision to leave to Georgia in the next three weeks.

"Alicia, believe me I understand." Mrs. Brenda said to her. "I'm sure going to miss my grandson and I don't want y'all to go but I know as woman and as a mother it is best for you to leave. My son has you out here basically on your own with his child and he should be doing so much more that what he is. But trust me, when y'all are gone it will hit him."

Alicia didn't really care if it hit him or not. She just knew that the best thing for her was to leave and start over with and for her son. What made Alicia finally realize that Cameron just wasn't shit, was that even when she told him that they would be leaving in three weeks he still wasn't making any attempt to spend time with his son. What kind of man, let alone father, does that? She decided not to stress about it and just let nature take its course.

On the day of the move Cameron showed up just as Alicia was putting the last suitcase into her car. She wanted to go off on him for that but felt as though it would be pointless. He hasn't showed any care that his son was leaving and still didn't spend time with him so what would it change? He went into her apartment and picked up his son. Cameron stood there holding him with a sad look on his face. *He is such a pathetic con artist.* Alicia thought to herself, not understanding why he was trying to front like he was sad. He gave Alton a hug, placed him in his car seat, and buckled him in. "Daddy loves you little man. I'll see you soon." He told then closed the car door. He turned towards Alicia as she walked to get into her car. He stopped her before she got in. "I just want you to know that I did talk to Maria about that stuff she posted a few months ago. I'm going to try to come and see my son as soon as I can." He told her.

Alicia scoffed. "Okay." She didn't really have anything else to say to him. He tried to embrace her, but instead she gave him a one-arm hug, got into her car, and drove off leaving all of the bullshit behind her.

The Road to New Beginnings

Alicia had dealt with a lot of turmoil during her time in Georgia and it only got worse in Tennessee. Cameron was completely absent from dealing with their son in any type of way. He would rarely answer when Alicia called to talk to him about things regarding Alton and he was always late with child support payments for Alton. They constantly argued about everything and it came to a point where all of their communication had to be done through texts. Alicia found out about another female that Cameron had begun dealing with named Christine. Ordinarily Alicia doesn't comment on others' physical appearance but this girl was so ugly and she lived with her mama. But that's neither here nor there.

Alicia had gotten an opportunity for a really good job in Tennessee but she didn't have enough money for daycare for Alton due to having pay for his doctor's visits, medicines, and immunizations out of pocket because Cameron still had not put him on his free health insurance with the military. He kept making excuses as to why he wasn't able to do it yet so Alicia had to keep paying out of pocket for it all. She asked Cameron to pay for half of the daycare fee so that she could start the new job. He said he would send her the money in the mail because it cost too much to send it through Western Union. Alicia felt like it was just a way for him stall since he had been sending payments through them. A week after he was supposed to send it, she still had not received it. She called him and he claimed he put it in the mail. Another week passed and it still hadn't arrived. Finally after almost 3 weeks he told her that it must have gotten lost in the mail so he sent her the money western union, but only after she had already gone into the negative on her account to pay for it.

She had asked him to keep his son for a month while she got her living situation together in Tennessee but he told her no because he had to do training for a month so he wasn't able to. Alicia later found out that was a lie, he didn't have training to do. He also went and got his daughter Kennedy and kept her for that month that Alicia had asked him to keep their son, and even more so, they went out of town to Augusta just to attend his grandmother's 70th birthday party. Alicia was beyond pissed when she learned of that. On top of neglecting his responsibility to his son, she also learned that he was indeed the father of the baby that Maria was pregnant with. At first he lied and told her that they had only sex twice and both times she tricked him into having sex while he was drunk at a house party and that the condoms broke. Of course his story sounded like a lie from the start to Alicia. The truth was actually that Cameron had been seeing each other since Alicia was six months pregnant when Maria was only 17. They kept it under wraps and claimed they didn't have sex until after Alton was born because she was only 17 years old. He had known that Maria was pregnant way before Alicia had ever seen the post on Facebook. He hid the truth form his parents as well but Danielle had told them and Alicia about Maria's baby after she was born, they named her Camaria.

Things were still not going well for Alicia in Tennessee so once again at the urging of her family, she packed up and moved back to Texas with her sister Ralonda. Almost immediately she had gotten a job as a director for a before and after school program. She had gotten an apartment and things were looking up a little bit for her. Cameron had still not enrolled their son in his health insurance so Alicia was still spending a lot of money on his health expenses. The turning point for Alicia to stop taking bullshit from Cameron came when he refused to help her with any of Alton's medical expenses. Cameron had been taking multiple trips out of town, splurging on clothes and electronics, and just throwing money away. Alton had been diagnosed as having reactive airway disease, eczema, and seasonal allergies. He was also constantly having to go to the doctor because he was getting frequent ear infections. Alicia had to continually leave work early to pick him up from daycare because he kept having fevers. On the day of Alton's first birthday Alicia took him for immunizations. She called Cameron to ask him for help paying. She explained that since she had been paying for all of his doctor's visits and every other medical expense, she felt it be fair if this time he paid for something. She even tried to compromise and told him that she would pay for the immunizations if he would just pay for the office visit, which cost less than the immunizations. He flipped out and told her she was money hungry and that he shouldn't have to pay for any of that because he gives her $300 a month for child support. He told her to use the child support money to pay for it. She told him that his child support barely even pays for half of his daycare which was $145 a week. Not to mention that she buys all of his clothes, keeps a roof over his head, food in his mouth, diapers, wipes, and everything else that he has all are from Alicia's pockets. Not to mention that she has already come out of thousands of dollars by herself to pay for all of his medical expenses. She couldn't understand how he thought that what he said was okay. He didn't even send Alton a gift for his birthday. It was at that moment when she decided that she would no longer ask him for anything or any type of help for his son. That very moment she hung up the phone with Cameron, Alicia called the Attorney General's office and filed for child support. He was an asshole throughout the whole process. Alicia only asked for $400 a month because she didn't want him to be completely broke seeing as how he had three children by three different women. He didn't even want to pay that. He decided to be sneaky and underhanded and told the courts that he didn't know if Alton was his child or not and that he wanted a DNA test. He knew that it would buy him some time before he had to pay. He and his mother tried to convince Alicia that the court forced him to take a DNA test even after he told them that he was certain Alton was his son. She knew that was a lie because when the test comes back positive then the father has to pay for it. So why would they force you to take a test if you tell them that you are the father. It didn't matter to Alicia though because it was him that had to pay it. Once the order came back that he had to pay and when he had to pay, Cameron stopped sending money altogether because the order was dated for a few months away. He didn't even buy Alton Christmas gifts. By this time Alicia had also had a fall out with his family because they began treating Alton differently. They stopped calling and stopped answering Alicia's calls and even stopped sending Alton birthday and Christmas gifts. Alicia didn't really care anymore she had tried so many times connect with Cameron and his family. She had tried so many times to make sure they were a part of his life even volunteering to bring Alton to visit on many different occasions as well ass, offering to bring him to them to spend the summer more than once. She was going to foot the bill for all of it and they still always came up with an excuse why he couldn't come. Alicia just accepted it and moved on. On the rare occasions that he did attempt to contact her about Alton she would answer and she would be cordial but he always made it out to other people like she didn't want him in Alton's life and even tried to say she was bitter because he was with Maria instead of her. That was hardly the case though. Alicia didn't want Cameron, she had moved on and closed that chapter long ago. All she wanted was for him to be a father to his, but she wasn't going to beg him to do it. He had gotten deployed and while he was gone Maria had sold his stuff out of his apartment, had men in his home, stole money from him, got his car impounded, and was doing drugs. He tried to get Alicia to feel sympathy for him but she had none because he still wasn't being a father to their son. He would email her all the time but rarely asked about or mentioned Alton. His emails were always him trying to explain to her why he was even with Maria and telling her that he always loved her and that he doesn't love Maria and never. He told her that the only reason he was with her is because he messed up so bad with Alicia that he felt the only person that would want him was Maria. Alicia didn't care and she wasn't trying to hear any of that. She had been over Cameron for a while and the only thing she wanted from him was to be a good father. She made sure that he knew that. He told her he understood and that he would come to visit him when he came back from deployment. Alicia agreed to let him stay in the guest bedroom if he came so that he wouldn't have to come out of pocket for a hotel room. Instead, when he came back from deployment he chose to go Vegas with his friends instead of visiting his son that he had not seen in over two years. Alicia didn't get upset or go off. She just simply kept on with her life. He didn't send Christmas gifts that year either. Months later when it was time to file taxes he asked if he could claim Alton on his. Alicia told him no after she remembered that he cheated her out of money when she let him claim Alton two years prior. Besides that, he doesn't do anything for their son so why should he be able to claim him. He then went on to say that he was going to try to come visit him but he needed her help financially to get out there. He had spent $800 to help Danielle get her truck fixed so he didn't have enough money to get out there to visit his son. Alicia told him that wasn't her problem and he should've put his son before helping his ex-wife who has a man and kids of her own. Of course Alicia was every selfish bitch in the book for not helping that time. The summer came around and Alicia decided to take her son and her niece, Tekerri, (who was now living with her) to Orlando for a vacay to Disney World. Alicia decided to try and see if Cameron would like to see his son while they were near. Orlando is a four hour drive from Hinesville so she didn't mind cut the trip a day short so that Alton could spend a day with his father. Cameron agreed that he would like to spend the day with him. Once Alicia got there it was a not so good experience. Cameron neglected to tell Alicia that he was on extra duty because he had gotten into trouble at work so he only had a couple of hours to spend with him that day. He also told her that he asked his mother if she wanted to see her grandson and she said no. While Cameron was there with them he didn't even know how to interact with his own son. He got angry with Alicia because he while he was trying to play with Alton, he started crying and didn't want to go to him. Instead of stopping and showing him reassurance, he kept annoying him and trying to make him play. Alton wouldn't go to him and

Alicia wouldn't make him. She tried to tell Cameron how to approach him but instead he got angry and accused Alicia of babying him and said that she needed to tell Alton to come to him. Alicia refused. She told him that she was not going to make her son do something that he was uncomfortable doing and that if he had been a part of his life all this time then he wouldn't be so distant towards him. She told him that he doesn't know him. The next day when they left Alton did allow Cameron to pick him up and hug him. Cameron hadn't seen Alton since that visit.

Throughout all of the nonsense, Cameron still had not gotten health insurance for their son so Alicia had to go through Medicaid in order to get Alton coverage. He's still been an absentee father and even more so, he went to jail for a pulling a gun out on Maria because she had his daughter around some guys, doing drugs. His going to jail was the last strike for him in the Army and they kicked him out. Luckily for him the military gave him an honorable discharge. At least that is what he told Alicia. He had become about $3,000 in the rear on child support because he would either only pay a portion of it or he would skip paying some months altogether. He tried to get Alton's social security number and date of birthday as well as Alicia's home address but wouldn't tell her why he needed the info, so she didn't give the data to him. He got angry with her and told her that they can never get along because all Alicia does is worry about Alton. He begged her to care about him a little bit and not so much about Alton. She told him she would never care about him more than she cares about her son and if cared a little about his son then she wouldn't mind helping him. She let him know that Alton his her priority even if Alton is not his priority. Of course he got upset again and decided to stop paying child support. When she asked him if he planned on paying so that she could enroll their son in drum lessons he starts accusing her of only contacting him when it's about money. That conversation was probably the dumbest to date.

Alicia picked up her phone to send a message to her sperm donor on Facebook messenger: *Are you planning on paying child support this month? I'm trying to enroll our son in drum lessons and winter swim lessons. I'm already paying for him to do boxing and I'm paying his afterschool childcare.*

Cameron responded: *I'm paying it a day before the first. As long as it's still in this month, I'm good.*

Why is it about YOU being good? Shouldn't it be about Alton being good? She asked him in the message. *And technically, you're not good when you are already $2778 in the rear. I'm just saying. But it's okay, I'll pay it all on my own like I've been doing. I do everything for our son on my own anyway. Have a good day.*

Alicia had no intention of continuing the conversation but Cameron came at her like she was the wrong one but he had the right one that day.

He messaged back: *You contact me about money...some of us have to try...you get money...you have no issues in your life...I do...so it's about Alton having a roof over his head and clothes on his back. Not experiences a fun life. Thank you. For once try to understand when people struggle...we can't all be on SnapChat showing off...enjoy your day sweetie.*

Alicia was done being nice: *Don't come at me because you chose to do stupid stuff that got you in the position that you are in now. Take responsibility for your actions like a man and not some little boy. And if I only contact you when it's about money how do you have pictures and videos of your son? I'll wait...oh ok thought so. And you don't contribute to the roof over his head, the clothes on his back, his medical bills, or anything else so what you are saying right now is irrelevant. And on SnapChat showing off? Lmao! Oh I get it now, you're bitter because I'm living and loving life and you are still doing the same bullshit that you've been doing since I met you. At some point you will have to grow up and want to do better. I don't know when or if you will ever get there but good luck. And you love trying to talk shit about when I contact you but you never even attempt to contact your son...don't know anything about him and it's sad but hell he doesn't know you either so I guess it balances out. The foolery that comes out of your mouth is almost laughable.*

Alicia was hoping that he didn't respond but no such luck: *I did take responsibility to raise 2 lil girls by myself. So you got it. I'm doing what think is right. You will get the money before the deadline.*

Alicia laughed so hard that her side begin to hurt. She had to respond to that: *Was that supposed to hurt my feelings or something? Sorry sweetie didn't work at all…I actually laughed! You are raising them because their mothers aren't shit…you don't get accolades for doing what you are supposed to do you moron. I'm going to pray for those little girls though because having you raise them is just as bad as having their mothers' do it lol! You can't teach my son how to be something you don't even know how to be…so I guess it's a good thing that you are a deadbeat to him. No need for further convo…I'm over it and I won't respond.*

No matter what he said in his next message (which Alicia was sure he was going to send) she wasn't going to respond, there was no point. Her phone chimed with a message from him.

I don't even know Alton so he is a stranger to me…Imma deadbeat…um no…I don't know y'all. So who cares. Let your boyfriend be his father like you told me once little girl. And I know my girls love me no matter what…no matter what…that's love…money got y'all all fucked up…dumb folks…go to hell and swim in the lake of fire…devil.

Alicia just shook her head and laughed. He is definitely a lost cause. Time continued to pass and Cameron had become completely absent from Alton's life. Alicia had accepted that he was going to do the right thing by his only son so she didn't stress about it or push the issue. She never contacted him again. She felt as though she had tried her hardest and had done all that she could to get him to be in his son's life but, he never put forth any effort. Even when she made it so easy for him to be in it. She used to feel sad about it and often wondered why he didn't want to be a father to this amazing little boy that he helped create. Alton had so many characteristics and personality traits from the both of them but when it comes to physical features, he was purely his father. He had the same big head and long face. He had the same nose, same mouth, same thick eyelashes, and even his teeth were just like his father's. Alton was a miniature, lighter skin version of Cameron with the same pretty smile. How could he not want to know him? It also used to bother

Alicia that Cameron would lie to people and have them believing that Alicia wasn't allowing him to be in Alton's life. He had people thinking that she was just this bitter "baby mama" who was using a child because they were no longer together. Alicia learned not care about whatever lies he was telling folks because they both the knew the truth and one day it would all come to light without her having to do a single thing. And even more so, Alton would see the truth for himself and know who has always been there for him as well. Alicia did however, make it a point to never speak negatively about Cameron to Alton or to anyone else for that matter. She never spoke of him at all to Alton, and he never asked her about his father.

Alicia had moved on since her hard times in Georgia and Tennessee. Settled back in Killeen, Texas for the past 5 years she had gotten a job a site director for the YMCA afterschool program. She was promoted to a site coordinator and now oversees 5 schools. She bought a house and was living much more comfortably. She joined a car club called One Life to Live, OL2L for short, and had made some pretty strong bonds with new friends. She had dated the President/Co-Founder of OL2L, Jacob for about two months but they broke up when she found out that he was messing with another female. Jacob was a real asshole when they had broken up. One night the club had met up to go greet Noise, one of the club members that was coming back from deployment, at his welcome home ceremony. Alicia and the club treasurer, Ravyn, were standing by Alicia's car talking to Knock when Jacob pulled up with three females in his rental car with him. They had only been broken up for a week and he was trying to disrespect her by bringing the females. They exchanged words and Knock and Ravyn had to hold Alicia back from putting her hands on Jacob. Luckily the night didn't get completely ruined and they were all able to welcome home their brother Noise. Alicia and Noise had been like brother and sister ever since that ceremony. Ravyn had also become one of the few members of the club that Alicia had formed an instant connection with as well as another female named Tika. During the course of the break up with Jacob, Alicia had met a guy named Rick Swolles. They bonded over being from neighboring small cities in Louisiana. He was a very cool guy and she liked hanging out with him. Rick was interested in Alicia on more than a friendship level and he made that very clearly on more than occasion, even telling her that she was like a breath of fresh air and he enjoyed spending time with her. They spent a lot of time together over the course of about three weeks but Alicia decided not to be more than friends with him for two reasons, she was considering giving Jacob another chance, and Rick was married. He told her that he was very unhappy and that they were getting a divorce, but Alicia had learned that it's better not to start anything with a man until he is free of all baggage. She didn't know if he was really getting a divorce but what she did know is that she wasn't going to be entertaining a married man. Period. So they eventually became very good friends. Her relationship with Jacob was better than it was first go round but it was a lot more stressing. Although he was home every day and they went everywhere together, their age difference definitely put stress on the relationship because he did not have his priorities in order and he was untruthful about his debt and living situations. Not to mention he also had a teenaged sister in his care. Alicia felt trapped because she had let him and his sister move in with her and her son, as well as Alicia's niece, Tekerri. He made sure that Alicia had her own password to his phone and her own key to his car. Since he was a cook in the Army he did know how to cook a little bit so he would cook meals for them sometimes. A big problem in their relationship was that he would blow all of his money and leave Alicia to pay for all the bills in the household, which were way more than she was used to because of him and sister living there. Grocery bill and light bill had almost tripled since they had moved in. They didn't clean up anything unless Alicia told them to, and Alicia paid for everything for his sister. The relationship was definitely becoming more than what she wanted and she was beginning to feel trapped and suffocated. She felt as if she was taking care of him and that's was something Alicia would never do…take care of a grown man that is fully capable of doing for himself. Especially when he wasn't even trying to better himself. That was a major for turn off for her. Slowly she began drifting away from him. The summer of 2015 Alicia went to a car show with Jacob, Tika, Knock, and Rick. There were various other local car clubs and organizations that showed up as well. One in particular was Top Notch Boys and Ladies. This was the first time that Alicia had laid eyes on their member, Trevion Williams, whom everyone called Tre Will. Apparently Tre Will and a couple of his fellow members were once prospects for OL2L. They had just come back from doing a year in Korea and have decided to join Top Notch. As they were all checking out cars and chatting, Alicia noticed Tre Will eyeing her as he was having a conversation with some people. Alicia guessed his age to be about 24 or 25. Although at the time she was 31 years old, she looked younger than her age so she had boys from 18 years old all the way to men 50 years old trying to get with her. Typically she didn't have a specific age that she preferred when it came to dating because she learned from experience that some younger guys were very mature and put together, and some older guys were full of crap and didn't have a thing going for themselves. That's why she always dealt with whatever man she chose according to his own character and the way he presented himself. This Tre Will guy wasn't the finest guy in the world or anything like that, but Alicia thought he was cute, and definitely her type. Smooth, dark skin, nice defined arms and chest but he wasn't super muscular or bulky. Alicia hated big muscles. He was almost the same height as Alicia so she guessed that he was only about 5'5. His lips looked so soft and kissable. Although Alicia hated the word "swag", she had to admit that he definitely had a lot of swag about him that caught her attention. She was attracted to him especially once she heard him speak. It was clear he was from the South and one thing Alicia loved more than a chocolate man, was a chocolate man from the south. They exchanged glances throughout the day but Alicia wasn't interested in trying to start anything with him. She was still with Jacob and even if she wasn't, she never went looking for a man. They came to her, and depending on how they approached and what point she was at in her life at the time, she would either give them a chance or curve them. Most of the time, it was always the latter. There had to be something special that Alicia sees in a man that makes her want to pursue anything with them. Alicia put the young man out of her mind and continued her relationship with Jacob. There were so many ups and down and soon he became so disrespectful towards their relationship. He was going out and coming in at five in the morning, wasn't pulling his weight around the house, was in the inbox of different females on Facebook, having inappropriate texting conversations with his females co-workers, and even was talking to his ex-wife again. To top it all off, they would get into physical altercations at least once a week when the kids would go to sleep. Alicia was always thankful that their bedroom was on the other side of the house away from the kids'. They had gotten into some bad fights. Alicia had broken her cell phone once when he had made her so angry that she threw it at him and he ducked so the phone hit the wall and shattered. Another incident they were fighting so she threw a fan at his head. The final straw was one day when they were fighting he had her on the couch trying to choke her as she was punching everywhere that she could land one in at. He tried to stand over her and when she lifted her leg to stop him she accidentally kneed herself and busted her lip. The fight continued to the other side of these house by the front door and due to all of the bumping against the walls and doors, it woke up Alicia's niece and she came running out of her room towards them yelling to stop fighting. Alicia sent her back to her room. She knew this relationship was over and she didn't have any feelings for him any longer so she decided right then that he had to go. She gave him a month to find somewhere else to live. The next day while Alicia was getting her son ready for the school and the girls were getting ready, Jacob tried to start an argument with her. She didn't like arguing or fighting in front of the kids so she ignored him but he called her a bitch in front of Alton and Tekerri so she told him right then he had to get out that day. She refused to let her niece believe that it was okay for a man to speak to her in that way. She was always trying to lead by example, which is why she never argued in front of the kids. After Labor Day weekend Alicia went to Jacob's new place to return some of his shoes that he had left even though he took a lot of her stuff from her house when he moved out and wouldn't pay her for the money she let him borrow to get a plane ticket back from Georgia when he went there for his dad's funeral. Alicia didn't see the point of keeping his stuff because she couldn't fit his shoes. When she went, she found him there with this female that had tried to come at her sideways with her friends one night when Alicia and Jacob had gone to TGI Friday's with a group of friends. Alicia was the non-confrontational type. She didn't like fighting or entertaining drama. She would defend herself if anyone put their hands on her because she wasn't a punk, but she was at an age where she didn't the purpose of fighting. Especially over stupid stuff. The female named Carly had come out of his bedroom with her hair looking a mess and he was only wearing basketball shorts with no shirt. Alicia laughed then cursed him out. Just earlier that day he was trying to get back with her. Carly must have thought Alicia was going to do something to her because she kept saying that she thought that they had broken up and that she and Jacob were only friends. Carly looked scared but Alicia was not going to do anything to this hideously ugly chick. She doesn't do that type of stuff. She went on about her business. A few days later Jacob had contacted her to get in touch with Rick because their friend Danny Ruiz, who was Rick's best friend, had gotten into an accident on his motorcycle and passed away from his injuries. It was a horrible loss for Rick and Alicia tried to be there for her friend in any way that she could. OL2L had a carwash at Joker's Icehouse and after the carwash was over they were heading to a church where Holy Rollerz Christian Car Club were having their annual car show and this year they were incorporating a memorial tribute for Danny. As they were leaving to go to the car show, Alicia saw Tre Will pull up on the side of her and yelled something to her out of his window. She didn't hear him at first so he repeated it then started laughing. He said was going to take the eyelashes of her car. She told him to try it. They ended up at the car show at the same time. They spoke but didn't really have a conversation because Alicia and Tika were trying to make sure that Rick was holding up okay. They were like the three amigos. All from three different neighboring cities in Louisiana. As they were watching Danny's wife standing by his car crying, they went over to her. There was a small box with a slit in the top that people could write a message to his young daughter Mercy, who was only 3 years old, or write down a memory about her father for her to read when she got older. Alicia wrote her message then looked behind her where Rick was standing a few feet away trying to hold back tears. She and Tika glanced at each other at the same time and without words they both rushed over to their friend before he finally broke down. Alicia and Tika had both started to cry as well and it became too much for Tika to handle, so she stepped back and allowed Alicia to continue to console Rick as he cried. Alicia wrapped her arms around him and let him cry into her shoulder as she rubbed his back and told him it was going to be okay. He kept repeating "Why man? Why?" and "I can't believe he is gone. What am I going to do without my brother?" Alicia knew that Rick had not cried until that very moment and that he was trying to keep it together and be strong for Danny's wife and daughter, but she also knew that it would eventually come out and that he needed it. Alicia didn't say anything else, she let him cry until he couldn't anymore and then she just stood there with her friend. When Alicia had gotten home that day she showered and laid on her bed with her Alton and Tekerri and watched movies. Her phone vibrated because she had a notification from Facebook. It was a friend request. When she clicked on the notification it was from Tre Will. She accepted the request then logged off.

Chapter 42

It was the end of September 2015 and Alicia sat at work bored out of her mind. She had made her visits to all of her schools, had gone home for her two-hour lunch and took a nap, then came back to work and finished up her payment books. She had nothing else to do for the day until she left the office to go to one of her schools for the rest of the day. She decided to check out what everyone had going on with Facebook to pass some time. As she was scrolling down her timeline she noticed a post from Tre Will. She clicked on profile just to see what type of stuff he had on there. Nothing out of the ordinary. She clicked on his pictures and browsed through a couple of them. She saw that he had a son that looked to be about 2 or 3 years old. *What a cutie!* She thought to herself. She clicked "like" on 3 pictures and then went back to her timeline. She browsed for a little while longer then logged off and finished her work day. After work Alicia headed to Purser Village Elementary school to pick up her 9 year old niece, Tekerri, and her 4 year old son Alton from the after school care program. As soon as they got into the house and got settled in Alicia went to start on dinner. Just as she was putting the garlic bread into the oven she received a Facebook message. It was from Tre Will.

I see a big dog showing me a lot of love today. She read the message from him and laughed out loud.

She responded, *I just liked a couple of pictures that's all.*

Mhhmmm ok ok. He wrote. *How you doing today beautiful?*

Alicia smile as she typed back. *I'm great, how are you?*

I'm wonderful, especially now that I'm talking to you. He said.

Oh is that so? And why is so wonderful to be talking to me? She asked him.

He took his time responding back to her. *Because I am interested in getting to know you and possibly spending time with you. If that's okay with you.*

Alicia was surprised at how forward he was, but she liked it. She also liked that he actually talked with some sense. That's something that men seemed to lack these days. *That is definitely okay with me. What would you like to know?*

Everything about you. That simple statement that he made was just enough to send chills down her spine. They talked a little while longer on messenger before exchanging numbers.

He called her a little later that evening after she had gotten home from work and got the kids settled.

"Hey gorgeous. What you up to?" He asked through the phone when she answered.

Alicia smiled, "Just relaxing on the couch. What about you?"

"Not much. I'm at my people house. How was your day?"

"It was kind of long and tiring but not too bad. How about you?" she replied.

"It was great." He said. "Glad the day is over though."

"I agree. So Tre Will, tell me about yourself." She asked him.

"What would you like to know?"

"For starters, where are you from?" she asked him.

"I 'm from Alabama, but I've lived in Georgia for years and graduated school there."

She scoffed, "I hated Georgia when I lived there."

"What is your age? If you don't mind me asking." He said to her.

"I don't mind and I am 31."

He paused before speaking. "You do know that I'm 20, right?"

Alicia blinked rapidly trying to make sure she heard him correctly. It's a good thing they were speaking on the phone and not face to face because her face was twisted up at the moment. "I did not know that you were so young. I mean I knew you were young but not that young." She said to him.

"How old did you think I was?"

"I honestly thought you were around 24 or 25." She told him truthfully.

"Oh yeah?" he asked.

"Yes." She responded. "That's a bit of a difference. Did you know I was this much older than you?"

"I thought you were in your mid-twenties actually." He said to her. "You look much longer than 31."

"Good genes, I guess."

He paused again. "So is my age going to be an issue for us? I don't mind the difference, I like older women."

"It won't be a problem as long as you come at me correctly and you handle your business. Show me maturity and that you have your stuff together and there will be no issue at all." She answered him. "But, I don't how cool we will be for football season though, you know we are college rivals." She joked with him.

"Oh that's right, you are from that shit hole place called Louisiana." He said laughing.

"Oh don't go there country boy! Alabama is so trash!" she said laughing.

He let out a little chuckle. "It's all good. As long as we're good, I could care less."

Alicia smiled. He asked if it was okay for him to stop by and see her. Since the kids were in bed and it wasn't her first time meeting, seeing, or talking to him she figured it was ok. She usually doesn't allow men to come over to her house so soon, especially not while the kids were home. He arrived within 15 minutes of getting her address. When Alicia opened the door he stepped in and gave her a warm hug. She almost melted in his embrace. He smelled like he was fresh out of the shower and his deodorant smelled so nice. She loved the scent of a man. It turned her on. She showed him to the couch she had been sitting on and they sat, him on one end and her on her on the other. He didn't seem nervous but she felt that he purposely put space between them so as to not be disrespectful. They made small talk and cracked little jokes here and there. Alicia learned that he became a father at the age of 17 while he was still in high school. His son would be turning 3 in November, the same birthday as Alicia's mom. She told him that she had a son and that her niece also lived her with as well as her 15 year old brother. He told her that he had 24-hour staff duty the next day but that he would still like to see her tomorrow if she had free time. Alicia agreed. He stayed and talked for another 20 minutes before they decided that it was time for him to go. She walked in front of him, leading him to front door. "Girl, you luckily I'm a gentleman." He said to her seductively. She turned and looked at him. "What are you talking about?" she asked smiling with her hand on her hip.

"I love how you look in those tights. Making me weak." He said while licking his lips.

Alicia looked down to check out what he was referring to. She was wearing purple leggings that hugged her curves just right, showing off her thick thighs, nice hips, and somewhat plump butt. She had on a white tank top and different colored socks on her feet. Her hair was pulled back in a messy ponytail and even though she was in comfortable house-wear, she definitely did look hot. She was happy that he was able to see her dressed down but was still turned by her appearance. Blushing, she walked closer to him and leaned in close to his ear. "I appreciate you being a gentleman." She wrapped her arms around his neck as he slid his arms around her waist and pulled her in closer to him. Her breast were pressed against his chest as he ran one hand up and down her back. "You smell good." He told her. "And you're so soft. I don't want to let you go." He placed a soft kiss on her neck. That little kiss felt like a thousand to Alicia. She let him hold onto her for a few seconds longer. Then she kissed him back on his neck very lightly and stepped out of his embrace. She opened the door and waited for him walk out. Once he was out of the door he turned to face her. He looked deep into her big, almond shaped eyes. "Goodnight gorgeous. I'll talk to you tomorrow."

Chapter 43

The next morning Alicia's alarm on her cell phone went off at 600 am, waking her for work and to get the kids up for school. She swiped the phone to silence the alarm and noticed she had a text message from Tre Will. *Good morning gorgeous. You probably aren't up yet but I just wanted you to wake up to this. Text me when you get up.* Alicia smiled so big. That was unexpected but it made her feel wonderful. She sat up in her king size bed and began typing a reply. *Well this was a pleasant surprise. Good morning love. You put a smile on my face.* She laid her phone on her dresser and went to the other side of the house to wake the kids up for school. Her son had peed in the bed as usual so she brought him into her bathroom and put him in the shower. While he was showering, Alicia brushed her teeth and made her bed. Tekerri put waffles in the toaster for herself and for Alton. Alicia loved her 11 year old niece, she was a big help with Alton. Alicia's brother Kyle was in his room getting dressed. Once every one had eaten and dress, they all got into the car so that Alicia could first drop Tekerri and Alton off at school around the corner, then take Kyle to his high school near her sister's house, and finally head to work downtown.

Alicia was sitting at her desk when her phone vibrated. It was a text message from Tre Will, whom she had saved in her phone as Trevion. That was his real name and she preferred to call him by his real name instead of Tre or Tre Will or even just Will, which are all the names that everyone called him. She smiled when she read his text.

I thought about you all night. All I could do is smile.

She texted back. *Oh yeah? What were you thinking?*

I was thinking about how I just wanted to hold you all night.

That does sound nice. I want that walk in the park, holding hands that we talked about. She responded and quickly added *I know I've already said that but I'm just reiterating. Lol.*

He sent a text back. *Nothing is wrong with that. Just reiterate those kisses and hugs from last night and it'll be okay.*

Alicia laughed. Trevion asked to stop by and see her when she went home for lunch and as she pulled up into her driveway she noticed that his car was already there. They went inside and she made them both sandwiches with chips and sodas. She thought it was weird, but cute, that he didn't like anything on his sandwich. Just the meat and bread. After eating he took their plates in the kitchen and put them in the sink. Alicia had come back from the bathroom and was putting her shoes back on. She had to go back to work and he had to go back to staff duty. His break was about over. She was happy with the little bit of time that they were able to spend together. They walked out of the door and he walked her to her car. She opened the door and before she got in she turned and gave him a kiss on the cheek. He got into his car and they went their separate ways. He called her as soon as she made it back to her office. "I enjoyed you." He said as soon as she answered.

"Me too. It was nice to spend time with you again."

"Let me find out that you're really feeling me." He said with a chuckle. "And your scent is on daddy."

She laughed. "Maybe I am. I hope the feeling is mutual though."

"You know it is." He told her truthfully. "I been feeling you since I first saw you at that car show this past summer."

"Oh yeah? I kind of thought you were checking me out then. Why didn't you ever say anything?' she asked him.

"I just didn't want to be rude and start any drama a while back. You know?"

Alicia thought back to that day. "Oh so you knew I was checking you out too?"

"No." he responded. "Probably. I don't know. All I know is you were just sexy to me."

"Well now that you've gotten the chance to spend time with me one-on-one, are you still feeling the same?" she asked already knowing the answer.

He sounded as if he was smiling through the phone. "Yes ma'am. I get butterflies when I see you anywhere." He said. "I get all excited now."

Alicia laughed. He sounded so cute. She loved his personality. They both loved the Fox series Empire so they made plans for him to go on another break from duty so that he could come and watch the show with her at 8. The kids would still be awake because bedtime wasn't until 830 but she would introduce him as a friend, like Noise, and they have go into the room for wind down time until bedtime.

Alicia's close friend Tika called her after her call with Trevion.

"What you doing heffa?" she said as soon as Alicia picked up the phone.

 Alicia laughed. "Why I gotta be a heffa?"

"Cause I'm always one so today you are too!" she said laughing in her loud crazy way.

"Touché' my friend." Alicia said laughing too.

Tika started to speak. "I was going to come meet up with you today during your lunch but by the time you went on lunch it was damn near time for me to be back at work." Tika was in the army as well but she and Alicia tried to have to lunch together at least a couple of times per month.

"Yeah I know. I had just left my office when you said never mind."

"Where your boo at?" Tika asked her.

"He just left my house before I came back to work."

Tika had attitude in her voice. "For real for real?" she asked. "How long was he there?"

"Only for about 30 minutes or so." She answered. "He wanted to see me before I went to work."

"Mmm." Was all Tika had said.

"Mmm what?"

"Mmm nothing my nigga." Tika spat.

Alicia laughed. "Nooooo! What? He came at like 1:06." She said, knowing why Tika had the attitude.

"Oh okay." She laughed. "I guess I'll be watching this Law and Order: SVU at 8 while eating dinner at your house!"

Alicia laughed again "You selfish!"

By now Tika was cracking up with laughter. "How though?"

"But um, we are only gonna catch the last hour of SVU cause Empire comes on at 8 also." Alicia told her. "And I know you were thinking 'this heffa canceled me coming by but let him come by'." She laughed.

Tika laughed again. "You right." Then she sighed. "Then I will be there for the second episode."

"It's only one episode but it's the premiere so its two hours long.

Empire goes off at 9 though."

"Well what time will dinner be ready?" Tika asked.

Again Alicia was cracking up with laughter. "I guess about 730. But FYI, Trevion is supposed to be coming by on his break too."

"What break? What time? Well I will just come get my plate and leave so I can make it back to my room in time." She said and then burst into laughter.

That had Alicia holding her stomach in laughter. "You so greedy!" she shrieked. "I think his break is around 8. I'll have your plate ready. You lucky I love your spoiled butt!"

Tika laughed again. "I love you too!"

After work, Alicia picked up her son and niece from school and headed straight home to make dinner and get them settled in. She made sure Alton and Tekerri had bathed while she made fried pork chops, macaroni and cheese, homemade mashed potatoes, green beans, and cornbread for dinner. They ate their dinner and then did their homework before grabbing their IPads and tuning Alicia out. Tika came at 7:30 on the dot to get the plate that Alicia had put aside for her. After she thanked her, Tika told her to have fun tonight and to text her in the morning. Alicia made a plate for Trevion as well and put it to the side for him. She quickly cleaned up the kitchen and then took a quick shower. She applied her Victoria's Secret Love Spell body lotion to her skin and put on a pair of black boy shorts with a white t-shirt and long socks, one pink and one green. She braided her hair into two pigtails and just as she was walking out of her bedroom, Trevion texted her that he was pulling up into her driveway. It was 7:52. He was kind of early but she was okay with that. When she answered the door he stepped in and gave her a quick hug, noticing that the kids were sitting in the living room on their IPads.

"You are so gorgeous." He said in her ear after hugging her.

Alicia blushed. "Thank you." It was weird to Alicia that no matter how many other men had told her how beautiful, pretty, gorgeous, cute, or whatever that she was (and there were many), it still made her blush every single time she heard from Trevion. He walked into the living room and spoke to Alton and Tekerri. Kyle was in his bedroom. After he had a quick conversation with the kids about school, Alicia gave him the television remote and asked him to put it on Empire. Then she escorted the kids to their room and made them put away the IPads. They knew that it was wind down time so they got into their bunk beds and lay down to watch television for thirty minutes before lights out.

Alicia walked back into the living room where Trevion had made himself at home. He was on duty so he had come over in his Army ACUs. He had taken off his jacket and boots and had made himself at home on the couch.

Alicia stood in front of him. "I fixed you a plate in case you were hungry. Do you want it?"

"Thank you. Yeah I do. I haven't eaten since earlier." He told her.

She warmed the food up in the microwave then brought it to him with some hot sauce, a napkin, a fork, and a glass of fruit punch. He thanked her again then devoured the meal. He told her that is was delicious then took the plate to the kitchen. They were sitting on two opposite ends of the couch again making sure to not be too close to each other. Alicia had told him that she didn't want the kids to see them interacting in an affectionate way too soon. He completely understood and agreed to keep his hands to himself whenever the kids were around or could come into view. The show went to a commercial at 8:26 so Alicia took that opportunity to have Alton go use the bathroom and to tell the kids goodnight and turn off their television. She closed the door and headed to Kyle's room to let him know that he had thirty minutes to bedtime. Alicia and Trevion watched Empire intently and had quick, light conversation during the commercial breaks. Alicia caught him gazing at her a few times out of the corner of her eye. When she would look at him, he still gazed. He wouldn't look away. She smiled. "What?' she asked him. He didn't smile. "You really are beautiful." He said to her. She just smiled and continued watching the show. At 9:00 the show went off and Kyle come out to say goodnight before heading back into his room and going to bed. Alicia went to get some water from the kitchen and when she came back Trevion sit in the spot on the end of the couch that she had been sitting in. She walked over and sat down in the spot right next to him and pulled her feet up under her sitting Indian style. They talked and joked for a little bit, she could see him getting more relaxed with her. He pulled her left leg from under her and laid it across his lap. He was caressing her leg at first as they talked, but then he took off her sock and starting playing with her feet. She squirmed as he tickled the soles. She laughed quietly and tried to pull her foot away from him. He didn't let go. He laughed at her trying to get away. He stopped tickling her feet and just looked into her eyes. Then he leaned over and kissed her. Not a little peck like he had done on her neck the night before, but a real deep slow passionate kiss. His tongue swirled in her mouth searching for hers, and when he found it, they danced in perfect step. He caught her bottom lips in between his teeth then began to suck and tug on it slowly. Alicia felt her whole body get warm just from his kiss alone. She kissed him back with as much as passion as he was giving her, caressing the side of his face with one hand and rubbing the back of his head with the other. Alicia wanted more than kissing. She was yearning for him at that moment. Alicia rubbed her thigh on his leg as he lifted up her shirt and started rubbing her erect nipples. He began planting a trail of kisses on her neck, then to her breasts, down her stomach, and to her inner thighs. He pulled her boy shorts off and tossed them to the side. He began kissing around her bikini line and licking her inner thigh. Just when Alicia thought that she was going to crazy from anticipation, he dove face first into her womanhood. Alicia moaned and rotated her hips as he licked, sucked, kissed, and pleasured her box. She let her fingers roam all over his head as he pushed her legs further back while he gripped her thighs. Alicia was almost to her exploding point when he suddenly stopped, picked her up from the couch, and carried her to her bedroom. He closed the door then walked over to her king-sized bed and lay her down gently. She lay there breathing heavily awaiting next move. He bent down tasting her box once again until he was satisfied that she wanted him. She heard the buckles on his belt loosening and then his pants dropped to the floor. He came up and began kissing her mouth with more aggression than before. Alicia loved that. She was ready. She took off his shirt and rubbed his back and chest waiting for him to enter her. He looked her in her eyes. "You ready?" he asked her with a low, seductive tone. Alicia licked her lips and whispered. "Yes." He positioned his manhood at the opening of her vagina and slowly begin sliding inside. Alicia gasped as he filled her insides up. She wasn't expecting him to be working with that much but she pleasantly shocked. Now the question remained, does he know what to do with it? She soon found out. He started off slow and steady, thrusting inside of her like he wanted her feel every bit of what he was giving her. Alicia met his rhythm, throwing it back at him as he kissed her again. He moaned into her mouth as she grinded beneath him. "Damn. You feel so good." He whispered to her. Soft moans escaped Alicia's mouth as he went deeper inside of her. Before she realized it, she cried out in pleasure as she released all of her juices on his piece. Her legs quivered as she continued to pulsate. He removed his member from her and turned her over, positioning her on her knees. Alicia was on the bed balancing on her knees and forearms with her butt up in the air, her back arched, and her face buried in the pillow. He entered her again, this time like he was on a mission. He pumped hard and quick as he gripped both sides of her waist keeping her exactly where he wanted her to be. Alicia reached behind her and grabbed a hold of his forearm digging her long nails into his flesh. She felt the veins popping out as he held her tightly. The faster he thrusted, the deeper she dug. The roughness felt so good. He was giving her everything he had inside and Alicia was working hard to give him the same pleasure he had just given her. Trevion let out a loud, deep growl then quickly pulled his manhood out and let his seeds spill out all over Alicia's lower back and butt. She collapsed on her stomach as he collapsed on his side laying right next to her. They lay there panting trying to catch their breath for a few minutes. He grabbed her hand, intertwining their fingers, then he kissed her hand. He got up and headed to her bathroom. Alicia heard water running, then she heard him gargling mouthwash. He came out of the bathroom carrying her towel that he had wet with warm water. He wiped his semen off her back and butt then threw towel in the laundry basket in the corner. He fixed his uniform then helped her up off the bed. She grabbed a pair of shorts from her dresser drawers and put them on as he watched her. She knew he had to go back to duty so she was going to wait until he left to shower again. He lay on her bed running his fingers down her back while she lay her head on his chest. Neither of them wanted to move but unfortunately he had to leave. She walked him to the door and pulled her close to him and kissed her good night. Once he had gone she hopped in the shower and then got into bed without putting on any underwear or pajamas. As she was drifting off to sleep she received a text message. It was from him. **Sleep well bae.** Alicia smiled as thoughts of a man who is ten and a half years her junior evaded her mind. *This may be one worth exploring.* She thought before sleep overtook her.

Chapter 44

The week had gone by pretty fast for Alicia. She had her regular routine of work and activities with the kids, but she also added Trevion to her agenda as well. They hadn't been talking for a whole week yet but she had to admit, she was into him. He didn't really seem like the typical 20 year old guy. Yes he was young, and had a few young guy tendencies but Alicia could easily look over them. He had already decided that he was going to make the army his long-term career, he was studying to go to the promotion board to become a Sergeant, he wasn't in debt, he managed his finances well, he a had a pretty good credit score, he paid child support for his son, and made sure that he was a part of his life as much as he could be. All of that was positive in her eyes. What started to draw Alicia in more was the way he was towards her. He made sure that he called every day, at least twice a day, sometimes more. He would send her a "good morning beautiful" or "good morning bae" text every day, even if he had stayed with her the night before. He made sure that between phone calls, he would still text her throughout the day even though they wouldn't be texting about anything important. He respected her wishes about not interacting affectionately with her while they were around the kids, and he even made sure to really play with the kids and talk and listen to them. He found out that Tekerri loved hot wings as much as he does so he just popped up one day with WingStop for her. Alicia liked that he paid attention and remembered everything that she told him and everything about her.

She smiled. He just might be a keeper.

Alicia and her club was having a cookout at the club CEO's house that Saturday. Tekerri had a volleyball game that morning and Alicia needed to wash her car afterwards but didn't have time to vacuum it out before the cookout because she still had to make the macaroni and cheese to take over there. Trevion had already called earlier that day and asked what she had planned that day. She told him about the cookout and he told her that he had a few things that he had to do with his club that day as well. He told her that he needed to go clean his car out today.

"I need mine cleaned out too." She joked to him.

"I got you." He told her.

She thought he was he joking. She was at the cookout talking to Ravyn when he called back a few minutes later.

"Where ya at?" he asked her.

"I'm at Chill's house. I told you we having a cookout today."

"Okay text me his address. I'm about to come get your car and clean it out." He said nonchalantly.

Alicia looked at Ravyn and smiled. "Okay." She said into the phone, then she hung up and sent him a text with Chill's address. Ravyn looked at her. "Why you smiling all hard? Who was that?" she asked Alicia.

"Trevion."

"Who the hell is Trevion?" Ravyn asked.

Alicia laughed. "Tre Will, girl."

"Oh! Well next time say that." She laughed. "Is he coming over here?"

"Yes. He is about to come get my car and vacuum it for me."

"Oh okay, then." Ravyn said with a sly grin. "I'm glad Jacob here, too. So he can see how a real man treats a lady." She laughed out loud.

Alicia loved Ravyn. She always spoke her mind and was one of her most loyal and close friends. She didn't like the way the situation happened with Alicia and Jacob so she was glad that Jacob was going to see her happy with another man. Alicia went and checked with Chill and the others to make sure they didn't mind if Trevion stopped by. Most of them didn't even know who Alicia was talking about until she described him in great detail. They didn't care if he came though. Alicia was still inside talking to Ravyn and the others when Trevion sent her a text saying he was on the way. She grabbed her keys and she walked outside with Ravyn so that Ravyn could smoke. She wasn't even aware that Jacob was already outside on a phone call with someone. When he realized that Alicia was outside he began talking louder so that she could hear that he was speaking to a female.

"He so stupid sometimes." Ravyn said to her. "I hope he still out here when Tre Will pull up to get your car."

Alicia just giggled. "Girl, I'm not even thinking about Jacob and I don't care if he talking to a female. Even if I wasn't involved with Trevion, I still wouldn't care cause I definitely do not want him." She matter-of-factly.

"Yeah, but still." Ravyn laughed.

Trevion pulled up and parked on the side of the road in front of Alicia's car. She walked over to him. When he got out her pulled her into his arms and hugged her.

"You smell good, beautiful." He said.

Alicia grinned. "Thank you." She said. "You gonna stay for a little bit when you bring my car back?"

"If you want me to I will." He told her. He saw Ravyn and Jacob standing outside so he went over to Jacob first and dapped him up. Then he walked over to Ravyn and gave her a hug and chatted with her for a minute. Alicia gave him her car keys. "I don't have any quarters for the vacuum." She told him.

"Don't worry about that, I got you." He said as he handed her his car keys. "In case you need to run somewhere before I get back." He answered her question before she asked.

When he pulled off Alicia turned to walk back to Ravyn's car and noticed Jacob looking at her. He tried to hurry and look away but she had already saw him. She laughed to herself. Ravyn had told her that he was watching the whole time she was talking to Trevion. She didn't care because she wasn't checking for him. Trevion brought her car back about 40 minutes later. It was clean and it smelled good. She thanked him. They stayed at the cookout for another hour then gathered up the kids and headed to Alicia's house where they stayed for the rest of the night.

The next day while Alicia was talking to the president of OL2L, who just happened to one of her best friends Noise, they decided on an impromptu day at the lake in the Belton. Alicia called Trevion to see if he wanted to come. He said he would bring a few of his friends as well. Tika had surgery on her eyes a few weeks ago to correct her vision but she still wanted to go to the lake. She said as long as she had her shades on and didn't just sit directly in the sun for too long then she would be fine. So Noise, Tika, and Alicia rounded up their camp and we all met up at Noise's house to convoy together to the lake. Alicia and her son and niece, Noise and his wife and two daughters, Ravyn and her boyfriend C-No (the club's co-founder), the Sergeant-At-Arms Brock, Rick, and a few other people from their club all met up at Noise's house. About ten minutes later Trevion pulled up to the house with his friends McCool and Slim in the car with him and his friend Black B in the jeep behind him. Black B was the only white boy in the crew that day, but everybody thought he was a cool guy.

They got on the road and made that 30 minute drive to the lake. As they got farther out of the city the guys began speeding and swerving in and out of traffic. Ravyn was driving in front of Alicia but Alicia could still see Trevion driving in front of Ravyn. He was hanging out of the window as he drove, he drove on to the shoulder of the road to pass up Rick's truck, and he was swerving all over. Alicia didn't think that was cool at all. What if he caused an accident? She didn't drive reckless and she preferred if the people she was with didn't either, especially when they had been drinking. Alicia didn't drink because she wouldn't put the kids in jeopardy by trying to drive after drinking. When they finally made it to the lake Rick turned the music on from his truck and let the tail gate down so that the ladies could sit on the back. C-No let the tailgate down on his truck as well. Everyone was just laughing and having a good time. The kids were playing with a ball together in the dirt. The guys were throwing the football around. Some were drinking beer that they brought. Brock, Trevion, Rick, and Noise went over to play with the kids for a little bit. The ladies sat on the truck and talked.

Hannah, Noise's wife, asked Ravyn, "Who is that over there playing with the kids with the other guys?" she pointed at Trevion.

"Oh!" Ravyn said and looked at Alicia. "That's her little boo."

"Oh…Ms. Thang!" Hannah laughed. "You're a cougar!"

Alicia just laughed. "Y'all leave me alone."

Tika chimed in. "Y'all know Alicia like them young men." They all laughed.

"Sometimes they are more put together than some of these older guys." Alicia said truthfully. She looked over at him playing with kids. That melted her heart. She loved that he liked kids.

As if she was reading her mind, Ravyn said "At least he is good with kids and he is taking an interest in interacting with them." Hannah and Tika agreed.

Trevion came over to the truck a few minutes later while Alicia was standing on the side talking to the ladies. He walked up behind her and palmed her butt discreetly so that no one saw. She turned around and put her hand on her hip. "Just what do you think you're doing?" she asked him.

"I haven't been able to touch you since earlier this morning. And you out here looking all sexy in those shorts. I couldn't help myself. I just wanted to feel what's mine." He was standing so close to her face that if he leaned a half an inch closer their lips would be touching.

Alicia smiled, "Well, you gotta keep your hands to yourself for now. The kids may be watching." She leaned in and whispered in ear. "But later, you can put your hands anywhere you want to." Her lips brushed his neck ash she moved to walk past him. He grabbed her hand and pulled her back. When she turned around he pecked her lips quickly, discreetly, and softly. Then he winked at her and walked over to where the guys were chatting it up. The sun looked like it was slowly starting to set so they all packed up everything and decided leave. They lined up and pulled out heading back towards the city. Alicia was towards the end of the convoy and most of the guys and the trucks were in the front. She thought that the guys were driving more cautious now because they had all been drinking more. As she rounded the curve on the road that they were driving on, she had to slam on her brakes in order to avoid running into the back of Ravyn's car. She parked on the side of the road behind Ravyn's and got out. Hannah got out of Noise's car behind her and brought her kids into the car with Alicia's son and niece so that she could watch them. Alicia walked up the road and saw that everyone that was in front of her had parked their car on the side of the road as well. There was also a black truck parked on the opposite side of the road. Alicia began to get nervous. She didn't know what had happened. As she walked farther down the road she was taking a count of everyone's car. *Noise is behind me. Ravyn is in front of me. There is Brock, Black B, Rick, and C-No.* She thought to herself as she walked. *Okay so far everyone is good. Where is Trevion?* She thought. She looked around and still didn't see him or McCool or Slim. Then she stopped dead in her tracks. She looked over to the other side of the street and saw his car in a ditch, wedged on top of a tree. She looked a little farther up the street and saw them talking to Rick, Brock, and C-No. Alicia exhaled. She was so glad to see that everyone was okay. She asked Rick what happened. He told her that Trevion was trying to pass C-No when they were going around the curve but he couldn't see past his truck. When he went over to the other lane the black truck was coming so he had to swerve off the road and ended hitting the tree in the ditch. Now his car was stuck on top of the tree and they were trying to get it out before the police got there. Luckily, they had a lot of guys there. They had McCool, who is actually a lesbian female but dresses like a boy, to sit in the driver's seat and push the gas while the men pushed the car off of the tree and out of the ditch. It worked, and they all fled before the police came.

By the time Alicia had made it back to her house, everyone was already there waiting for her and Trevion had already taken his car and parked it at Black B's house. Alicia went into her house and had Tekerri give Alton a bath and told her that after she showered they need to eat the pizza she brought for them and get into bed because they had school the next day. Alicia went back outside to her driveway where everyone was hanging out talking. They were all just basically talking about what had happened and what they should do. Trevion was drinking and he was underage and he was driving. That wasn't going to be good for him, especially with him trying to go to the board in October. McCool or Slim couldn't say that they were driving because they had both been drinking as well. Alicia felt that she could help him out of the situation. She agreed to say that she was the one driving. She would get a ticket at the most. The police had already contacted Trevion's Uncle. The guy at the lake wrote his license plate number down and gave it to the police. His car registration had his uncle's address on it. She went into the house with Trevion and went to her bedroom to speak with the police on the phone. Trevion handed her his phone with the officer on it. As she talked with the officer and told him what happened, Trevion stood next to her with his arm around her waist and head on her shoulder with his face buried in her neck. The officer told her that she would only get a ticket and that it should arrive in the mail by the end of the week. He told her that as long as she paid the fine there would be nothing else that needed to be done since no one was hurt and no property was damaged. Trevion assured her that he would pay the fine. He said as soon as it came in the mail to tell him how much it is and he would take care of it. He thanked her for being willing to help him avoid trouble. They went back out front and hung out for a little bit longer but Alicia was exhausted. After about thirty more minutes she told them that she needed to get inside and get settled. She had work in the morning. She told Trevion that she would see him tomorrow. He kissed her goodnight and they went their separate ways. She showered and put on her pajamas but she didn't have an appetite so she didn't eat dinner. She checked on the kids and just as she made it back into her bedroom Trevion called. He only wanted to make sure she was ok and to tell her goodnight. Alicia liked him but now she had to think about if his behavior driving like that today was a normal occurrence.

Chapter 45

Alicia was laying in her bed talking on the phone to her other best male friend, Rick. They had the best relationship ever and it was in part due to the fact that even though they had initially wanted to date each other, they ended up becoming the best of friends. They met when Alicia had broken up with Jacob the first time and they talked for about three weeks before Alicia decided that it would be better for them to just be friends because Rick was married even though at the time he was supposedly getting a divorce. Once she decided to get back with Jacob, their relationship became strictly platonic, even adding Tika into it and they basically became the three amigos from Louisiana. It was rare that you didn't see the three of them together, or at least Alicia with Rick or Alicia with Tika. But in truth, Alicia and Rick kept a secret from all of their friends and family. They had indeed hooked up one time before. After she kicked Jacob out of her house and before she started talking to Trevion. It was actually about a week and a half after their friend Danny had passed away. Alicia didn't really remember how it happened though. She barely even remembered the night. But she did know that she, Rick, and maybe Tika had gone out to TJ's Bar and Grill one night to drink and shoot pool. They ended up very drunk and Alicia remembered Rick kissed her in the bar. Everything else after that was a blur. The next thing she remembered was waking up at around 4am in bed with him, both of them naked and a condom wrapper on the floor. She gathered her clothes and left. They talked about it the next day but luckily, it didn't negatively affect their friendship. If anything, it actually made them closer friends and better at being there for each other. It bonded them somehow. Rick had wanted to continue being "lovers and friends" but Alicia on the other hand, didn't think that would be a good idea. Of course Rick would still try but he respected her enough to fall back when she started dating Trevion. They confided in each other about everything. There were no secrets between them. They had truly become best friends. The conversation they were having now was about the incident at the lake.

"So aside from driving stupid as hell," she asked him. "What do you think about Tre Will?"

He paused for a second as if he were thinking. "Well I mean I don't know how he treats you but I think y'all could be okay if he chilled on the young nigga shit he does cause that will drive you crazy."

"You are right about that!" She told him. "It's like I understand he's 20 but I ain't got time for shit like today. But on the flip side, I don't have to ask him to do certain things like I had to do with Jacob."

"Like what things?" Rick asked her curiously.

"Small things." She said. "He was at my house the other day and saw that the trash was full, so he just went ahead and took it out without me asking him to. Came and picked up my car and cleaned it out for me. He make sure he sees me every day. When he isn't physically around me he texts and calls me throughout the day. He respects that I don't want him around the kids so deep just yet. Like it's a different type thing with him than with Jacob. And I'm not comparing them, I'm just saying. Only thing I don't like so far is his reckless driving."

Rick thought about his response before he spoke. "Yeah, I mean with anybody you gonna have good and bad, and if him doing those things for you is good and the driving thing can be worked on, if he cares he will consider your concern with his driving. Sounds like he is off to a good start. He seems cool though but you gotta remember how young he is and that he still gonna do young nigga shit."

They talked for a little bit longer before they hung up. Rick always her best interest at heart and he was usually right about most things that he said. She was truly thankful for her friend.

Trevion came over to see Alicia during their lunch breaks. He told her that his car was being totaled out so he had to rent a Dodge Challenger until the insurance company sent his check to get another car. He said this time he wanted to get Ford Crown Victoria. He wasn't trying to have a car payment and he loved big body older model cars. Of course he was going to hook it up with big rims, sound system, and T.V. screens inside. He was excited talking about it. A boy and his toys.

They were sitting at her kitchen table eating wings and talking when his phone rang. He looked at it then rolled his eyes before answering. "Yeah." He waited for what the person on the other end said before responding. "I'm at Alicia's house." He waited again before saying "Yeah." Then hung up and said to himself "Man that bitch crazy." And he shook his head.

Alicia looked at him, waiting to see if he would tell her what that was all about without her asking him. He didn't so she asked. "What was that about?"

"My crazy ass ex." He said looking at her. "You'll meet her one day. She is in Top Notch Boys and Ladies, too."

"What was the call about?"

He sighed. "Nothing. She asked where I was at. I told her I'm at your house. She said 'okay bet.' And then she hung up."

Alicia didn't really like how she felt about that. Why was she worried about where he was? "So what's the deal with y'all? Is there still something there? When did y'all break up and how long were y'all together?"

"There is no deal. We are not together but she still wants me. You can say that we broke up about 4 weeks ago, it was like the first week in September. But technically we were never in a relationship." He told her.

"Wait, what? What do you mean?"

He began to explain. "We were just cool at first and we basically started fucking after my grandma died when she came to check on me one day. Then we stopped fucking and when we were in Korea I was engaged to someone else and she was talking to somebody else, too. When me and my fiancée called it off and we all came back to Korea a few months, ago we started hanging out and fucking again. Then we stopped fucking about 4 weeks ago."

Alicia didn't really know what to say to what he just said. "So you were going to do a contract marriage? And are you sure you are really done with the "ex" for real this time?"

"No it was going to be a real marriage. I don't believe in contract marriage. If I'm going to get married it's going to be for real." He said looking her straight in the face. "And yes I'm done with Nikki for real. She just do way too much."

"What does she do that's way too much?"

"Just everything." He said. "Like, she always wanna argue and fight and blow things way out of proportion. She childish and petty. I just don't want to deal with all her drama. Like she goes overboard with everything. It's cool to get mad sometimes but to always be mad and always trying to start shit. I can't explain it but she just be doing way too much." He said before pausing and speaking again. "Like she tried to be slick one day. A few days ago as a matter of fact. McCool wrecked her car, right. So Nikki told her she could keep her car. Now we all work in the same unit. So I see McCool in Nikki car and I'm like what you doing? She told me that Nikki told her that she would just ride with me and that she could keep her car. I told her fuck no! I told her nah, take her muthafuckin' car back right now and where ever you need to go I'll take you."

Alicia only had one more question for him. "Well four weeks isn't really that long to have be broken up from someone. Do you love her?"

He took a second to respond as if he was thinking about it. "I will say that I have love for her but I am not in love with her. I was never in love with her. But I do care about her and I have love for her. She not a bad person, I just don't like her ways and things that she does."

"Well how do you know that you are not in love with her?"

"I just know. I know what I feel. I don't feel it. I didn't want to change anything that I was doing when I was fucking with her. I didn't really care if I spent any real time with her. Like, I was in love with my baby mama. My son's mom. I was in love with her. What I felt with and about her, I never had any of those feelings for or about Nikki. That's how I know. You get what I'm saying?" he asked her.

Alicia did understand. As long as he wasn't in love and didn't still want her then she wouldn't sweat it. She changed the subject. "So I don't won't be put into any odd situations, right?" she said only slightly joking.

"Nah not at all. I really like you. I don't even usually do this type of stuff with other females." He said to her.

"Do what type of stuff?"

"Like texting all day, talking on the phone, spending so much time." He explained. "I literally want to see you all the time. I spend the night almost every night. Wake up go to PT, go to my room and shower get dressed for formation and then come back to your house to see you before we both have to go to work. Then I come here during our lunch, go back to work, and when I get off I go to my room and shower and change. I'll go stop by and see my people or do what I need to do while I'm waiting for you to get off, get home, and get settled. Then I'm right back here with you. If you want to go somewhere we go. If I didn't get to finish doing whatever I needed or wanted to do before you get home then I come here and after you got the kids in bed then I take you with me to go do whatever. I even showed you all of my hangout spots and where my people live. I don't stuff like that for other females." He said all of that with such seriousness.

"Then why do you do it for me?" she asked sincerely.

He looked her in the eyes. "Because I know that I can't bullshit and half ass with you. I gotta come to you the right way. You're not like these other females out here."

That made Alicia smile. *Wow. He just gets better and better.* She thought to herself.

Chapter 46

Alicia and Trevion had been spending almost every single day together and she loved it. They had been to cookouts at Chill's house together, a couple of times he brought his club members over as well to race their cars against her club members. He had begun to be around so much that King, who was Chill and C-No's best friend, had begun to call him Alicia's "little Top Notch friend". Alicia thought that was funny because King was also from Louisiana but he talked with a country accent and he was kind of dumb so that made for pure comedy when he was around. King had wanted to holler at Alicia before she even knew who he was. He had been messaging her on Facebook but she wasn't interested in him at all so she just kept it friendly, nothing more. When he realized that she wasn't going for him and saw that she was dating Trevion, he set his sights on Tika. But she didn't want him either.

Things were going well between Trevion and Alicia. He smothered her with attention and affection and took an interest in things that were going on in her life. He made sure to ask her about her day, about work, engaged in talk and play with the kids, told her things that were going on his life, learned and remembered her favorite things and when she wanted something he went above what she asked for, even with the smallest things. He even thought her sense of humor was cute and when she cracked jokes he would always "Once again, you're so lame, Bae." But she loved when he said that because she knew he liked it. They were talking on the phone one evening before he came over and she had mentioned that she wanted some ice cream, she was thinking about ice cream from McDonald's. When he came by that night he asked her to go ride with him somewhere. While they were out he took her to this place called Mango Cup to get the ice cream she was craving. She had never even heard of the place before. It was those simple things that made her begin to fall for him. When he learned her middle name was Leona, he shortened it and started calling her Leon as a funny pet name. She thought it was cute. Although things were going well between the two of them, it was inevitable that they had their first interference and subsequently their first fight.

It started at a football tournament at LongBranch Park. Trevion's club, Top Notch, had entered to play. Everything was great that day. Trevion had stayed at Alicia's house the night before. At the tournament he was all over place but they did manage to talk a little bit, here and there. While he was playing a game, Alicia was standing on the side lines talking with Ravyn and some other people. She felt that someone was watching her but she really didn't know who it was. Eventually she noticed two females also standing on the sideline and whispering to each other. One was really skinny and short with a hat on and the other was tall like Tika, at least 5'9, but she had some meat on her bones. She wasn't fat but she wasn't slim either. She had an onion booty and she wore some little shorts with her butt almost hanging out. Alicia thought she looked kind of sloppy. The two females kept looking at Alicia. Then they would say something to each other and look at her again. She also noticed that they were watching Trevion very closely but didn't seem to pay anyone else any attention. Alicia had put it together. One of them was Trevion's ex, Nikki. She assumed it was the small one, since Trevion was only about 5'5. She walked over to C-No's truck and started talking to Tika and King. She told them she was about to go the store across the street from the park and they asked her to bring them back some drinks. Trevion's game had ened and as she was walking to her car he walked up to her.

"I'm about to go across the street to the store." She told him. "You need anything back?"

He wiped the sweat from his face. "Nah I'm good, thank you though. I'm tired as hell."

"Did y'all win that game?" she asked him.

"Nah we didn't but we still got one more game to play though." He said.

She started walking away. "Oh okay. Well I'll be back in a few."

"Okay." He said and started back towards the field.

When Alicia got into her car she saw that she was wrong about who Nikki was. She was actually the bigger one. She had walked over to Trevion when Alicia walked away. She saw them walking and it looked as Nikki was trying to grab his hand but she wasn't sure. As she drove to the store she called his phone. He didn't answer. She didn't like that. As she was getting the stuff for everyone from the store she called Tika. She was telling her about what had just happened. As she was talking, Nikki and the short friend whose name was Tasha had walked in. They didn't come by her though. They walked towards the back of the store, turned to look at her, and they walked out. Alicia saw them looking at her car as they walked to Nikki's car which ironically was the same kind of car as Alicia's. A white Kia Optima. Only difference was Nikki's was completely stock and Alicia had black rims, tint, and had accented her car with black door handles, side mirrors, spoiler, and moldings. *Yeah, hate on it sweetie.* Alicia thought to herself as she watched them check it out. When she went back to the park Nikki and Tasha were still there but Trevion was gone. He had called Alicia while she was still in the store and told that he was about to leave instead of playing the last game. Then he told her that Nikki was trying to be messy and he had to "chump her ass out" for the stunt she tried to pull. Alicia asked what he meant. He said after she had left Nikki came up to him and tried to hold his hand but he snatched his hand away from cursed her out because she "knows what she be doing". He said they are not together so she didn't need to be all up in his face or trying to hold his hand. He also told her that Nikki knew exactly who Alicia was and she was doing that on purpose. Either way Alicia felt like he needed to make sure that she didn't feel like she had a place in his life or heart as long as he was involved with her. That little bit of interference had her starting to feel like something was amiss. Alicia was sitting in Rick's truck telling him about what had happened. Rick told her not to worry too much about it. He said that if he had cursed her out like he said then that means he took care of the situation and there was no more need to think about it. He told her that all she could do was trust that he handled it unless he gives her a reason to doubt him, but at the same time pay attention and keep her eyes open. That's the basically the same advice that Tika had given her, too. Alicia watched as Nikki left the tournament she noticed on the back of her car along with the Top Notch decal it also 'Will's 1st Lady' on the back window. Alicia remembered Trevion telling her that Nikki had gotten that put on her car but he hadn't wanted her to do it. He had told her that he'd been telling her to take it off, especially after they stopped fucking.

A few days after the tournament, Alicia was leaving the mall when she spotted Nikki driving past her in the opposite direction. She noticed that she had went and put chrome rims on her car and when Alicia looked in the rearview mirror she saw that she had removed the 'Will's 1st Lady' from her window. Alicia smiled. *He handled it.* She thought to herself. She was already on the phone with him when she saw Nikki. He was joking with her about getting him something from mall. Alicia felt compelled to test him and see where his mind was at with the Nikki situation. She didn't know why she did because it was childish.

"Oh I see ya girlfriend. She got some rims for her car?" she asked him nonchalantly.

"Yeah." He said like she was getting on his nerves.

"Oh so she IS still your girlfriend?" Alicia asked him.

He was annoyed now. "Man stop saying that shit. I already told you she not my girlfriend. That shit gonna piss me the fuck off."

"Well excuse the fuck out of me!" she spat at him, then hung up the phone.

He didn't call or text her for a whole day and she didn't either. It seemed like they were trying to see who break down and hit the other one up first. Alicia was stubborn so it wasn't going to be her. The next day while Alicia was over at Chill's house with the club she got a text from Trevion.

No kisses or nothing today I see. I guess you gonna make me sleep alone again tonight. That's cool. I just love sleeping alone. Don't you?

Alicia shook her head, but she smiled. He was so extra. *You were the one who cursed and yelled at me.*

He sent a text back. *Because you said that dumb shit when I already told you. I didn't like that. It really aggravates me.*

Well you could've just said that instead of getting an attitude and cursing and yelling at me. I don't like being talked to like that. She typed to him.

He was responding very quickly. *I apologize gorgeous. I wasn't trying to be mean or come off like that to you. For real.*

Alicia waited a few minutes before she responded. *Okay…so that means your my boo still? Lol.*

Damn you was trying to get rid of me that fast? He said.

No, but I'm stubborn and you hurt my feelings so I was like well damn, okay. She answered honestly.

But what did I tell you? He asked her.

I meant earlier before you told me that. Damn why you gotta be all dramatic?

He hit her right back. *I'm not dramatic.*

She didn't waste a second. *Well you are something today.*

I'm ready to go to bed. Was his response.

Alicia raised an eyebrow. *At 8 o'clock?*

He made Alicia smile so big with his next text. *Not really. I just miss my bae.*

How much? She asked him, not prepared for the answer he was about to give.

Enough to eat that pussy in the kitchen when the kids are asleep. Now go home. I'm on my way.

Alicia did as she was told. They pulled up to the house at the same time. He played with the kids a little bit before they had to bathe and get to bed. Once they had fallen asleep Trevion and Alicia went to her bedroom to get in bed. Before Alicia got into the bed he asked her for a cup of ice, no water in it. Alicia thought he liked to ice like she did so she obliged. When Alicia got back into the room he had stripped down to only his boxer briefs and was laying on top of the covers on side of the bed that was closets to the bathroom and night stand. He knew that was her side of the bed. They fought over it every night because neither of them liked sleeping on the side by the wall. She felt like he tricked her into going to get the ice so that he get her side of the bed. She laughed but she wasn't giving it up without a fight. She jumped on top of him and they began to wrestle. Of course she wasn't going to win against him but she liked play fighting with him for some reason. They rolled around in the bed for about three minutes until he straddled her thighs and had her arms pinned down by her wrist. He was hovering over her in victory, smiling, looking devilish and delicious. She loved his chocolate skin and toned arms. She even loved his hairy chest which was weird to her since she didn't usually like hairy men. He eyes pierced hers and before she knew it, play time was over. He covered her face and lips with kisses galore before he reached over turned the bedside lamp off. He kissed her deeply and began making that familiar trail down her neck, chest, stomach, and inner thighs. He paused for a moment and Alicia heard a smacking noise. She felt his hands grip her thighs and then he dove in face first. She jumped at the shock he sent through her body. This time felt different. She felt this cold warmth between her legs and the sensation was absolutely mind blowing. She had realized that he had the ice cubes in his mouth when he started eating her womanhood. He expertly ran the ice all over her clitoris using only his tongue. When the cube melted he devoured her box like it was his last meal. Alicia was moaning so loudly that he released the grip on one of her thighs and used his hand to cover her mouth. It wasn't long before she was shaking and jerking from the orgasm that his tongue had just given her. He slurped up all of her juices then kissed her clitoris again before coming up and kissing her mouth, allowing her to taste her own sweetness. He entered her slowly at first, then picking up speed. He placed her feet on his chest and began stroking deeper. He grabbed one of her feet and kissed the ball of it before placing her toes in his mouth and sucking them. Alicia was on the verge of another orgasm. When he placed his hands under her butt and began whispering in ear that she felt so good, it pushed her over the edge and released her second orgasm, just before he pulled out and spilled his semen all over her belly. As usual, he collapsed next to her, almost putting his arm on her belly in his semen. Alicia caught her breath then got up and headed to the bathroom to clean herself up. She returned with a warm washcloth for him. They lay wrapped up in each other's arm. "I missed you." He told her.

He felt her smile. "I missed you, too." And with her head on his chest, they drifted off to sleep.

Chapter 47

The days passed on as usual for Alicia. Work, kids, car club, Trevion, and friends. They had begun to have a standing Empire date night every Wednesday night. They never missed watching an episode together. After this week's episode they had talked and played for hours before finally falling asleep while they both were laid stretched out across Alicia's bed. She woke up to him giving her oral pleasure at 4 in the morning. She didn't complain. Although she knew she wasn't going to be any good at work in a few hours, she didn't want him to stop. After he made her cum with his mouth, he mounted her and they had a quickie session. Then they lay down for another 45 minutes before the alarms went off to get up. He was at Alicia's house so much that he had clothes, shoes, underwear, work uniforms, toothbrush, toothpaste, deodorant, body wash, and razors there. Not all of his stuff, but a good bit of it. She didn't mind at all. This Friday Alicia had met up with Tika in the parking lot of K-Mart. They were waiting for a few of their other club members to arrive so that they could attend a party that another local car club was hosting. Trevion had gone to Austin that night with his friend DJ and some other people but she sent him a picture of her outfit for the night. She was wearing a bunt orange and tan printed t-shirt dress that hugged her body and showcased her curves and a pair of tan, strappy, open-toe heels. While Alicia and Tika were sitting in their cars talking to each other through the window, he called. She could tell he had been drinking a little bit because it seemed as though he was saying came to his mind at that moment.

"Hey beautiful, I miss you."

Alicia smiled. "I miss you too. Y'all made it to Austin yet?"

"Yeah we chillin right now though. I can't wait to get back to your sexy ass. I don't know what it is but you do something to me. For real. You bae." he said to her.

"Oh is that right?" she asked him.

"Yes it is. I wish I could just taste you right now. You taste so good. I'm gonna eat that pussy in the garage on top of the washer when I get back to you." he said making Alicia laugh.

Tika heard her laughing and asked who she was talking to. She told her Tre Will. He then asked if she was with Tika. When she told him yes, he asked to talk to her. Alicia got out of her car, walked over to Tika's and handed her the phone.

Whatever he had said to Tika caused her to burst out in uncontrollable laughter. She said a few things back to him then looked at Alicia started laughing again. Alicia looked at her with a half-smile. "What is he saying?" she asked Tika.

"He said you got some good stuff and you taste sweet. He said you got him hooked and wanna eat your vagina when he gets back." Tika laughed the whole time he was talking to her. After they hung up the phone he sent Alicia a text message. *I wanna fuck you with just your heels on.* He told her. Alicia felt playful so she replied. *Too bad you'll be out all night...*

She smiled when she saw his response that simply said *Grrrr.*

Are you growling at me? Lol. She texted him back.

Yes I am. He said.

Mmmmm...Turning me on babe. She typed back.

Alicia loved the little back and forth thing that they did sometimes. So playful and cute. He responded to her previous text with *Muahhh I like you. Gimmie kiss.*

Muah!! A hundred times back... she wrote to him. He had her blushing.

The last text from him that night was *I miss you.*

I miss you too. She told him.

Alicia and her club, along with Rick, were all hanging out at Noise's new apartment that he had moved into to save money instead of continuing to live in that big house that his family didn't need. Trevion had called and asked her where she was. When she told him, he asked if him and his club could stop by and hang out for a little bit too. He said they were supposed to be going to a kickback a little later and invited them to come as well. When they came over they all were outside just hanging out and talking and chat. The guys of course talked about typical guy stuff; whose car was fastest, whose gun was better, and who had a better stereo system. All of that stuff that Alicia didn't care anything about. Alicia caught a glimpse of Trevion though, she licked her lips. He was on his fly guy trip that night. He wore dark rinse Levi's jeans, a pink Ralph Lauren Polo shirt, and some brown leather loafers. She thought he looked very cute. It was nice to see that he can switch it up from t-shirts and Jordan's sometimes. Tika wanted to go out and do something but she didn't really want to go to a bar. They decided to go to a strip club. Alicia, Tika, Rick, Black B, and McCool were the only ones that wanted to go. Trevion didn't care for strip clubs so he opted not to go. He told Alicia that he would come to her once she got back home though. He was texting her while she was there but as the night went on he began to say that he was getting sleepy. Alicia asked if he was still going to wait up for her. He said yes and that she all she had to do was text or call him and he would be there. If Alicia had been having fun she wouldn't have really been thinking about as much as she was. The strip club wasn't much fun at all. The dancers weren't attractive and they weren't great strippers. The drinks were overpriced and she was mad that she had paid twenty dollars to get in but it wasn't even worth ten. They all agreed that it was trash so after only an hour and a half they left. Since Trevion wasn't answering his phone, Alicia assumed he was asleep and decided to go eat at IHOP with Tika, Rick, Black B, and McCool before heading home. She texted Trevion to let him know she made it home so that he wouldn't be worried when he woke up the next day. She hated that she had decided to go out tonight because she remembered that he had 24 hour duty the next day so he wouldn't be sleeping over tomorrow night either.

He called her the next morning as he was going in for duty. "Hey gorgeous. I apologize for falling asleep last night. I was so tired." he told her when she answered.

"It's fine. I missed you last night." she said.

"I missed you too." he told her.

She smiled slightly. "I wish I would've stayed home with you last night."

"You should've." he said warmly.

She sighed. "I know. Tonight will make four nights in a row of sleeping alone."

"Stop baby. You making me feel bad." he pleaded with her.

"I'm not trying to make you feel bad, I just miss my boo." she said in a baby voice.

He chuckled at her silliness. "I miss you too with your fine ass. All your soft kisses and touches."

"Oh yeah?" she smiled.

"Yep you make me cookoo for cocoa puffs." he joked with a laugh.

Alicia laughed too. "You're so silly."

Chapter 48

It always seemed like when things are going well in Alicia's life somehow, trouble isn't far away. Of course over the weeks Trevion had been pretty much everything that Alicia wanted and needed him to be. They both had attitude problems and were stubborn so they had an occasional spat or disagreement. Sometimes they would make up and be finally immediately afterwards, sometimes they would need just a day to themselves, and sometimes they would end up going two or three days without communicating until one of them stops being childish and hits up the other. They had an issue one day that stemmed from a visit to a home improvement store to go see Ravyn while she was bored at work. Alicia, Tika, Trevion, and DJ all went to go keep her company for a little bit. They walked around the store with her just laughing and making jokes. Trevion held Alicia's hand and gave her his hoodie to wear because she was cold and she had forgot her jacket. They snuck in little kisses when they thought no one was watching them and snuggled up together creating warmth in his hoodie. Alicia had gone on her SnapChat while they were in Ravyn's break room and recorded Trevion and DJ being silly and Tika and Ravyn laughing at them. After they left Ravyn, Tika got sleepy and decided to head back to her barracks room and Trevion and DJ went to hang out with some other friends. Alicia went home and relaxed until came over and they cuddled and went to sleep.

A few days after hanging out with Ravyn at work, Alicia received a message on Facebook from someone named Tameshia Gray. She had no idea who this female but she found out when she opened the message.

Hey! This Nikki. I know you know me, but anyways, what you and Tre got going on?

Actually I don't really care about the what, but how long?

Alicia read but didn't respond to either message. She didn't feel the need to. It seemed as though Nikki was trying to start some sort of drama and that was something Alicia did not engage in. She didn't even know why it mattered to her what they had going on or even for how long. They weren't together and Nikki definitely knew that Alicia and Trevion had something going on. She made it obvious the day of the football tournament. About an hour later she received another message.

Aight! Bet! With the laughing emoji behind it. Alicia didn't know what that was supposed to mean but she was not about to entertain the foolishness.

Trevion called her a little bit after that and asked her if she had told Jacob that they are in a relationship. She hadn't told anybody that they were in a relationship. Alicia and Trevion had talked about just dating and eventually working towards a relationship but she had always told him that for the moment she was content with how things were between them and she wasn't trying to rush into anything. Noise had even told her that when he talked to Trevion one day that he told him he wouldn't mind being in a relationship with Alicia but that she was the one that said she didn't want one. Trevion had told her that Jacob's girlfriend is a friend of Nikki's and that he and her were watching Alicia's snaps and saw Trevion on it. Then Jacob had told his girlfriend that they were dating, she then told Nikki. When Alicia didn't respond to her message she pulled up on Trevion at Black B's house and started a big commotion. She was cursing and yelling while his son was inside. In order to get her to calm down and leave he had to tell her he would meet her over at her house to talk to her. He was heading that way now while he was on the phone with Alicia. He told her that he was going to calm her down and that he would be over to her house afterwards.

Alicia called and told Tika what had happened. The first thing Tika said was, "Why is it a problem if someone told Nikki y'all are in a relationship? If that's his ex then what's the issue? I'm not saying anything is going on but I think you should kinda step back and really find out what's going cause she isn't acting like this for no reason. I just don't want you to get hurt." She said sincerely.

Tika and Alicia rode over to Jacob's house to ask him why he and his girlfriend were talking about Alicia and Trevion's situation. Jacob explained that he was watching Alicia's snaps one day and his girlfriend was sitting by him and saw DJ and Trevion on it. She asked him why Tre was on Alicia's snap and he told her that they had been talking for a minute. Then his girlfriend said that he was over at Nikki house that same day that he was on Alicia's snaps. Alicia had gotten angry but she wouldn't let it show. So not only were these three assholes trying to interfere with her situation with Trevion, but also apparently he was at her house recently. Oh he was going to have to tell her what was up or it was a done deal between the two of them.

Trevion made it over to Alicia's house about an hour after the phone call. He walked in like he was so tired. Not physically tired, but emotionally. He sat on her bed while she stood in front of him. He looked up at her. "That girl is really crazy."

"How do you mean?"

He let out a deep exhale. "She showed up to Black B house clowning and acting a fool because she wanted to know if I got something going on with you."

"I don't understand why it matters. Or why you had to go over there to talk to her. Are y'all trying to work shit out or something? You can be honest with me. I can't see how she would be sending me messages, flipping out on you, and doing whatever for no reason." Alicia questioned him. "And did you go over to her house that night we went to see Ravyn at work?"

He didn't deny it. "Yes I did. DJ wanted to go over there cause he been trying to get at her friend. It was nothing like that though. I was just there for him and all we did was play cards. I came back here to you that night."

Alicia folded her arms across her chest. "Well why did you have to go to her house tonight to talk to her?"

"Because if I didn't she would've stayed at Black B house causing all that shit. I didn't want all that in front of his house." He explained to her. "But when I went to her house I put her in her place. I told her she was tripping and it was pointless for her to be showing out over me cause she is my ex. She was asking me how long I been talking to you and if we are in a relationship and I told her it ain't none of her business because, well, it ain't none of her business. Then she started talking dumb shit saying that she gonna fight you whenever she see you again. I told her she sound stupid as fuck and that you ain't with all that stupid shit. I told her straight up that you are older and you don't do all that fighting shit and that you are too grown for that. But she kept saying she was going to fight you so I told her that if she put her hands on you that I was gonna beat the fuck out of her. Then I left and came over here."

Alicia appreciated that he at least told her what the conversation was about but she wasn't sure if there was more to what he was saying. She tried to put it out her mind. He needed to go to his barracks to get more underwear and his PT clothes for the next day so she rode with him. They made it back, showered, and went to sleep.

Chapter 49

A couple of days before Halloween Chill stopped by Alicia's house to chat with her about some club things. While he was there Alicia talked with him about her situation with Trevion and Nikki. Chill told Alicia that he knew Nikki as being a hoe. He told her not to worry about Nikki and that until Trevion gave her a reason not believe him then she should put her reservations aside and just enjoy what they have. Later that night some of the club members had to attend a trunk or treat event that Top Notch was throwing at a local restaurant. When Alicia and Tika showed up with the other club members they immediately spotted Trevion, McCool, Slim, and Black B. They went over and spoke to them and exchanged hugs and pounds. Alicia acted like she wasn't going to give Trevion a hug but then he laughed and she leaned in to hug him. Tika and Alicia walked around the parking lot of the event checking out how everyone had decorated their trunks. When they stopped to speak to some members of another club Alicia saw a white car driving slowly through the parking lot and the people inside of the car were looking around as if they were trying to find somebody. She realized that it was Nikki and Tasha. She saw Tasha point at her and say there she go right there. Then they drove around back to where Top Notch was at and parked. Alicia asked Tika if she had saw that, but she hadn't. When they walked back around to where the other club members and Top Notch was at they saw that Tasha and Nikki were out of the car and standing near Trevion's car with everyone else to. Alicia and Tika walked over there with Alton and Tekerri in tow. Trevion started playing with and talking to the kids before they ran over and started playing with toys in the dirt. Alicia was standing by passenger side door while Trevion was sitting on the hood of his car. He turned to her and something silly then he smiled. Alicia just laughed and started talking to Tika. A few seconds later she heard someone say "So! I don't care hoe!" when she looked up she noticed that it was Nikki talking while she was smoking a cigarette and trembling as if her nerves were bad. Alicia frowned up her face. Tika looked at her and told her "Don't even entertain her. She didn't direct it so let it go." Alicia just nodded her head. Then Noise commented "Besides, the kids are out here. We don't need no bullshit in front of them."

Alicia nodded again. She heard someone ask her "Who is that big Shrek looking ogre ass bitch anyway?" she wasn't sure who had asked her but she responded simply "Oh that's Nikki. Trevion's ex." She gathered up the kids and was getting ready to leave. Trevion walked over to her and told whomever he was speaking on the phone with to hold on. He gave her a hug and kissed her cheek and told her that he would be at her house when the event was over. Alicia stopped by the store to Ravyn since they were nearby. After filling her in on what had happened she headed home. She was surprised to see that Trevion had beat her there. They went about their usual routine and cuddled up to fall asleep.

The last event that Alicia was attending for Halloween was another trunk or treat at the park hosted by a different club. It was a pretty decent event. OL2L entered two of their members' cars to decorate the trunk and hand out candy. While they were there, Alicia took Alton and Tekerri around to collect candy from other cars. When they got to the area that Top Notch was in she was surprised that Nikki wasn't being an asshole that she actually talked in a nice a voice to the kids and gave them a big hand full of candy. Alicia smiled and kept walking. While Alton and Tekerri kept walking to other cars with Ravyn, Alicia stopped at Trevion's car, which was parked near where Nikki was passing out candy. He was sitting in the passenger side with the door open messing with something inside of his car. She stood inside the door. He looked up at her. She told him to give her a kiss so he snatched his mask off and kissed her three times on the lips. She smiled and walked back to the kids and her club. She didn't know if Nikki saw it or not but she just got satisfaction knowing that he would kiss her in public with Nikki being around. That put her at ease a little bit.

Halloween day Alicia had decided that the kids' weren't going to go trick or treating. They had been to two trunk or treats already, they didn't need any more candy. Earlier that day Alicia had gone on post to the commissary to get groceries for Tika. She had surgery on her feet so she couldn't drive or go anywhere or even walk around really. Alicia genuinely loved Tika so she didn't mind helping her out at all. She did however, hate that Tika lived on the third of her barracks. Hauling those groceries and the cases of juice and water up those stairs was no easy task. But she did for her. True friendship.

Chapter 50

First weekend of November and Trevion had gone out of town. He was heading to Georgia to see his son and be there for his third birthday. He had a few mishaps that morning when his friend took him to the airport in Austin. He had overslept so he missed his flight. He had to pay for another flight and unfortunately the next flight was hours later, so he was stuck waiting at the airport. He called Alicia and talked to her for about two hours before she had to get off the phone and actually do some work. During their conversation she could hear the frustration in his voice but she tried to keep him positive and reminded him that at least he would still be able to see his son and spend some time with him. He was not really trying to hear all that though. He wanted to continue to be mad. He made her laugh when he told her that he "wanted to take all of my frustrations out on your cooter." That was funny to her because unless she was extremely mad, Alicia never said the word pussy as he did all the time. She always said cooter. He finally got into a better mood by the next time she spoke with him. He had landed and gotten situated and was waiting for his son's mother to bring him over.

That Saturday Alicia and her club attended a car show at Whiskey Creek Saloon. Alicia hadn't intended on entering her car but they told her all the proceeds go to charity and that she was going to win an award because they had over 40 places and not nearly that many participants. So the whole club entered including Tika, Noise, Ravyn, and C-No. Chill had convinced King to enter as well and to say that he was apart OL2L in order for the club to win most represented award. Although, Trevion was away for the weekend he still made sure to be in almost constant contact with Alicia the entire. He called her multiple a day while he was gone and if they weren't on the phone he was texting her. She was surprised when he called her during the car show, though.

"Hey love." Alicia answered her phone.

"What you doing gorgeous?" He asked her.

She rolled her eyes, playfully as if he could see her. "I'm at this car show, remember?"

"Oh yeah, I forgot. Well I got somebody that want to talk to you." He said with a mischievous tone.

For some odd reason, Alicia was half way expecting it to be his son's mother, or his son. "Someone wants to talk to me?" she asked. "Who?"

He didn't tell her. He simply said, "Hold on." and then he passed the phone to someone.

"Hey. How you doing?" The female voice said into the phone.

Alicia didn't think it was his son's mother due to the maturity of the woman's voice. She was hoping that it wasn't who she began to expect. "I'm pretty good. And you?"

The woman replied, "I'm fine. This is Tre's mother. I'm Lisha."

Alicia knew it. "I'm Alicia. Nice to telephone meet you." She said with a giggle.

Lisha chuckled. "You too." she said before continuing. "So, I was just talking to my son and he has been telling me about you. He says that he really likes you and that y'all have a good thing going."

"Yes. This is true." Alicia said.

"That's good. But I'm sure you know because of y'all age difference that it made me want to know this woman that he is so into it. I believe he said that you are 30 or 31. He isn't 21 yet. I guess I'm just curious as to what interested you about it enough to make you give him a chance." She said sounding like a mother with sincere concern, and woman with honest curiosity.

Alicia thought for a minute before speaking. "Truthfully, Lisha, you have raised a decent man. I was very skeptical about giving him a chance at first because of his age as well but he is not the average 20 year old male. I initially thought he was a few years older when I first saw him. The times that I had spoken with him before he actually approached me, he didn't come off as most young guys do. He was very respectful, he is very charming, and he knows how to make a woman feel as she should. I gave him a chance and he showed me that he is very responsible, he has his priorities in order, he respects my feelings, and he does things that I don't have to ask him to. There are so many reasons why I gave him a chance and he hasn't made me regret it yet. I chose to overlook his age because I've dated older men, younger men, and men my age and what I have realized is that age doesn't make a man do what he is supposed to do. He boils down to the man. If he ain't shit he just ain't shit regardless of age. So until your son shows me that he isn't the right guy for me, I'll continue to give him a chance." Alicia spoke those words with so much truth and sincerity that she scared herself. She didn't realize that she had begun to fall for him.

"You are right about that." Lisha said into the phone jarring Alicia from her thoughts. "He is very mature and responsible and for his age and I'm so proud of him. Well I just wanted to speak to you, that's all. I don't know if he told you but I'm 37. Only a few years older than you." she laughed.

Alicia felt weird but Lisha seemed like a pretty cool lady. She heard

Trevion's voice through the phone. "Baby."

She smiled. "I'm still here." she said softly. "Your mom seems cool."

He laughed. "Lisha don't play." he laughed again. "What did you say to her?"

"Nothing really. I just answered her questions. What made her want to talk to me anyway?" she asked him.

"Remember when I was talking on the phone with her that time at your house?" he asked her. "Well, I was talking to her about you today, too, and she was surprised that I was still involved with you. So she wanted to talk to you."

Alicia smiled again. "Oh, I see."

"So what did you tell her?" he pressed.

"I told her the truth." she said coyly. "Ask her what I said."

"Mm mm...okay." he said. "I miss you."

"I miss you too. I really do." she said to him.

"Why do you miss me?"

"Cause I do. No hugs and kisses and rubs and laughs, and shit talking." she said to him in a playful but serious tone.

He laughed. "You miss that?"

"Yep!" she laughed. "Cause you are sweet afterwards." They talked a little bit longer before hanging up. The continued to text for the rest of the day. As Alicia was sitting on Tika's car during the show, this guy named Niko came over and started talking to them. Alicia had seen Niko around quite a bit but she never really cared for him. She thought he was too arrogant and full of himself. He just gave off this really annoying vibe. She and Tika were both friends with him on Facebook and they had recently had a whole conversation on one of the pictures that Alicia posted and tagged Tika in. He was interested in Tika. Surprisingly, Niko wasn't as bad or as annoying as

Alicia had initially thought. He and Tika hit it off instantly and that made Alicia happy. She knew that her friend just wanted someone to call her own. She deserved happiness with someone who wouldn't play games with her. Niko seemed like he was for real about trying to date her. They left the car show together that day and after going to eat at Razoo's Tika and Niko spent that evening together and they were still together the next day. Tika had called her and Niko took the phone from her and began talking to Alicia about how much fun they were having. He told Alicia that he and Tika had sex multiple times since they left the car show the day before and he even told her that he was certain that she was going to be pregnant soon because he spilled his semen inside of her. Niko was laughing and she heard Tika in the background laughing so she assumed that they were just joking around. He was very playful and Alicia began to feel bad that she had thought so negatively of him before she actually knew him. She was happy that he and Tika had hit it off. Later that day they had gone to a barbecue for all of the clubs in the city to attend. It was cool at first but then Top Notch showed up. It was okay because Alicia was cool with all of their members, except of course Nikki. In truth, she really didn't have an issue with Nikki but of course Nikki had an issue with her. While OL2L members was standing outside talking to some Top Notch members, Trevion's name was brought into the conversation and both clubs were making jokes and obvious comments about his and Alicia's relationship/situation. Nikki didn't say anything though, she just stood there listening and looking angry and uncomfortable.

That Monday had gone by so slow for Alicia. Trevion was coming back that evening and she was going to pick him up from the airport. She was so happy when she pulled up to the pick-up and drop off area. He had already texted her and let her know that he had landed and what gate he was exiting from. She instantly smiled when she caught a glimpse of him walking towards the baggage claim. She wasn't sure if he had seen her because she was sitting in her car looking out of her window. He had on white jeans, a red t-shirt, and red Jordan Futures. She had missed him so much. Once he got his bags and walked outside, he spotted her car and came right over. Alicia popped her trunk and he placed his bags inside. He hopped in the passenger seat then leaned over and kissed her lips. They talked a little bit as she drove back to Killeen from Austin. He told her about his son's party, what he had done all weekend, and that he missed her. He did tell her that he stayed at his son's mother's house the previous night, Alicia wasn't too happy about that. He told her that he only stayed so that he could spend the last night with his son, and so that she could bring him to the airport this morning. He was sure to let her know that he slept in the bed with his son. Although she felt uncomfortable with him staying at her house, Alicia appreciated that he was honest with her about it. After talking about that and the both of them having brief attitudes, they discussed what they were doing as far as their situation was concerned and what they wanted to do. They decided to keep moving slow. Alicia was fearful of jumping into a commitment so they decided that they would continue to date and do what they have been doing but now they were working towards being in a relationship. Slowly. As they made it closer to Killeen she got a text from Tika. *Hey heffa! Niko wanna know what you think about us. Lmao he been talking about we need to call Alicia lol talking about I wanna talk to Alicia.*

Alicia laughed. *Ask Niko what the hell he want!*

Tika sent a text back with several laughing emoji. *He got in his feelings and was like 'tell her I don't want nothing nomore'.*

That made Alicia laugh even harder. She began her response with the laughing emoji followed by *Ole sensitive ass! Tell him I'm sorry.*

Lmao I did. I just took him home. Tika texted about 15 minutes later.

Alicia asked, *is he still salty? Lol.*

Lol! He was like shit tell her I'm always in my feelings. Still telling me he'll cut me. That lil mother fucker puts hands on me earlier. Grabbing the back of my neck. Alicia could see the playfulness in Tika's text. She wasn't worried at that moment because their crazy asses sent her pictures yesterday afternoon of him playing with her knife. Then another a picture they were both smiling as he held the knife up to her throat. Alicia thought it was weird but they seemed to be having fun with it so she didn't think much about it.

Alicia asked Tika, *Why did he grab the back of your neck?*

Tika sent back a long message. *Lmao I think I said somebody was cute on Facebook. Then my ex had been calling and texting me. He asked me to help him study for the board. Niko told me to tell him I can't because he said so. And to let him know he that nigga and will cut both of us. I'm the first to get cut though.*

Alicia was laughing so hard reading that text. Trevion was looking at her like she had lost her mind. She didn't pay him any attention though. That had her stomach hurting from laughter. *Lmao! I don't know what to say to that shit! Niko is crazy! You better tell your ex to move around lmao!*

Lmao you stupid. You picked your boo up yet? Tika asked Alicia.

Alicia looked over at Trevion and smiled. *Yeah we just got back to Killeen. We are at Popeye's getting Noise something to eat to take to him cause he is on staff duty tonight.*

Oh ok...well I'll let you enjoy your boo. I'll talk to you tomorrow.

Chapter 51

Tonight Alicia went out to eat at Chili's with Noise, Tika, Ravyn, C-No, TC and his girl Lanay, and a few other people for Veteran's Day. They all got free meals for their affiliation with the military. Alicia and Trevion were supposed to have their Empire date tonight as usual but because they had gotten into the previous night, they weren't speaking today. He kept telling her that she had an attitude when she actually didn't. She told him that if he kept telling her that she had an attitude it was going to cause her to really get one. He was in his feelings, so that made her get in her feelings. They hadn't talked at all today except when he came to her house to get his dirty laundry so that he could go wash them. Even then they barely said two words to each other. He was stubborn but so was she. As they were waiting on their food, Tika turned to Alicia and began talking to her. "Where you boo at?"

Alicia rolled her eyes. "I don't know and I don't care."

"Oh lord, what he do now?"

"We aren't speaking at the moment. He be catching attitudes but then get in his feelings when I get one back with him. I'm about to just fall back from him a little bit because he been doing a lot of flip flopping lately." Alicia told her truthfully.

"Well I can understand that. But don't be too quick to just cut him off though, you know never know what's going on. Try to talk to him first."

Alicia rolled her eyes again. "Blah blah blah Dr. Joyce." she laughed. "I wonder if he brushed his teeth or put on deodorant...hopefully he bought another toothbrush and hygiene items."

Tika burst into laughter. "You petty as fuck!" she said still laughing.

"I'm serious though! You know he has his personal hygiene items at my house along with clothes and like two pair of shoes." she said seriously but still chuckling.

"Yeah, but I think he bought more personal hygiene stuff though." Tika said smiling.

They ate their meals and after the server brought out the to-go meals that Alicia had ordered for her son, niece, and brother, everyone said their goodbyes and went their separate ways.

Two days had passed since Alicia had last spoken to Trevion and she was missing him. Usually he would be the first to break the silence and contact her but she didn't want to wait anymore so she picked up her phone and texted him.

Trevion... she wrote and waited for his response.

Yes Leon.

With that text she knew his attitude was gone and that he was missing her too. It was always in the subtle things that he would say and do that let her know when he missed her. *So we just go MIA for two and three days without a word?*

A few seconds later he responded. *I've been at King's house everyday chillin and working on my car.*

Yeah and obviously not thinking about me... she wrote to him. She didn't believe that he hadn't thought about her but she wanted to be an ass.

I thought about you everyday, faithfully. But you know that though. His response made Alicia smile. They talked for a little bit longer and later that evening he came over to her house. They talked like they had never argued and of course they pleasured each other almost the whole night. This night was the first night that Alicia had given him oral pleasure. He had never given her the chance to do it before because he always took charge. He loved tasting her womanhood so the thought of her putting his member into her mouth never occured. But tonight, she wanted to show him just how much she missed him. She pleasured him with her mouth like a pro and before he got his point of climax she let him fall from her mouth. He grabbed her by the waist and pulled her up to mount him. As he entered her she gasped and a moan escaped his lips. She was rolling her hips while he grasped her ass and plunged deeper inside of her. She cried out as she came hard on his penis then she began moving faster while bouncing up and down. When he said that he was about to come she lifted herself off of him and moved to the side so that he didn't spill his seeds inside of her. After they cleaned themselves up, they lay back in bed. He lay on his side and she lay behind him facing his back. He pulled her arm around him and placed her hand on his heart and then covered her hand with his. She lay her face on his bare back, oh how she loved his back. They lay there falling asleep in silence.

Things were back on track between Trevion and Alicia even though she didn't like that he had suddenly began hanging out with the guys of OL2L so heavy. When he wasn't with Alicia during his free time he was always at King's house. She tried not trip though because she knew where he was and those guys were like her brothers in a sense so she was welcome over there any time she chose to go. Trevion's birthday was coming up in another month and when Alicia asked him what he wanted he told her he wanted a flip down TV screen to go in his car. It only cost a little over $100 so Alicia said she would get it for him. He had been very good to her and almost anything she asked him to do he did without any hesitation. He was there for her and he showed her that he truly had feelings for her. He did the simplest things sometimes that made her smile. Like the other day when he called her while she was out grocery shopping. She told him she was on her way home and when she pulled up to her house he was already there waiting for her in the driveway. She parked in the garage, gave him a quick kiss, and ran into the bathroom because she had been holding her pee for an hour. When she came back out he had already taken all of her groceries bags out of her car for her and began unpacking them. She stood there and smiled. Little things like that were things that he did all the time and those things were a part of the reasons why she had fallen for him. She went ahead and ordered the tv screen for him a month before his birthday because he was doing upgrades to his car and she wanted him to have it right then.

When it arrived she called him and told him that it was here.

"What time do you get off?" he asked her.

"I'm getting off at 5:45 then you know I have to go pick up the kids. I should be home around 6:30." she told him.

"Meet you at the spot." he said.

She laughed. "Man shut up and okay."

"Trap house." he said and they both laughed.

She was smiling. "It's funny to me how we are."

"I like it like this for real." he told her.

Truth was, she liked it too. She was in love.

When he came by her house later that evening he asked her to take a ride with him. He needed to go by his Aunt and Uncle's house out near Chaparral Road. They had a beautiful house and Alicia loved that it was ducked off out of view. After stopping by his folk's house. They headed back to Alicia's house but detoured to Wing Stop when Trevion had received a text from King that he was there with Chill, Tika, and another friend Doosie. When they pulled up he parked on right in front on the curb. They were all sitting at the first table in front of the window. They hopped out both wearing sweatpants and slides looking like they were at the house chilling. They walked in and began talking and laughing with the others as they ate.

"Y'all look cute or whatever." Tika said laughing.

"Oh is this really your boo?" Doosie said to Alicia and everyone started laughing.

They talked for a little while longer.

"Alright girl come on." Trevion said to Alicia. She kept talking to Tika.

"I'm about to leave your ass here. You better get your ass up and come the fuck on." He said to her trying to sound serious.

Chill decided to be an instigator. "Oh we see who wears the pants in this relationship! You better get your ass up!" he said to Alicia.

Alicia kept talking to Tika.

"I don't know about that bruh, she still sitting there and haven't moved so he may just run his mouth." Doosie said playfully.

"Oh you right, touché." Chill said and they all laughed.

"Y'all know that's bae." Trevion said. "She know what's up. She know how we do in public and in private so she don't trip." They said their goodbyes and went back to Alicia's house with no interruptions for the rest of the night.

Chapter 52

Alicia was sitting at her house talking to Tika when Trevion called her.

"Hello?"

"Baby." Trevion said to her.

"Yes, love?"

"Why you didn't tell me about Rampage's birthday dinner tonight at Plucker's?" he asked her.

Alicia frowned. "I did tell you."

"When you tell me?" he said sounding like he was pouting.

"The other day when you came over here while Tika was here. Remember something was said about Jacob being there. Tika said you should come because you weren't going to play with Jacob. Then you said nah cause you would beat his crippled ass." she recalled to him.

Trevion laughed. "Oh yeah. You right. Well the gang is going so let's go."

"Okay. I'm going to ride there with Tika. I know you probably going ride with King so I will see you in a little bit." They hung up and Alicia hopped in the car with Tika heading to Plucker's.

When they walked in they saw Rampage and his girlfriend Sandy sitting at a big table with Ravyn, OL2L secretary Nella and her husband Barton, and also Jacob and his girlfriend. When Tika and Alicia walked towards them Jacob's girlfriend frowned up her face, looked at Alicia, and then rolled her eyes. Alicia just laughed to herself then smiled. *Bitches always got an issue with the kid.* She thought to herself as greeted everyone at the table with hug. Everyone except Jacob's girlfriend of course. She and Tika grabbed the table behind them since they knew Trevion and the others were on the way and they would need more room. They heard Trevion, King, and Doosie talking and laughing as they walked over to their table. They greeted everyone except Jacob and his girlfriend. Trevion stopped being cool being him a little after he and Alicia started dating. She didn't know the exact reason why, though.

Trevion sat next to Alicia. "Did you order yet baby?" he asked her.

"No not yet. Can you get order me some nachos though. That's all I want." she told him. "And a strawberry lemonade."

"I got you." he said and placed their orders when the server came over.

So far everyone was enjoying their time together. They were all laughing and cracking jokes. Someone made comment that Alicia couldn't hear, but whatever was said turned Trevion up a little bit. "I'll beat his muthafuckin ass." he said.

"Who you talking about Tre?" Doosie said being messy. "Put a name on it."

King, Rampage, and Tika all laughed because they knew who he was referring to.

Trevion stood up and pointed to Jacob. "That little crippled muthafucka right there. That little bitch Jacob on the crutches. I can't wait 'til he get off them thangs."

Jacob pretended like he didn't hear what was being said. A few minutes later he and his girlfriend got up and left.

Trevion got a phone call while they were sitting there finishing their meals. "Hey bae." he said to the caller on the phone. Alicia looked at him. He was always calling his friends' bae, baby, boo, and other little names all the time so didn't trip too much on it. Usually he would say something that would let her know who was on the phone, if not she simply asked and he would tell her. She couldn't figure out who was on the phone this time after a few minutes of the conversation so she asked. He told her it was McCool. After all the chatting up with everyone Alicia was full and ready to go home.

Trevion paid for their meals and they all said their good byes. Once Alicia and Trevion got her house they went straight to her bed. They were both extremely tired and although he fell asleep fast, for some reason Alicia couldn't. She got on SnapChat and scrolled through a few of her friends snaps. She watched Trevion's snap. It was him riding in his car earlier that night with Alicia's favorite Lyfe Jennings song playing. The song called I'll Always Love you. She loved that song so much. The words written on the snap video said 'for one of my snappers'. Alicia immediately got a little skeptical. She texted Tika and told her about it.

Ask him who it was meant for. Tika said simply. Alicia didn't really want to, but how would she know if she didn't ask?

He was laying on his stomach in a deep sleep. She tapped him on his back but he didn't wake up. She shook him forcefully and he lifted his head up a little bit and looked at her. "What girl?" he said groggily.

"Who was that snap for today with the Lyfe song playing that said 'one of my snappers'?" she asked him.

He didn't even hesitate. "It was for you cause you said it was your favorite song of his."

Alicia smiled, but felt like a dumb kid at the same time. He was so sweet and the fact that she could wake him up out of his sleep and he answered her with no problem, that was something to her. "Okay, she told him. That's all I wanted to know."

"Go to sleep girl." he said before pulling her close to him and going back to sleep.

Chapter 53

Alicia and Trevion had started having more arguments lately and were spending less time together. He would say that he was at King's house or hanging with Top Notch but Alicia felt like it was more going on that. She knew that King and the other guys were some whores that tried to screw every female that they could and she beginning to think that Trevion may have stating falling into the same pattern as them. She felt things between changing them but she didn't want to be that person that was always questioning and never believing what he said. If that was the case then she may as well not even be with him. Still, something was amiss with them and she didn't like it at all. They were supposed to go see a movie but they ended up arguing so they didn't go. He was at King's house one day and she went over there but because they were into it, he didn't even acknowledge her when she walked in, so she didn't say anything to him either. There was another day that Nikki sent her a friend request on Facebook but Alicia didn't accept it. She did however go and take a look at her profile. Nikki had posted a video from her SnapChat on her Facebook. It was her in a barracks room with Trevion sitting on a bed and her sitting on his lap. Alicia's blood was boiling. When she called him he said he was at the Dollar General store near her house getting body wash. She went there to talk to him. When she asked him about the video he said that it was an old video and that he didn't know why she posted it. He told Alicia that he cursed Nikki out for posting it. Alicia wasn't sure if the video was old or not but she didn't think that Nikki just decided to post the video for no reason, whether it was old or not. After they left the store he called her on the phone. He was in the middle of explaining to her when he got another call. He told her he would have to call her back in a little bit because he had to handle a situation. Alicia went over to Ravyn's house and as she was telling Ravyn about what had just happened King walked in. He listened to their conversation for a few minutes before he chimed in. He told Alicia not to think anything of the video of Trevion and Nikki because that video was old. Then he said that Trevion went to check on Nikki and her house because a suspicious car was parked out front of it with the lights turned off. Alicia didn't know how that concerned Trevion though. What she did know was that Trevion hadn't called her back that night nor did she hear from him for the next couple of days. When she talked to Ravyn a few days later she had told her that she had a quick conversation with Trevion at King's house a few days prior.

"I asked him what the problem with y'all is." Ravyn said. "He said that y'all are always arguing and that you always want to talk to him lately. But you fuss and always questioning him about stuff. Then I asked him if he thinks he does stuff that makes you feel the way you do and question him and fuss at him and he said yes he knows does sometimes but he really don't be doing anything."

Alicia frowned. "Well if he knows my behavior and feelings are justified then why does he keep doing what he does and then gets mad when I have something to say about it?"

"I don't know. But y'all need to talk and sort it out." she said.

Alicia was sitting at home reading a book when her phone chimed. It was a text from Tika. *I think I kind of forgave Niko.*

?????? Was all that Alicia texted back.

You asking why? Lol. Or you saying so? Or some smart ish? Tika asked.

Alicia smiled. *I'm asking you how/why? I have no smart mouth tendency lately.*

Tika took her time responding back. *I didn't officially forgive him. He apologized and what not saying it wasn't supposed to happen that way and he never meant for it to happen at all. He'll do whatever and he'll do anything. He wanna make it right etc.*

Alicia had to choose her words carefully. Tika didn't always take things in the best way. *HHmmm...I don't know...I mean I can't tell you what to do but what he did is serious red flags...he didn't just scare you, he physically put his hands on you and threatened you...I don't know...I'm just saying it wasn't a reason for it and if he is doing stuff like that this early on who is to say he won't do it again but next time actually hit you. And then he apologize again then do it again and it becomes a pattern of abuse...I can't really tell you what you should do or believe or what you should tolerate. Only you know that but he just seems to me like even though he may be cool and funny or whatever, I believe he might be slightly abusive but then again I really don't know.*

Tika took so long to respond that Alicia thought she may have been upset with her long response. She texted back about 20 minutes later though but didn't say much. *Yeah. You right. But I still don't know what to do. Oh well, I will just talk to you tomorrow. I'm sleepy. Good night.*

Thanksgiving was weird to Alicia. Usually her dad and step mother comes from Alabama to spend it with her but due to her step mother's new job, they weren't able to make it this year. Her friend Shamelle had come over for the day though and her mom was there as well. As Alicia was sitting around talking with Shamelle, Trevion pulled up to her house. He came in and Alicia immediately was agitated. Although she missed him, he had been being an asshole for a few days now. He walked into her house and expected her to jump for joy at the sight of him. He tried to make small talk but she wasn't really in the mood for it. He had made her start feeling like he was out there spending time with other females and she didn't like it. Alicia's mom walked into the living room and instantly started smiling when she saw Trevion.

"Hey ma." He said to her.

"Hey my little chocolate son!" she said as she hugged him. Alicia didn't know why her mother loved him so much but he was definitely one of her favorites of any guy that Alicia had ever dealt with.

They walked into the kitchen and he stood by her then laid his head on her shoulder. He was pouting and trying to look sad. Alicia's mom looked down at him. "What's wrong with y'all?"

"That's her, Ma. She crazy. She always mad at me." he told her.

After about 20 minutes of playing with the kids and Alicia not talking to him, Trevion decided to leave. Alicia walked him out to the door and he told her he would be back later. He kissed her lips softly, but quickly then got into his car and left. As they were outside talking her sister, Ralonda was pulling up to the house. She walked inside and immediately began to irritate Alicia. "Oh you know you wrong for that little young boy!" She said to her. "What is he like

18?"

Alicia rolled her eyes and walked right past her. She wasn't in the mood for her judging and nitpicking today. She just let her have that one.

Later when Alicia went over to Ravyn's house Trevion had come over there as well. He said he had been with his family and then with Top Notch for most of the day after he left her house. They didn't really talk much at first while they were there but then Alicia called him into a backroom to talk privately.

"What's up?" he asked her.

"I want to know what's going on. You haven't been around much lately. We barely communicate like we used to. Be for real with me, what's the deal?"

He looked down and shook his head. "Nothing is up. I've been chilling. Just hanging with my Top Notch family. That's all." he said.

"No. Something is up with you." she paused. "Did you get back with Nikki?" she asked him looking right into his eyes.

"Man, no, we didn't."

"Well are y'all trying to get back together?" She pressed.

He sighed. "No we are not. I don't know why you think that."

Alicia was feeling herself get upset but she tried to keep her composure. "I ask that because you have been hanging around her a lot more lately and have barely been seeing me. You're not the same as you once were with me. I just want the truth. If you are back with her or trying to get back with her or anyone else then all I ask is that you tell me. There will be no hard feelings and I will let you be." she told him honestly.

"It's not even like that. You really tripping right now. I promise it's not even like what you thinking. Just chill." he was beginning to get annoyed by Alicia's questioning now.

"Then what is it like? She's posting videos of y'all, sending me messages, making little side bar comments. You've been telling me that it's nothing and to trust you and I have been trusting you but when are you going to show me that my trust is deserved? Have you told her that you deal with me still and have feelings for me as you say?" by now she was talking in an angry tone but still trying not to yell.

He stood up and spoke with force. "I told you it's not like what you think it is but you don't want to listen. I'm trying to protect you. She keep saying that she gonna fight you. When she run up on you cause you want her to know that we are together or whatever then I don't want to hear nothing cause I'm trying to tell you."

Alicia stood there in disbelief. Was he seriously saying this stupid shit to her right now? "You know what, whatever. You saying some real dumb shit right now and just listening to what you're saying I clearly have my answer. I don't have time for whatever games you playing so it is what it is." she walked off and went back into the living room with everyone else and he left out of the front door. She wasn't going to allow him to make her look like a fool.

Alicia was sitting at King's house hanging out with the guys. She hadn't spoken to Trevion since the day after Thanksgiving when he told her that he didn't care for how she acted towards him and he felt like they should cool it for a little while. She felt like he just wanted to mess with other people so she wasn't going to beg him or keep trying. That's what he wanted to do so she let him go. Besides she had started talking to her old friend Carson back in October but at that he really was just a friend. She had known him for about 2 years yet they had never actually hung out or talked on a consistent basis. She began talking to him more when Trevion would have his attitudes and go missing for days. She had never had sex with him while she was involved with Trevion but she had kissed him twice. Alicia was not as attracted to Carson as she was to Trevion. She thought he was cute but he didn't excite her like Trevion did. He had his shit together though. He had a Camaro and Corvette, he always dressed nice, he had his bills and priorities in order, and he was really just an all-around cool guy. She liked that he was silly and loved to laugh and joke around but his conversation was boring and they didn't have much to talk about. He seemed a little shallow to be honest. But still he was cool to chill with when she bored. He was friends with Chill so naturally he wanted him to join OL2L but his best friend Christian was in Top Notch so they were also trying to get him to join them. He didn't really want to join either one them, he wasn't much for clubs.

Alicia was at King's house talking to him about her situation with Trevion. He told her that Trevion and Nikki were not back together and that she shouldn't worry about all that. He also told her that maybe she should just have fun and talk to someone else to take her mind off of him for a little while. Alicia didn't know if that was good advice though. She decided to just put everything out of her mind and enjoy the company of her boys that night. She remembered Tika was supposed to be back today so she called her.

"Where ya at heffa?" she said as soon as she picked up the phone.

Tika laughed as usual. "Still in Irving."

"Oooohhhh." Alicia said. "I'm lonely as fuck, I'm kid free and I can't locate Ravyn. Just uuuggghhhh right now."

"I'm coming back today." Tika said.

Alicia rolled her eyes as if she could see her. "The day is bout over."

"Well stop complaining then."

"Uuuughhh." Alicia said.

Tika laughed. "Man you better get out your feelings! What y'all doing tonight?"

"Rampage trying to go to Country Rock, but I don't know. I'm bored as hell."

"Let me know. I'll get on the road and come with you." Tika said to her.

"Well Rampage said he really just want to get drunk." They laughed.

Tika got quiet. "Well I'm about to take this test."

Alicia was confused. "What test?"

"This pregnancy test." she said solemnly.

"Ooooohhh." she said. "Well?"

"Positive." she said in disbelief.

Alicia's mouth dropped. "Oh fuck!"

"Yeah girl, I know."

"Well what are you gonna do?" Alicia was concerned.

"I think I'm gonna keep it. I don't believe in abortions."

She was glad to hear Tika say that. "I don't either so I am happy to hear that. When are you going to tell Niko?"

"I did already. He didn't really say much."

"Well what did he say?"

"He only asked how many I took and then he said oh okay." she said sounding like she was fighting back tears.

Alicia was holding her own tears back. "The fuck? Have y'all been talking like before you told him this?"

"He was cool earlier until we had a small argument. I was supposed to go with him tomorrow to the Paul Walker meet but I don't know." she sounded so sad. "That's what I get for being stupid."

Alicia kicked into gear then. "Hell no! Don't even do that. Both of y'all did this so don't take all of the blame on yourself. And don't think you are stupid because we all feel strongly about a person sometimes when we first get with them and sometimes it's simply that our expectations don't match the reality that's all. It's nothing to feel stupid about, it happens to all of us and trust me even at my age I still do it too sometimes. And who knows, he may turn out to be a good father. Maybe he is just in shock and it has to wear off." Alicia said trying to console her.

"You right." she said simply. "At least I'm not crying though. My cousin over here laughing at me cause she is excited."

Alicia smiled. "Well are you excited? You did want a baby at one point before."

Tika paused. "Not really but somewhat."

"Well you will get excited as you start to feel your baby move."

"I'm going to take more test to be sure. But anyway what are you doing?" Tika asked.

"I'm at King's house with Rampage, Barton, and Nella. And take it first thing in the morning."

"Oh okay. They annoying?" she asked. "I wanna come but I don't wanna drive and then y'all probably gonna be gone by the time I get there."

Alicia laughed. "Nah they got me in here cracking up. I really just need to drink and laugh that's it. But yeah, I'll be gone before you get back. I ain't gonna be over here all night."

They said good bye and hung up. When Alicia was getting ready to leave she noticed that King had been playing on her phone. He had been sending crazy messages to Tika and she didn't realize it until Alicia told her that he had been. She went home and crawled into her bed. Lonely as hell in her house without the kids and without Trevion.

Chapter 55

Alicia was sitting at work barely working when she received a text from Trevion. *Hey. How are you doing?*

I'm okay. You? She responded.

He took his time responding. *I can't even explain it. I'm just really stressed and frustrated. I want to be unbothered at times. I just wanted you to know that you've done nothing wrong. I promise it's all me. I be tripping.*

Alicia didn't know what to make of that so she just kept it simple. *I appreciate you for telling me that. I really do.*

Over the next week or so things were up and down for Alicia. She and Trevion had not talked at all except for him calling to tell her he was going to come and pick up his things from her house. Alicia didn't make a big deal out of it. They talked and he told her he just had some things he needed to work out and that she hadn't done anything to warrant his actions. She was going to mull over it. She packed up his things and had them ready for him when he arrived. He couldn't even look her in the face. She had been doing fine this whole week of not talking to him and not seeing him. Even though she wasn't really feeling Carson in that way, he had become an awesome distraction from Trevion. Then all of sudden, Trevion called.

"First and foremost, good morning." he said into the phone. Alicia didn't respond so he continued. "I'm gonna be straight up with you. I like you way more than I had planned to. I want to fuck with you but I'm not ready to be in a relationship just yet. I don't want to answer to no one right now. I'd rather come and go as I please with no problems than to have to be questioned about my moves. I'm not saying that I don't want to fuck with you, I'm just not ready to be in a relationship. If you don't want to fuck with me after hearing this I totally understand. I don't want you to waste your time if you don't want to or have to."

Alicia sat quietly for a second trying to understand why he even decided to hit her up at all. "So why couldn't you have said that before when I asked you repeatedly? I told you it was fine if yu didn't see a future with me but all I wanted you to do was tell me that honestly."

"I do see myself being with you, but not right now. I enjoy us. You're a wonderful person. I just don't want an anchor right now." he seemed sincere but Alicia wasn't about to get suckered in.

She simply replied, "Okay." and then she hung up the phone.

That night she met up with Carson at the park. They talked for hours and listened to music while he danced for her. Somehow he ended up leaning on his car with her standing in front of him and his arms wrapped around her waist. They enjoyed the embrace and the silence. He kissed her on the neck. Soon their lips were locked in a deep kiss. Alicia felt herself getting hot. Since the kids were gone she invited him back to her place. On the way home she texted King.

I'm taking your advice and definitely doing me now.

Lmao! Aww shit somebody is about to get that wet! He texted back.

She laughed so hard after he sent the emoji of the eggplant and strong arm.

I was with him at the park when you called that's why I didn't really talk like I wanted to but yes, it's about to go down! Lol! She responded to him.

Lmao! You just nasty!

No I'm not lol! I'm horny and I'm single!

He responded right back. *Fix that then! Lmao!*

Oh I'm about to soooo good night! Lol.

Lmao good night!

Alicia hadn't been calling or texting Trevion at all since they fell off but out of the blue he began texting her again. Every morning she would get a 'good morning beautiful, have a good day' text from him to which she would simply respond 'thanks you too'. She didn't want to be a part of whatever game he was playing. A couple of times he asked to come see her during lunch and she allowed him to. When he would come over it wasn't the same though. She sat on the opposite end of the couch, she wouldn't make him lunch, and she didn't allow him to kiss, touch, or show her any affection. She noticed that he started only trying to come see her during lunch and barely hit her up at all after work. She knew he must have been talking to someone else so she just kept him at a distance and continued her thing with Carson. She was determined to get over him.

Chapter 55

Can I come lay with you?

Never mind. Alicia had received these texts from a number that she didn't recognize one morning. She debated if she should respond, reluctantly, she did. *Who is this?* She asked the mystery person.

Nobody.

Okay, Nobody. Have a good day. She answered even though she now had an idea of who it could possibly be.

Ya.

She knew then who it was. *Tre?*

Nah.

He was being so childish. *Okay well whomever this is, why did you text me in the first place if you don't want me to know who you are? Just curious.*

I don't even know. I apologize though. It won't happen again.

Okay. Was all she said back to him.

He kept texting. *So can I come lay with you?*

Nah, go lay with one of your chicks from SnapChat since you being childish putting on there that you want some head and sex.

He was answering her texts immediately. *How is that childish, Alicia? It's childish because I wanna have sex?*

No it's childish because you putting the stupid shit on social media. She wrote in annoyance.

He tried to pull out his old tricks. *I know you want some of me. If you wanna fuck just say so.*

Alicia literally laughed out loud. He really tried it. She didn't bother to respond to him. He was so extra. She redirected her mind and started thinking about hanging out with Carson later that evening. Carson spent the night and all Alicia could think the next morning was that even though Carson always got the job done in bed and thoroughly enjoyed sex with her, she was so happy that she hadn't had sex with him the night before because she was currently laying in her bed, spread eagle while Trevion was slurping on her womanly juices. He had called and texted her all morning asking her to come stop by and see her since she was off that day. At first she was saying no but when he texted her that he was outside, she let him in. He walked in and gave her a long tight hug. It had been a couple of weeks since the last time she saw him. They lay in bed for a couple of hours. They were both laying on their side facing each other with their faces so close that their lips were almost touching. He was rubbing her face and back and telling her how much he missed her as he kissed her forehead. Alicia was fighting back her tears. She didn't know how she allowed herself to be laying here with him again. She didn't know why she still had feelings for him. She didn't know why he wouldn't just leave her alone or why she allowed him to stay. She told him that shouldn't be doing what they were but yet she didn't want him to stop licking her. She was fighting with herself about what she wanted to do. After they had sex, they lay for about an hour before she had to get up and shower and run errands. She didn't know why that had happened but she did know it was going to happen again. Especially after Tika had just sent her a screenshot of Nikki's Facebook page from the previous day where Nikki posted a screenshot of her on facetime with Trevion with the caption 'when it becomes more than just a silly crush #mancrushmonday' Alicia's breath got caught in her throat as she held back tears of anger. She was done and she meant it. She put him on the spam message list and auto reject on her phone and told herself to just get over him because he didn't mean her any good. That was it for her. She didn't talk to him anymore afterwards.

Chapter 56

Alicia woke up so excited this morning. She had been waiting for this weekend to get here because Rick was coming down from Louisiana to visit. She hadn't seen him since he got stationed back home in Louisiana and she really missed her friend. Even though they talked and texted on the phone almost everyday, it didn't compare to actually being physically in his presence. After she had started dating Trevion, Rick respected the boundaries and stopped trying to push up on her because he knew how she felt about Trevion. Once Alicia and Trevion started having these problems and she decided to fall back, Rick began trying to ease back into the mix as more than just a friend. Although she had love for Rick, Alicia didn't want anything to jeopardize their friendship so she tried not to go too deep into more than friendship with him. He wouldn't give up though. He was constantly expressing his feelings of wanting to be more than friends with her. Every time she would get dressed to go somewhere he wanted her to send him a picture, and when she did he always gushed over how good she looked. He was always telling her how much she missed her and that he loved her. It was strange but their friendship worked like that. She didn't know how it was going to feel being around him and Tika at the same time knowing that feelings have been involved in their friendship.

Alicia took off from that Friday so that she could be available once Rick touched down. He made it early that afternoon and when he texted Alicia to let her know he was pulling up to her house, she jumped up and ran out her front door to greet him. As soon as he stepped out of his truck she jetted to him and jumped on him. He caught her as she wrapped her legs around his waist and hugged him tightly around his neck. He laughed while he stood there holding her for a few minutes before he put her down. They went to lunch at their favorite place, Plucker's Wing Bar, and then made plans to meet up with Tika later to go out to Club Fuego. Unfortunately, Tika had staff duty that night so she couldn't come. Rick and Alicia linked up at King's house later that night so they could all ride out to the club together. Rick brought his cousin Iesha and friend from back home, Joe. King and his best friend Lady D as well as a few other club members all went to Fuego and had an awesome time. Trevion was supposed to go as well but he bailed at the last minute, insinuating that he was about to go be with a female. He was purposely making it known to make Alicia feel some type of way. It was a good thing that he didn't go seeing as how Rick was all over her as if she was his woman. He stayed glued to her side the entire time in the club. He kept telling her good she looked in her black and white patterned mini dress that hugged her curves just right. She wore red pumps to give it a splash of color. She had her hair pulled back in a loose curly ponytail with loose strands falling on the sides of her face. They both got pretty tipsy but she made sure not to drink as much as she did the night in September when they had crossed the line of friendship. After a night of partying and much fun they all headed to Denny's to grab something to eat. Alicia pulled into the parking lot right behind Rick. He parked and walked over to her car, waiting for her to get out. As she got out and closed her door, he grabbed her by her hand and they walked hand-in-hand inside the restaurant. They sat down with King, Iesha, Lady D, and Joe. They placed their orders and waited patiently for the food to arrive.

Rick was sitting next Alicia with one hand on her thigh under the table. He was leaning in close to her as they talked and was looking her deep in her eyes. Lady D picked up on their chemistry and called them out.

"That's ya boo?" she asked Alicia.

Alicia's eyes widened. "No! We are just really good friends."

"Nah, y'all are more than just really good friends." she said. Rick looked at Alicia, then at Lady D and King. He didn't say anything, just laughed.

"Seriously...we are just friends." Alicia repeated.

Lady D and King both laughed. Lady D told them her theory. "Mmm mmm. I'm not buying it. Either y'all are fuckin now, or y'all fucked one time and never did it again, or y'all want to fuck but haven't done it yet; in which case, y'all will eventually do it"

Alicia just laughed. She didn't see the point in trying to convince her otherwise. After eating, Rick paid for their meals and they all left. He took his cousin home and he and Joe went back to their hotel room. Alicia went home and as soon as she got into her bed her phone rang. It was Rick.

"What you tryna do?" he said when she answered.

"Huh?" she said. She was confused about what he was talking about.

He referred back to the conversation that they were having as they left Denny's. He wanted her to come to his hotel room. "I still think you should come."

"Man I'm not about to be up in there like that with Joe in the next bed."

He still pressed. "That nigga gonna be knocked the fuck out."

"Nah, I can't do it. You can come to my house though." She responded.

"When?" he asked, then spoke again before she could respond. "Just come and stay with me."

Alicia gave in. "I'll come stay with you but we aren't doing anything with him lying in the next bed. Sleep or not." She told him firmly.

He laughed. "Okay. That's cool." then he continued. "I know ya mom just moved back in with you so I don't want to stay at ya crib and have ya mom speculating. But this nigga already almost sleep." he said talking about Joe.

"Well she isn't here and I thought about that earlier because she would be like 'why mike stay over here with you?'." Alicia laughed.

Mike laughed too. "Where the fuck she at?"

"At work."

"Oh ok." He laughed. "He already sleep. Well anyway, I'm at Holiday Inn Express, it's by HEB."

Alicia had to back out of coming. "I rather you come here. My son is laying in his bed awake and I don't feel comfortable leaving him while everyone else is asleep."

"Okay. I'm about to come then." he told her.

"Okay call me when you get here, so that I can come to the door."

He arrived about ten minutes later. They lay in bed cuddled up and before long they were both sound asleep. No sex and Alicia was happy about it.

The next day, which was a Saturday, they had decided to go out again but this time Tika was able to join them. They went to Club Country Rock and at first the night started off great. Alicia had decided to only have two drinks since she had gotten drunk the previous night and still hadn't fully recovered from it. She was standing next to a table where Tika was sitting and Joe and Rick were standing nearby going back and forth to the bar behind them. Tika saw Niko in there and when he was walking past their table, she grabbed him by the arm. Tika had told Alicia a few days ago that she and Niko and had resolved to be in a committed relationship. She was happy that they made the choice and even happier that he seemed to be accepting fatherhood now. He stopped where they were and had some words with Tika. Alicia didn't know if it was a good conversation or not but he was smiling and saying something in her ear, Tika wasn't smiling though. After a few minutes he walked away and the ladies noticed that as he was walking a petite, light brown skin female walked up and hugged him from behind. They disappeared into the crowd. A few minutes later the female came back over to Tika and began asking her questions about Niko. She wanted to know if they had something going on. Tika didn't respond immediately. The girl kept talking to Tika and asking her questions. When Tika finally asked who she was they girl told her that she was his girlfriend and that they had been in a relationship since April that was about 8 months. Tika didn't respond after that. The girl kept talking as Tika just sat and stared at her. Her friend looked at Alicia so Alicia tried to be peacemaker. She told the friend that little petite was beginning to get a little bit disrespectful and if she would take her friend and go. The friend said she was just trying to find out what was going on. Alicia told her that Tika was pregnant with Niko's baby. The friend looked over at the petite one to clarify that she had heard what was just said. All hell broke loose then. The other females walked away to find Niko. They came back a few minutes later saying that he denied getting Tika pregnant. They kept trying to ask Tika questions but she wasn't responding. She was still sitting in the chair fuming. The girls walked away but kept walking by making petty comments and hyping themselves up. When they walked by again they had another girl with a short blue haircut with them. So it was the petite chick, the chick with blue hair, and another chick with a fur vest on walking by saying stuff towards Tika and acting like they wanted a fight. Alicia had realized what was going and she automatically went into protection mode. Tika was pregnant and Alicia didn't think she needed to be in this situation. She asked her if she wanted to leave. "Nah, they not about to have me leaving. I want that bitch hands because she keep trying me." Tika said.

Alicia didn't think she should be trying to fight so she kept trying to convince her to go. It wasn't working so Alicia became more alert and on guard, keeping a look out for in case they tried to attack Tika. She saw the girls go behind them so she turned around to face that way and make sure they weren't trying anything funny. She and Tika saw the girls talking to Lady D and they all walked over to Tika and Alicia. As they approached Tika stood up from her sitting position and immediately the petite girl got a slightly spooked look on her face. Alicia assumed that is was because she didn't realize Tika's actual size while she was sitting down. Tika was about 5'10 and she wasn't a super skinny chick. She wasn't anywhere near being fat but she did have a little meat on her slender body. The petite one was about the same height as Alicia only about 10 or 15 pounds lighter. Her friends were all about the same size.

Lady D was explaining to Tika and the other girl that she didn't know what was going on and she didn't realize that Niko was messing with both of them. The other girl called Tika a bitch and Tika warned her to stop calling her out of her name. She told her she hadn't disrespected her so she would appreciate the same. The girl ignored what Tika had said and called her a bitch again. Tika punched her in the face. As soon as Tika threw the punch Alicia stepped in front of her and starting trying to push her back away from the girl. When Alicia turned around to try to push the other girl back the petite girl and the blue haired girl both begin throwing punches at Alicia. Because she was caught off guard, they got a few punches in on her but Alicia wasn't going to let them get the best of her. She started throwing punches back and landed a couple on the blue hair girl before grabbing the petite girl by the hair and punching her continuously in the face and head. The petite girl had fallen to the floor but Alicia didn't let her go nor did she stop swinging. Security rushed to them and grabbed Alicia by the waist trying to pull her over off of the girl and as they were pulling her back, she was dragging the girl with her by her hair. More security guards came to separate the two and as they were both being pulled in two different directions the blue hair girl came out of nowhere on the side of Alicia and started trying to hit her. Alicia stopped punching the petite girl but still held her down by her hair with her left hand and began throwing punches at the blue hair girl with her right hand. She guessed the blue hair girl was trying to sneak some hits in because once she felt Alicia throwing punches she backed up without security coming for her. Alicia was about to start punching the petite girl again but Joe suddenly appeared and grabbed her arm. She let go of the petite girl and allowed Joe to usher her out of the building. Outside she felt something wet on her face. When she reached her hand up to touch it she saw that it was blood. She was fuming hot. She didn't see Tika or Rick so started to panic. She hoped that nothing happened to them during the fight. Alicia noticed that Joe had somehow collected her and Tika's keys, phones, and wallets. She was thankful to him for that. As they walked through the parking lot she heard Rick calling her name. She was happy to see him and Tika were okay. He grabbed her by the hand and walked her to her car. When she got into the car she called Brock and told him what happened. He then called Chill and King and they all met up at Rick's hotel room with Lady D in tow. At the hotel room Joe was really quiet, Tika was crying, and everyone was trying to hear what had transpired. Rick and Alicia had told them everything. In between sobs Tika had told them that Alicia had been jumped by all three of the females, not only two of them. She said she had started fighting the one with the fur vest on when she realized what was happening. Alicia felt some type of way because she was sitting there with a bandage on her face right above her eyebrow because one of the girls had cut her face with her ring when they first started fighting. She had blood dripping and the only person Chill and King seemed concern about was Tika. She was concerned about her too because after all, she was pregnant and just found out her boyfriend has another girlfriend and is denying her baby, but damn, Alicia had just been jumped by three bitches because she didn't want to walk away from a stupid fight. Why didn't they show a little concern for her as well? They stayed in the room for about an hour then everyone had to leave because the hotel was getting complaints of too much noise from the room. Alicia went home, cleaned her face, put on a new bandage, and crawled into bed. She checked to make sure Tika had made it home safely and told her she would talk to her tomorrow. Rick called to make sure Alicia was home and then she went sleep.

Chapter 57

Alicia lay in her bed the next morning, head pounding and not wanting to move. She couldn't believe what happened last night. She hadn't been in a fight since her early 20's, with the exception of fighting her boyfriends. As she lay there replaying scenes from the night before her rang. It was Rick. "Good morning. You okay?" he asked.

"Yes but I'm sore as hell." she replied.

He let out a sigh. "I hate that shit had to go down like that."

"I do too, but I couldn't let Tika go out like that." she said honestly. "You okay?"

"I'm good. I wish Joe would've got to you quicker though. I told him to be ready if something pop off cause we needed to get you and Tika outta there." He said sounding remorseful. "I didn't even know you was fighting. I snatched Tika up then when I saw you I told him to grab you. I was trying to avoid all of that."

"It's okay though. I think Joe couldn't really get to me on time because we were moving as we were fighting. But he came out of nowhere and snatched me up and got all of our stuff too."

He continued trying to explain things to her. "Yeah cause when I seen security had you and they were still trying to get you I threw something at him and said go get her! And Tika pregnant, she gotta chill. That's why I didn't leave her cause I woulda came and grabbed you myself."

Alicia shook her head. "That was my main reason for stepping in front of her cause she's pregnant and really don't need to be fighting at all. But I'm gucci though. Mad I left my shoes."

Rick laughed. "Yeah I think Tika mad at me but she can't be doing that pregnant and in the club when it's real easy to get hurt. And that's what pissed me off cause when security grabbed you, nobody had the other chicks."

"I don't think she mad at you, I think she is just in a really bad head space right now cause of how everything went down and her finding out all that she did." she tried to reassure him.

"Yeah but she was like 'why the fuck you grab me and they jumped on Alicia after you did that' and other stuff."

Alicia thought about it. "I think it was more her being angry because she feels like she was at fault for it and wasn't able to help."

"I'm sorry though. It was probably some things I could've done better." he said sincerely.

"Nah I think you and Joe handled the situation as well as could be expected. We left with all of our stuff, no one went to jail, and even though I got jumped I still beat one of them up!" They laughed at her silliness.

Almost as soon as Alicia hung the phone up with Rick, Tika was calling.

"Hey girl." Alicia said into the phone.

"I'm sorry again. I really am" she said.

"It's cool. You weren't wrong, she was and you did what you felt you had to do. You know I got your back."

Tika exhaled loudly. "I know and I'm still sorry."

"You okay?" Alicia asked her.

Tika replied. "The question is are you ok?"

"Yeah I'm good. I'm still cute." They both laughed.

Tika stopped laughing. "Oh okay, but I'm sorry again. Is there anything I can do?"

"It's fine chile." Alicia laughed again.

"You think we need to get your eye checked out at the hospital or something?"

Alicia fell out laughing. "No girl."

"You sure?" Tika asked her. "And stop laughing."

Alicia got serious. "Okay. And yes I'm sure."

They talked a little bit longer. Tika made Alicia promise that if her eye started bothering her she would go see a doctor. Alicia had only gotten two hours of sleep and she was sore so she got off the phone and lay back down to get some sleep.

Chapter 58

Alicia lay awake in her bed staring at the ceiling. Her mind was blank yet she couldn't fall asleep. She didn't have a cuddle partner tonight because Carson had gone home to Shreveport for the holidays. She lay on her side and begin to stare at the wall. Her phone lit up in her dark room. When she looked at it she saw it was a text message. She really wasn't in the mood to talk to anyone so she didn't bother to read it. Then a few minutes later she got another message. When she picked up her phone and opened the messages she saw that they were both from Trevion. She had not talked to him in almost two weeks and she was completely fine with that. She didn't know why he was texting her now.

Good night.

I care for you A LOT. Idk why but I do. That's it. Good night.

Alicia just laid there looking at the messages. She didn't have a response so therefore, she didn't reply. She didn't really care to talk to him.

The next day, Christmas Eve, she received another text from him. *You think you love me?* Alicia was caught off guard by this question. It didn't matter if she did or not. She thought about her response to him. She did in fact think that she loved him. Actually, she knew that she did. But she wasn't going to tell him that. Instead she lied. *I could have and I almost did, but no I don't.*

His response, *Okay, cool.*

Why do you ask?

I was trying to see something but it's nothing major. No big deal. He told her.

Alicia smacked her lips. *What were you trying to see?*

Nothing we good. Fuck it.

Alicia didn't respond anymore after that. There was no point.

Christmas day and the kids were gone with Alicia's mom. They opened their gifts on Christmas Eve every year and this year was no different. Trevion had come over today to move the WII from the living room to Tekerri's room and to set up the PS4 in the living room. Alicia thought that he was going ot text or call her when he was on the way. She assumed she had at least 30 minutes before he was going to come so she decided to take a quick shower. As she was stepping out of the tub, her doorbell rang. She rushed to wrap a towel around her and ran to the door. When she looked out the peephole she saw Trevion waiting on the other side of the door. She didn't expect him to be there so soon and she didn't want him to think that she had come to door like that on purpose to entice him. She decided to keep it cool. She unlocked the door and opened it just barely to a crack then dashed back to her bedroom. He caught a glimpse of her but she didn't want him to see at all. When she came back out of her room fully dressed in a pair of leggings and a t-shirt, he was kneeling on the floor in front of her television already hooking up the PS4. She sat on the couch and watched him worked. She was trying to keep her mind from wandering but she couldn't help but to think about him touching her again, kissing her, and holding her like he used to. He was looking so delicious in a black Adidas sweat suit and his chocolate skin just glowing. Alicia knew that she could easily have him all over her right now but she wasn't trying to go there with him again. She was trying to really keep her distance, but at the same time she still wanted him around. She just couldn't leave him all the way alone. He seemed a lot quieter than he used to be. He gave off this feeling like he knew he was wrong for how everything had gone with them over the past few weeks and she sensed feelings of guilt and him missing her. But it was weird to her because even though they were not really talking, she could still feel that chemistry, that bond, that magnetic force between the two of them. She wanted him to hurry up and leave. He finished within 45 minutes but somehow she knew he could have been done in much less time.

Later that day she received a text from him asking if he could see her for a little bit. She was a little skeptical at first but agreed. She didn't want him to come to her house and she didn't want to go to his room or wherever it was that he had been staying. She agreed to meet him at Lion's Park at 5 that evening.

As Alicia was sitting in the living room just relaxing and listening to music before her meet up with Trevion, she thought about Tika. She decided to text her just to check up on her. She sent her message with some uplifting words. *Sometimes the best thing you can do is not think, not wonder, not imagine, and not obsess. Just breathe, and have faith that everything will work out for the best.*

Thank you for the words of encouragement. She responded.

Alicia smiled to herself. *You're welcome my love.*

It's gonna be hard but eventually I will.

*Well...*Alicia started to type. *You definitely will. Here's some positive outlook. I was five months pregnant with Alton and I found out his dad was cheating on me with a 17 year old, then he got her pregnant when Alton was only 4 months old. I was devastated and I thought I would never get over him or that situation...that's how bad it hurt. But, you see how I am now? I don't think about him or the situation. I look at my son and I find it easy to forgive his dad and still be thankful that I met him because no one else could have given me Alton exactly as he is and I wouldn't trade my baby for anything in the world. Just think about that. I promise you are going to be okay.*

Tika sent her a text with seven kissy face emoji. *You're awesome!!!! I love you Alicia.*

Love you too thugga thugga lol. Alicia responded. Then they made plans to go see a movie later in the week.

Alicia pulled up to Lion's Park at 5 on the dot. Trevion was pulling up at the same time. They got out of their cars and leaned on the side of his. He tried to pull her into his arms for a hug but she stepped back. He raised his eyebrows then nodded his head as if to say he understood.

"What's up?" Alicia asked him.

"Shit you tell me."

"Well I guess I'll start." she said. "So are you ready to finally tell me the truth about shit?"

He looked at her. "Such as?"

"If you are back with Nikki. Why you just went ghost on me then come out of the blue with the texts the other day. Why you do the things you do. Everything." Alicia truly thought he was going to dance around the subjects but to her surprise he opened up and poured everything out.

"I started fucking with Nikki again but we are not in a relationship. She knows that and she knows what's up. I was trying to do the right thing and stop fucking with you because I didn't want to keep going back and forth and doing what I was doing and having you questioning what was up. But I be missing you so that's why I sent those texts. I really do care about you and I want to fuck with you but I'm still young. I admit that I haven't really grown up yet and I still do childish shit. But it doesn't change that I truly care about you. I don't know why I do but I really do. I just can't let you go. I don't want to see you with somebody else but I still want to do what I want to do. That's just how it is. I told you before that I can definitely see myself being with you but I still have this other stuff too." He said sincerely.

Alicia just stood there for a moment trying to collect her thoughts. "So basically you want me to be loyal to you and only fuck with you while you still fuck with Nikki and any other female that you choose?"

He just looked at her. Alicia shook her head. "You got me fucked up. I'm not going for that shit." she said to him. "If you care for me like you say then why don't you just leave me alone? You know you don't want to do right by me so why keep coming?"

"I told you, because I still want you. I don't want you with anyone else. It may be selfish as fuck but it's the truth. I'm sorry but I can't help it" he stared into her eyes.

Alicia looked away. "So what were you trying to see when you asked me if I loved you?"

"You said you didn't love me so it doesn't really matter now." he solemnly.

"Well do you think you love me?" she asked him.

He cocked his head to the side. "I could have, but no." he said sarcastically throwing her words back at her. That didn't faze Alicia. She smirked.

"I don't know why you want to play these games with me. I'm not for it. And I'm not going to be fucking with you while you're out here fucking with Nikki and other bitches. I'm not doing that." she stood in front of him holding back tears. He walked up closer to her and grabbed her. She tried to step back from him again but this time he wouldn't let her go. He pulled her into his arms and wrapped her in his embrace. She didn't hug him back. She just stood there allowing him to hold her. He began speaking softly in her ear. "I'm sorry for hurting you. I didn't mean to hurt you at all. I'm sorry for everything. You hear me? I'm sorry" he said and he kissed her cheek before burying his face in her neck. He kissed her neck and said he was sorry again. Alicia was determined to be strong and not cry. She succeeded. He stepped back a little bit but kept his arms around her. Then he kissed her lips. Alicia didn't know whether to kiss him back or not, so she didn't. He opened his car door and sat down in the driver's seat. He grabbed her by the hand and pulled her onto his lap. They sat there staring at each other with him gently caressing her cheek. They talked and laughed and talked some more. They even had a facetime chat with his best friend McCool. When they parted ways at the end of the night he kissed Alicia and told her he would call her tomorrow. They had been at the park talking for 6 hours. On Christmas Day.

Chapter 59

Trevion came by the next day and spent a few hours with Alicia and the kids. It was a good time, no pressure or any awkwardness. The friendship was there. Later that day a member of OL2L, TC, came over to get a plate of Christmas dinner leftovers. Alicia very rarely ever saw TC by himself without one of the boys with him, so she took the opportunity to get his advice on the situation with Trevion and Carson.

"So let me ask you something." she started as he was eating. "You know I've had this situation with Tre since September and we aren't like we used to be. I've started to talking Carson more and he really likes me but i still have feelings for Tre. Every time I choose to stop dealing with him he keeps coming back with how much he misses me and cares for me. Like he told me finally that he started fucking with Nikki again and other females but says he still wants me. I understand why though. Like if you dealing with all of these other females then why are you so adamant about being in my life. Why won't he just leave me alone? And what if my situation with him messes up what could possibly come with Carson?"

TC thought about his response. "Well, do you like this Carson guy?"

"I mean, he is cool. I like hanging out with him sometimes but I can't say that I am really digging him deep like that or anything." she told him truthfully. "But I don't want to just push him off when he could possibly be something good for me."

"Here's what you do." He said finishing up his last bite of food. "Just be honest with this Carson guy. Tell him that you like him but you were dealing someone else but now that's over and you want to try and see what can happen with y'all but that you want to take it slow. As far as Tre, if you feel like you don't want to deal with all that comes with him then just do what you feel is best for you."

He made it all sound so simple and Alicia knew his advice about Trevion was generic simply because that was his friend so he didn't want to look as though he wasn't being loyal by telling her anything that she may actually need to hear so he just kept it at 'do what's best for you'. Carson called Alicia that night. He was still at home in Shreveport but he said she was on his mind. They talked about the usual random stuff and then he got serious. "So I have a question." he said to her. "What are we doing?"

Alicia was dreading the conversation. "What do you mean?"

"Are we trying to have a relationship? Do you want to be in a relationship? Is it just me and you?" he questioned.

She didn't want to lie to him so she answered honestly. "I honestly don't know if I want to be in a relationship right now but I do like spending time with you and I would like to continue to talking to you and dating and see where it may go."

"Isn't dating a relationship though?" he asked.

"No, not to me. Dating is the stage before a relationship, it's getting to know a person in order to determine if you want a relationship with them." she explained to him.

"So are we supposed to talk to other people as well?"

She didn't care if he didn't but she didn't want to come off crass. "Well I would say no."

"With us doing what we are doing, if you saw me with another female, what would you do or how would you feel about it?" he pressed.

Alicia honestly wouldn't be mad but she wouldn't like it either. "I would probably feel some type of way but I wouldn't go off on you or anything because we are not in a relationship so therefore you're free to date anyone you want."

"I would feel some type of way too if I saw you with another guy. But what you said is true though."

They talked for a little while a longer before they hung up. Alicia knew that eventually she would have to stop dating Carson because he seemed to want a relationship and she didn't, well at least not with him.

Alicia had met up with Hannah and a couple of Hannah's co-workers at a restaurant called Cheddars for dinner. Hannah was Noise's wife and had become a friend of hers due to Alicia being so close with him. They were drinking frozen margaritas so Alicia knew that she would end up a little tipsy by the time they left. When their server came over to take their orders Alicia and Hannah both had to do a double take. He was hot! Alicia asked how old he was and he told her 19. She shook her head, she wasn't going that young. He was tall with a slender frame. Light brown hair, grey eyes, and very kissable lips. His forearm was covered in tattoos and he had a slight goatee. The fact that he was a white boy didn't matter to Alicia or Hannah, they didn't discriminate and this young guy was gorgeous! When he came back with their food Alicia put a video of him on her SnapChat with the caption 'when your server is super fine'. She and Trevion were already through text messages because she was out with the ladies, and drinking, and looking super cute with a mini dress on. He didn't like that at all. When he started being a real asshole she sent him a text saying that she hated him. He texted back being all dramatic like always. *I hate your ass too. I hope that nigga fuck your ass so good that you forget about me! You ain't shit folk. Stay with your FB friends! Goodbye fuck nigga.*

Alicia laughed so hard she almost peed herself. He was so over the top sometimes. She told him he was crazy and told him to stop trying to act like that's what he really wanted to happen. She knew that he had watched her snap and was in his feelings because when she asked him if he cared about her he replied with *Ask your waiter does he care.* She laughed again. They texted a little more here and there the rest of the night but she wasn't going to argue all night.

Over the next couple of days things were crazy. Trevion would send crazy ass texts one minute, then would be all sweet and loving the next, then act like an asshole the next. She was tired of his flip flopping but she still loved him being in her life. She had a meeting with Tika, Chill, and King to see if she could salvage her friendship with King. Thad fallen out because he had become friends with Nikki and started trying to treat Alicia like shit. Alicia didn't really care but she thought it was stupid. At the meeting King told them that he had a problem with Alicia because he would give her advice about what to do with Trevion and she wouldn't listen. He said Trevion would show him texts from her asking him to cuddle and stuff like that. Alicia and Tika both told him that he was only seeing the messages that Trevion wanted him to see because there was way more and he would always say things to her that made her say those things in her texts to him. It was a pointless meeting because Alicia didn't care to be friends with King anymore and he was only mad because he had become friends with Nikki and Alicia had stopped talking to him. That was the bottom line. The good thing that came out of that meeting was that Alicia had decided to stop dealing with Trevion. She realized that he was trying to paint the picture of her just chasing and begging him when that wasn't the real deal at all. She was good on all that. The night before New Year's Eve he saw a post she made on snapchat that said 'ain't no feeling like being free.' He immediately texted her. *Free huh? Ok.*

She rolled her eyes. *I love how you think EVERYTHING is always about you...I'm not in the mood for nonsense right now. Goodnight Trevion.*

Ohhhhhhh Ok, Alicia. Good night. Sleep well love. When she didn't respond to him he sent her picture of himself. Then he sent another text. *I guess you don't want this but it's cool. Good night though!*

Night. She replied.

Twenty minutes later he sent another text. *I wanna stay with you tonight.* She didn't respond. He texted again. *No reply?* She didn't respond to that either. She didn't know why he thought she was supposed to jump at anything he wanted. About an hour later he sent another message. *Alright cool. I hope that nigga you with can fuck you better than I can. Just don't ask me to come cuddle with you nomore. I'm not spending the night with you or nothing. As a matter of fact you can lose my number good bye.* Alicia saw that texts the next morning when she woke up for work. She didn't care though he was childish. When she made it in to work her co-worker and close friend Lena was already there. Lena knew a lot about the situation with Trevion and even though she didn't know Nikki personally and had never seen her in person, she didn't like her and wanted to beat her up. Once Alicia got settled at work she sat at her area and waited for the kids to start coming. Since it was Christmas break she worked at the site most of the day. She decided to go ahead and respond to Trevion's text from the night before. *I wasn't with a nigga but you can think whatever you want because at this point I'm not even tripping over your bullshit anymore. You are out here talking shit about me, trying to make people think that I'm chasing you. You fucking with Nikki again and fucking with other bitches as well but you wanna try to trip out on me and say dumb shit like you did last night. I'm done. I am too good of a person and woman to settle for the bullshit that you try to give me. You fucked us up so remember that when you get a bitch that just don't give a fuck about you. I'm good. Enjoy your life.*

Alicia was satisfied with her message and she really didn't even think he would respond. But he did. *Okay Alicia, whatever. If that's how you feel okay then. I won't bother you anymore.*

She didn't respond. Tika sent her a screenshot of Trevion's Facebook post though. He put up a video of his car with busted windows and key marks. The next post said 'two different cars. Two different bitches. Same situation. Leave these crazy hoes alone Tre.' with the laughing emoji. Alicia was confused. She went and looked at his post and read the comments. From what she gathered, Nikki had done that damage to his car. She was kind of happy that she did that. Alicia would never do anything like that but she believed he deserved it. Alicia had told Ravyn and Rick about what happened. Rick told her that he had already saw it. All he said was damn that's crazy. Alicia asked Ravyn if she was wrong for being happy that Nikki messed up his car. Ravyn's response was no because of how the situation with them happened. It was funny to Alicia that it happened last night. He was trying to come stay with her last night. She laughed and then went on about her day, no longer thinking about him.

Chapter 60

Alicia and Tika had decided to go to Austin to bring in the New Year. They were going to meet up with their friend Strut at his hotel room that was located within walking distance to Sixth St, which is where everyone partied at in Austin. Strut was also the brother of Tika's baby father, Niko. Strut was the Vice President of another car club but Alicia had met him a couple of years before she entered car club world. They had talked very briefly and although they technically never had sex, she did let him pleasure her orally. They had been only friends after that but he still had a crush on her and still pursued. She never gave in though. Alicia had just gotten off the phone with Hannah and she laid down to try and take a nap before it was time for her and Tika to head to Austin. Almost as soon as she laid down her cell began to ring. She looked at it and saw that it was Trevion. She was debating on if she should answer or not, and finally gave in.

"You gonna start over with me or what?" he said as soon as she answered.

"What?" she said to him.

"You heard me. Are you gonna give me another chance?"

Alicia wasn't sure what to say. He just came out of the blue with this. She didn't think now was a good time to even have this conversation. "Um, I think this is something we should talk about in person, not over the phone."

"Alright man, what you doing?"

"I was trying to take a nap before me and Tika get ready to go to Austin." she told him.

"That's what y'all doing tonight for New Year's Eve?" he asked.

"Yep."

He paused. "Alright man, I'll just to you later."

"Okay." Alicia said then hung up and laid back down. About 20 minutes later he was calling again. Alicia was getting annoyed. He was interrupting her much needed nap.

"Yes?" she said groggily into the phone.

"Baby." he said, sounding either sad or desperate, Alicia couldn't decipher which. As he continued to talk she realized that he had been drinking. She knew he was in a car and at first she thought that he was driving until she heard his friend's voice talking in the background and the sound of the pipes. She knew it was the President of Top Notch, Van. Trevion began making his plea to Alicia. "Baby, I know I hurt you and I know I've been wrong and I'm sorry. No, wait, I'm not sorry cause I ain't no sorry ass nigga. I apologize. I really truly apologize. I love you, I am in love with you." he paused. "Wait, no. I'm not going to say that. I mean I think I'm in love with you. I really think I am."

Alicia was speechless for a second. He has never told her that he loved her before. He always said he cared but never loved. "Why do you think you're in love with me?" She asked him.

"I don't know. I just feel it. I never felt like this before. I don't what it is about you but it's like I just feel it. It's something about you that makes me think about you all the time. I know I act crazy sometimes and send you crazy messages but that's only because you be ignoring me and I just want your attention. I know it's childish but I can't help it sometimes. I just want another chance." He sounded so sincere.

Alicia melted. Where she was trying to be cold, he had broken through. She heard a saying that a drunk mouth speaks a sober truth, so she wondered if he was speaking his truth to her right then. She didn't want this heavy thinking to go on while she was trying to party tonight so she agreed to call him when she got back into town later after bringing in the New Year. The drive to Austin was a lot of laughs between Tika and Alicia. They enjoyed the car ride but things got off to a slow start once they made it to the hotel. When they finally got in contact with Strut it took another hour before they left the room and went out to Sixth Street. They had been drinking in the room so Alicia was feeling pretty good. She had some tequila and vodka shots, then she had some other brown liquor that Strut had given her when they all did a toast. They were a part of an entourage of about 10-12 people, Alicia really couldn't get an accurate count. She remembered all of them in the lobby getting ready to go out. Alicia and one of the other guys had started randomly singing a song in the lobby and an older white couple joined in. As they were walking to Sixth Street Alicia struck up a conversation with a white female that appeared to be about as tipsy as she was. They danced in the middle of the street! She didn't remember much else about the outing except that they went inside of a club and were invited to the VIP where they gave them more liquor, a sour tasting drink that Alicia didn't like. Alicia wasn't sure how she made it back it to the hotel room at all. She knew that she had vomited on the bed of one

Strut's friend and he got a little angry so Tika and Strut took her back to his room because Tika was going to curse his friend out. Once they were back in Strut's room, they realized that Alicia was wasted. Tika took her into the bathroom and stripped her naked before putting her in a cool shower. Strut had laid out a pair of his basketball shorts and a t-shirt for her on the bed and stepped out of the room while Tika got her situated. She remembered that she kept telling Tika that she loved her and thanked her for helping her. Strut let them stay the night in his room, he had two beds in it. He didn't want them driving all the way back in the wee hours of the morning with Alicia drunk and Tika pregnant. They appreciated him for that. Alicia had tried to call Trevion to let him know she wasn't coming back until the morning but his phone was dead. She assumed that he was drunk as a skunk anyway. On the drive home the next morning, Alicia tried not to talk too much because she was sure her breath smelled horrid and she didn't want Tika to get sick from the smell of stale vomit and liquor. Alicia barely remembered the night and Tika kept telling her all kinds of stories. They laughed so much. Tika had even had videos and when Alicia watched them she was cracking up because she really didn't remember any of that stuff. She had even saw a post that Tika put on Facebook that night. It was a picture of the two of them that she had tagged Rick in and said 'bet you wish you was here muthafucka!' with the laughing emoji. They could be so silly sometimes!

When Alicia got home at about 9am she showered and laid down. She planned to take a nap before she had to go pick up the kids from her sister's house later that afternoon. Trevion called her at around 10. He told her that he was supposed to go out last night but he got drunk and fell asleep at his cousin's house. She had let him know that she just got home that morning. He asked if he could come over for a little bit and talk. She said yes.

He arrived about 20 minutes later. As soon as he walked in he pulled her into a long warm hug. She missed him but she didn't say it. They lay in her bed on their backs, side by side. Her leg was draped over his and he was playing with her hand and intertwining their fingers. At first they lay there silently, just enjoying each other's touch. Then they began talking. He told her he wanted them to start over and try again with a clean slate. She asked him why he wanted to. He told her simply because he can't let her go. He told her that i would fuck him up to see her with someone else. He told her that he was in his feelings because it birthday had passed and she didn't tell him happy birthday, even when they talked at the park on Christmas. She told him that she was in her feelings because he didn't check on her after she got jumped at the club, and she knew he knew about it. He apologized for it. When she asked him about what happened to his car, the conversation got too real.

"Nikki did that to my car." he told her.

She already knew that much though. "Yeah I know. The question is why."

"Well she got mad at about something I don't remember what, and told King to tell me to come get my shit from her house. It was stuff that had been there a long time since I stopped fucking with her before. I went to her house and we started arguing. She tried to run up on me like she was gonna fight me so I took off my hoodie and told her if she hit me I was gonna beat her ass. So she got mad and went and got this big ass piece of wood and started breaking my car windows, while I stood there laughing at her. When she was finished, I got in the car and drove to King house."

Alicia thought that was crazy. Then she thought about something. Nikki was only a private first class. "How is she living off post?" she asked him.

"She is in a contract marriage." he told her.

"That figures." Alicia said. "Does she have any kids?"

He hesitated before answering. "She got one on the way." he said solemnly while looking at her for her reaction.

Alicia looked at him and squinted her eyes. "By who?"

He looked down, then back up at her. "Me."

Alicia's heart dropped. She snatched her hand from him, sat up in the bed, and just stared him in the face. They just sat there staring at each other for what felt like an eternity. Alicia couldn't formulate words for a few minutes until the initial shock wore off. "You talking about trying again but you weren't even going to tell me about this?"

"I was definitely going to tell you. I was waiting for the right time and I didn't really know how to say it" he said looking her in her eyes.

"How long have you known?" she asked him.

"Not even a week."

"So you just been nutting all up in her?" she spat at him.

"Nope I wasn't. I did one time. I was drunk and caught up in the moment. I know exactly when it happened. It was towards the end of November. That week of Thanksgiving I can't remember the exact day though."

Alicia didn't know what to say. She just stared at him.

"I'm telling you because I didn't want you finding out about it any other way."

"So what now? What's supposed to happen now?" she asked him.

"Well, I don't know. She was supposed to have an abortion. We agreed that was the best thing to do. But after she fucked up my car she said she was going to keep it" he pulled out his phone and showed her some texts from Nikki. The texts were basically her telling him that this was going to be another baby whose life he wasn't going to be able to a part of and that child support was going to eat him up. She was basically letting it be known that she was going to use the baby against him or for her own personal gain. Alicia thought that was despicable. She would never use a baby as leverage.

"So since you want to try again with me, how am I to know that you are really done with her?" she asked him.

"Because I am telling you and I really am."

"You told me before that you were done with her but yet you end up getting her pregnant...excuse me if I feel the need to question it" she said matter-of-factly.

He sighed. "You right, but I really am done this time. That was way too much for me. I don't need to be dealing with females that do shit like she do. It's way too much."

Alicia decided to stop talking about it. She was hurt and angry and she just didn't want to discuss it anymore at that point. She laid back down and he pulled her to him to lay her head on his chest. She couldn't deny that she had feelings for him still and she loved being in his arms but she wasn't sure if she was able to handle the situation and she definitely didn't know if she could trust him. They lay there for a little bit longer silently, until she fell into a nap.

Chapter 61

Alicia had decided to give Trevion another chance but she was nervous about letting him all the way back in. He was acting like he did when they first got together again but she still didn't trust that he was going to continue to do the right thing, so she continued her dealings with Carson. Top Notch was throwing an event that Alicia had to attend and Carson had come back from Shreveport two days early to attend the event with his friend and to see Alicia. When Alicia arrived at the event, of course Trevion was already there since it was his club that was hosting it. She came with Tika of course and a few other OL2L members. They made the usual rounds of greeting and hugging everyone from different clubs and organizations, then settled in a corner over by the pool tables. Alicia liked playing pool so she struck up a game with a guy form a different club. Trevion had made sure to let it be known in a subtle way that he was involved with Alicia. He kept whispering things in her ear and resting his hand on her lower back and leaning in close to her when he spoke. Eventually he started to give her some space and begin roaming around the club and mingling with crowd, but he made sure to keep his eyes on her and periodically attempted to lock eyes with her from across the room. When Carson showed up, Alicia was nervous yet kind of happy to see him because she hadn't seen him in almost two weeks. He walked in with his friend and when he spotted sitting in her corner at the back bar by the pool tables with Tika, he came right over. Alicia smiled when she saw him. She stood in front of him and he slid his arms around her waist and pulled her close to him for a hug. She wrapped her arms around his neck as he dipped his head and grazed her neck with his lips swiftly. If anyone was watching then they could tell that hug was way more personal than the hugs she had given anyone else there that night. When they finally let go, she introduced him to Tika. As they sat and talked, Alicia kept looking around the room. She noticed Trevion would be looking at her but trying to act like he wasn't. He had a look on his face that read jealousy and embarrassment at the same time. Alicia went to go play another game of pool while Carson ate the wings that he ordered. While she was playing Trevion kept coming over to her making small talk. He would stand so close to her that it felt like he was going to kiss her. When she finished playing her game she got caught in conversation with Van. He was a pretty cool guy for the most part but he was very long winded and kind of annoying. He held her there talking to him for about 15 minutes but he wasn't really talking about anything that Alicia cared about. When she was finally able to get away from him without being rude, she went back over to Tika and Carson. Carson looked at her and smiled.

"What?" she said.

"You seem to have a lot of admirers." he said teasing her.

She blushed. "What are you talking about?" Even though she already knew what he meant. Alicia wasn't the baddest female around by any means, but she was cute and she had nice curves. She was also super friendly and was very silly which made people gravitate to her even more. She did indeed have a lot of admirers, most of which had no problem letting her know that they were interested in her. From presidents of other clubs, all the way down to random men she would she at events. She turned so many people down that anybody that did get a shot with her had to really have something about them that she thought was worth exploring.

"Remember when you told me that you used to deal with someone in Top Notch? But you wouldn't tell me who it was cause you said it wasn't important." he asked her.

She didn't know where he was going with this. "Um, yes."

He smiled. "I think I figured it out. Well I narrowed it down between two possible suspects." he said and then laughed.

"Mm, okay. Who do you think?" She asked curious to know who he thought it was.

"I'm thinking Van or Tre Will. But my bet is Van." he said confidently.

Alicia laughed. "What?!" she screeched. "Why do you think them? Especially Van."

"I see how they are kind of all over you. I see how Tre Will keeps looking at you and when you were shooting pool he kept coming over there saying stuff to you. And Van's body language and how he was holding that long conversation with you." he smiled. "I'm a guy, I can tell just by their behaviors."

Alicia laughed again. "Oh okay."

He cocked his head to the side. "So which one was it?"

She hesitated at first then answered. "Tre Will."

"Yeah, I can see that." he said. They talked for a little bit longer before he decided to leave with his friend. They made plans for him to come stay over after she left the event. About an hour later she was text Carson to let him know that she was about to leave and go home. He said he was still up and asked her to text him when she made it home and he would come. As she was driving home Trevion called her and asked if he could stay over. She much rather preferred his company than Carson's and she felt that if she had said no, he would've still come by her house and would've saw Carson's car there. Since she was giving him another chance, she didn't want that to happen. She chose to cancel with Carson and spend the night with Trevion. She told Carson that she had an emergency with a friend from another club and that she didn't know when she would be home. He understood. She felt so bad for lying to him and cancelling but her heart wanted Trevion. By the time he arrived Alicia had showered and put on only a t-shirt, no bra or panties. He had called her when he was on the way to see if she needed him to bring her anything. She had a sweet tooth and told him to bring her a Three Musketeers candy bar. He walked in with a Walmart bag full of candy. There was 8 king-sized Three Musketeers bars and about 5 king-sized Twix bars. She laughed. He always went so extreme with the simplest things she asked him to do. That night he fucked her like he missed her and never wanted to miss her again. She was so engulfed in the passion of being with him again that she forgot all about everything that had transpired between them, including him getting Nikki pregnant. They fell asleep with her laying on his chest, like they used to do.

The next morning, while he was still asleep, Alicia lay awake in bed next to him. Her mind was racing and her heart was aching. She had such strong feelings for him but she had come to the realization that she couldn't and didn't want to deal with his extra baggage. They had something great going and he made the decision to be untrue to her and to creep back to Nikki, ultimately getting her pregnant. She remembered her relationship with Alton's father and she remembered how she told herself that she would never allow herself to be that broken and hurt by anyone ever again. That was the worst pain that she had ever felt and she didn't want to feel it again. This situation with Trevion was going to have her feeling that pain again. She was already hurting now and she knew she needed to protect her heart from anymore damage. She couldn't trust him. She already saw that Nikki was going to be one of those baby mama's that will use the baby to hurt him. She didn't want to be involved with anymore drama. She had made the choice to let him go.

"Trevion," she said to him about ten minutes after he woke up. "I care so much about you. And I really wanted to give you another chance. I love what we had, but I don't think I can handle all this other stuff that comes with you now."

He sat up and looked at her. "What are you talking about?"

"I don't trust you. I don't trust your situation with Nikki. You lied to me once already about her, how do I know you won't go back to her again. Especially since she is pregnant with your child." she said her voice cracking a little.

"Because I told you that I'm done with her for good this time. I came back to you for another chance." he said looking into her eyes.

Alicia sighed. "Yeah but you told me that before and look what happened. I can't do this. I have to have my own back."

He sat there quietly staring at her for a few minutes. Then he got up, put his clothes on, slipped on his shoes, and walked out of the door.

Chapter 62

It was the end of January and almost a whole month had passed since Alicia had made the choice to end things with Trevion. She saw him very often throughout the month though because he, along with Slim, McCool, Tru, and a few other Top Notch members left that club and joined OL2L. They had quite a few run-ins and situations with each other during that month as well. One night they had all gone out to Club Fuego, Alicia left early with Carson and when she woke up the next morning she saw that Trevion sent her two texts after she had left at 1 in the morning. *Who you took home? I hope he fuck you way better than me!* Then a minute later he sent, *You're mine forever. I don't care who you fuck with. I'll fuck all that shit up.* Alicia didn't bother responding. He was texting and calling her at all hours of the day and night for days. He was at Ravyn and C-No's house one night before they were all supposed to go out to a club called City Lights. Alicia hadn't made it over there yet but Tika had called her and told her that Trevion was there telling anyone who would listen that he was never going to leave her alone. He always made comments in the club's group page about how much he wanted Alicia, even saying she was always going to be his and that he would never stop fucking with her. He pulled up to her house one day and Alicia wouldn't open the door for him. He took a picture of him outside of her house and posted it to the group page telling the whole that she wouldn't open the door. Even though she was trying to get over him and didn't want to deal with him, he made it hard for her to just ignore him and not talk to him. They had a conversation on the group page that made even Tika laugh.

One of the prospects asked a question on the page. "So only designated people can talk in the page? Like the prospects?"

Alicia explained it to him. "Technically I'm not supposed to be on this page, but I created it sooooo yeah." she laughed.

Trevion chimed in. "Well bye, Leon."

"Shut the fuck up Trevion." she told him.

He shot back. "Make me."

"I can." she said.

"How?"

"Put these paws on you."

Just then Tika came in the conversation. "Take it somewhere else!"

One of the prospects added. "Please." and laughed.

Another prospect laughed and said. "Nope continue on."

Trevion ten said to Alicia. "You got my number."

"And you got mine." she said to Trevion, then said to Tika and the prospect. "Dang what's wrong with y'all?" she laughed.

"Nothing." Tika said.

Trevion replied. "You don't answer."

Tika fell out laughing. "Why she don't answer? Hmmmm."

Alicia laughed. "Tika so petty today!"

Tika responded. "I'm staying out of it." while laughing again.

"Good night y'all." Alicia said laughing.

Things like that were why it was hard for Alicia to stay mad at him. That night before City Lights he had been texting her but she had him on the spam list so didn't know that he was texting her until Ravyn mentioned to her that he said she blocked him. When Alicia went and checked her spam messages and call logs, she saw that he had called multiple times but they were automatically rejected since he was on her reject list. He sent her a few texts as well. They were asking her if she missed him, talking crazy to her, then the last one saying 'oh I'm blocked...cool'. She unblocked him but still didn't respond. He wasn't aware that she was in the club already when he got there. She was on the second floor with Tika looking down on the big crowd downstairs. Alicia had seen the girls that they fought at Country Rock the previous month but they didn't seem to have any beef so luckily nothing popped off. As Alicia was peering down onto the dance floor she spotted Trevion. Then she saw a female walk up to him. They exchanged words and he hugged her with one arm and kissed her on the neck. Alicia's eyes widened. The girl started to walk away and he slapped her on the butt. She turned around and smiled at him then walked off. He winked at her. Alicia was furious but she wasn't going to check him about it because that wasn't her man and she wasn't dealing with him anymore. She was mad though because he was still trying to get back with her. Alicia and Tika were waiting for Ravyn to get there. She had lost her ID card and only had the paper replacement until her hard copy came in. Alicia's friend Valerie was able to get her into the club that night though, because her father was part owner. She had him come out and get Ravyn out of the line and escorted her inside the club. Once they were back inside they got drinks at the bar and then went to the dancefloor where the guys were at. Alicia spoke to everyone and gave them all hugs, everyone except Trevion. She walked right past him and he reached out and grabbed her arm. She turned around and snatched her arm back from him and looked at him with so much anger in her eyes. She tried to turn and walk away again but again he grabbed her arm. This time, despite her trying to pull away he didn't let go. He pulled her back towards him and started talking over the music in her face. "What the fuck is your problem?" he yelled at her.

"Go talk to that chick who face you was just in."

"What are you talking about?" he said. "Don't fucking pull away from me!"

Alicia got in his face. "Nigga don't fuck with me! I saw your ass over there with that chick. You kissed her neck and smacked her ass." His eyes widened and he didn't know what to say.

"Yeah nigga, you didn't know I was in here, huh. I was right up there looking dead at your ass when you did it" she spat.

"Man, it ain't even like that. You tripping." was all he could say.

Alicia just shook her head. "Yeah, what the fuck ever dude." she tried to pull away again but he wouldn't let go. By then, King had walked over to them and was standing there watching. Alicia snatched her arm away again then pushed Trevion out of her way. He went to grab her again but King stepped between them and told him to chill out. Alicia walked over to where Tika and Ravyn were dancing. A little later Trevion was fighting some guys and Alicia saw that he was on the ground covering his head while they were trying to stomp him out. Once the OL2L guys realized what was going on they all ran over to him and started fighting the guys that were stomping him. Someone helped Trevion up and then all of the guys got kicked out. Alicia rounded up Tika and Ravyn and went out to where the guys were. In the parking lot, Alicia saw that some of the boys were leaning on King's car. She went over to Rampage first to make sure he was okay. Rampage and Alicia were extremely close. They had each other's back on a lot of things and Rampage was always one of the one's that had a huge crush on her since the first day he met her. They would jokingly call each other bae or boo but Alicia wasn't interested in him as anything more than a good friend. She would talk to him about her problems with Trevion and give him advice on his relationship as well. They went to play pool one night when they were both depressed before he went home for Christmas and to her surprise he kissed her. She pushed him away but he had been happy that he was able to do that. She told him not to do anything like that again. After checking to make sure Rampage was good, she went to King next. He had busted his knuckles and she joked that if she was in her car she would've been able to fix him with her first aid kit. Tika and Ravyn had made sure everyone else was accounted for then they left walking way over to the back parking lot to go get C-No's truck. That's what they rode in that night to the club. The last person she went to check on was Trevion. Even though she was mad with him she still wanted to make sure he was okay too. He was standing there looking embarrassed but trying to play it cool.

"You okay?" she asked.

"Yeah, I'm straight." he said then tried to pull her to him. She resisted.

"Give me a kiss man, quit acting like that." he said.

"Nah, you was up in there all on another female. I ain't with it." she said seriously. They stood there arguing for a few minutes. He tried to tell her that weren't together so she shouldn't be mad. She told him that didn't matter, he had been trying to get back with her knowing he was fucking with someone else. He said he wasn't fucking with her though. As they were talking this chick came up to him super hype telling him that she was fighting the guys in club too because she fucks with Trevion so she had his back. Alicia just assumed that she was one of his friends because he was standing there just nodding his head and saying he appreciated it. She let the girl finish talking and when she walked away he came back over, leaned on King's car and started talking to Alicia again. In the middle of the conversation she turned around and looked at the girl again, she was standing a couple of cars away from them with three other females. A light bulb came on in her head. That explains why he barely said anything when the girl was talking to him and why he kept looking nervously at Alicia. She turned back to him and said in a low tone. "That's the girl whose ass you slapped inside the club."

"Man, I don't know what you're talking about." he tried to act cool.

"Yes you do. Stop trying to play." she said. Before they were able to finish the talk Alicia heard some commotion behind her. When she turned around she saw the girl and her three friends trying to get past

Slim, Rampage, Tru, and McCool to come and fight Alicia. She was confused. Why did these girls all of a sudden have beef with her? She didn't know them, she didn't say anything to them, and she didn't say anything bad about them. She assumed it was because the girl realized that she had dealings with Trevion and didn't like it because she apparently had dealings with him too. But one thing Alicia never did was engage in beef over a guy, especially one that was obviously community dick. If the chicks wanted to fight though, she would've been cool with squaring up but the fact of the matter was it would've been 4 against 1 because Tika and Ravyn had left to go get the truck. Alicia was smarter than that. Fighting was one thing, but purposely putting herself in a situation to get jumped again was just stupid. She stood there for a minute watching the girls try to get past her people. Trevion just shook his head and got in the passenger seat of King's car. King was already sitting in the driver's seat. Alicia heard someone tell her to get in the backseat of King's car. She didn't know if it was him or Slim. She was heated all over again, not at the girls though, but at Trevion. She got in the car and a few seconds later they drove off. She immediately began going off on Trevion.

"That's what the fuck you do?" she yelled. "Just get in the car when your bitch and her friends was going to jump me?"

"Man, those girls were not trying to jump you." he said coolly.

"Then what the fuck were they trying to do asshole?" she spat at him.

King chimed in. "Man chill out. Nobody was going to jump you."

She shot him a hateful glare. Even though they were cordial and would laugh with each other when they were around, they still hadn't become friends again. Alicia felt like he was a fraud so she didn't really care to be friends with him again. "Man shut the fuck up, King. Yes the fuck they were." she turned to Trevion. "And this bitch ass nigga sat there like a fucking coward and was going to let it happen when he is the reason for it in the first place."

He shot her a look. "I ain't going to be too many more names bruh."

"Man fuck you. You a pussy!" she yelled at him. "A fuckin coward ass pussy nigga!" she yelled at him. He knew she was mad because not only did she not talk to him like this, but she also never said the word 'pussy' unless she was extremely mad.

"That's how you feel?" he asked her.

"Fuck yes that's how I feel you pussy! Gonna allow me to be in harm's way all because you wanna keep fucking the bitch. I hate your pussy ass!" she said as they pulled up the corner store across the street where Tika and Ravyn were waiting for her. As she got out of the car he yelled out to her. "Stop fucking talking to me like that."

"Fuck you, you ole hoe ass pussy." she said then got into the truck with her girls. He started texting her while they were driving to IHOP but she wouldn't respond to him. When they got there she went to use the bathroom. Once she came back out they had gotten their table and Trevion was walking in. She tried to keep walking past him but he grabbed her from behind and wrapped his arms around her waist. He kissed the back of her neck. "Baby." he said to her. "Stop acting like this." Everyone was watching them, she didn't care she was still mad as hell. She peeled his arms from around her and tried to walk away. He grabbed her and pulled her back so that she was facing him now. He pulled her by her hips to him and tried to kiss her. She resisted and leaned back away from with her face frowned up. "So you gonna act like that for real?" he asked.

She answered him. "Look how you acted at the club. I don't know who you think I am but fuck all that."

He let go of her. "Alright, bet." He said. They both turned and walked to the tables with the rest of the group. He was texting her while they were sitting there but she was cursing him out through text messages still. He was in his feelings now and about twenty minutes later he got up and left. Someone at the table said "Where is Tre Will?"

Everyone looked around, just now realizing that he was gone. King spoke up. "He went home cause he mad and in his feelings." King said smirking.

"Why?" Tika asked.

"Cause of Alicia." King said with a laugh.

Everybody began asking her what she did to him. She ignored them, ate her food, and cracked jokes with the crew.

About a week after that happened they were getting along again. Alicia had eased up in talking to Carson because she didn't think it was right when she knew that wasn't really feeling him like that. She did however began to hang with a guy named Chris and was having conversations with a few other guys. She didn't really like them much either though. They were having a family day cookout at Ravyn's house and before she went over there she had met up with one of the guy's that was interested in her. His name was David. She wasn't attracted to him but he was a really sweet guy. But she just couldn't see herself dating him. She only met up with him so that he wouldn't feel bad. Once she left from meeting him she went to the cookout. Everything was normal. Everyone was drinking and laughing and having a good time. For it to have been the middle of January it was a pretty sunny and cool day out. The whole day Alicia and Trevion had been flirting and showing little bits of affection towards each other. He cornered her in the bathroom when she first got there and forced her to talk to him. She told him that she didn't want to fuck with him because he fucks with other bitches. He countered that and told her that he fucks with other bitches because she won't fuck with him. They argued, then talked for about twenty minutes in the bathroom before they finally made up. He kissed her so deeply that she thought they were going to go at it right then and there. Once out of the bathroom, the enjoyed the rest of the cookout. He would smack her butt when she walked by. She would stand next to him and play with his hair while he was playing cards. It was like old times, only they weren't actually dealing with each other again. He gave her money to go buy herself the kind of alcohol that she liked to drink and when he was eating a sausage she wanted some of it so he fed it to her. Everyone thought they were so weird. They didn't understand why they were the way they were. She didn't understand it either. They were running low on beer so Trevion and Alicia went to Wal-Mart to stock up on some more. As he was driving there he held her hand and played with her fingers. She really did love him, but she would never tell him that. In the store

Alicia had a taste for some ice cream so he bought her two half gallons of Blue Bell. She was greedy and he knew that the easiest way to make her happy was something she could put in her belly. Driving back someone was trying to face time him. Alicia saw the name Kim. He tried to hide it but she had already seen. He didn't answer. She questioned why he didn't answer he said because it wasn't anyone important and that if he did answer she would've gotten upset and it would've started an argument. Alicia felt that he was fucking the chick which is why he didn't answer in front of her. Immediately the mood had gone sour. They began arguing the whole drive back to Ravyn's house. When they got back to the house, they continued arguing in the garage. Luckily the only people in the garage were Barton, McCool, and C-No. Alicia was angry and she felt stupid. She quietly and discreetly walked past everyone else in the house and went into a back room and laid on the bed trying not to cry. She had one arm over her face so when she heard the door open she didn't know who had walked in. But then when the person began speaking she realized it was C-No. He was standing by the door on the wall but someone was sitting on the bed as well. It was Tika. She asked if Alicia was okay but Alicia didn't respond. She didn't really feel like talking. So Tika just sat quietly while C-No talked to Alicia. He told her that she shouldn't keep letting him control her moods. He said not to let him see that he affects her in that way. He told her that he looks at her like a big sister and he tries not to get involved in their business but he doesn't like to see her sad and crying. He just told her to be strong and remember what she's worth and what she deserves. Although, Alicia didn't respond she was listening. They left. A few minutes later, McCool came in. She and Alicia had developed their own friendship stemming from her being with Trevion so much. Alicia liked McCool she was honest and really had a good heart. Even though she was best friends with Nikki, she still remained good friends with Alicia when she and Trevion were on the outs. Alicia talked with McCool for about 15 minutes in the room. She basically told her that Trevion is still young and he doesn't really know what he wants. That he is doing him and she doesn't think he is going to stop anytime soon so instead of being sad and dealing with the rollercoaster emotions with him she should just do what's best for her. Alicia appreciated the talk and the honesty.

When Alicia talked to Ravyn the next day she told her that she felt so foolish for her behavior at the cookout. Ravyn said she shouldn't feel foolish because knew they were arguing or that she was crying. And she knows the different emotions that she is going through dealing with Trevion right now. She let her know she would always be there for her. Another couple of weeks had passed and it was the last Wednesday of January. Trevion had been texting Alicia all day long. He asked her repeatedly if she loved him. She wouldn't answer him but, he made sure to tell her that he loved her. He told her that he didn't want her with anyone else. He posted a picture on the group page and Alicia knew the parking lot looked familiar. He was at the hospital on post. Apparently Nikki had a doctor's appointment. He was very active in her pregnancy so he went with her to all of her appointments. He called her and continued the conversation that they were having during the texts. He was now verbally telling her that he loved her and that he missed what they shared before. She didn't want him to ask her if she loved him again so she switched the subject. She told him that she had some loose screw in her car battery terminal. He told her to bring her car over to King's house later and he would tighten it up for her because that's where his tools were. When she went over to his house he wasn't there. She tried calling him but his phone was going straight to voicemail. King tried calling him but the same thing happened. Then King called another number and got a hold of him. King told Alicia that he was on the way and that he had been asleep. When Alicia asked how he got in touch with him, he smirked and said that he called Nikki's phone. Alicia was heated. When Trevion pulled up he got his tools and tightened the screw for her. When he was finished he came over to Alicia and tried to kiss her. She pulled back. He gave her a puzzled look. She started talking. "So you over Nikki house, partially still in your work clothes, and you were asleep when I called?"

"Yeah." He said looking as if to ask 'what's her point?'

"Oh so you with her now?" She asked him.

"No I'm not. I told you she just my baby mama." he said.

"Just your baby mama but you've been with her all day and you over her house asleep tonight." she said.

"I told you she had an appointment today. After the appointment I was just hanging out at her house and I fell asleep. I was tired. She is just my baby mama nothing else. She was sitting right there when I was on the phone with you earlier telling you I love you. You think I would do that if we were together. That's just my baby mama." He explained to her. When he saw that she wasn't going to argue about it he pulled her in for a kiss. She didn't resist. After they talked a few more minutes she got into her car and went home.

The last weekend in January had come and the club had an event to attend. They all met up at the parking lot of K-Mart as usual. It was lot of cars coming and going. It was a lot loud music. It was lot of keeping emotions in check. Alicia was determined to not allow anything that Trevion did that night get under her skin. Alicia didn't really feel like dressing up for this event so she threw on some black tights and black and gold t-shirt dress with long splits on the side. She put on black combat boots and gold accessories. Trevion and King were being extra petty the whole time at K-Mart. They saw a car with rims and a female driving it so King told Trevion to see if he could recruit her since he is the prospect manager. Trevion had stayed over there talking to her for about 15 minutes. Alicia didn't like that but she didn't say anything. As they were lining up the cars in the convoy to roll out, King yelled out to Trevion. "Man I should have known better than to send you over there to talk to her. You were probably getting her number." Trevion laughed and said to him. "You already know how I'm rockin'."

Alicia knew what they were trying to do but she was done with him so she wasn't going to give them a reaction. Once they got to the event and everyone was parked, Trevion came walking to Alicia's car as she was getting out. He walked up to her trying to hug her but she pushed him back. "Nah don't come over now. Go hug that chick you was just talking to at K-Mart since that's how you rockin'." She said with attitude.

"Man what you talking bout? I was talking to her about joining the club." he tried to explain to her. Before she could say anything else King started laughing loudly. "Aye y'all, Alicia jealous!" he yelled to the other members who had no idea of what was even going on. "Tre tried to come hug on her and she told him nah go hug that bitch you was talking to at Kmart." he laughed again and as well as a couple other members. Alicia just looked at him and kept walking. Once they got inside they made their rounds greeting other clubs that were in attendance. Alicia had come and sat at the bar with Nella and ordered a drink. As she was sitting there talking Trevion came and sat down in the empty seat next to her. He started making small talk trying to get her to stop being mad at him. Just when she was start being nice to him, the president of a motorsports club came over and started talking to her. She hadn't even realized that he interrupted their conversation without saying excuse me and without even acknowledging Trevion sitting there at all. The president grabbed Alicia by the hand and pulled her up out of her seat for a hug. He was smiling and Alicia smiled back at him, she was interested in him, she was just being her usual friendly self. She looked to her side and saw Trevion get up and walk away. The president was asking Alicia out on a date for the hundredth time. She laughed and then declined again. Finally she was able to ease away from the conversation and rejoin her club. She looked for Trevion and spotted him on the dancefloor with the guys. She went over and tried to dance with him but he was in his feelings and he stepped away from her. She wasn't going to let him have her looking like she was begging him so she went on about her business. She danced with a few members from other clubs and clowned around with Barton, Nella, Tika, McCool, and Ravyn. She had been drinking the whole night so she was pretty tipsy and feeling really good. After the event everyone went back to Ravyn and C-No's house. They were waiting for the address to a kickback at someone's house that they were going to. They all raced down Fort Hood Street towards the house weaving in and out of traffic, doing at least 60 in the 40 mph zone. They were all feeding off of each other's energy and luckily no police were out and no one was in an accident. When Alicia pulled up to the house behind Ravyn the driveway and most of the street was already full, so she pulled up in front yard and park right in the grass. Trevion pulled up beside her 15 seconds later. She had barely put her car in park and had just turned off the ignition when she saw him jump out of his car and rush around to her car. He snatched open the driver's side door, leaned in, and began kissing her so deeply that she didn't even have time to react. She simply melted into him and kissed him back. They would've been out there kissing all night if C-No hadn't come over and kicked them out of her car so that he could move it from being so close to the neighbor's yard. Alicia ran into the house and went straight to the bathroom. Drinking always made her have to pee a lot. She used the toilet, washed and dried her hands, and opened the door to walk out but as soon as she opened the door she was surprised by Trevion standing on the other side waiting for her. He pushed her back into the bathroom and closed and locked the door behind them. She didn't know what he was doing, so she just stood there looking at him. He picked her up and sat her on the sink counter. Then he stood between her legs and began kissing her again. He kissed her all over her neck and face, biting and sucking her bottom lip. She just couldn't get enough of him. C-No interrupted them when he came banging on the door. They came out of the bathroom and he started fussing at Trevion for shooting his gun outside and causing the police to come to the house. After all the confusion died down, Trevion and Alicia were in the garage talking by themselves while everyone else was in the house or outside. He took her phone and put it in his pocket so that she wouldn't be ignoring him. Her phone started ringing and when he went to hand it to her, he caught a glimpse of the caller ID. It was a call from 'cute Chris'. He immediately got upset and tossed her phone to her. "Cute Chris calling you, go ahead and answer it" he said to her as he walked out and left her there alone. She didn't bother to answer the phone. She went back into the house and tried to talk to Trevion but he was ignoring her. She was so tipsy that she thought she was going to start crying. She didn't want to cry in front of everybody so she went outside. There were people outside as well so she tried to go sit in her car but remembered her keys were inside. She didn't want to go back inside so crawled into the front seat of Trevion's car and was asleep in minutes. She was awakened about 30 minutes later when everyone was getting ready to leave to either go home or go to the kickback. Trevion got in his car and saw her there. He was surprised. He told her that Tika, Ravyn, and Nella had been looking of her but no one knew where she was. He asked her why she was asleep in his car. She didn't answer him. He told her he was about leave but she didn't get out of his car. They sat in his car arguing for half an hour. He was mad at her because he said she disrespected him tonight by dancing with other people and being too friendly. He had heard the president ask her out on a date. She reminded him that he was trying to talk to the chick at K-Mart. He maintained that he was just trying to recruit her. Alicia's phone began ringing. It was Cute Chris calling again. This mad Trevion mad again. He started cursing at her asking why this nigga was calling her at 1 in the morning. She didn't respond. He began to chastise her and try to make her feel bad for the things he mentioned before and for the calls. She told him that he had no right to be upset about anything that she does because he got Nikki pregnant while he was still dealing with her and he was fucking another chick name Kim (the one from the club), and he almost got her jumped. All he could say was all that was in the past and it doesn't have anything to do with now or tonight. Just as she was about to respond he got a text from the girl Kim. He looked at his phone then looked at Alicia. He didn't check it, he just put the phone back down. A few seconds later Cute Chris was calling her phone again. Trevion grabbed her phone and threw it in the backseat. She pushed him. "Well that nigga need to stop calling your phone." he said to her. Then his phone rang. It was Kim calling. He didn't answer. "Answer your phone." she said to him.

"Chill out man." he said smiling.

"Nah you had so much to say about my phone. Why this bitch calling you at almost 2 in the morning?" she said to me. She didn't really care but he tried to trip on her so she put it back on him. She snatched his phone from his hand and threw it in the backseat with hers. HE tried to reach back there and grab it but she was wrestling with him so he couldn't get to it. He got frustrated and told her he was going to slap her. "I wish the fuck you would." she told him. He reached out and slapped her for real. Her natural reflexes made her hit him back. They went back and forth hitting each other a couple of times. Finally she yelled "Stop fucking putting your hands on me!" He told her not to hit him then, even though he was the one who hit her first. One thing about Alicia, she didn't like to fight and even if she knew she wouldn't win, she would never allow anyone, man or woman, to put hands on her without her fighting back. They argued some more about her dancing with other guys and about him fucking other bitches. Alicia was sleepy and didn't feel like fighting anymore. She reached in the backseat and found her phone then reached for the door handle to get out. "I don't have time for this shit." she said to him as she was getting out. While she was trying to get out she felt him push her so when she got out she slammed his car door. She went towards her car with her keys in hand. He got out and walked in front of her. "What the fuck is wrong with you slamming my door man?" he said to her.

"Get out of my face! You shouldn't have tried to push me out."

She tried to push him out of her face but instead he grabbed her by the neck and choked slammed her on the hood of her car. She fought to get him off of her and when he released her she slid down to the ground. He walked over to her to try and help her up but she kicked him. He grabbed her by the leg and tried to drag her on the ground. She kicked him again. He let her leg go and stepped back. She tried to get up and again he came over and tried to help her up off the ground. "Get away from me." she said and got up on her own. She walked over to the driver's side of her car. She reached for the door handle but as soon as she opened the door a little bit he slid between her and the door and closed it back. He blocked her from getting in. He was leaning back on the car door looking at her. Exasperated, she let out a heavy sigh. "Move so that I can get in my car and go."

"Nope." he said to her. "You wouldn't let me leave when I wanted to."

Alicia couldn't take any more. She didn't know if it was the alcohol or the constant back and forth with him, or the fighting that night. She didn't know what it was but at that very moment right in front of his face, she broke. She broke down crying. With tears flowing uncontrollably down her face she threw up her hands in defeat and started walking from him towards the neighbors' yard. She didn't know where she was going but she wasn't going to just stand there with him. He ran up in front of her surprised by her break down. She stood still sobbing loudly with her wet face buried in her hands. "I can't keep doing this with you." she cried to him. "I can't do this anymore. I don't want to do this anymore. All you do is hurt me and I don't know why." she cried so hard releasing everything that she had been holding in. He grabbed her and held her in an embrace so tight that it made her cry harder. He rubbed her back and buried his face in the side of her neck as she cried into his shoulder. "Come on, stop crying" he said to her. "You made me act like this. You was dancing all up on them niggas tonight. You know I don't like that shit. You were disrespecting me." he told her in calm but accusatory tone. Alicia couldn't believe that he was really trying to blame her. "And you got this nigga calling you at 1 and 2 in the morning." he said to her. "Why he calling you so late?" he asked. Alicia looked up at him. "Probably the same reason Kim was calling and texting you at 2 in the morning. You are so fucked up for trying ot blame me for all your bullshit. You got somebody pregnant, you fucking other bitches, you played the fuck out of me but you're blaming me?" Alicia shook her head. "Let me go. I'm going home." she broke free from his embrace and started walking to her car. He called out after her. "I'm coming too. I'll meet you there."

She looked up at him. "Nah ain't you supposed to be going to Kim?" she said with attitude.

He looked her in the eyes. "Yeah, I was supposed to, but did I go? You see where I'm at right? You see where I'm trying to be right? Fuck her. I ain't worried about her."

Alicia just looked at him. She got in her car drove off. He called her as she drove home. She didn't answer the phone. When she pulled up to her house he was already there waiting in her driveway, parked behind the side of the garage that she parked on so she couldn't pull in. He wouldn't move. She was so tired that she didn't even put up a fight. She got out and went into the house with him following behind her. She changed into her blue cookie monster night shirt and crawled into her bed while he was in the bathroom. Trevion emerged from the bathroom wearing nothing but his boxer briefs and socks. He crawled into bed with her and snuggled up close.
"Baby." he said from behind her.

Alicia exhaled loudly. "What?"

"Turn around please." he asked her.

She didn't feel like fighting anymore so she obliged. He stroked the side of her face with his hand and then he kissed her lips. She pulled back from him but he caught the back of her head and brought her face back into his. He kissed her deeply and she submitted to him. She knew she loved him but she also knew that she had to end this rollercoaster situation with him. Tonight was too much for her. She didn't know when or how she would get out of this but she knew it was going to have to be soon. Her heart couldn't take anymore. But in the meantime one last sexcapade wouldn't hurt. Hell, she deserved some pleasure after a night like this.

Trevion laid her on her back and moved down her body, spreading her legs apart. She didn't have on any underwear so he had easy access. His face was between her thighs, his tongue working overtime to please her. She rubbed the back of his head the way he liked for her to do when he went down there. He always knew how she liked it. After a few minutes he came up for air, rolled over on his back, and pulled her on top of him. He positioned his manhood at the opening of her vagina and slid right in. She gasped as he filled her completely up. She began riding him slowly while he moaned and gripped her butt. She was in paradise as they moved together enjoying every minute. Then her phone began to ring again. She already knew who it was but she ignored it.

"That's that nigga again, ain't it?" Trevion asked her. She didn't answer. "Baby, why he keep calling you at 2 in the morning?" he asked in a pleading tone.

"Probably the same reason Kim was calling and texting you." she said smartly.

"You better stop disrespecting me" he warned her.

"Don't dish what you can't take." she replied. She began riding faster as he pushed his pelvis up to go deeper. She knew he was closing coming so she stopped and climbed off of him so that he could be on top. It was easier for him to pull out like that. Once they both obtained orgasms they fell asleep with their legs intertwined and the covers half off the bed.

Alicia didn't sleep well that night. She didn't sleep for very long either. About 3 hours after falling asleep she was lying in bed staring at the window as the first signs of morning started to peak through. Trevion's phone was ringing. He couldn't hear it because it was on silent. Alicia looked at the phone it was Nikki calling. She had called twice already and then called again two more times. She sent him some texts but his phone was locked so Alicia couldn't see them. Nikki tried to Facetime him. Alicia hit the reject button. She tried again. Alicia hit reject again. So she called. This time Alicia nudged him and said here Nikki is calling, then she swiped the phone for him to answer it. She handed it to him but he just looked at the phone, pressed the end call button, and went back to sleep. Nikki called about 5 more times. Alicia wanted to know why she was calling so early and so many times. He said that he was not in a relationship with Nikki and that she was just his baby mama, so why was she blowing up his phone? Alicia decided to find out the truth. She picked up his phone. He had a passcode on it. He had told her once before that she would never guess the passcode to his phone. Alicia sat there staring at the phone, thinking of what it could be. She tried his son's birthday. She didn't think that was it because it was too simple and that would be the first thing most people thought of. But obviously he thought it was clever enough to deter a person from guessing it. Alicia's heart was racing. She had complete access to everything in his phone. She hesitated. Did she really want to go through his phone? She went back and forth in her mind but ultimately decided to look. She had to know. The first thing she went to was his text messages. Of course the first message she saw was from Nikki demanding to know where he was at and telling him he had her fucked up. She scrolled up through their messages and what she saw hit her like a ton of bricks. He had been lying to her all this time. Reading some of the texts she came to the realization that he was living with Nikki. They had conversations about what time he was coming home, what he wanted her to cook for dinner, her telling him she bought him some new shoes and jeans, even her telling him she loved him and him telling her he loved her, too. If that wasn't a relationship then her name wasn't Alicia. She went through his other messages. There were multiple females that he was carrying on with, it was obvious that he was either fucking them already or was trying to fuck them. He had a conversation with a female where he was trying to finesse $80 from her. Alicia looked over at him to make sure he was still asleep. He was. She went through his Facebook messages and saw even more females. Some of the conversations he initiated, others were thirsty chicks trying to get at him. Alicia's mind was racing. Her mind was blurred and she couldn't think straight. She was blinded by her rage. She began crying quietly. She covered her mouth to muffle her cries. Although she was hurt by what she saw, that wasn't her reason for crying. She cried because she knew that even if she confronted him with this information, even if she told him never to contact her again, to just leave her alone, even if she blocked him and cut him off completely he would still eventually try to come back. She cried because she didn't think she would easily just walk away from him. Why he had such an effect on her, she didn't know. She decided that she would have to do something extreme to make him not want to deal with her anymore. She was going to make him want to leave her alone.

She went onto his snapchat and recorded him laying naked in her bed. She made sure she got his face in the video and she made sure to caption it with the date and time. Then she saved the video and sent it in a text message from his phone to Nikki and some of the other girls he was texting. She then took screenshots of text conversations between the two of them and sent them to his phone, from his phone she sent them in texts to Nikki and the other girls. They had begun replying back already. They were cursing her out, telling her they were going to beat her ass when they saw her, and even calling as if she was going to answer the phone. Nikki was the most upset of all the girls. At first she was saying that she was going fuck Alicia up. Then she started trying to convince Alicia that she wasn't out for her, that she only wanted him and that Alicia should tell her where she lived so she could pull up and fight Trevion. Alicia wasn't stupid, why would she give her the place where she and her children lay their head. After about 15 minutes of texting Nikki, Alicia had come to her senses. She regretted doing what she had done, feeling so childish. Only little girls did stuff like she had just done. She felt sick to her stomach. She called Tika, but she didn't answer. She called Ravyn hoping that she was up. No such luck. She didn't really know what to do next. She had caused a big commotion hoping that it would be the way that he would want to stop fucking with her, but she didn't think it through. She didn't think about making enemies. She didn't think about how he would initially react when he woke up and saw what she had done. She wanted someone to be at the house when he woke up so she tried calling McCool. Unfortunately she couldn't come right then because she was getting an oil change. Tru had called his phone. Alicia answered and he talked to her calmly. She guessed that Nikki or McCool had called him. He told her to wake him up and tell him that he was on the phone. He said that he wasn't going to do anything to her and that he would distract him from what was going so that he wouldn't realize it until he was gone. She did what he said. Trevion got on the phone with Tru, Alicia watched as his facial expression changed when he realized what was going on. He got dressed and walked out of the door without a single word to her.

King called her about 30 minutes later as she was still reeling from the emotions of what she had done. "Alicia! Why the fuck did you do that? You had Nikki at my house at 7 this morning. She wanted me to tell her where you live but I wouldn't. She said when she see you she is gonna beat your ass. You done brought your personal drama into the club. I'm about to tempted to kick you out." he scolded her.

"First of all, you don't have the authority to kick me out. Second of all I felt it was something at the time that I had to do but after I did it I regretted it, but I can't take it back. And I didn't bring any personal drama to the club. This is a personal situation." she told him.

"No you putting the other females in the club in danger because aside from Nikki, those other females talking about fighting you too! What if the other girls get hurt for trying to protect you because of your bullshit? Alicia I'm not playing if one of the other girls get caught up because of this you out!"

Alicia instantly got pissed off. "Man fuck you! You wasn't saying this shit when Trevion almost caused me to get jumped by four bitches. You just sat there and watched. You wasn't saying this bullshit when I got jumped by three bitches trying to protect Tika after she hit that girl first at Country Rock. Now all of sudden because it's me you got a problem. You didn't care when y'all pulled guns out on those guys after that fight at City Lights or when y'all are out here fighting every weekend in the club. They know our club colors and anyone of us could be a target because of y'all bullshit but you ain't saying shit about that. You think I haven't already figured out that you trying to find any little reason to kick me out because you want Nikki to join? Get the fuck out of her with that bullshit my nigga!" she spat at him then hung up the phone.

That Sunday they had a club meeting. After the whole club met, Chill asked to have another meeting with just Tika, King, Alicia, TC, Trevion, and C-No. They discussed making sure that Trevion and Alicia do not have anymore dealings with each other on a personal level. TC was unbiased in the meeting, trying to see all points of views of the situation and how it played out. He said he didn't care if they still dealt with each other but wanted them to be able to find a way to keep their emotions in check. Trevion sat quiet the whole time, stealing quick glances at Alicia every so often. C-No didn't really say much he just mainly listened. Chill listened and spoke when he needed to. King of course went to bat for Trevion, blaming everything completely on Alicia. He tried to convince them that Alicia always came to Trevion and started situations with him. He said she would get drunk and get in her feelings and they would either end up fighting or being lovey-dovey. Then he said that she was always bringing their personal business into the club. That's when Alicia cut him off. She told him that most of the time nobody even knows what be going on with the two of them until King decides to put it on blast. He denied it so she reminded of him of the night of the fight when they were in the parking lot of the event and she and Trevion were arguing and he yelled out to everyone that they were arguing because she was jealous. No one knew what was going on until he told them. That was only one of many examples. King tried to flip it back again saying that he always sees Alicia up in Trevion's face. That's when Tika spoke up and came to Alicia defense. She told him flat out that was a lie. She told the group that it's not just Alicia. She sees the texts he sends her. She sees when he be up in her face. Sometimes she tries to walk away from him but he keep trying until she talk to him. She basically said it's both of them not being able to leave each other alone, and sometimes it goes good and other times it goes bad. She told him he can't sit up there and put everything on her. Chill interjected and agreed with Tika. He said he also sees that they both can't leave each other. Then he said that they would have to. He said they can't deal with each other anymore on a personal level and still be in the club. Alicia was fine with the ultimatum, she hoped it would be enough to end whatever this thing was that she had with Trevion. She was also happy because she knew he was heading to NTC training for a month in California in a few days. That meant she wasn't going to see him or talk to him for at least 30 days. She was happy because that meant she would be able to begin the process of getting over him. A couple of days after the meeting and a few days before he was set to leave, Trevion met up with Alicia at the kids boxing class. He needed to purchase some bands for an anniversary event for when he came back. Alicia had the bands. While the kids were inside the gym, she was sitting out in her car reading a book. She saw him pull up. She expected him to keep the car running, get his bands, and go. But he didn't. He parked. Turned his car off and walked over to her car as she was stepping out. They handled the business first. After that he stood for a second just looking at her.

"You have to something to say to me?" she asked him.

I'm getting there." he said. "I want to apologize to you."

"For what?" she said, wanting to know the real.

He stepped a little closer to her. "For everything. I didn't mean to drag you into all of this and I apologize for hurting you and lying to you." he said sounding sincere.

"Why did you lie to me at all? I told you to go and try to be with her and be faithful and make it work. So you didn't have to lie to me." She said to him.

"You just don't understand. I gotta do what I gotta do so that I can be in my child's life. It doesn't matter about being happy or whatever. I will not miss out on being in my baby's life."

"I can understand that. So why didn't you tell me before that y'all were together? You kept saying that she was only your baby mama but this whole time you been with her. Even living with her. I saw it in the text messages in your phone." She asked him. She didn't mean to even be having this conversation with him but it felt like closure.

"She was just my baby mama. I was not in a relationship with her for this entire time. I promise, we were not together."

"But yall are together now." she said.

He looked down. "I mean, yeah. We just decided on it like Sunday after our meeting. May as well." he said.

"So that's where you want to be. That's where you've always wanted to be." she looked at him. "What I don't understand is why keep trying to fuck with me? Why not just leave me alone after I said I was done?"

He looked her straight in the eyes and without hesitation he answered. "Cause I can't just turn off my feelings. I care about you. But I gotta be in my child's life. So like I said I gotta do what I gotta do."

Alicia understood what he was saying without him coming all the way out and saying it. They talked for a little bit longer before he got ready to leave. He asked her for a hug. She obliged. He held her in his arms for long time before letting go. Then he got in his car and drove off.

But wait there's more....

From that point forward Alicia tried her hardest to move on from Trevion and to get back to the person that she once was. She didn't like allowing the club, people, or situations to get her out of character. Things were happening that were showing her what she needed to do and where she needed to be. For her 32nd birthday in February, which she celebrated all weekend long, Ravyn and Nella had accompanied her to Alton's school to have a pizza lunch with him and then to Chili's for her birthday dinner with them and the kids. The next day she picked Tekerri up early from school so that she, Ravyn, Nella, and Tika could have a ladies day with her getting manicures and pedicures. She didn't want to go out to a club at all so the final element of her birthday weekend consisted of getting tatted up. She let Tika pick out her tattoo. She chose a bushel of flowers to go on her thigh with the writings 'always a lesson, never a failure', Tika said she liked it because of the words. Alicia agreed. When they had a club meeting she them all the tattoo and King yelled to everyone that she had gotten the tattoo because of Trevion. Alicia didn't even bother responding because he was trying way too hard to throw shade. He was a little bitch. Time was passing, Alicia found out that Trevion was still keeping in contact with her mother while he was away for training. She didn't understand why though. She hadn't spoken to him since the night he left for training. He called her when he got there but the conversation didn't go as he assumed it would. It told her that he missed her and once again said that she need to learn how to stop disrespecting him. He asked her if she missed him, she told him she wouldn't answer that. She didn't see the point in them even having this conversation. He was with Nikki now, officially so why was he even hitting her up. She wasn't going to knowingly and willing, deal with someone that had a woman. He got an attitude because she was being cold and distant so he hung up on her. He didn't call her for the rest of his training, she was happy about that. Ravyn was having a cookout at her house and the whole club was going to be there. TC had planned to bring Nikki since she was now officially Trevion's girlfriend and because she was pregnant and he wasn't there, TC was looking out for her while he was gone. He told Ravyn that he was going to bring her but she told him that she wasn't welcome to come the cookout because Alicia was coming. TC had forgotten about that situation. He was friends with both of them and he wasn't the type that started drama so he understood why Ravyn said no. Tika told Ravyn to ask Alicia if she minded if Nikki came. At first Alicia said hell no and Ravyn was in agreement. But then she thought about it. She would have to be around her eventually since it's out in the open now that she is with Trevion, and Alicia didn't have a problem with her, she hadn't done anything to her so why not allow her to come. Ravyn told her that she had such a good heart because she didn't think she would be able to do that. Ravyn made sure to let it be known that if Nikki tried to be shady or start any mess that she had to go and would not be allowed back at her house again. Ravyn was super tiny, but she was a firecracker. At the cookout, things started out awkward, Alicia was annoyed by Nikki's presence but when she went on a Wal-Mart run with Tika, she changed her mood. Nikki was being cordial so she didn't see a reason to be annoyed by her. She wasn't trying to be petty or throw shade or anything so Alicia was cordial as well. She even laughed at a few things that Nikki had said that day. She was definitely not trying to be friends with her but she didn't see a reason to have beef either. Besides it was good to know that they could be around each other without pettiness. Tika told Alicia that she could the change in her mood from when the cookout first started to when they came back from Wal-Mart, she said she was happy to see it. Alicia had explained to Tika and McCool that she understood Nikki's position and how she must feel. She was so in love with Trevion and she was having his baby, her first child so of course she wanted it to work out with him. Her anger and hatred towards Alicia wasn't because she was horrible person, it was because she was hurt and she didn't know what to do with those feelings of pain, jealousy, and insecurity. Alicia understood. She had been there before. So she just let it go and tried to be the bigger person. That didn't last long because the closer the time came for Trevion to get back, that's when Nikki decided to start getting petty. At a car wash they had she got in her feelings because she heard Alicia refer to Tre Will as Trevion, she thought she was trying to be funny by calling him that because she didn't realize that was what she called all the time. She felt some type of way so she began to make loud comments about 'daddy coming home soon' and making gestures of a head between her legs. Alicia just shook her head. When Trevion came back they had a cookout at Ravyn's house. This cookout Nikki was prancing around like she owned the place, she made a few little comments here and there but Alicia paid them no mind. Everyone had their dogs at the house that day and Alicia had been making jokes about the dogs the entire time. Trevion made a comment about saving the bones for the dogs and Alicia said 'fuck the dogs', but she was only joking. Nikki immediately got angry and stormed out of the house causing an unnecessary scene. The house was quiet for a minute, then once she and Trevion were gone they began enjoying again. The next day Alicia found out that some of the people at the house, mainly King, said Alicia was being messy with the joke about the dog but Ravyn had come to her defense telling them that she wasn't being messy because she had been saying fuck the dogs all day long. Nikki just wanted a reason to blow up. Alicia was thankful that Ravyn was a true friend. Alicia noticed that the more Nikki started coming around the more tense it felt when she was with certain club members. She noticed that Trevion would still try to talk to her and be around her when they had functions to go to and then Nikki would make sure she was super close to him. Alicia was really not even worried about them but it seemed like Nikki was going out of her way to be seen. Alicia just laughed because she was trying way too hard to put on the facade that she was happy and confident in the relationship. At a fish fry that they went to for another club's anniversary, Ravyn and Alicia had gotten a plate and sat down a table to eat. Nikki and Trevion sat down at a different table a few feet away. When Trevion went outside Rampage had gone over to the table where he was sitting and attempted sit in his seat. Nikki, trying to get attention from Alicia, jumped up and declared loudly "No! You can't sit there! I'm saving that seat for the love of my life!" then she glanced over at Alicia with a smirk on her face. Alicia just laughed to herself and went on about her business. When they went to the main party that night, Nikki didn't go. They ended up going to Club country Rock afterwards and Trevion was trying to hit on every female that came near them on the dance floor. Didn't matter if they were ugly or not. Alicia had come to the conclusion that it was because he was trying to make her jealous. She was having a great time with Ravyn and their new member Windii so she didn't even care what he was doing. She did notice that he was getting turned down and snubbed by almost every chick that he tried to talk to. Alicia thought it was funny. He didn't stop trying to make her jealous though. When they left the club he was trying to convince some random chick to get in his car. When they went to IHOP they were waiting in the entry way for a table and he sat right in front of Alicia trying to hit on a female. He was lying to her that he was single and lived in the barracks. Then he looked at Alicia and smirked. She ignored him. He was so pathetic at that point. The last time that Alicia had gone out with the club was a Friday night at Club Fuego. The whole night Trevion was trying to get at her. She looked so good with a little black mini dress on and he wasn't the only who was checking her out. He cornered her over by the pool table and tried to convince her that he missed her. When she told him that it didn't look that way because of how he had been trying to get at all those females in her face and being with Nikki, he started trying to explain. He told her that she knew the reason he was with Nikki and that he still cared about Alicia a lot. She didn't want any part of whatever game he was trying to play so she left him standing there. Later that night she noticed that he was all up in Tasha's sister face. Asia, Tasha's younger sister, had come down to live with her for a little while. She didn't have a pretty face but she had a banging body. She was kind of quiet, like Tasha.

Alicia began slowly distancing herself from the club. She didn't feel the same family vibe that she once felt and she didn't even like being around them as much anymore. All they did was party and fight. Some of the members began to be really two-faced and Alicia just didn't want to be bothered. She would only come around for meetings and mandatory events. Aside from Tika, Ravyn, Nella, Windii, and Brock she didn't really communicate much with the others unless it was about business. Noise had quit the club a couple of months prior but she still made sure to get with him from time to time. Alicia and Tika had gone out to grab a bite to eat at McDonald's one night and Tika felt the need to come clean to Alicia about something.

"So I wanted to tell you that, I have become cool with Nikki, or whatever." Tika told her.

Alicia looked at her. When she didn't respond, Tika continued. "We aren't friends or anything but we have pregnancy PT together so we talk there but we haven't exchanged phone numbers or anything like that. I just wanted to tell you so that you wouldn't be surprised by anything."

Alicia spoke then. "Well I can't expect you not to be cool with someone just because she doesn't like me. That's high school stuff. I appreciate you for telling me though."

"Well yeah but just know that we never talk about you or y'all situation. Like my friendship with you is way above anything I would have with her. Our friendship is way different." she said sincerely. Alicia felt good knowing that. Those sentiments didn't last long however. Tika had begun to get moody and really slick at the mouth. She would get attitudes with Alicia, Ravyn, and Nella all the time. Alicia would just brush it off as her pregnancy hormones. She made sure to check on Tika often and tried to be there for her as much as she could because she was basically alone in her pregnancy. Tika had begun trying to hang out with the boys more so there was an unspoken tension within the group of ladies. Eventually she and Alicia fell out and ended their friendship. Alicia felt like Tika would talk to her sideways and do petty things towards her but if Alicia said anything back then it was a problem. She was tired of the club being wishy washy and began ending friendships with not only Tika, but Rampage and Barton as well. The final straw that drove her away from the club came after an event they attended. They were all outside of the event waiting to leave. Windii told Alicia that she saw Trevion in Asia's face and that he was feeling on her butt. When Alicia looked over in the direction that that they were in she saw them. Trevion was standing super close to Asia. She was smiling and he had his hand on her waist. It was obvious that they had something going on. Alicia snapped a couple of pictures of them and she sent it in the group chat that she had with Ravyn, Windii, and Nella. She including the laughing emoji and the caption 'when he community dick so he start fucking the sister of his baby mama's best friend!' The message and the picture was only supposed to be a joke for the ladies in the group text. They did things like that all the time in their group text. It was a place for them to be petty and make jokes about people without it getting out. Unfortunately, Nella had decided to be messy and send it to Nikki. That's when all hell broke loose. She threw Alicia under the bus and made it seem as though Alicia had told her to show the picture to Nikki. Alicia was livid. She couldn't believe that Nella would do that. It wasn't her intention at all for Nikki to see the picture. If she wanted her to know she didn't have a problem sending it herself. She didn't have anything to gain by showing the picture Nikki. She went to hang out at her friend's house and got a call from King while she was there.

"What?!" she answered the phone.

"Alicia if I found out you sent Nikki that picture you are out of this club and I mean th-" he started saying to her before she cut him off.

"I didn't tell Nella to show her that picture she did it on her own but at the end of the day I am so sick of you muthafuckas anyway! You been looking for a reason to get me out because you in ya feelings for whatever reason. I am too old for all of this drama and I don't have time for the bullshit. So on some real shit, fuck you, I quit!" she said with venom dripping in her voice and hung up in his face. C-No called her after that but she didn't answer. She was done. Once she left the club, Alicia had decided to that she didn't want to in any other club. If it was anything like being in OL2L she didn't want it. Things really it the fan after she quit. She had been seeing Nikki talking so bad about her on social media and Tika, Nella, Rampage, and Chill were all egging her on. She took the high road though because she could have easily put every one of them on blast and hurt feelings at the same time but that wasn't her style. She didn't engage in unnecessary beef and she didn't like her business all over social media so she just ignored it. Besides, it made them look bitter and childish to be trying to keep up mess with a person who hadn't been worried about them in the least. Nikki went so far as to use her friends to send Alicia friend request on social media and then send her messages from their pages. She tried hard to paint Alicia as a slut that started fucking Trevion while they were together. Alicia didn't care though because she knew the truth and the people that mattered knew also. That type of petty behavior continued to go on. Later, it had come out that C-No was sleeping with a new member named Shan. Shan was a young, big, female that was supposedly Trevion's cousin from Georgia but was rumored to have slept with him as well as most of the other male members in OL2L. Simply put she was a hoe. Windii and Alicia had gotten word that Shan was supposedly pregnant for C-No and was planning to announce it to everyone in OL2L at the next meeting. Alicia loved Ravyn and she didn't want her to be caught off guard with the information. She went over her house with Windii to tell her about the information she had learned. Nikki, Tika, Nella, and Rampage were all over there when she arrived. In order to keep the peace she would usually not come over when they were there because she didn't want to make Ravyn uncomfortable but today was an exception because she had to clue Ravyn in. As soon as she walked into the house the petty comments from Nikki began. Tika and Nella laughed like she was the funniest thing in the world. They were entirely too obsessed with her. She ignored them and went into the garage with Ravyn and Windii. She told her about the revelation and listened to her vent about it. A few minutes later Ravyn called Tika into the garage. As the vice president of OL2L she felt that Tika should know about the situation and wanted to know what she had planned to do about Shan as far as her role in being in the club.

"Well, I'm not sure about exactly what could be done about it." Tika said to Ravyn.

Ravyn frowned. "What do you mean? You could have her kicked out. She already broke rules in the by-laws and she doesn't even have a car anymore. So why is she still in?"

"That's not really my choice and I'm not even sure that should happen." Tika said nonchalantly.

Alicia just shook her head. "This is really fucked up." she said to herself.

"What did you say?" Tika asked her

"I said this is really fucked up." she responded.

"Why do you think that?" Tika asked her sounding as if she really wanted Alicia's opinion.

"Well, I mean because Ravyn is family and she has been putting in work and been loyal to OL2L from day one. I don't think that it's right that she has to feel uncomfortable in this situation. It's not cool." she said honestly.

Tika immediately got an attitude. "Well it ain't ya business anyway. Why you even speaking on it. Ain't you TGL now? You didn't have to say anything." She said referring to the fact that Alicia had joined the motorsports club The Good Life aka TGL, at the urging of Rick who was President of the Louisiana Chapter. Alicia had already knew a few members of TGL so after careful consideration she joined them despite being approached by other clubs that wanted her to join.

"Well you asked me why I felt like I did so I don't know what me being TGL now has to do with anything and yes I am TGL, so what?" she said.

"I don't care that you are TGL, I kicked you out. It was my choice. I didn't want you in anymore." she said raising her voice.

Alicia laughed. "You are so simple. How could you have kicked me out when I had already quit before you even knew about the situation that went down? Please get your life honey but if it makes you feel important to think that you kicked me out go right ahead and enjoy that." She sat back and folded her arms while Tika kept getting louder and repeating that she kicked her out. Just then Nikki came walking out of the house into the garage trying to bait Alicia into an argument.

"Nah you a hoe. That's why you got kicked out. You got kicked out of OL2L cause you a hoe." Nikki said to Alicia. She thought that was going to make Alicia feel bad and she really believed that Alicia wasn't going to say anything back to her. She was wrong. Although Alicia never said anything back to her on social media, and she really didn't care too much for confrontations and fighting at her age, one thing was certain. Alicia would never allow anyone to be in her face talking crazy to her and think she wouldn't say anything back. She didn't want to fight but she was ready to square up if she needed to defend herself. Say whatever they wanted to about Alicia, she wasn't a punk and she wasn't scared of anyone.

Alicia stood up just in case Nikki or Tika tried to attack her. She looked Nikki right in the face and crushed her whole world with one statement. "I'm a hoe because your so called man wasn't claiming you?" she tossed at her. "How does that work?"

Nikki walked towards her. "He was claiming me! You a hoe cause you fuck everybody." she said visibly angry at Alicia's clap back. Alicia stood her ground even though Nikki was in arm's length. She could've easily swung on her but she didn't. "Nah he wasn't claiming you at all. But whatever though. You salty that ya man wasn't claiming you and that's that." Alicia said and was done with the situation. Ravyn grabbed Alicia by the arm and walked her into the house. They talked for a minute inside then Alicia decided to leave before things got even more uncomfortable. As she was heading out the door she saw Nikki, Nella, and Rampage by Trevion's car in the driveway. Nikki didn't have a car so she was driving his. She was sitting on the hood while Rampage was standing a few feet away in the grass and Nella was standing next Nikki by the car. Alicia started walking down the driveway, purposely walking between Rampage and Nikki. She could have gone through the grass or walked around the car to get to her car but she wanted it to be clear that Nikki put no fear in her at all. Even as Nikki was talking shit as she walked passed. She slowed her walk as she walked through. Nikki threatened her. "You better be ready cause I'm gonna dog your ass. Wait til I have this baby. I can show you better than I can tell you." she said with malice. Alicia smiled at her and gave her a condescending little wave. "Do what you feel. You know where I live." she told her. Nikki spoke. "I sure do 1202. I'll be there don't worry."

Alicia looked at her. "Well I own my house so I will definitely be there." She finally got to her car and got in but didn't drive off. She started it and then search through her music to find a song to listen to. As she was sitting there she heard Nikki still talking shit to her. She didn't care. She put her car in drive and as she was about to drive off she saw Nikki out of the corner of her eye. She stopped. Nikki had gone to the garage and got a golf club and was coming towards Alicia's car with it. What was with this bitch and trying to fuck up cars? Rampage and Nella had begun trying to hold Nikki back. Alicia laughed. As big as Nikki was and as little as Rampage and Nella was she definitely could've gotten away from them if she wanted to. Alicia let down her window. "Let her go, I have full coverage. Go right ahead." she said to them. Alicia was done entertaining her. She concluded that Nikki just wanted an audience and she had shit to do. She drove into the driveway of another house to turn around. As she was driving past Ravyn's house Nikki stepped out onto the street almost in front of her car. She didn't even bother to stop the car. After that incident there wasn't a whole more that was going on. Mainly because Alicia was busy with work and TGL events. She wasn't going ot let insignificant people get to her. The rest of the year went by in fast blur. She found herself in a fight against two females that she didn't know at Cub Tabu. Apparently Trevion had made a comment right after the picture incident that he wanted Shan to fight Alicia. The night at Tabu C-No had supposedly told her not to do it so she asked her two friends to fight her. Noise and Kanitra had gone out with her that night and he had realized that something was about to go down so he told them to go walk around off the dancefloor. As they were walking Alicia turned around to make sure Kanitra was good but as soon as she turned around the two girls started fighting her. Kanitra jumped in to help. Alicia didn't know who she was fighting but she was going toe-to-toe with whomever it was. Security came and broke them up. As they were escorting Alicia out of the side door some woman that was standing next to Alicia on the dancefloor tried to run up on her. Alicia took off her heel and starting swinging at the woman. She connected a few hits before the woman backed up. Alicia had heard that Kanitra was escorted out of the front door and when she saw Shan she ran up and started fighting her. Kanitra was little but she had heart. Alicia appreciated her for having her back too. This was her second fight in less than a year, she wasn't feeling this. The members of OL2L were upset with Ravyn because she was still friends with Alicia and because she was loyal to her and defended her when people tried to tell lies about her. Every time Alicia was out somewhere that Nikki, Tika, King, and Savage was at they always tried so hard to be petty and to get to her. They spent too much time worrying about her and not even time getting their lives together. Alicia had stopped being cool with Nella after the whole picture situation but Nella always tried to speak to her when she saw her. At Rick's constant urging Alicia became cordial with Tika again. She saw she was having a hard time during her pregnancy and she felt sorry for her. Even though she wasn't friends with her anymore and they had that argument and Tika talked a lot of trash about Alicia, she was told from a couple of different people that Tika would tell them how she missed having Alicia in her life and that she loved her and wished things were different . She even made sure to find out if Alicia was ok after the fight at Tabu. Alicia still had love for Tika too but she had no desire to be her friend again. She had done way too much. Alicia had bought her baby a bassinette and a bunch of other stuff while they were not friends and she checked on her after the baby was born. Even after all of that Tika still showed up at with Lady D,

Nikki, Shan, and two other females at a skate party that TGL was hosting so that they could fight Alicia. Fortunately, Alicia had already decided a week before that even that she was not going to attend, instead she was at her house getting her hair done by Ravyn. Then there were comments made by Tika on a post on Facebook when Theo, the President and founder of TGL was defending Alicia. Tika said that Nikki was going to fight Alicia and that there was nothing he could do about it because it had been play since before she joined them. Alicia didn't really expect Tika to have her back since she became best friends with Nikki but she felt like she should have at least not said anything or showed up with them to fight her. She had lost all respect for Tika because she was a follower and wanted to fit in so bad that she switched up on the very person that was always there for her even after they fell out. Alicia didn't understand how she could publicly talk shit about her and act like she was so hard but then behind closed doors was sad about the demise of their friendship. The members of TGL had Alicia's back on all the stuff that was going on. They didn't like her constantly being messed with. Things had died down with all of the nonsense between Alicia and Nikki and OL2L. And surprisingly TGL had begun getting along with OL2L also. They were supporting each other's events and even being friendly with each other again. At an after party for another club's meet and greet event in September, Alicia saw Trevion squash his beef with Jacob. A year-long feud had finally come to an end. Trevion had been watching Alicia that whole night but they didn't speak a single word to each other. As she was leaving she saw him sitting on the stage by the DJ area. He was watching her leave and they locked eyes for a long time. He had this solemn look on his face and it looked as if he had a lot he wanted to say to her. He held the gaze until she broke it and walked away. Nikki texted Alicia some bullshit about still wanting to fight. When Alicia didn't fall into her trap she kept trying to get to her. She told Alicia that she had been disrespectful during her whole pregnancy but she wasn't pregnant anymore so she wanted her one. Alicia told her she need to get over herself and just accept the fact that she used to date Trevion. She told her she wasn't worried about her and that when she sees her then just do what she feels because she wasn't going to be going back and forth with her. Nikki tried again to make Alicia feel bad telling her that she was only fucking Trevion not dating him. She then told her that all she did was spend a lot of money on him and she enjoyed spending the money from the she bought him that he sold. Alicia laughed hysterically she really tried it. She knew was trying hard to prove a point now because the only time Alicia spent any money was to buy him the flip down for his birthday and it was only $100. She was clearly just making stuff up. Besides Alicia could really hurt her feelings if she wanted to seeing as how Nikki was the one that bought all of his shoes and clothes. Alicia just quit responding, she didn't see the point. Alicia had dealt with a lot that year and she felt she was in a much better place by the end of it. Things were better for her going into the New Year.

Chapter 62

Almost a full year since the drama had begun with Nikki, Trevion, and OL2L and things were unbelievably calm. Alicia didn't have any more people beefing with her, well at least not that she was aware of. She had gained about 15 pounds but surprisingly the weight looked great on her. She was finer than she was before, now with thicker thighs and wider hips, she carried the added weight very well. After the whole situation with Trevion she had tried to get back on the dating scene but her tolerance for bullshit was very low. She had men coming at her from all over trying to talk to her, date her, fuck her, marry her, whatever. But as many men that tried to get with her, she turned down about 97% of them. She wasn't picky, in fact she was the opposite, but she didn't just get down with anybody because they showed her interest. The couple of guys that actually did get a chance with her either blew it or presented themselves as something other than what they really were, and like she said before she wasn't pressed for the bullshit. There was Stiggz, he was a member of another car club and she had met him at a car wash when she was still a part of OL2L. He had started a conversation with her telling her that he thought he was her friend on social media. She wasn't sure because he didn't look familiar. He told her his name and it still didn't ring a bell. From that brief conversation they had she felt that he seemed like a pretty cool guy, but she wasn't interested in him. Physically he wasn't her type. He was tall and dark skin, which was definitely a plus because she liked chocolate men. But he was kind of on the chubby side, he had a lot of acne on his nose, was in need of chap stick, and he looked a little sloppy with his basketball shorts, wrinkled t-shirt, and Nike slides. She liked her men well put together even when they had on something as simple as basketball shorts and a t-shirt. She wasn't a shallow person by far but she was into heavy set men either. She has dated many different types of guys but they ones that she wasn't attracted to physically, had other qualities that attracted her to them. This was the case with Stiggz. He had a nice smile and he had great conversation, plus he was silly and came off as a very respectful and decent guy. That's what made her lower her standards and give him a chance. She felt that she could overlook his weight and acne and his sloppiness. Unfortunately, after dating him on and off for about seven months, she knew she had wasted her time. She wasn't too happy to find out that he had bitch tendencies and he was a big liar. He engaged in gossip and told other people's business. He tried to be a player and he didn't have his finances or priorities in order. Alicia couldn't take someone seriously that didn't take his finances and priorities seriously. He had confided in her that he was having money troubles but then went out and financed some rims for his car, after she advised him not to. She thought it was stupid to add an unnecessary $400 a month bill to a budget when you're already living paycheck to paycheck. Besides that, she believed that if you can't afford to buy your rims straight out then maybe you shouldn't have them. Why go broke trying to stunt? She was pretty much done with dating him about 5 months into it but he caught her off guard after she stopped fucking with him and became friends again. He text her one day out of the blue after she stopped dealing with him. He had tried hitting her up a few times before but she never responded. He baited her this day though.

I can't do this without you. He sent to her.

Alicia didn't know what the hell he was talking about. *Do what?*

Be here. I'm missing you way too much. He replied.

Alicia rolled her eyes as if he could see her. *You weren't missing me while you've been out here with other females.*

He took a minute to respond. She was hoping that he wouldn't send anything else but no such luck. *It's not females Alicia, I went on a date. Honestly we have had heart to heart conversations but we've never established anything or made a decision to be in a relationship. I didn't lie to you about it, never have and never will. I looked at your pictures the other day and my heart broke down. I fucking miss you. If you're going to leave me alone I won't argue only because I messed up but I will ask you to let me take you out so that we can talk.*

Alicia laughed out loud. He was trying way too hard. It wasn't that serious. They were not in a relationship and they were not in love, well at least she wasn't so why was he talking like they had been together for 10 years or something. *Right. So I'm just supposed to give you another chance? What happens when you feel like it's cool for you to take another female out again? Or when you get in ya feelings because you heard something about me from a nigga that couldn't get me or a bitch that's jealous of me? Then what?*

I'm not doing any of that no more cause I see where my heart really is and where it wants to be. That was his response. Alicia wasn't that interested in being with him but she at least concluded that they could be friends again and if he acted right as her friend, then maybe she would consider fucking with him again. She told Rick about the messages. He told her that was just a way for him to get back in good with her because regardless of if they verbally agreed on a relationship, he knew what was up with them and knew it wasn't right to be doing whatever he was doing. She wasn't sure if Rick was giving her that advice from an objective view or not because he was still trying to have a thing with her as well. He had still consistently been there waiting for her no matter who she was dealing with at any time. Rick made sure that she knew that he loved her. He told her that we wanted them to date since they low-key been dating this whole time anyway. He said he felt that they were in a relationship without actually being in a relationship and he loved her as more than just his best friend. She loved him too. They had this super strong bond and love for each other than was unlike any other. In truth he was the most stable and consistent male relationship she had ever had. But deep down she knew she couldn't be with him because he was married and even though he maintained that he and his wife April were not on good terms and were leaning towards divorce for real this time, she was pregnant so she wasn't going to get invested in that situation. But it turned out that Rick's advice was solid because not long after Stiggz begged Alicia to let him back in her life, he was back to his bitch tendencies and listening to gossip. He had even became friends with Nikki and Tika because his friend was fucking Tika. After that, she really cut him off. If she would see him out at an event or the club she would speak, maybe even have a laugh or two but never more than that. He tried to get at her again many times after that but she kept shutting him down.

In between those months with Stiggz she met Geoff. She liked Geoff because he was really low key and liked to stay in the background. He was a very down to earth and just super laid back. Probably because he smoked weed. She really dug the fact that rode a motorcycle. Something about a man on a bike that turned her on. He used to be a part of one of the biggest clubs in the city but he had gotten out. He was still extremely close to the members though, they were his family. Geoff came into the picture once Alicia joined TGL. When she accepted his friend request on Facebook after it had been sitting there for weeks, he sent her a message making a joke that he was beefing with her because he sent her a request before and she never accepted it. He grasped her attention from the start. *I've seen you before, a while back. I like your style.* He wrote to her. She smiled.

Where did you see me and what style is that sir?

I'm sure it was some kind of car club event, not sure which one and that's for me to know ma'am. Just know that you caught my attention. He responded.

Alicia was interested. *For you to know but for me to find out lol.*

Only if I want you to find out. He said sending her the winking emoji.

She laughed. *Why be stingy though?*

Stingy? Not at all. I can't give you everything you want when you want it...that's boring. Got to have some fun with you lol. She could tell he was a jokester like her. She liked that.

Lol but it's pleasing to me.

I'll please you...sometimes...other times I'll have to punish you. He said sending the winking emoji again.

Alicia fell out laughing. *Lmao! Okay 50 shades of gray.*

Lmao! That's not fun enough for me. Lol anyways how was your day? And that was the start of their friendship. He made sure to hit her up every day, was always checking on her, was interested in every aspect of her life, when she would make trips out of town he always made sure to check on her and see that had made it safely no matter what time it was, he came out to her club's events just to support her, and her favorite thing was that he wasn't putting any pressure on her for sex or anything. She would go hang out with him at his house and they would watch movies, play fight, talk shit, crack jokes, and laugh the whole time. She was physically attracted him because he was short and dark skin with a full grown beard. And her two favorite things about him physically was that he had nice teeth and he was pigeon-toed. She always found that to be so cute. Geoff wasn't an emotional or sentimental guy by far, but the couple of times that he did express them, Alicia was pleasantly shocked. She liked knowing that he felt some sort of an emotional connection with her. That came from them taking the time to be friends instead of jumping straight into bed. She wasn't sure exactly what eventually caused them to stop communicating so much but she was happy that they weren't on bad terms. They still talked from time to time and hung out every now and then. Whenever they see each other they jump right back into the groove. She will never just fall completely out of touch with him. Oddly enough though, she never told Rick about Geoff. She didn't know why though because she tells Rick about everyone else.

Around the same time that Alicia had met Geoff, she met a guy named Tricky. The dynamic with Tricky was weird because he had told her that he saw her a while ago when she was still a part of OL2L. His cousin was in a motorsports club and he went to the fish fry event with him. When he was there he saw Alicia pull up in the convoy with her club. He didn't talk to her that day but somehow they met later on down the line just as she was getting out of OL2L. Ironically, the last weekend that she went to Fuego with her old club and they got into fight, he had almost gotten into a fight with Trevion. Killeen was super small. Initially, he was interested in her as more than a friend. They talked every single day and they went out to the movies a couple of times, they even met up a few times at various places and hung out just talking. Alicia wasn't really attracted to him at first even though he was kind of short and dark skin, but eventually he became attractive to her. By the time she was physically attracted to him it didn't matter because she realized that even though they got along well, they had two completely different mindsets on a lot of things and she couldn't see anything more than a friendship between them. Luckily, they had never done anything physical. He kissed her hand once at the movies but that was about it. From the beginning he was a person that she felt she could trust and talk to about anything. He listened to her vent about the bullshit that was happening and would give her honest feedback. He was one of the reasons that she never felt pressed to play into Nikki or Tika's foolishness. He told her that even though it doesn't seem to be totally her fault, she is involved in a lot drama. She didn't want to give any reason for the drama to continue or to be associated with the drama so stayed low key and never responded. Tricky and Alicia had one argument before because she told him about himself and he didn't take it too well. He got defensive and tried to play her out but after a few days of her not speaking to him and him having a chance to think on it, he realized that he was wrong and apologized to her. Even though they would take shots at each other sometimes he made sure to let her know that he missed their friendship and that she was a friend that he didn't want to lose. He got deployed a couple of months after they first met but they remained good friends.

Chapter 63

December 2016. The last month of the year. Alicia couldn't believe how fast the year had flown by. So many ups and downs over the past year that she felt she could make a movie of her life. It was the middle of the month and that Saturday OL2L was having a glow party at O'bok nightclub. TGL was planning to go show support and turn up with them. Alicia was tired so she decided not to go. As she was laid out on her couch watching TV and partially dozing off she got a message from one of her club members, Frannie. It said that she was told to give her a message. The message was to tell Alicia that he loved her and missed her and that was real talk. Alicia was confused. Then Frannie told her the message was from Trevion. She continued to tell her that they had a conversation and the first words he said when he saw TGL walk in were 'Where my baby at?' referring to Alicia. Frannie said he was a little drunk so he kept talking to her. When Frannie told him that she didn't want to have to beat his girlfriend up because he was still in love with Alicia, he told her that he didn't have a girlfriend. Frannie was trying to record him saying that he loved Alicia and that she was the best he ever but by the time she got her phone ready he was eating a peppermint laughing saying it was the best peppermint he ever had. Frannie was laughing so hard. She thought he was funny. Alicia just found it so crazy that after all this time he still had an effect on her. She hadn't fucked with him in almost a year and hadn't spoken two words to him more than 8 months. She would see him at different events here and there but she would be mingling and doing her own thing not worrying about him. They would catch glances of each other and maybe even lock eyes for a minute but no words were ever exchanged. Crazy how the chemistry was still there though. She didn't want to believe that she still had feelings for him but it was obvious that she did when a few days after Frannie passed her the message, she sent him a message on Facebook.

I heard you had some kind of message for me. She said.

He responded within seconds. *Who you heard that from?*

Whoever you told it to.

I already passed the message. I'm pretty sure you got it.

I don't believe in passing messages...if you have something to say

then say it to ME. She told him. Instead of sending her a message back he video called her. He asked her if he could meet up with her one day so that he could give her the message face to face. He apologized to her for everything that had transpired over the past year. He told her that he had grown up a lot and he was trying to be a better person. He sounded sincere but Alicia knew from past experiences with him that she needed to just keep her distance. They talked for a few minutes before getting off the phone. They hadn't met up or even had another conversation for almost a week after that. He had gone home to Georgia for the Christmas break. He had video called her on Facebook a couple of times while he was there. He seemed to enjoy just looking at her. Alicia didn't know if was a good idea to be talking to again or so much. She knew she had feelings still and didn't want to allow him back him, but she also was dating someone exclusively.

Taylor Johnson was not the type of guy that Alicia was usually into, she liked that he was tall but he was light skin and looked like he had a permanent frown on his face. He was slender but he had a little beer belly and he had absolutely no definition in his arms. Alicia didn't like muscular men but he didn't even a visible muscle when he flexed. Honestly the only reason Alicia even gave him a chance is because he looked good on paper. Everyone always told her that she needed to start giving guys a chance. They said date different guys and you make get different results. Taylor was about a year younger than Alicia but he looked older than 32. He was from Alabama and he was a Sergeant First Class in the army. He told her that he one daughter that was 11 years old and was never married. He also told her that he had been single for the past almost 8 years due to constantly being deployed. He was a nice enough guy but Alicia didn't like few things about him almost immediately. He seemed to think that he was better than other people. She was all for having confidence but not to the point of arrogance or feeling superior to others. He bragged a lot about money and materialistic things. The first time they went out he spent almost the whole time talking about his house that he owned in Tennessee and all of his cars that he had including the electric blue Dodge Charger that he drove that day to meet her. He also had a white Nissan Maxima, an orange Dodge Charger that was back home in Alabama, a Mercury Grand Marquis with a custom paint job that was also back home in Alabama, and a motorcycle. Alicia didn't know if he really had all those cars or not but she didn't care. That didn't impress her. He always had to tell her the price of something, he always talked about what he had already bought and what he was going to buy next. That irritated Alicia but she figured that if had other good qualities she could brush that off. He loved to pay for everything when they went out and even when came over to the house to just hang out. He always told her what type of person he was, meaning that he would tell her stories of how his female friends would get drunk and call him to come pick them up and he would let them stay at his house and would take care of them while they were drunk. He would always say "You can ask anyone of them, I never tried anything with them just helped them that's all." She thought it was weird that he always had to say ask somebody else about all the so-called good deeds that he did. She felt he was trying too hard to paint this perfect image of himself. Alicia always kept that in mind. He also knew a couple of people in the car club world. He seemed like he was trying to portray himself as being cool or important but he seemed to really be the type that wanted to be relevant. He would tell Alicia that he trusted her he wasn't the jealous type. He saw that she had quite a few admirers and that she was a friendly person. He would always say that he loved the way she dressed and he didn't mind other guys wanting her. She realized later on that he was actually quite the opposite. He was very insecure and exhibited suspicious behavior but would try to flip on her when she called him out. There was one time when they were in bed asleep and she woke up to have Alton go use the bathroom. When she rolled over she accidentally rolled on Taylor and woke him up. He had his phone lying next to him. She rolled back over debating on if she wanted to get up or not. He thought she went back to sleep. She saw the light from his phone behind her. When she turned back to see what he was doing she saw that he was in his text messages. He tried to hurry and exit out of it but she had already saw that he was going to go read a text. He tried to put the phone down but as he was lowering it she saw the message icon still had a 1 on it because he had an unread message.

"Why did you exit out?" she asked him.

He put his phone down and laughed. "Oh cause I was done sending the text."

"Who were you texting?"

"I was texting my brothers. We have a group text that we do every night when my younger gets off of work."

"So why didn't you read the text then?" she asked.

"I did...and I replied back." he said.

"No, you still had an unread message. You tried to hurry and exit out when I turned around." she said getting annoyed.

"No I didn't." he said. Alicia didn't respond she just got out of bed and headed towards her bedroom door to wake Alton up for the bathroom. She opened the door then closed it behind her. She made sure to leave a tiny crack in it though and then she stayed standing there. Not even 10 seconds after Alicia had walked out of the door. She saw the light from his cell phone. She pushed the door open and he scrambled to make the screen go black and tried to lay in the bed like he wasn't just on the phone.

"So why did you feel the need to wait til I left the room to get back on your phone?" she asked him.

"Huh?" he said trying to come up with a lie. "I wasn't on my phone."

Alicia frowned. "You're gonna sit here and lie to my face? I didn't go anywhere. I stood right outside that door and watched you get on that phone as soon as I walked out. That is suspicious as fuck, especially since you trying to lie about it."

"I told you that me and my brothers have a group text every night." he said

"Okay so if it's your brothers then why did you put the phone did when i turned over earlier and why did you wait til I walked out to get back on it then lie like you weren't on it when I clearly just saw you?" she questioned him.

He began to get angry. "You know what I see that you don't trust me."

"It's not about trusting you. What you just did was suspicious and instead of answering the question and making sense, you are lying and getting upset." she told him, her own annoyance beginning to show.

"You know what, fuck it. I know you don't trust me. You just insecure. I don't say nothing when you be getting text from people all the time." he tried to flip it on her.

"First of all, I don't hide my phone. I don't wait til you leave the room to text, and I'm far from insecure, you're just being suspect. But whatever, you can get out if you going to be getting an attitude because you are wrong." she told him and then walked towards the door. He left and she went back to sleep.

Chapter 64

Taylor had called and texted Alicia numerous times over the next couple of days apologizing and trying to explain to her that he was just feeling like she didn't trust him that's why he got angry. He told her that he would do whatever it took to make things right. Alicia only gave him another chance because Ravyn and her other two close friends Talia and Shamelle had urged her to hear him out, let him know that shit was unacceptable, and give him another chance. But if he messed up again, kick him to the curb. Alicia had met Talia through her wife and the car club that they used to be in. They ended up joining TGL and even though they had a little hurdle at one point, she and Talia ended up being great friends. Shamelle had been around for a few years. She was originally friends with Alicia's sister Ralonda, but because she was closer in age and similar in personalities, she ended up vibing more with Alicia and that had also become great friends. So Alicia's circle of close friends were limited to Ravyn, Talia, Shamelle, and her best friend Cookie that lived in Louisiana. Of course she also had the brotherly bond with Noise and after he split up with Hannah and began a relationship with his now pregnant girlfriend, she became friends with his girlfriend as well. Tandis was the same age as Alicia and she had a daughter Tekerri's age and a son Alton's age so it was perfect when they wanted playdates.

Although Alicia agreed to give Taylor another chance she still didn't really like him so therefore she tried to refrain from any type of physical affection with him including sex. Over the course of four months she could count on one hand how much times they had been intimate. He always tried to eat her booty even though she constantly told him that she didn't like that. She was really turned off by his touch and she even hated the way kissed. She didn't know what is was about him but she really almost could not stand him. Ravyn thought it was because she was still in love with Trevion. She didn't believe that was the reason but just to make sure she continued to date Taylor to see if her feelings would change. Meanwhile she was getting close to Trevion again but she tried to keep her feelings in check. They would talk every single and he was constantly trying to see her. She remembered how bad he did her before and the hurt she felt because of his actions and she didn't want to feel that way again. She was afraid that he would get her open again and then hurt her all over again and she didn't want that. That was part of the reason she put up with Taylor's annoying ass. In order to keep her feelings for Trevion in check she would constantly tell him that he was community dick and would always talk about him fucking with other females. She would even ignore his calls, texts, and attempts to spend time with her just so that she could remind herself not to fall too deep again. He was so persistent though and she liked how he made her feel ad all the attention that was giving her. He didn't care who knew that he had feelings for her. He let it be known to C-No, King, and Swag Billie (whom he always seemed to be with). He made it known to the members of Alicia's club and he even made it known to her friends. She didn't really want to let the world know that she was back talking to him because she didn't want anyone judging her or calling her stupid. Trevion was just as charming as he was in 2015 when she first began dealing with him. Truthfully here it was in 2017, he was actually even more charming and loveable. They conversations became so frequent that it felt funny when they didn't talk.

Alicia's friend, Angel, from middle school had moved to Killeen from Alaska back in October and she had been meaning to get up with her. Angel had told Alicia that she was tired of sitting around not doing anything and that she was lonely and bored. Her daughter wouldn't be there until the summer time and her friend that lived here was married and never wanted to do anything or go anywhere. So Angel would constantly be going out of town to see other friends and family, or at home drinking by herself and being depressed. Alicia was so busy that months passed and now finally way in January she hit her up to go out to Club Tabu with her and her ladies, and Angel was thankful and excited. Alicia, Talia, Shamelle, Ravyn, Angel, Mina (Alicia's friend from high school), and Sunshine (first lady of another car club) had met up that night for their ladies night that they tried to do at least once a month. They didn't always go to the club they also went out to eat, to the movies, or to shoot pool. All of the ladies were ready to let loose and cut up that night and they already been drinking so they were pretty much already tipsy. When they stepped inside the club and began walking towards the bar Angel was taking in everything. Alicia was dressed in a burgundy mini dress with olive green flower prints on it and olive green Nine West gladiator heels. Talia and Alicia had a good laugh earlier that day about the dress because Talia said it looked like something she would wear to a funeral. However, when Alicia put it on, the way it hugged her curves made them reconsider. Alicia made that dress look good and she got many compliments on it that night. All the ladies had worn dresses that night except Angel. She had on and powder blue spaghetti strap jumpsuit. Angel was tall and slender but she had a big butt. Alicia didn't knock anybody for their fashions choices and the outfit didn't look bad on Angel, it was just something that neither Alicia nor her ladies would wear. As they moved through the crowd, Alicia was stopping every few steps to give people hugs and say hello. Angel didn't know that Alicia knew so many people. She was a friendly person and she was the public relations officer of a car club, she had to be a people person to do her job. Alicia preferred to be low key and out of the spotlight. Alicia saw Stiggz and he immediately came over to give her a hug. For the rest of the night he was all up in her face but she didn't want to be bothered with him. As she was walking to the dancefloor she saw him standing near the entrance of it, when he saw her approaching he stood there and waited for her. She didn't know why though because she had planned to walk right past him. Before she reached the floor she felt someone grab her arm. When she turned around it was Carson. He smiled at her and tugged on her arm gently so that she would come over to him. As she began to turn around to go to him she felt her other arm being pulled. She looked back and it was Stiggz, he was pulling her towards him. She laughed and pulled her arm from his grip then went straight to Carson. Stiggz stood there watching as Carson wrapped his arms around her waist just barely above her butt. Her squeezed her tightly and told her she looked good. When they ended the hug he was still holding her hand and he looked her up and down. They talked for a few minutes before she headed back to the dancefloor with the ladies who were all having a good time. Alicia had forgotten that Carson and Stiggz knew each other. In fact they were friends from Shreveport. Alicia had met Carson a couple of years ago before she ever knew Stiggz existed. She was already involved with Stigggz for months before she found out they were friends. She never told either one of them that she knew the other. She didn't see the point.

Trevion begin texting Alicia while she was dancing. He asked her what she was doing but she figured he already knew because his friends were in the club and she had spoken to them. She told him where she was anyway. He told her to go home because he wanted to come over. She told him no because she was out with her ladies. He called her an ass. When she asked him how she was an ass, he said because she was busy with her friends and he wanted to kick it.

That doesn't make me an asshole.

If you say so. He replied.

She laughed because he was in his feelings. *Rolls eyes.*

Let me physically do it to you. You know I can do it. He was referring to giving her an orgasm.

Her smile disappeared. *I can't go there with you.*

Come talk to me? When you leaving there? He asked her.

She didn't know when they were leaving but she was sure it wasn't soon. *Idk, I guess whenever they are ready to leave. I drove.*

So come talk to me. He requested.

Afterwards? She asked him.

Now. Was all he said.

Alicia shook her head as if he could see her. *No not now.*

Guess I'm not important. Ok. Just hit me up whenever you're free.

Alicia laughed. *I wish you would stop being so dramatic lol.*

I'm not. You got a thang for me. He said randomly.

She threw it back at him. *You got a thang for me.*

That wasn't a question I asked. That was a statement. He replied.

She smirked to herself. *Mine was too. Wyd?* She asked him as she sat in the drive through line at Jack in the Box at 2am after leaving the club.

I'm posted in Tabu.

Wtf?

Waiting on you. He typed.

She replied back. *I left.*

You didn't tell me.

You didn't tell me you were going there. She told him.

Can I come over?

I don't think that's a good idea.

Smh ok.

Why are you shaking your head now? She asked.

He replied. *I just want to see you.*

That thawed Alicia's heart a little. *You can meet me somewhere to talk.*

Where? You pick the place.

They met up at the parking lot of Walmart at 2:30 in the morning. She didn't really want to be out there but she didn't want him at her house either, she thought it would lead to something that didn't need to happen. He pulled up beside her two minutes after she got there and hopped in her. At first they just sat in the car listening to music and looking at each other. He started messing with everything in her car and then drank her soda. She just stared at him. How could she still feel so strongly about him? She just wanted to reach out and caress his face and lay in his arms all night. But she was trying not to go there. Maybe she shouldn't she be talking to him again. She didn't know but she couldn't deny that chemistry was still there between them.

"I missed you." he said to her.

She looked at him trying to put on her tough girl act. "After a whole year? Yeah, okay. You were not thinking about me. I don't know why you even passed that message to Frannie in the first place."

He stared into her eyes. "Because that's how I felt. I know I fucked up on so many levels but I can't help how I feel."

"How is it that you feel?" She questioned him.

He looked out at the parking lot then looked back at her as if he was hesitant to tell her." I can't really explain it or put it into words but," He paused. "I feel like you're my forever. You're everything." Alicia held back tears. She didn't know why that made her so emotional but it definitely touched especially since he seemed so sincere. Of all of the things he has ever said to her, including 'I love you", that had to be most touching. He leaned over towards her and asked her for a kiss. She obliged. He brought his hand up to her face and stroked her cheek as their tongues danced in sync to their own melody. He kissed her so deeply and passionately that she almost forgot about everything that he done in the past. After breaking free from the lip lock, Alicia sat there quietly as he held her hand, caressing her palm with his fingers. Eventually they began talking again but it wasn't as deep as before. They stayed out there for almost two hours before Alicia got sleepy and decided it was time to go home. He kissed her goodnight, got into his car and they went their separate ways. By the time Alicia had made it home and stripped down to her bra and panties he had sent her text saying that he really wanted to lay with her, then another that said good night. Alicia wanted to just lay down and got to sleep but she wanted him next to her. She wrestled with herself for a few minutes then said fuck it. She called him and 15 minutes later he was in her bed fucking her for the first time in a year.

Chapter 64

Every day since she let him come over after that night at Tabu, Trevion had been adamant about sending Alicia 'good morning beautiful' texts everyday as well as texting throughout the day when she was busy and calling when she wasn't. She enjoyed the conversations that they had even though they argued a lot and talked shit to each other. All of the clubs in the city had gotten together to donate things to a local shelter for victims of domestic violence and afterwards, Alicia took the kids out to eat with Noise and Tandis. Trevion was texting her and when Noise asked who was blowing up her phone, she told him Tre Will. He shook his head and then asked. "Seriously sis, are you dealing with Tre Will again?"

"Not in that way we are just cool. I'm still dating Taylor." She said not wanting him to worry and cringing at the thought having to see Taylor later on that day. She still wasn't feeling him and he was still annoying as hell.

"Okay. Well just be careful. Y'all been talking a lot lately. Every time I see you, you're either on the phone with him or texting him. I don't want you to get caught up in all that drama again." he said.

Alicia understood Noise's concern and she knew he was looking out for her so she didn't trip. His heart was in the right place. He always had her back. Just as the food came out to the table her phone rang and of course, it was Trevion. "Don't play with me folk." he said to her as soon as she answered.

"What are you talking about?"

"These little niggas that got your attention."

Alicia burst into laughter. "What little niggas?" she asked.

"All these niggas that be up in your face that you be friendly with."

"I don't know what you are talking about." she said truthfully.

"So why don't you text me back?" he asked sounding like a child whose puppy just died.

Alicia sighed. "Because of some of the stuff you text me."

"Okay Alicia." he said.

"Look at what you texted me last night." she said. "Get up I wanna fuck you til come on my dick. What kind of shit is that?" She said mocking him.

"Your point?" he asked.

"No point. You got that." she said before replying to a statement Tandis had made to her. Then she began talking to Noise.

"Got what?" Trevion asked.

She said something else to Noise then responded to Trevion. "Nothing."

He got an attitude and said. "Man bye Leon." Then hung up in her face.

She texted him. *So you just hung up on me.*

Just hit me up when you have free time. I don't want to distract you. He replied acting like a spoiled brat.

She told him he was rude. He said okay. He tried calling her later that night but she was mad at him for hanging up in her face so she didn't pick up. He got in his feelings and sent her a text. ***You know what? I'll just leave you alone. You got it. Enjoy the rest of your night.***

Idk why you act like that. She replied. He didn't respond back to her. The next day he called her. She debated on answering but decided to see what he wanted. "Hello?"

"Are you busy?" he asked her as soon as she answered.

"Um, no not really."

"Okay. I just wanted to call and tell you that I love you. That's it. Okay bye." he said and hung up in her face. Alicia stood there holding phone. She was happy that he hung up. She didn't want to say it back. She did love him but she felt that if she told him it would be letting him get too close again and she couldn't risk it. She texted him and told him he was rude for hanging up in her face. His response was back handed. ***I just had to tell you that one thing. I mean, I know you don't fuck with me so I just kept it simple.*** Alicia didn't respond. She just enjoyed the feeling of knowing that he loved her.

While things with Trevion were pretty good most of the time, things with Taylor were horrible. Alicia tried to keep an open mind and see if she could end up liking him but he was making difficult. Not only was he annoying with this superiority complex, he was also beginning to show him as a liar. It seemed as if the more she tried to give him a chance the more he started doing suspect shit and making her reconsider. He would go MIA sometimes not answering text or phone calls when they had planned to do stuff and then get an attitude when she would something to him about it. The only time he would have anything negative to say about something she was doing is when she called him out on stuff that he did. She told him that she didn't like that comments things under females' pictures on Facebook. Not just regular comments but things would be considered inappropriate for someone one who was trying to pursue a relationship with her. It was okay to like pictures but to be under them with the heart eyes or talking about how sexy they are, or wanting to hop in their inbox looking thirsty. She had talked with about that multiple times yet he continued to do even after he said he would stop. She would text him sometimes and he wouldn't respond for hours if at all, but he would have just been on Facebook messenger. When she brought that up to him he tried to flip it on her. "Why you noticing everything. I be on messenger because I have family that don't have my number so they hit me up on there. If it's a problem cause I be on then something is wrong but when you are on messenger and making live videos do I say anything no cause that don't matter to me." But she felt like it must matter for him to bring it up especially during a conversation where it doesn't even make sense. He would take her out on dates but he always wanted to pick the time and place and date, he would ask her what she wanted but then complain until it turned into what he wanted. He always wanted to talk about himself and he never really took the time to listen to her and pay attention to what she likes. When he did things for her it started to feel as though it was only to make himself look like such a great guy. Usually the only time she could depend on him was when it was a situation that involved money. Not actual effort and reliability. They had a conversation about shoes one day. He has seen her closet and she has told him that she doesn't actually like Jordan's shoes. She owns a couple of a pair but only got them because of the need for a certain color shoe. She buys them for her kids because they like them but she personally prefers Converse All-Stars and Adidas Samoas. He cut her off and begin to tell her about shoes that he spent $300 for but never wore so he gave them to his brother. Alicia just looked at him. She didn't care. He had a pair of metallic blue Nike running shoes that Alicia liked because of the color. He decided to tell her that he was going to order her some along with a red pair. She didn't ask him to do that she gave him a compliment on his shoes. A few days later he told her that he had ordered them and that they would be there by the end of the week. Then it was the next week. Then 3 weeks later they had supposedly arrived at his cousin's house and sent her a picture holding the shoe in his hand. He said his cousin had opened the package and took a picture to send to him and to show his wife. When Alicia looked closely at the picture it looked like it was taken in a store and that was definitely Taylor's hand. She didn't understand the point of that whole lie. He kept saying he was going to bring the shoes but oddly, he kept forgetting them in charger whenever he came by and he barely drove the charger so it was in storage and he pulled it out every so often. But then one day he came over to her house and handed her a shoebox. It was face down he said because he wanted her to be surprised when she flipped it over. She did but she wasn't impressed. She opened the box and saw that they were a black and gray pair of Jordan 13's with a pink sole. She was annoyed because she had verbalized to him that she didn't care for Jordan's. He sat there smiling like he had just done the best thing ever then bragged about them costing $150 dollars. She thanked him but she was annoyed. If he was going to surprise her with a gesture from the heart then it should have been something she wanted, not just what he wanted her to want. She didn't like them very much but she would still wear them because they were a gift. Then there was the matter of his little lies. He had recently moved into his cousin's house because the lease on his duplex was supposed to be up and he was getting out of the Army soon and planning to buy a house. Well he showed her the duplex he supposedly lived in, but when it was up for rent she asked him what real estate company he rented from. He told her Longhorn Properties but the sign in the yard said Morris Real estate. Later when she asked him again he said it was a private landlord name Marvin Williams. She didn't understand the point of lying and was starting to believe he never lived there. She asked to see a picture of his daughter he told her he didn't have any pictures of her, he didn't have a picture of her on Facebook. That was odd to Alicia. When she told Talia and Shamelle about her suspicions that agreed that a lot of things he was saying and doing didn't seem right. They advised her to keep her eyes open. She didn't want to keep her eyes open she wanted to stop dealing with him because he got on her nerves so badly. Part of the reason she kept him around though besides to give him a chance, was because it helped her not be as available for Trevion. If she wasn't always available for him then she wouldn't fall to deep back into a situation with him that could hurt her. She was figuring things out.

Chapter 66

TGL hosted a party at O'bok in which the only member of OL2L
that came through was Trevion. The rest of his camp had gone to
Austin but he stayed behind. He and Alicia pretty much hung out
together the whole night at the party. He even rode with her to go
pick up Mina. She loved that she didn't have to tell him to get in the
backseat so the Mina could sit in front. He saw she was a female and
got out on his own. That's why she loved him and knew he had the
capacity to be a good boyfriend or husband. He knew the right things
to do, even the simple things. Towards the end of the night Alicia
walked out to his car with him. She was just going to tell him bye
but he wanted to shower her with affection. Ordinarily she loved
when he did that but because she hadn't wanted to let anyone know
just yet that they were talking again, she tried to refrain from it. She
knew that the people inside could see them out in the parking lot and
even more so that a couple of the more nosey ladies in TGL were
watching. They talked for a few minutes then he gave her a quick
kiss on the lips then went home. They were texting and he asked her
if he could stay over. She said yes and he said he was on the way but
he never showed up. She sent him a petty message telling him to
enjoy his thots. He texted her the next morning telling her that he fell
asleep and asking her please not to be mad at him. She believed him
because usually even when he was wrong he never asked her not to
be mad at him. He came over that morning and they spent son
quality together. He even played with the kids like the old times.

Although they texted and talked on the phone every day, Trevion
didn't get to see Alicia as much as he wanted. So whenever he got
the chance, if he had time, he took it. They decided to meet up at the
duck pond Central Texas College. He had never been there before
but it was one of Alicia's favorite places. She had come here to think,
sometimes to read, and sometimes just for some fresh air. He had
told Alicia that he didn't care where he saw her at as long as he got
to see her.. They walked around the duck pond. Alicia laughed
because he refused to get anywhere near the ducks. He claimed he
wasn't afraid of them but she could see that he was. After walking

around the pond, they sat on a bench and talked and enjoyed the breeze. He kept finding ways to touch her and kept looking her deep in her eyes. They were really just talking about anything that came to mind. The really enjoyed each other's company. They had been out there for about two hours when they decided to go. He walked her to her and she didn't know why he get but he did. She started her car and they were sitting in there for about two minutes when phone rang. Her phone was connected via Bluetooth to her radio so the caller ID displayed the name Him and the phone number. Trevion looked at it and said who do you know with an Alabama number? She simply stated that she knew people. He told her she didn't know anyone in Alabama and she told him her dad was from Alabama. He looked at her with face that read, 'stop trying to play me like I don't know that wasn't your dad'. When she got home later she texted him and told him thanks for the duck pond. He had to go into staff duty so she knew he was going to be up the rest of the night. She would told him good night anyway. When she woke up the next morning, she had text from Trevion that read. ***Whenever you wake up, go to Mitchie's page and see what he posted at 11:44 last night. I was crying when I saw that shit.***

She went and looked. It was a meme that said 'When you know he got community dick, so you sign up for community service'. Alicia fell out laughing. She was always telling Trevion that he had community dick so that really made the both of them laugh. She texted him about 20 of the laughing emoji then typed ***I can't deal with you or him...not today Satan. Not today lmao!***

Lmao! It's not true though, I just that I would point that out. He replied.

Later that afternoon Trevion calls and the conversation is rather interesting. "I really wanna fuck you though." He said as soon as she answered the phone.

"I'm sure you do." she replied. "Unfortunately for you, I don't fuck."

"What do you do?"

"Wouldn't you like to know." she teased.

"Yea." he said.

She laughed. "Well."

"Tell me."

She laughed again. "I make love."

He answered quickly. "Bet, let's go!"

She laughed out loud. "You don't know how to do that."

"Think so?"

"Yep."

She could hear the smirk in his tone. "I'll show you one day."

Chapter 67

Alicia and Trevion had been talking so much on a daily basis and spending so much time together that she almost completely forgot about Taylor and his lies and suspicious behavior. She liked that things were going so well for her with Trevion, but she felt herself falling deeper and it was scaring her so she began to pick random fights with him just so that she could keep herself at bay. She knew it wasn't right and it definitely wasn't fair to Trevion but she didn't know how else to protect her heart other than this. Even if she went all in and he ended up doing the right thing by her he was going to Germany for two years in May. That was less than 3 months away. Either way her heart was going to be broken. When he called her that day she started an argument about him acting like he couldn't talk to her like he normally does because he was somebody's house with some bitches. He really had no clue what she was talking about. He had just told her that he was hanging his home girls Faith and Nyla but he was talking to her normal though. She made herself have an attitude though and when he told her she had one she hung up in his face. She didn't want to be so childish but she felt it was necessary. She didn't call or text him at all for the rest of that day and for the whole morning the next day. He texted her though. *You and your attitude. I got something for that.*

What attitude? She was trying feign innocence.

I haven't heard from you since you caught your little attitude yesterday.

I didn't catch an attitude...and why aren't you asleep? She asked him knowing that he had staff duty again yesterday.

His response made her smile. *Because I'm not next to you.*

She thought that was cute. She told him so, then told him to go to sleep and to just hit her up when he got up. Of course he obliged.

Since Alicia had been basically ignoring Taylor and she needed to pace her emotions with Trevion, she agreed to go out on a date with Taylor. He kept bugging her to spend time with him and it was getting on her nerves so she said yes. They were going to regular old dinner and a movie. Fifty Shades Darker was out and Alicia was excited to go see it. Taylor wanted to go to the movies in Temple which was at least a 25 minute drive from Killeen. She liked the theater in Copperas Cove but he claimed that he had already bought the tickets for Temple online so she didn't press the issue. She pulled out a long brown and gold printed maxi dress that hugged her hips and butt like a glove. She paired it with gold sandals and gold hoop earrings with a gold bracelet. She flat ironed her hair and wore it down. As she was getting dressed for her date with Taylor, she was having a whole texting conversation with Trevion. He had asked her what she was doing and when he told her getting dressed, he asked if she was wearing panties. She laughed and sent him a picture of her in her outfit. He texted back quickly. *Nice, but answer my question.*

I have some panties on you perv. She answered him.

When are you going home? He asked.

She didn't know what to tell him and she really didn't want to lie so she just told the truth. *I'm home now but I'm about to go in like 5 minutes.*

Where you going?

To eat and to the movies.

Enjoy the rest of your night. Night.

She would rather have been going to the movies with him but she wasn't going to sulk. *Night.*

Get the fuck up. He texted her about 5 hours later.

Huh?

I'm finna come stay at your house.

I'm not at home. She told him, even though she would be there within the next 10 minutes.

Oh ok.

You're so weird.

K.

Lol GN.

Whatever Alicia.

Um...ok Trevion...I really don't know what your problem is but I didn't do anything to you so good night. Hope it gets better.

He didn't respond so she went on about her night. Taylor had annoyed her the whole night and she regretted agreeing to go out the movie with him. When they arrived at Chili's in Temple, he found a decent parking spot in the front of the building. When he lifted up his armrest to grab his money Alicia saw his military ID. When she picked it up to look at it, he quickly grabbed it from her hand then started laughing. Alicia asked him to let her see it. He said no because he hated his picture. She told him she wasn't going to laugh but he still wouldn't let her see. He even went so far as to put it in his wallet and put his wallet in his pocket and brought it inside with him. Alicia felt like he was obviously hiding something on that ID card that he didn't want her to see because he never brought his wallet in. It always stayed in the car, even when he came over to her house. She began to think that he lied about his name because although she didn't see the names on the card, she could've sworn there were 3 names; a first, middle, and last. But he had always told her he didn't have a middle name. She had asked him at least twice before about a middle name. Alicia was going to get to the bottom of it though. Somehow, someway.

Chapter 68

Alicia had a club meeting with TGL on a beautiful Sunday afternoon. During the meeting Trevion had called her. She sent him text and let him that she was in a meeting. He texted back and she wasn't prepared for what he said. *You have a boyfriend?*

What do you think? She countered, not really wanting to have the conversation because she didn't want to lie to him.

I'm asking.

What made you ask?

Just asking. That's all.

Gotta be a reason for it. She pressed. She knew that one of the boys had told him, that's why he was asking. Process of elimination said either TC or C-No, since they were at Ravyn's house one day when Alicia was talking about Taylor. She doubted that it was TC because he didn't really care to be in anyone's business like that. Either way it wasn't something that she wanted to be told. She was dating, but she didn't have a boyfriend, not technically anyway. She didn't even really like Taylor.

Ok. Trevion responded.

Ok what?

Just ok. I see you're not going to answer me so ok.

Would it matter if I did?

Whatever Alicia.

What's your problem? For real talk to me.

I don't have one. He told her, trying to hide how he was really feeling. That was a problem Alicia had with giving him 100 percent of her again. He didn't want to look or be vulnerable so a lot of times he would try to hide his true feelings, especially of it meant keeping his pride.

Then talk to me.

About what? You don't even answer the phone.

We were having a meeting when you called.

I understand that.

Then why are you trying to make it like I never answer when you call? She pressed.

You don't though.

Yes I do...I even call you sometimes.

The lies.

I don't lie.

I hear you. He was being an ass, but Alicia understood why so she wasn't going to just get an attitude. She was kind of in the wrong so she kept trying to talk to him. Even trying to put him on a guilt trip.

You just do me so wrong. She said.

I definitely don't.

Right...I guess I'm just a horrible lying ass person.

Your boyfriend must have told you that? I didn't.

You basically did tell me that.

Okay Alicia and you still haven't answered my question.

Do you care about me at all? She said trying to divert his question again.

Yea.

"Yea" Mmm...yeah that shows you don't.

I don't see how.

It sounds so bland and not genuine.

She got him talking again, and not about a boyfriend. *Meanwhile I hit you up more than you do me.*

You can't say that I don't hit you up.

You don't. When we text, sometimes it takes you forever to text back.

I do hit you up and sometimes it takes a while because I be doing stuff or I'm not by my phone...you don't always reply right back.

Definitely do, Alicia.

Not always. Stop acting like that.

Just answer the question I asked you earlier. He asked her again.

She wasn't going to answer. *What are you doing? Is that the only reason you called me today?*

Just answer it.

IS THAT THE ONLY REASON YOU CALLED ME TODAY? She asked again.

Why can't you answer the question? Is it that hard? Yes that's the only reason I called you.

So you didn't actually want to or care to talk to me today....

You didn't hit me up all day so I should be asking you that.

This conversation lasted for another hour through text messages. She was still at the meeting at a member's house but the official meeting was over. She told him he was acting like he was upset with her and he assured her that he wasn't but he didn't want her to beat around the bush either. She was hoping that he wasn't going to distance himself from after that. Regardless of what she was doing or not, she really loved him and loved having him back in her life, everything that she did was only to protect her own not to hurt him. She would never try to purposely hurt him even after all that he had done to her. That was the love that she had for him. Able to see the good in him even when memories of all the bad tried to come back. Besides that, she knew he wasn't just sitting around waiting for her and not doing anything. She knew him better than that. She was certain he had a female or two waiting in the cut for when he wasn't getting what he wanted from her. She wanted to see him tonight so that she could know that his heart was still with her. She asked him to come help her fill out the kids Valentine's Day cards that they had to send to school tomorrow. He said yes. She told him she would be heading home within the next thirty minutes and he said he would meet her there.

Alicia was driving home when out of the blue she got a call from Stiggz. "Make me go upside your head." he said to her when she answered the phone.

"What are you talking about?" she asked him.

He laughed. "I just feel like you doing something you shouldn't."

She rolled her eyes and laughed. "Nigga I'm driving home."

"Oh! My bad." he said laughing again. "Sorry. But I have a question. How do you know Carson?"

So that's why he was calling, because he was jealous that I chose to go over and talk to Carson instead of him that night at Tabu. She would always prefer to talk to Carson over him. There was no question about that. She was settling when she was dealing with Stiggz, but she genuinely liked Carson as a person and liked being around him. She was wondering when he was going to ask her about him, though. It was funny because she spoke with Carson a few times after that night and he didn't feel pressed to ask about Stiggz at all. That was the difference between a man with confidence in himself and one that knew he was barely even considered as mediocre. She laughed to herself. "I've known Carson for a few years. He's a very good friend of mine."

"Oh." Was all he said, then he just held the phone without speaking.

"Why?" she asked him.

He tried to act nonchalant. "I was just curious, didn't know y'all knew each other. I be seeing shit."

"Seeing shit like?"

"His hand was a little bit too low." He said as if he had any claim to where anybody's hand was on her body.

"When?"

"When you walked away from me and he was talking to you." he recalled.

"I could've sworn after he hugged me he was holding my hand while he was talking to me." She said not owing him any explanation though.

He laughed. "I don't know, too many flashing lights."

"Yeah right." she said laughing. Then she ended their call. She didn't have any desire to continue the conversation.

Trevion showed up to her house about ten minutes after she got home. He walked into the house with this solemn look on his face. Alicia could tell that he had an attitude with her because he barely spoke to her. She tried to make small talk with him but he would barely respond to her if at all. He acted like he was so focused on fill out Alton's cards. When he finished, he attached the lollipops to the cards with tape. She stole a few glances at him as he lay across her bed prepping the Valentine's cards. It was moments like this that made her really care for him. It was something so simple yet it spoke volumes. Oh she really did love the person he was, flaws and all. She didn't like him not talking to her though. So she told him he was being a childish asshole. He smiled a little. Probably because he knew that not talking was making her feel bad. He really was childish like that. He eventually started talking to her normal, but the fun conversation didn't last long. He asked her again if she had a boyfriend.

"Oh my goodness!" she exclaimed. "Why is that so important? Like my goodness would it matter if I did?"

"I just want to know but you acting like you can't answer the question." He said. She was beginning to feel like a shitty ass person because he usually didn't show emotions like this in regards to her dealing with other guys. He would usually just threaten her and drop the issue. But tonight he sat there with this look on his face like all he wanted was to know the truth. She knew that feeling all too well because she used to feel it all the time when she would ask him about who he was dealing with and with Alton's father. It was a very powerful emotion to not get the needed answers to the questions you seek. "Don't be trying to do me like I'm a side nigga or something." He said to her then laughed it off. She was glad that he did. There was no more awkward conversation. He told her that he had duty on Valentine's Day and the talked about a few other things. He left about 20 minutes later after giving her a little kiss on the cheek. She texted him and told him thanks for helping her. He said she was welcome. She asked him not to be mad at her. He said he wasn't. When she asked him to stay over he said he was tired and already in bed. She told him he was lying. He simply responded with 'whatever and night'. She just crawled into bed and went to sleep.

The next morning he began texting her at 5:58. It was an emoji that she couldn't see. Then ay 6:14 he sent the emoji eyes. Then at 6:18

he texted her *Baby girl.*

Alicia's alarm went off at 6:30. She read his texts and simply responded that she couldn't see the emoji.

Kiss me. He wrote to her.

She sent him the emoji that was winking with the tongue sticking out.

I wanna kiss you between your thighs.

She responded with the 'speak no evil' monkey emoji and the surprised face emoji.

Can I? He asked.

She felt like being petty since he didn't stay with her last night. *Did you kiss your girlfriend between her thighs last night?*

Don't have one of those.

Are you sure about that? She baited him.

He clapped back. *Unlike you, yea 100%*

Mmmhhh yeah cause you have a girlfriend...you have side bitches...you have hoes...and yet you're too deep in love with you girlfriend to ever really break up and stay apart that's why y'all always get back together. I'm sure y'all will be getting married soon and she will be on that plane to Germany in May, too. She didn't know why, but she was really trying to provoke him this morning. She was really just talking out the side of her neck.

I don't have a gf and you can keep thinking that. It's ok, knock yourself out with these assumptions.

Oh my bad a fiancée then...that's why you were at Y'ALL apartment last night right? She said going in for the kill.

That either but ok.

She didn't think he was at the apartment for her, but she knew he was there. There was no question about that. *I see you didn't deny it either. Smh. You make my heart hurt.* For the first time since they started talking again she openly told him the first real truth about something that she felt.

You don't think you make mine hurt? He asked her.

No I don't...at all...that's impossible.

He sent her the emoji blowing a heart kiss.

She sent him the blank stare emoji and told him that he avoids the topics. He asked her to kiss him back. She told him to stop avoiding the topics. He said he wasn't. She didn't respond. He sent her a text a few minutes later asking where she was at. She was at the DMV. Her Louisiana licensed had expired before she got a chance to go renew it so she had to get a Texas one. She really didn't want to. He called her.

"No work today?" he asked.

"At 11. Hopefully I will be out of here way before then." she shook her head.

"Ok cool, let me know." He said.

"Okay." She smiled.

"You miss me?" he asked her.

She had to be difficult, she didn't know why though. "Do you miss me?"

He sighed "There you go with that BS."

She frowned as if he could see her. "Why is it BS when I ask?"

"Why can't you just answer my question?"

She went back at him. "Why can't you answer mine? I'll answer when you do."

"Bet." Was all that he said in response.

She was being childish for no reason now. "See there you go being that asshole again. That's why I can't answer your questions first cause I feel like you wanna make me look like a fool, Mr. attitude."

He chuckled a little. "You thinking too much."

"I'm not."

"Stop being extra."

"I'm not being extra and you got your nerve with your dramatic ass." She said to him. More people had come into the DMV so all the different conversations mixing with the intercom calling the next numbers was making it extra hard for her to hear him. He got an attitude and hung up in her face. She texted him.

See that's what I say the shit that I say to your ass. The fuck is your deal? Just fucking rude and shit.

You act like you can't hear. He told her.

She was pissed off. *Nigga I'm in the fucking Dmv, people are talking, there's a loud ass intercom, and you were moving too much on your end...and even still me not being able to hear aint got shit to do with you being rude and talking about oh I see you don't want to talk to me then hanging up in my fuckin face...that's that bullshit there that I be talking about. But what the fuck ever, you got that.*

He responded almost immediately. *Are you yelling at me? If so, stop it. You're hurting my feelings.*

Yes I'm yelling at you and cursing you out and I'm definitely not hurting your non-existent feelings. She thought he was trying to be funny.

You are.

Valentine's Day. Alicia was kind of dreading it because she had to see Taylor that night. She really didn't want to spend it with him. She wanted to spend it with Trevion but he had staff duty. She could see him on his breaks but she was sure Taylor would be there by then.

She had gotten the kids and her brother some gift bags with all kinds of goodies that they each would like and some perfume or cologne. It was something that she did every year. Trevion texted Alicia that morning trying to make small talk but she was mad at him. She hit him up last but he didn't answer so she was pretty sure that he was with a female cause he text her like 3 hours later. She didn't respond. His text this morning said 'Bet'. She responded with whatever. It told her it was too early. She shot back at him telling him not to start shit then. All he said was cool. She only said whatever. Guess he got annoyed with her smart remarks so he called her.

"What?" she said.

"I'm gone choke ya ass out when I see you."

"Not worried." she kept it simple.

"Good." He said.

"Bad."

"O."

"P." She was really being a dick right now.

"You bringing me something to eat today?" He asked her.

"I'll bring you a corndog." She said sarcastically.

"Oh yea?"

"Yep."

"Bet." he said.

"Cool." She mocked.

He playfully told her, "I got a corndog for you."

She snapped at him. "Nah you have it for whomever you were with last night."

"Chill."

She didn't say anything back to him. She just held the phone in silence.

"Baby." He finally broke the quiet air.

She wasn't done being petty. "That's what you call whomever you were with last night."

His tone changed from playful to concerned, "What's wrong with you? Why are you being an ass today?"

"I'm not being an ass. You were an ass yesterday and Sunday, so..." She stopped talking.

He exhaled. "I just miss you and I want you in my mouth."

"You don't miss me, you miss my kitty." She said getting in her feelings. "And you had someone else in your mouth last night."

"I didn't."

"On your dick then." She had a comeback for everything.

She knew he was getting annoyed. "Stop assuming."

"I'm not assuming anything. So whatever." A few seconds after she said that he hung up in her face. She texted him and let him know that would be the last time he hangs up in her face. He said she was the one with the attitude though. She told him it didn't matter because she never hangs up in his face. He tried to avoid an even bigger. He told her he missed her. She wasn't in the mood to be sweet with him. She told him she couldn't tell that he missed her. He said it didn't matter because he did. She just sent the emoji exhaling a deep breath. He responded with the heart eyes and emoji blowing a kiss. Two hours later he texted her saying Baby. She replied Trevion. He immediately got in his feelings. *Never mind.*

See there you go. Smh. She typed.

He was being an ass now. *I guess.*

Whatever man...I'm really getting tired of the bullshit.

Shit me too. He countered. She couldn't believe they were fighting right now. On Valentine's Day. Then she still had to deal with Taylor coming over in an hour.

She spazzed on Trevion. *Well then go back to your girlfriend/baby mama and be happy then...the fuck!*

Oh yea? Bet Alicia.

Yeah! You act like I'm so fucking difficult as if I don't have a reason to be, but yeah whatever man. She was really upset.

He was trying to stop their argument after she made that comment. He knew she had reason to be difficult with him but with all the effort he had been putting in over these past couple of months he wanted her to recognize that he was different. *You gone open the door when I get a break?*

Alicia really wanted to say yes. She really wanted him there with here even if it was only a couple of hours. But, she had already made plans with Taylor. She wished she was cold hearted cause Taylor would've been kicked to the curb of instead getting a chance with her. *I will open the door tomorrow and don't say alright bet Alicia.*

Ok deal Leon.

Lol okay. She thought everything was fine.

Taylor came over at about 8 that night with a dozen red roses in a beautiful vase, a pink teddy bear, a white teddy bear, and a huge heart shaped balloon. Alicia thought they were cute gifts but she could tell that he put absolutely no thought in it at all. His presence just immediately annoyed her. She really wanted him leave but she would have felt bad. She watched movies with him until she got tired. They crawled into bed and she tried to go sleep but he kept trying to touch her and kiss her. His touch made her skin crawl for some reason. She didn't know how much longer she would be able to give him a chance. She was hoping that something would happen soon so that she could have a reason to stop dealing with him. She knew he was trying to have sex but she didn't want him to touch her. She lied and told him it was that time of the month. He said he didn't mind a little blood. Alicia shut him down. He was not her husband or even her boyfriend so that was not about to happen. He finally stopped trying and they went to sleep. Alicia woke up to her phone ringing around 10pm. It was Trevion. She wanted to talk to him but she would never be so disrespectful to him that she would hold a conversation with him with another man lying in her bed. She loved him too much to do that. She wouldn't be able to look him in the eye after that. He texted her after she didn't answer and said Night then sent her the laughing emoji. She figured he knew or at least assumed she was with a guy.

Chapter 69

Today, the day after Valentine's Day, was Alicia's 33 birthday. She didn't have big plans for the particular day, just going out to eat with the family. Taylor said he wanted to come by to bring her gift. She knew he was going to try and stay over and she knew Trevion was going to want to see her today especially since he didn't see her yesterday. She was going to make some time for him today somehow. He started in on her early this morning though. At 6am he was already sending texts with his attitude evident. *How many of your boyfriends told you happy birthday?*

Omg! You gonna start on my birthday?

I mean you did try the fuck out of me last night. He was really on one today.

Her response was simple. *I didn't.*

You definitely did.

Definitely did not.

So which one of your hoe ass niggas tell you happy bday? He was tripping now.

I don't have "niggas" lol.

Answer my question.

Your hoe ass haven't said it yet. She sent to him.

And I won't until you answer my question.

I did answer already. She told him.

He was quick to text back. *You didn't.*

I don't have niggas.

He was getting annoyed with her. *Let me rephrase that. How many of your little friends that likes you, told you that?*

Quite a few of them...the day is still young though so I'm sure it'll be plenty more. She told him since he wanted to be an asshole this early in the morning and on her birthday.

All he said was ok. She asked if he had a problem. He said no. Then told her happy birthday when she pointed out that he still hadn't said it. She called him later that afternoon to see what he was doing. He immediately went into seduction mode. He told her he was wanting some of her. She told him no. "Omg. I miss it." He told her.

"Exactly." She said.

He started getting in his feelings. "You don't want it from me?"

"I don't want it from anyone she told him."

"Whatever. Am I going to see you at some point today?" He asked her.

She answered with a question. "Would you like to see me?"

"I asked you a question." he said.

"When are you free?"

"After 6."

"I will only be free til around 7:15. I'm expected at a little shindig at

7:30." She told him, happy to know that she will get to spend even a little bit time with him.

"What shindig?" he asked.

"My people are feeding me, doing cake and ice cream and such. It is my birthday ya know."

"I know nigga."

"Well act like you know nigga."

"I do. Bring me some cake."

"Sure." she said.

"Can I eat off of you? Just eating. I'll just eat it and leave. I just want to taste It." he said to her.

He already knew that if she let him eat it she was going to want the dick too, he wasn't slick. "That can't happen." She told him.

"Why not?"

"Cause we shouldn't be doing that. It complicates things."

"Ok." He said with disappointment.

She was looking forward to seeing him but they have a horrible time communicating with each other. He hit her up at 5:40 asking her where she was. She was heading to Noise's house to hang out with them until Trevion was free. He said he was at King's house. He hit her up again at almost 6:30 and told her he had been waiting on her. She didn't know that he was waiting on her he didn't say he was ready. He got a little attitude and asked her why else would he be asking where she was. She figured most logical people would have made it known that they were available sooner than anticipated.

I guess I won't see you then. He said.

It's your fault though. She told him.

He clapped back. *It's definitely yours. I told you I was free after 6.*

Okay Trevion.

He texted her 30 minutes later. *I wanna see you. But you're too busy for me I see. It's fucked up how you do me. I'm just gonna fall back. No hard feelings we're still cool.*

How do I do you?

Nothing.

I treat you fucked up because I won't let you spend the night?

Yeah.

She didn't even bother responding to that. She hung out with Taylor for the rest night. He walked in and handed her $50 dollars talking about Happy Birthday. She said thanks but she was annoyed that yet again he put no thought into the gift. He made it even worse when he had the audacity to say to her, "You see how I just walked in and handed you $50 like it was nothing, it's nothing to me." Alicia just looked at him because she had to bite her tongue. In truth the little bit of money was nothing to her either. She didn't need and it barely bought a meal for her and the kids. That was the shit she was talking about when she would tell Ravyn, Shamelle, and Talia that he was annoying and narcissistic as hell.

Alicia, Shamelle, Angel, Talia, and two other ladies had planned two days of events for her birthday. Her birthday was yesterday but nothing was popping so tonight, they were going to hit up cub City Lights and get faded. Then Friday they would head out to Dallas to relax at SpaCastle and go to a club that night. Alicia was taking a nap before getting up to get ready to go out with the ladies. She woke up to a barrage of texts from Trevion. She didn't even hear her phone going off. *I'm coming over. You gone open the garage. Ok Alicia. You got it mane. I understand.* He sent all of those one by one within an hour and a half. She told him that she had literally just woke up. He asked if he could come over. She told him truthfully that she was about to get ready to go to City Lights. He said he was shaking his head and said ok. She asked him why he was acting like that. She only wanted to have fun for her birthday. He told her to enjoy her night. Alicia had showered and spread her Victoria's secret

Love Spell lotion all over body. She wore White mesh t-shirt style dress with a black tank top and boy shorts underneath. She put on black open-toe boots that came all the way up past her knee to her thighs. She decked out her ensemble with silver accessories. Shamelle wasn't feeling well so she decided to stay home and save her energy for Dallas tomorrow. Talia had pulled up to Alicia's house to drop her daughter off. And Alicia's friend from back home named Courtlynn met them there. She had just moved here a few weeks ago and she wanted to get out and have some fun. She had also planned to come to Dallas with them. The three of them headed to the club together to meet up with Angel and her friend Aaliyah. Talia and Alicia rode together and Courtlynn drove her own car. When they got there Angela and her friend were already inside with a table for them. They immediately started drinking and turning up as soon as they all linked up. Somehow Stiggz and his friends spotted Alicia and her ladies and came over trying to spit game. Stiggz was talking out of his ass trying to get at Alicia. She was ignoring him and then Talia told him that Alicia was her woman. Stiggz asked she was her woman when Alicia was his. Then he looked at Alicia and said, "Ain't that right?" She laughed in his face and told him hell no! Talia laughed too. He started begging Alicia and Talia for a threesome. She dismissed him after that and the ladies went to the dancefloor. Alicia had gotten super wasted but she truly enjoyed partying with her ladies that night. They wanted to go eat at IHOP afterwards but Alicia was so faded that Talia had to drive. At IHOP the love didn't stop. Their server came over and told Alicia that a guy at another table sent a message that she was beautiful. Then he brought his ass over there trying get at her. He wasn't someone that Alicia would even consider but she wasn't a rude person at all so she held a friendly conversation with him until they left. She didn't know what time it was when they made it home but as soon as they got there she crashed.

When she woke up the next morning she was still tired and slightly hungover but she was ready for the trip to Dallas. She had been trying to get to SpaCastle since last summer and today she was finally going. All she thought about was their Aqua Bar. She showered, dressed in leggings and a t-shirt, and made sure she had everything packed. Talia was the first to make it to her house.

Shamelle showed up next followed by Angel. Courtlynn had hit Alicia up and let her know that she was getting a tune up and then would meet them in Dallas. They were just waiting on Shamlle's acquaintance named Kay. They were already an hour behind schedule waiting for her but they still gave her a little more time. She said that she was dropping her daughter off then would be on her way. Thirty minutes later she pulled with this sob story about her male friend hitting her and she only had $80 dollars because of some issue with bank fraud. Alicia felt bad for but not that bad. She could've told them all that before instead of them waiting for her to show up just to bail out. She wasted two hours of their time. Then on the drive there, they ran into traffic. Talia had driven her car and Shamelle rode with her. Alicia hopped in the car with Angel. She was going to stay the whole weekend there with her brother when Alicia, Talia, and Shamelle came back on Saturday. The drive to Dallas was cool though. Angel and Alicia were able to have a seriously deep conversation about men, love, motherhood, and even a little of their childhoods after Alicia left Alaska. Alicia knew that Angel had been through a lot and was battling all kinds of demons and depression. She also noticed that Angel had a bit of a drinking problem. She didn't judge her because she believed everybody had a story. Angel just made her want to help her and be there for here and continue to be a good friend. She was glad the she had introduced Angel to her circle of friends so that she would be around women with morals, goals, and standards that were also amazing mothers and some of the best friends she has ever had. Alicia didn't particularly like telling her inner most feelings and things has happened throughout her life with just anybody. If she divulged a lot of stuff then that meant she trusted you and deemed you be loyal and worthy enough to know all of her. There was only a handful of people that got that privilege. Talia, Shamelle, Ravyn, Cookie, Rick, Noise to an extent, and at one point in time Tika. After everything with Tika, Alicia was more cautious of how much she told to whom. So therefore even though she thought Angel might be worthy, she didn't know so she only told her things that could be a testimony for her. She talked about her past situation with Trevin and her feelings for him, she talked about Alton's dad, and she talked about she didn't really like Taylor but was trying to give him a chance.

Before they had made it to the hotel, Courtlynn called Alicia and basically flaked on the trip. She said something about her brother buying a car and leaving it parked somewhere because he doesn't know how to drive a stick so now she has to go help him find it. Alicia didn't know but she was leaving all bad thoughts behind because she just wanted to enjoy the trip with the ladies that made it. When they arrived at the hotel they were all thoroughly satisfied with the place that Alicia chose to stay at. The Renaissance Hotel was beautiful and even though Alicia was afraid of heights, she couldn't help but enjoy the ride in the glass elevator overlooking the lobby with beautiful water fountain and plants. The room was nice but it wasn't the room that Alicia had confirmed. She had checked with the hotel the night before to make sure the room had two beds and a sofa couch. Instead they only had one king size bed and a sofa couch. Then they told Alicia they didn't have any other rooms available that would accommodate the four of them better than the one they were already in. She was upset but she wasn't going to let it ruin her trip. They brought a roll away bed in. Angel and Alicia would take the king size bed, Shamelle would take the sofa couch, and Talia would take the roll away bed. She loved how her friends were such good sports and didn't complain just so that she could have a good time. After settling into the hotel the girls grabbed their swimsuits and headed out to eat. They found this smokehouse BBQ place in a beautiful shopping area. The food wasn't that great but it did the trick. They headed to SpaCastle and was blown away by how beautiful the building was from the parking lot. They couldn't wait to get inside. They had to lock their things away in two separate locker areas, they couldn't wear any outside clothes into the areas beyond a certain point, and they had undress in an open locker bay area in front of strangers and each other. It was weird. They had areas that you could only go in if you were naked. The entire spa looked exactly like the pictures. Even though it was kind of cool outside, all the water was heated. There was a beautiful cave outside with a waterfall of warm water. There were pools, hydrotherapy beds, Jacuzzis, anything you could think of relating to water. The water was not only warm, it was a beautiful blue green color. The ladies went straight to the bar and got frozen margaritas then headed to the pool in the middle of the bar. There were tables and chairs in the pool to sit at. It was so awesome. They stayed at SpaCastle for about

4 hours and once they felt super relaxed they headed back to the hotel for the night of turn up. The trip was turning out better than it seemed it would when the ladies had gotten on the road earlier. The ladies each showered and got dressed for the club. They were going to an upscale hip hop club with a dress code. The ladies had to be wearing heels. That was fine though because they always wore heel when they went out. Alicia opted for a black long sleeved body suit with a fringed leather skirt and black and gold wedges. She threw on some gold accessories to complement the shoes. The ladies all loved Alicia's outfit. That's one thing she was known for besides being cute and friendly, she was known for pushing the limits and making a statement with the way she chose to dress when they went out. She didn't dress for attention, she dressed in what she thought was cute and what would look cute on her. No matter how risqué some of her outfits were, she was a woman of class so an outfit that may look trashy on another female, looked a little more sophisticated on her. Alicia looked at her friends. Although they generally have different styles and things they liked to wear, they always looked good.

They headed out to the club. When they got there the parking lot was already full so they had the park in an area on the other side of the street. It was a three minute walk to the club from there but it seemed longer due to the crisp air and walking in heels. When they got to the door there was a line wrapped around the corner and a much shorter line that was VIP. They chose to pay a higher entry fee and go to the VIP. Unfortunately, they were not allowed in the club because Alicia's outfit didn't cover her whole butt. They went to a strip club instead. The strip club may have been dope as hell if they were drunk but since they were still pretty much sober, so to them it was ratchet. They had a few bad ass strippers but most of the ladies there looked a mess. The waitress left with Angel's debit card and they had to go find her to get it back. There was an old man that wouldn't stop trying to holler at them. Then there was a lazy ass stripper that went from stage to stage literally laying down and only moving one ass cheek for the entire song. It was a complete mess but it was good for some laughs. The ladies left after only spending about an hour in there. They got some Taco Bell, went back to the room and crashed. The next morning after checking out they went to Waffle House for breakfast and then said goodbye to Angel and got back on the road to Killeen. When they made it back, Alicia showered and took a nap. She was exhausted.

Chapter 70

Alicia hadn't talked to Trevion since Thursday went she went to City Lights with the ladies. He didn't call or text her so she didn't call her text. She just wanted to enjoy her birthday without any drama or fighting. Taylor hit up her but she didn't want to talk to him so she kept it short. She lied and told him that she was going out with the ladies tonight for the final night of her birthday weekend celebration. She had no intentions on going out at all. She really just wanted to relax and she didn't want to be bothered with him at all. Alicia woke up from her nap after she got back and saw that she had a text from Trevion. A big smile broke out across her face. He missed her.

It would be life to go to the duck pond and talk. It's okay though. Continue to be great.

Her smile disappeared. Why did he have to be so petty instead of just telling her he missed her? He got on her nerves when he did that. *You know, you could've just asked me that...instead of being sarcastic and throwing shade.*

I didn't know if you were busy. He replied.

She was almost going to dig into him but she didn't want to argue and she knew why he was acting like that. She just decided to keep the peace. Besides she missed him, too. *You should have asked...and you really didn't have to say "continue to be great".*

So what are you doing? He asked her.

At the current moment nothing.

Can I come see you?

I thought you wanted to go to the duck pond and talk.

He replied quickly. *Either or, I just wanna see you.*

That made her smile again. *I can come to the duck pond for a little bit.*

Okay let me know when you're about to leave your house.

Five minutes later she was on her way to meet him. He pulled up right behind her. It had just turned into night so Alicia didn't want to walk around the pond and startle the ducks. They sat on a bench near the front area looking out at the pond. He just looked at her for a minute. He had this young boy smile on his face. He told her he missed her and he really just wanted to see her beautiful smile. She blushed. He made her feel awesome. They talked about nothing in particular, they cracked jokes. He was being silly and making her laugh. He really showed her how much he missed her and enjoyed her company. He repeatedly told her that he missed her. She couldn't stop smiling. That was the most fun that they had together without any type of fussing or attitudes on a long time. They had only been there for about 30 minutes when the campus police came over and told them the pond was closed. He had told them that once it gets dark then they shut it down from visitors. He kept them out there for about ten minutes talking to them about the snakes that are in and around the pond. He warned them to be careful and keep a good distance from the water especially during the summer because they are out in abundance then. They thanked him then Trevion walked Alicia to her car. He gave her a hug and a kiss on the cheek then they parted ways.

At home Alicia couldn't stop thinking about him. She missed him and that thirty minutes wasn't enough for her. She called him.

"I had fun." She told him as soon as he answered.

She could hear his smile in his voice. "Well you're welcome."

"You didn't?" she asked.

"I did."

She didn't really have anything to talk about but she was going to keep talking to him. "You going out?"

"No ma'am. Not really in the mood. I'm not feeling it." He said sounding like he had somethings on his mind.

"When was the last time you went out?"

"I can't even tell you honestly."

"Mmmhhmm....Then what do you be doing?"

He paused. "Chilling for real."

"What are you doing?"

"I'm at King's house chilling with TC."

She nodded her head as if he could see her. "Oh. Okay. What are y'all doing over there?"

"Just talking about 99 different topics with TC, Lady D, and AP." She was surprised that he was really answering every single question with more than just one word. She asked him what time he was going to bed. He told her he didn't know but probably soon because it was so boring.

"Wanna come hang out with me for a little bit?" She asked him sweetly.

"Yea I can."

She rolled her eyes. "I didn't say can you, I asked if you wanted to."

"Do you want my company? That is the question."

"Why would I ask?" She said smartly.

"I'm coming bae." He said 10 minutes before he was in her driveway.

Alicia already showered and put on a nightshirt when she came from the duck pond earlier so Trevion came in she had on a short gray t-shirt gown with splits on the side. The back of the gown said boy bye. She wore it with no underwear. He was instantly turned on when he saw her but he kept it cool and tried not to be all over her. He wanted to watch Harlem nights so she popped the DVD in for him and lay down next to him in her bed. They talked a little bit during the movie and stole little touches of each other here and there. About an hour into the movie and them playing and wrestling, Alicia got up to go use the bathroom. When she came out he was laying on his stomach at the foot of the bed closer to the TV. She climbed on the bed and lay on her side next to him. She put her hand under his shirt and began caressing his back. His skin was so soft. "Baby can you give me a back rub, please?" He asked her. She was happy to oblige. She sat up and straddled him. She lifted his shirt and began running both hands across his back. She loved the way his back looked and the way his skin felt. Rubbing his back was putting her in a mood. She could tell it was doing the same for him but he was trying to behave. He wanted her to initiate things tonight. So she did just that. She didn't know what this strong feeling was that was urging her to kiss his back but she didn't try to fight it. She began placing a trail of soft, gentle kisses on his lower back, traveling up his spine with each kiss. She heard him let out a moan. She tried to kiss every inch of his back. She planted kisses on the sides, in the middle, on the lower area, across his shoulder blades and even his neck. She leaned up and lightly bit his right ear. Then she caressed the right side of his face ever so gently with her left cheek. He closed his eyes and used his cheek to caress back. She kissed his face, then the side of his mouth. He turned his head to meet her lips with his lips. They kissed softly. She used her tongue to trace his bottom lip, then she bit it, and tugged and pulled on it. He slipped his tongue out of his mouth and into hers. Alicia wasn't teasing him, she was ready and wanting him so badly. "Turn over." She whispered in his ear. She got off of him and lay on her side next to him so that he could do as she requested. He looked at her. "Touch me." She said. He sprang into action and took control from there. She saw the print of his manhood standing at attention through his sweatpants. She licked her lips. He begin rubbing his hands down the side of her body. From her shoulder, down her arm, down her waist, over her hips, caressed her thigh, then back up squeezing her ass. He pulled her closer to him so that she could feel his penis against her clitoris. He kissed her so deeply. He parted her lips with his tongue and before she knew it he was on top of her, grinding slowly, sucking and biting her neck. He lifted her shirt and began to play with the nipple of one breast with his fingers while licking and sucking the nipple of the other breast. He was driving her crazy. She wanted him so bad. She snatched off his shirt and helped him out of his sweatpants and boxer briefs. They were skin to skin now, just how Alicia liked it. He slid down her body, planting a trail of kisses as he went further down. He licked her clit once, then looked up at her. He did it again. And then he did it again. He was teasing her. "Stop playing." She said to him through her shallow breathing. He smiled with his lips up against her vaginal lips. Then he dove in. He ate her box and slurped up every ounce of juice that came from her. She was yearning for him to be inside of her. She couldn't wait anymore. She wanted it now. Alicia pushed his head up from between her thighs and reached into her nightstand for a condom. She handed him the magnum and watched as he rolled it on. She lay back and spread her legs for him. He slid right in with one forceful thrust and she gasped. Her breath was caught in her throat. He covered her mouth with his, and the deep kissing began again. Between kisses he whispered repeatedly that he missed her. He was stroking her so deep, yet so slow. It was agony, yet it was so much pleasure. He moaned in her ear and told her he loved her, so she began tightening the muscles of her vagina around his penis as she threw it back at him. He leaned back a little so that he could look her in the eyes. It was as if that was the final element that they needed that night because as soon as he looked deep into her eyes she came so suddenly and so beautifully. Not even 15 seconds later he was coming right behind her, hard. He let out a deep growl as he exploded and released all of his juices into the condom. She was glad she made him put on a condom, she didn't think he would've been able to pull out fast enough that time. He went limp inside of her and his "Bama Hamma" as he called it, slid out. He took off the condom and went to throw it in the trashcan in her bathroom. When he came out Alicia was still laying in the same spot and hadn't moved at all. She was damn near asleep. He crawled into the bed next her, and pulled her to lay on his chest. They fell asleep, both naked, with their legs intertwined. After a whole year, the love was still there.

Chapter 71

Trevion left Alicia's house at around 9 the next morning. He had only been gone for a couple of hours when he called her. She smiled when she saw his number pop up. "Morning." he said when she answered as if he didn't just leave her house that morning. "Good morning." she replied.

"Last night was different." he told her.

She cocked her head to one side. "How so?"

"You were kissing on me. I felt at home."

"You never felt at home with me before?" she asked him.

"Not with the kisses down my back and shit. I loved that." He said remembering the details of it.

Alicia smiled. "I know you did."

"My dick got so hard thinking about last night."

"Oh yeah?" She laughed at his frankness. "Why is that?"

"I want another round."

Alicia protested. "Nooooo. Savor the moment. Too much is never a good thing."

He countered her claim. "It wasn't enough. I didn't want to nut to just yet."

"So why did you?"

He laughed. "I couldn't hold that mother fucka! You too good for your own good."

"I didn't even do anything though." She said, faking modesty.

"I wanna hit you from the back. Smack your ass and pull your hair." He said seriously.

Alicia bit her lip at the thought of that. "So in other words, you wanna fuck me."

"Yes ma'am."

"Mmmm, what did I tell you about that?" she asked him.

"You don't fuck, I know."

"What did we do last night?"

He let out a lighthearted chuckle. "We made love."

She giggled a little. "Oh that's funny?

"It's funny because I'm the one who said so." he told her.

"Mmm ok. You loved it though. You were all into it. Feelings and all." She said teasing him.

HE teased back. "And you were too. You love this dick. You love when I slang this dick at you." He said trying to sound seductive. "You started it though."

"I didn't deny that I was into it. And I do not love the dick. I care for the person that it's attached to." She made sure to clarify that. "And I know I started it, you were actually behaving."

He came back at her. "I always behave baby girl. You sent chills down my spine with those kisses. I don't know whether to feel good or gay."

Alicia cracked up laughing. "I really can't deal with your ass."

"With the soft ass lips." He continued.

"You missed me." She was telling him that he did, not asking if he did.

"I did." He told her truthfully.

"You know how many times you told me that last night. And not just during sex either."

"It's the truth."

"I believe you." And she meant it.

Alicia was having an awesome Sunday. Her birthday weekend celebration was wonderful and being with Trevion on Saturday night was the best ending. She had cleaned up her house and she and Shamelle, had taken the kids to the Park at MTM for some quality time. While she was there annoying ass Taylor hit her up begging to see her that evening. She told him yeah but of course she would have much rather have had Trevion there with her. After they made it home the kids ate dinner and bathed, she let them play the PS4 for a half an hour and then it was time for bed. She didn't like allowing Taylor to come over while the kids were up. One reason was because she didn't want them seeing someone that she was pretty sure she wasn't going to keep around. The other reason was because they loved Trevion and even though there was no affection between him and Alicia in front of them, he was a man she allowed to be around and they could see the feelings for each other.

Alicia allowed Taylor to come over a little after 9. She was sleepy and she really just wanted to go to bed but of course he talked her ear off about shit that she didn't give a fuck about at all. He thought he was slick though. He knew she was ready to go to sleep so he tried to talk to keep her awake in hopes of getting some sex. That wasn't going to happen. When he tried to kiss her she pulled away. He got the hint and stopped trying. They lay down. It was weird how she could never fall into a heavy sleep with him in her bed, no matter how sleepy she was. The slightest movement or sound, whether it came from him or outside, always woke her up. But when it came to Trevion, unless they were fighting or mad at each other, she slept soundly for hours. Maybe it was because she wholeheartedly trusted Trevion because she knew him and she knew how he was. She didn't really trust Taylor, in fact she was very suspicious of him and she didn't know why. As she lay down and tried to close her eyes she got a text message. She didn't bother to grab her phone. A little less than an hour later, she got another one. When she looked at her phone they were both from Trevion. *Another back rub would be life. Bet don't worry about it.*

Alicia sighed. She hated that things were so complicated, but she knew she allowed the complications. *Please don't be like that.* She pleaded with him. He didn't respond.

The next morning he still hadn't responded, so she text him going off. *Get a back rub from whatever female you were with last night...or whomever you be talking to...you are still up to the same shit.*

I definitely stayed in the house last night but ok. He texted. She knew he was lying.

Exactly...you definitely stayed in the house last night with some chick...probably cuddled up and fucking.

He texted back fast. *At King house. Stop Assuming. I would have been at your house but you was probably with ya boyfriend and didn't answer or text me back.* He replied.

That kind of hit a nerve for her. *Oh you were fucking at King's house...got it. And I did text you back but whatever.*

Okay Alicia you got it SMH. He tried to end the argument.

Alicia went in. *You can say so much shit but you can't be real enough or man enough to admit that you went to Nikki last night? Do really think I'm that damn stupid? What the fuck is the point in you being in my life if you're not going to do anything but do the same shit that you did before? I will never understand why a person likes to fuck over and hurt people like you do smh.*

He wasn't fazed by anything that she had said. *Like you can't admit that you have a boyfriend? Oh ok.*

Unlike you I didn't sit up there and tell a fucking lie. You flat out lied my nigga but what the fuck ever. Go back to her ass, keep fucking her, have more babies, enjoy that fucked up ass relationship y'all got. Niggas don't even know how to tell the fucking truth....but swear you grew up and changed and then wonder why I don't believe shit...smh. She ended her rant with an emoji giving the peace sign.

That rant however, only caused him to come back at her as well. *I didn't lie about a bitch ass thang. I'm not going back to nobody. I'm going to remain SINGLE. You don't have to believe shit I say. You wouldn't be the first person to tell me that. And I have grown up. If you would answer my questions that I ask you, you wouldn't have nothing to worry about.*

That was his argument...because she didn't answer his stupid ass question. She noticed that he didn't deny having sex with her or any other female, though. She was done fighting. *I'm not worried about anything but like I said you did lie. Your ass was with Nikki last night and you just lied and said you weren't but whatever, you can remain single or remain a hoe...you make it to where a muthafucka don't believe you cause ya ass don't know how to be honest. But once again, you got that...do you.*

Alicia turned her phone on silent and went about the rest of her day at work without even picking it up. If someone needed to contact her in regards to an emergency they had her work number. She was tired of bullshit. Alicia left work and headed to go pick up the kids. She turned the ringer back on her cell and noticed that she had a bunch of text messages and a couple of missed calls. The texts and calls were from Ravyn, Talia, her mother, and her sister. Trevion had sent her a text almost every hour.

11am-What you mean "do you"? You cutting me off or something?

12:04-No reply?

12:56-Baby

2:44-Alicia

4:16-I see that you don't want anything to do with me anymore so I'll leave you alone.

Alicia was so twisted after reading the texts. She didn't want him to leave her alone but she was so afraid of history repeating itself. She just wanted to be able to love him without any extra drama or issues. Without any worried about getting hurt or looking or stupid. She knew it wasn't right to dwell on the negative things in the past when he was showing her so much better now but fear would not let her give in to him or her heart. Then keeping Taylor around wasn't helping their situation either. She sighed and put her game face back on. *I don't want someone constantly lying to me for no reason at all...enjoy Nikki.* She finally responded at 5:08.

Whatever dog.

You're the dog...but ok liar.

Not a dog nor a liar.

Alicia didn't respond, so he sent another text. *I thought you loved me.*

And I thought you loved me...guess that was dumb on my part.

Call me. He asked. She didn't see that text until she got out of the shower about thirty minutes later. She called him but he didn't answer. She texted him and asked him to call her. He didn't respond. She texted him again 45 minutes later and asked where he was. He told her at King's house. She was mad that she hadn't gotten a response or a call back for an hour and a half so she was back on attitude mode. *Oh you were with your girlfriend at King's house so you took an hour and a half to respond?*

I am single. Stop saying that shit. It's fucking aggravating.

I don't care if its aggravating...you shouldn't still be living with her and fucking her and maybe I wouldn't say it...smh good night. Alicia didn't believe the things she said to him. She didn't believe that he was still messing with Nikki and she knew for a fact that even he paid the rent at the apartment that he used to share with Nikki, he didn't live there. He moved out when they broke up in November and has been living with King. She only said these things to get a rise out of him sometimes. She didn't really know why she did it though.

She lives in MY apartment so ok. You're so childish mane. It's ridiculous. You don't even know what's going on and just be talking. If you have a problem for me to keep a roof over my child's head then you can stop fucking with me right now. And you have a whole boyfriend so you should be the last person to say anything about what I do. He really tried to check her but she wasn't having it.

She typed up a long response in less than ten seconds and went in. *I don't give a fuck if it is YOUR apartment muthafucka...it was Y'ALL apartment when y'all were together...she still lives there now so Y'ALL still live together...and stop trying to make it like I have a problem with you making sure your son has a place to live muthafucka...him having a place to live doesn't mean your ass has to live there too and it definitely doesn't mean you had to run to her last night so shut the fuck up with that...but since you can't stop fucking with her, you can stop fucking with me...now you don't have to lie about who you fucking with. Enjoy your night since I'm so childish and every other night too.*

She didn't think he would respond. She thought that was the end of the conversation and them as well. It wasn't. She was starting to think that he liked when she went off on him.

9:05pm-So are you done with me?

9:12-Hello

9:20-So you're going to be a little girl and not respond?

Are you going to be a little ass boy and not tell the truth? She texted back twenty minutes later. He called her.

"Nope." He said.

Alicia was confused. "Nope what?"

"To your question."

"What are you saying no to? No you're not going to tell me the truth?" She was trying to clarify but he was trying to change the subject.

"Are you done fucking with me?"

"Are you going to tell the truth?" She didn't know why he thought he was going to flip it back that easy. He knew she was a big ass kid and he knew she could do this all night. He got quiet. "Didn't think so." She said. "Good night." She was about to hang up in his face when she heard him say yes. "Okay I'm listening."

"What bae?"

"Truth." Was all that she said to him.

"About what?"

She groaned. "Never mind." He was trying to act stupid and she was sleepy and didn't have time for his shit.

"Can I come over?" he asked.

"My house is a mess and I'm sleepy." she said truthfully.

"So Leon."

"So what?"

He exhaled. "Your house or you being sleepy."

"Okay." she said feeling drained.

"Huh?" he asked.

Alicia shook her head. "What you asked."

He thought she was asking him what he said so he repeated. "Can I come over?"

"I gave you an answer."

His mood lifted. "Okay. Let me shower right quick."

"See you gotta do all this extra stuff and I'm sleepy." She complained thinking he was going to take 30 minutes or longer.

"I'll be there soon."

"You got 15 minutes." She told him and hung up. Twelve minutes later he texted her was on the way. Eight minutes after that she heard the loud music from his car as he was pulling into her driveway. As soon as he came in they went straight to the bed, he let her have her side of the bed without a fight and they were dead to the world.

Chapter 72

Alicia had recently quit working so that she could go back to school full time. She had one class online and 3 lecture classes. The lectures were only an hour and fifteen minutes long twice a week. Tuesdays she only had one class in the morning and nothing else for the rest of the day. When Trevion left her house to go to PT this morning it was an hour before she actually needed to be up so she laid back down. Not even fifteen minutes after he had walked out of her door he was calling her. He told her he she was lucky he let her get some sleep last night. She started laughing. "Boy go to work."

"You should've let me eat it." He said.

She was not about to play with him this morning. "I'm trying to sleep Trevion." She said playfully.

"So. I'm hungry."

She sighed dramatically. "Do not start that."

"I'm for real."

"I know you are." He had talked to her until it was time for her to get out of bed. She was still so sleepy. She went about her morning routine of making sure the kids were up and doing what they needed to do. Kyle woke up first before everybody else, every day. He would make his own breakfast then go about his morning rituals. Alicia always woke up Alton and Tekerri. Then Tekerri would make the both of them breakfast while Alicia supervised Alton in the shower. He had to shower everyone because he the wet the bed almost every night. She brushed her teeth and pulled her back into a single braid. Alicia didn't feel alert enough to sit in class today so she decided that she would just go and turn in her assignment then leave. She had planned to come back home and get back in bed. Trevion told her to let him know if she did that because he wanted to come lay down and go to sleep too. She ended up going to Walmart to get invitations for Alton's birthday party that was coming up on Saturday. As she was heading to the checkout line Trevion texted her. *When are you going home?*

Bout 20 minutes.

Am I invited or nah?

Yeah. She texted him as she was driving into her garage to let him know that she was home. She looked in her rearview mirror and saw that he was pulling up right behind. She smiled. She hopped out of her car as he walked up and grabbed the bags from her backseat. After she used the bathroom, she crawled into bed with him. They were laying on their sides facing each other. One of his arms was under her head and the other was wrapped around her waist. He was lightly stroking her back as she played with his chin and cheek. He kissed her forehead then just stared at her. She loved when he did that. The way he looked so deep into her eyes as if he was able to see in her soul and read her heart. She smiled and kissed him on the lips. They talked for a few minutes about nothing at all but she was truly sleepy and couldn't keep her eyes open for much longer. He was still awake when started snoring lightly. The alarm on his phone went off at 12:15 and jarred them both from their nap. He had to leave to go pick up his son. She loved that he was so involved in his son's life. It saddened her that he was no longer able to be a part of his other son life. Alicia didn't know the full details of what happened but when she asked about how his other son was doing he said he didn't know and then he mentioned something about his son's mother just started tripping a little after his new baby was born. She felt bad for him because she knew how much he loved kids, especially his own.

Later that evening after Alicia had gotten home she attempted to get the kids settled in and cook dinner. She had to pack their lunches and iron their clothes for tomorrow. On top of that she had to finish folding laundry and get Alton's birthday invitations filled out so that he could give them to his classmates tomorrow. She was overwhelmed. She was annoyed. She was tired. She was cranky. And, she was missing Trevion. He would always help her with things without her even having to ask. If he was there he would check to see if she had ironed and packed lunches already and if she didn't because she was being lazy he wouldn't talk to her until she did. He wanted her to be able to sleep longer in the morning instead of having to get up and rush to do those things. She really wanted him to come over that night but she had already agreed to Taylor coming by. He had been texting her earlier and she didn't know how it was possible to be annoying through text messages but he definitely was. She was making random small talk with him so she told him that she was going to have a ladies night on Thursday. He asked what they were going to be doing. Talia had suggested that they go to the Vault Lounge for their poetry night. He didn't even acknowledge what she said, which was something that he did often. Instead, he made a dumb comment trying to be funny, but it wasn't funny. In the same text, he tried portray himself to just have so much money. He still wasn't understanding even after her telling him so many times that she didn't care about money because she had her own. He thought that would make her want him but, it actually made him even more unattractive to her.

He texted her. *Me and the guys going to a twerk contest Thursday night and I'm going to take about 3 grand with me.*

Alicia rolled her eyes in annoyance. *Okay have fun.*

Are you sure you going there with the girls? You sure you not going on a date with some guy?

Anyway, I have to go run my friend a plate of this food I cooked real quick.

He replied. *Okay what time can I come? And you took your man some food huh?*

830 is fine. The kids will be in bed. That was all she said to him. She was trying to ignore his comments but he kept saying little slick shit like that then want to say he was playing. Alicia didn't think the shit was funny.

Alicia had fried some chicken wings and made homemade mashed potatoes and macaroni and cheese with some cornbread. She made a big plate and wrapped it up in aluminum foil to take to Trevion. She met up with him at the 7Eleven gas station across from Shoemaker High School. She could tell he wanted to ask her why she met up with him to bring him a plate instead letting him come over to eat. He didn't ask though and she was thankful for it. She didn't get out of the car. He walked over and opened her passenger side door and leaned in. He told her to give him a kiss. She obliged. She handed him the plate of food and they went their separate ways. She could tell by the look on his face that wanted to spend time with her. She wished she could. By the time she made it back home he texted her saying thanks for the plate and told her it was delicious. She joked that he probably didn't eat it. Taylor showed up at about 845 while Alicia was folding laundry and listening to music. She was visibly tired as evidence by the bags and dark circles under her eyes. She opened the door for him and he followed her into her bedroom where New Edition's If It Isn't Love was playing on her radio from her phone. She was in an old school music mood. Listening to music help her focus on doing what needed to do and getting done faster. He walked in and immediately started with the dumb ass comments. "Oh you're in her listening to these love songs thinking your other man huh?" he said smiling. She rolled her eyes. She hoped he didn't think he was her man. He went over to the TV and began to put on a movie. She looked at him. "Um, I'm listening to music right now." she said. He had the nerve to ask if she could turn it off. She told him no. She realized that she was being very rude so she tried to compromise. "Listening to music helps me get done with my stuff faster. When I get finished with this then I will turn the music off and we can watch a movie. If you help me fill out Alton's invitations then it will be faster." He looked at her and shook his head no then started laughing at sat down on the floor and proceeding to watch the movie. Alicia was in disbelief. She told him not to turn the volume up because she wasn't done listening to her music. Talia and Shamelle had already been texting Alicia in their group chat so she told them what had just happened. They didn't care for much him already as it was but now they were just as annoyed as she was with him. Her phone kept going off and the sound was annoying her so she put it on vibrate. Taylor started trying to rub against her but she turned away. He then tried to kiss her neck but dodged him. He then started making about another guy again. She had begun to feel as if had driven by her house and saw Trevion's car there or something. Or maybe her sister's truck. She remembered how he was so interested in knowing what kind of car each of her friends drove especially the ones that she would hang out with the most which was Ravyn, Talia, Shamelle, and Angel. He wanted to know who would be at her house when he stalked her at certain times. "If you were dealing with another guy while we were in a relationship would you tell me?" He asked her.

"If we were in a relationship I wouldn't be dealing with another guy but yeah I would tell you." She answered.

"No you wouldn't." he said.

"Okay." she responded not really caring if he believed her.

He began talking nonsense about how other guys ain't no good but he is honest and don't cheat and he isn't worried about females or anybody in Killeen and he wants to be with her. Alicia just looked at him. He wasn't making sense and it was obvious now that he was a liar and narcissistic person. Alicia sat on her bed with her back against the headboard and tuned him out. She was deep in her group text with Talia and Shamelle. Trevion had texted her and asked what she was doing but she wouldn't disrespect him by texting him while this idiot was at her house rubbing her feet and trying to suck her toes. She kept pulling her foot back from him he kept trying to grab to grab it and touch her in various places. She was getting upset and she felt disgusted by his touch. He had finally caught the hint and stopped trying to touch her, but then he became upset. He started going off telling her that she thinks he is stupid and think he doesn't know that she is fucking with all of her guy friends. He was carrying on about how he was sure anyone of the guys that be in her inbox would love to be with her and he don't hate a guy over some pussy, even used that old ass phrase that he doesn't hate he congratulates. Alicia was trying to hold in her laughter because she was elated that his crazy ass had flipped out for no reason so now she had a reason to be rid of him. She was calm and cool when she looked him in the face and told him to get out of her house. He was still talking mad noise as he walked out of the door and she didn't even bother to respond to him. He told her she wasn't shit as she closed the door in his face. As she walked back in her room she couldn't help but to get a little vexed because she had actually tried to give this lame annoying ass nigga a chance and he turned out to be crazy and insecure as fuck. She picked up her phone to call Ravyn and saw that Talia was texting her and Trevion had texted her and said goodnight. She Texted him back first and told him that she was filling out Alton's birthday invites and putting his gifts together then she told him good night. He sent her the kissing emoji and she sent him one back. Next she texted Talia and was telling her about what had just gone down with Taylor, at the same time she was talking on the phone with Ravyn telling her what had happened as well. Taylor sent a flood of texts to her phone at one time...every single text was crazy and he didn't make not a bit of sense.

All your male friends choose one of them and I hope they make you happy. I'm good hope you have a good life. You just like all the other females, U ain't shit tell all the niggas that want you they can have you I'm good. I'm pretty sure he will be over so he can fuck your ass tonight hope u enjoy and wish you nothing but the best. All those guys you cool with u think I'm stupid think I don't know u fucking with those niggas Alicia just tell the truth please. After sending all of those messages and not getting a response from Alicia he called her. "What?" She said calmly.

"You think I'm stupid. You ain't shit. You ju-." He got cut off by Alicia telling him not to call her again and then she hung up in his face. He tried calling back but she didn't answer. So his series of text messages began again. *Enjoy your niggas I'm done.* She laughed because he was saying he was done like they were in a relationship and she was begging him to stay or something. She didn't even fuck with him on that level. He was delusional but she was clap back if he didn't stop talking shit. She text him a simple response. *Smh, just smh...you are really insecure...go get some help because you are really fucked up.* She was still trying to be a little nice to him but he wanted to keep on with the bullshit.

I'm not fucked up I'm not stupid but u cool with your ex someone u was fucking get the hell out of here I'm good enjoy your life...Hope he makes you happy cause I never hate a guy over some pussy...do you and find that guy that can put up with your ways. Alicia didn't bother responding or answering the phone when he called yet again, it was a waste of time and energy for someone and a situation that she gave no fucks about. She lay down in her bed and snuggled up to her pillow wishing that Trevion was there. Just as she had that thought of him she got a text message. She almost didn't open it thinking it was Taylor still texting but she did. And she had the biggest smile ever on her face.

It was from Trevion. *I can't sleep so I hope you are sleeping enough for me. I'm just up thinking about you. You do something to me. I can't get enough of you.*

Alicia thought that was so sweet. She asked him what he was thinking about. He said just her all around, but specifically her trash ass sense of humor. Alicia laughed and told him he was hater and that she was funny as shit. He told her that she look funny as shit. She said she knew he was going to tell that lie and he said she has never seen her face during sex. She laughed. They said their goodnights and Alicia went to sleep with a huge smile on her face.

Chapter 73

Alicia woke up the next day feeling refreshed and in a good mood. She saw that she had new text messages. She was thinking that they were from Trevion but they weren't. They were messages that Taylor had sent after she had fallen asleep. He was still going off because last night during their argument she had told him that he was liar. She had caught him up in some of the dumbest lies. He had told her that he was in a relationship when he was in Tennessee and that it didn't work out because she was very jealous. He said that one of his female co-workers had called him one night while they were in bed asleep because she thought she saw his car at the store. He claimed that his girlfriend went off on him even after he had the female friend on speaker phone. The next time he told her a story he said that he had met this female teacher here in Killeen and that she had a crush on him but they never dated or did anything sexual. He said she had a cookout at her house and he was there and that he was cool with one of the other guys that were there. That part had nothing to do with the story though so Alicia didn't know why he had even told her that. He claimed that he had fell asleep on her couch and that a female co-worker had called him in the middle of the night because she thought she saw his car at the store (sounds familiar right?) and the woman who had the crush on him went off him because of that. When Alicia called him about the two stories he looked her right in her face and denied that he had told her the story about the girlfriend in Tennessee. She told him exactly what he said to her and he still denied. When she asked how he was in a relationship in Tennessee when he said that his last relationship was with his daughter's mother and it ended 8 years ago he switched up again saying the female in Tennessee wasn't his girlfriend and that they were just starting to date. He then tried to laugh it off and say that he was probably drunk when he told her the first story. Alicia just looked him. She felt that if he would lie about some stuff that stupid and simple then there was really know telling what else he was lying about. She would ask him questions and he either would allude to the answer or flat out tell a lie that didn't make sense or sound convincing. When she would call him out on his lies or his superior attitude that he had, his favorite response was always "you can think what you want." or "I know what I be doing or I know what I got." and in her mind she would be thinking *yeah nigga YOU know but I don't*. She got to the point where she had decided she was going to get to the bottom of his lies. One night Talia had invited her and Shamelle over for dinner. Talia was seeing a new guy and she wanted them to meet him and hang out. Shamelle brought her boyfriend Mitch, because they were all friends and always did stuff together. Alicia had known Shamelle's boyfriend for about as long as she has known Shamelle, years. When Talia's new guy couldn't make it for dinner, Shamelle had asked Alicia to bring Taylor along so that Mitch would have someone to talk to besides them. Alicia didn't want to but she did for them. As the guys were outside talking and drinking, Alicia took the opportunity to fill the ladies in on everything. She had told him about trying to kick Taylor to curb. They said that they already knew that she didn't like him very much and they could that his presence just annoyed her. She told them about his suspicious stories, behaviors, and attitudes. She told them all about his lies and he would get in his feelings when she called him out on them. Then she told them about her suspicions about his name and what happened when they went to Chili's. They were all in agreement that she needed to find out the deal. She told them she had come up with a plan. "I'm going to go buy a little cheap greeting card from the dollar tree and write a message like 'thinking of you' or some superficial shit like that in it. Y'all know he keeps his wallet in the car so while he is asleep I'm going to act like I'm going to wake Alton for the bathroom but I'm going to take his keys and go look in his car at his ID card."

Shamelle was little bit on the blonde side sometimes so while Talia understood every element of the plan, Shamelle had a question. "So what is the card for?" She asked.

Talia and Alicia laughed. "It's for me to take and put in his car when I go check his wallet."

Shamelle still was confused. "Okay...but why?"

Alicia broke it down for her. "If he wakes up while I'm doing it and I didn't find anything suspicious then how will I explain what I was doing in his car in the middle of the night while he was asleep?" She paused. Shamelle didn't answer so she continued. "I'll put the card in there so it will look like I was trying to surprise him with a sweet gesture."

"Ooooohhhh, okay." Shamelle laughed. "Smart plan lady."

Just then Mitch had come back in for another beer. Taylor was still outside. Mitch cracked a couple of jokes that had the ladies laughing. Talia asked him what he thought of Taylor.

At first Mitch seemed hesitant to answer. "Well I mean he seems kinda cool." he looked up towards the ceiling as if he was thinking about something. "He has a lot of cars." He paused again. "He talk too much about what he has. Like he brags and all he seems to talk about is materialistic stuff and money."

Alicia jumped up and shouted out. "Exactly!" She had been saying that about him and it was a real big turn off but he thought it made him look better to others. He was awkward in social settings and she was hoping that her investigation proved that he was a liar so that she could be done with him. He had told so many different lies and stories that it would take a month for Alicia to tell them all. Mitch went back out to talk to Taylor and the ladies resumed their conversation.

Shamelle asked Alicia about Trevion. "So how are things with you and Tre Will?"

Alicia smiled. "Y'all know how I feel about that man. We fight and argue and go days without talking. He's stubborn. I'm stubborn. But no matter what we always find our way back. He is the one guy that just touches every part of me inside and out."

They both looked at her like she was about to have an orgasm right at Talia's table. They knew the history of their situation including all of the drama with Nikki. Ironically, Trevion and Nikki lived in a duplex on the same street as Talia before they got evicted and had to move into the apartment that they were in now.

Talia spoke. "I know how you feel. Y'all are funny though. Some of the stories you be telling us about y'all be having me dying laughing."

"So I have a question." Shamelle said. "Do you think Tre Will is the reason why you don't like Taylor?"

Alicia took her time answering. "Ravyn asked me that one day too, after I had told her he was annoying me. But no that's not reason why. I don't like Taylor because he has the attitude that he is superior to others and he talks down about other guys yet he is a liar, temperamental, and just all out annoying as hell. Trevion, even though he can be an asshole sometimes, is actually the sweetest asshole you will ever meet. We have gone through all that shit but he has shown me who he is. I know his good and bad and I never have to question if he will be there if I need him. I can't say the same for Taylor because he has already shown he is not dependable. Trevion is a people person even though he tries to act like he's not. My kids love him. When he compliments me or tells me sweet things I know it's genuine and not just cause he wants something. He isn't always trying to be all over me or trying to get sex from but he gives just the right amount of affection. Taylor be trying to get some and is always trying to touch my ass like I have to literally tell him to stop touching me. His touch makes my skin crawl. If anything Trevion is the reason why I even gave Taylor's lame ass a chance in the first place." She had said all of that to them in less two minutes.

Shamelle made an observation. "It's seems as though you compare Taylor to Tre Will a lot."

"Yeah, I noticed that too." Talia agreed. "But how is Trevion the reason you gave Taylor a chance?"

"Well I do compare Taylor to Trevion. To be honest I compare every guy that I dated after Trevion to him. If they don't make me feel the way he does then or more than he does then why bother? Trevion was mad at me but I called him and asked him to come help fill out Valentine's Day cards for the kids. He came over right away with no questions and he did almost all of them. Taylor sat and watched me fill out Alton's birthday invitations and when I asked him to help he said no. Trevion always thinks about me and my well-being even with the simplest things such as getting enough sleep or getting to class on time. He remembers things that I say and takes the time to learn my likes and dislikes and my temperaments. And he does so much more than that. If a guy can't or doesn't do even half of that then I don't want them." she told them.

"Yeah, I get that." Shamelle said.

Talia asked again. "So how is he the reason that you gave Taylor a chance, with his annoying ass." They all laughed.

Alicia replied. "It's simple really. I'm afraid to give my heart to Trevion again. I'm trying to keep him at a distance even though I really love the shit out of him. But he is going to Germany for two years and he hurt me so badly before that I don't want to give him all that again. So, I felt like talking to Taylor until he leaves will help me keep that distance and protect my heart." She stopped talking and pondered what she just said. "I don't really know if that made any sense." They all laughed. The rest of that night went smoothly.

Alicia had recalled all of that as she sat reading the texts from Taylor. He kept texting her back to back. The shit he was saying was laughable.

I don't need you or any other female I'm good I hope you and one of your so called male friends get together and be happy. I'm sure one of them that's always in your inbox will love to be with you. Alicia wasn't responding so he called her. She didn't answer her so he started texting her again. *I was just calling to confirm so we are done right?*

We were not in a relationship Taylor. Idk why you are asking if we are done like we are breaking up. We were only talking but to answer your question yes I'm done talking to you. I was trying to give you a chance but you got too much shit with you for real. Even though she couldn't stand him, Alicia was not a mean person so she was still trying not to hurt his feelings even though he did try to talk to her crazy.

His barrage of text messages began again. *But all I want to say for you to think I'm always lying about stuff. My family knows about you and I was looking for us a house so we can be together and to purchase this for you.* He sent her a picture of what looked like an engagement ring. *But hey it's ok I hope you find the right guy for u and I wish you nothing but happiness.*

Alicia laughed so hard that she couldn't breathe. He was really crazy as hell. At first she wasn't going to response but her pettiness came out to play. *Mmhhmmm that's funny as shit! Why would you propose to someone that you've only known for a couple of months whom you're not even in a relationship with?! And after all that shit you said about me wtf would you want me if I'm that bad? So either you're lying or covering something up. Looking for a house? Negro I own my house! Lmao. You're funny. I hope you don't think that you just rubbed anything in my face cause I am not pressed for marriage honey, I've been proposed to more times that I can count.*

There you go always think somebody lying and what the fuck I'm trying to cover up. Nothing. He was stupid. Alicia didn't respond. She went about her day as usual. Trevion called her while she was waiting for her next class to start. "What are you doing?" he asked her.

"I'm at school…I do not want to be here at all today."

"Why not? What's wrong?" He said sounding concerned.

She sighed. "I'm just tired and feeling a little overwhelmed. I just want to sleep and not worry about having to do anything." She told him truthfully.

"Did something happen?" he asked her

"No not really, I'm just overwhelmed right now." She answered truthfully.

"Well," he said. "I mean you are a single mother."

"Yes I'm aware of that."

"But you're doing a good job." He complimented her.

She smiled. "I appreciate that."

Then he thought about it and changed it. "Well good is an understatement."

She thanked him again. "No problem." He said. "Miss me?"

"What do you think?" she waited for his response.

"Yes. A lot." He said with confidence.

She laughed. "Oh really? A lot huh?"

"Yes."

"Is that your way of saying you miss me a lot?" She asked him.

"Yes and cuddle tonight?" he stated and asked at the same time.

"Of course." She said smiling.

The rest of her day was going well and she was looking forward to cuddling with Trevion later that night. As she was in the kitchen making dinner for the kids Taylor texted her asking how her day was. She didn't respond so he texted right back saying he hoped she didn't mind him asking. She still didn't respond. So he texted again asking her if she just wanted him to leave her alone. Alicia didn't respond to that one either. He called her and she didn't answer. He sent her two more texts after that, both of them saying that he gets it. Alicia just carried on about her day. Trevion came over right before the kids went to bed. He talked and played with them for a little bit then they lay in Alicia's bed and watched movies and cuddled until they both fell asleep. When they woke up the next day so that Trevion could leave for PT, Alicia saw that Taylor had sent her a bunch of texts at 3am. She rolled her eyes. He was looking a crazy stalker. *You don't want to be bothered? I texted you at 4pm yesterday evening called you twice and you didn't answer. Really pretty sure you probably was busy with your friend and that's why you didn't answer the phone or text me smh. But just let me know if you don't want to be bothered with me or you got you a new guy now let me know and I will not bother you anymore. All I want is for you to be honest and tell the truth if you got another guy you hanging out with here which I'm sure you do just say it be straight with me. I was coming by your house to apologize I see your boyfriend was over there so you enjoy hmmm. I never cheated on you but I see just that quick you have another nigga over your house lol.*

Alicia was up at 6am cracking up from laughter reading his crazy ass texts. How can you cheat on someone when you're not even in a relationship? He really just kept texting her stupid shit even after she let him know she was never feeling him like that and she was never his girlfriend. She went ahead and responded to the texts he had sent 3 hours ago. *First of all, I don't have a boyfriend (that includes you as well) second of all if I choose to have someone over my house I can do that because I am single and grown and it ain't none of your business. We were never together so I can do what the fuck I want to do. Third of all, I highly doubt you were coming to apologize…you just wanted to see if someone was at my house because I wasn't responding or answering you. I read your text when you sent them and I saw you calling. You were right I didn't want to be bothered with you and your nonsense. I didn't need to tell you that! Anybody with common sense would've caught the hint already. But then you bring your ass by my house later last night and thought I was going to let you in? Boy bye!* She wanted him to know that he had her fucked up.

Of course he had to respond again. *I was coming to apologize and I don't care if you had a nigga over there but the same car was in your driveway this morning when I rode by so you tell me your friend a guy just stayed over get the fuck out here I'm not stupid.*

Alicia thought he had to be stupid because what he said was stupid. Didn't she just tell him that she could do what she wanted to do? Why the hell is he driving past her house at night and in the morning? He keep saying he not stupid as if she trying to explain to him or something. He was a psycho. She told him that he was crazy and she has been choosing not to answer his calls or texts because she doesn't fuck with him and he be trying to talk to her crazy. There really was no point in conversing with him.

Yea but your male friend just stayed over your house last night whatever I'm not stupid Alicia. So save that shit you talking cause it's funny the next day you have a guy over your house and stays overnight whatever I'm pretty sure it's someone you fucking with I'm not stupid.

Alicia laughed and laughed. He saying save that shit like she trying to be with him. *You keep saying stupid shit so I'm starting believe that you are stupid as fuck. Did you really think I was gonna want you after that crazed out episode the other day when I already didn't really want you before then? Nigga you lie about the simplest shit. I'm really not worried about you in the least bit. You just leave me be please. Enjoy the rest of your day.*

Instead of him taking that and moving on he still had to keep going.

Enjoy your day also and for your info I'm not worried about no female and I never will be. I'm not like these guys from Killeen all I'm worried about is making sure myself is established in the long run I'm not going around here chasing no pussy my money feels way better than pussy so if you think I am out here thirsty you out your damn mind and I had a few females try to talk to me and turned they ass down when I was talking to you and even before then but wish you the best in life.

He was like a bitch that was trying to sell herself to a nigga that didn't want her or care about her. Why was he telling her this shit like she cared or like it would change her mind? She wasn't going to keep going on with him. *Good for you! You take care now!* She brushed him off.

He wasn't taking the loss though. *I admit I was wrong okay and I apologize. Tell me what you feel I lied about because I have proof of everything. I even ordered you some shoes like mine that you liked and I wrote you a letter. I don't have to lie to you about nothing I've just always been a secretive person. I had plans for me and you for the future. I told my family about you and they wanted me to bring you home to visit. I enjoyed the time we had and I hope you and the next guy be together forever and I wish you nothing but the best. I will never talk to you the way I did before again and I rather for us to just be friends and you find someone that really deserve you. I was mad when I said the things I said and I apologize. I really care about you and want to spend my life with you that's all. I just want to make you happy and get a house and live our life together just give me a chance. But I need to know have you been with someone else since you talked to me? Just be honest I just want to make you happy. What do you want?* He had literally sent all of those texts separately throughout the entire day. Alicia hadn't responded to not one of them, and she wasn't planning on it. He called and she didn't answer. A couple of days later when they were leaving the house for Alton's birthday party she noticed a gift was left outside of her house. It was from Taylor. She assumed he thought that was going to make her deal with again. It didn't. She texted him and said thank you but that was it. The next night Trevion called her. "Let's make love." He said as soon as she answered.

"Are you in love?" she asked him.

"Yes."

"With whom?"

"Life."

She laughed. "Mmmhhmmm. So you're going to be making love to life huh?"

"Yep. Because you are life."

She laughed but at the same time she thought it was so sweet. "That was a good save." They Talked a little longer and made plans for him to drive her around tomorrow. She had to have some work done on her car so he volunteered to get her where she needed to be.

Chapter 74

Trevion had been such a big help to Alicia all week long while she was without her car. He had made sure that he was there every morning at least 15 minutes before he needed to be so that he could take her to drop off the kids at school and get her and the kids to and from school as well. One of those days the kids had doctors' appointments so he brought them for those as well. He waited in the car while they went in but as soon as they were called to the back, he had gotten a call that formation was changed to 3:30 instead of 4 and it was already 2:45. He texted her and informed her. She told him that if he needed to go it was okay and that she would call Noise and have him come get them when they were done.

Call him and ask him first. He typed to her.

It'll be fine. I don't want you to miss formation.

Man Call that nigga. He responded.

She laughed. *Okay geesh hold on. Okay he's gonna come get us.*

Tell that nigga don't have y'all waiting. He said referring to Noise whom he was also friends with.

Alicia smiled. *Awww you love me.*

Shut up.

She laughed so hard. She really loved that man. He texted about an hour later to make sure they had gotten home okay. Ravyn had let Alicia use her car the next day since she didn't like driving and barely ever went anywhere except to work. Alicia was able to get all of her stuff done with no worries. She loved that she had Ravyn, Shamelle, and Noise to help her out and get her where she needed to be without hassled but she liked that Trevion was always there to help also and he preferred for her to call him first before anyone when she needed help. They day that had actually drop her car off she was having a really shitty day. Her instructor at school had pissed her off, she had lost some money, her house was a mess, she was tired and no one was available to pick her up from the auto shop and take her home. Noise was at work, Shamelle was at school, and Mitch was at an appointment in Temple. She texted Trevion and asked if he was busy. She had forgotten that he had duty that day. It was no big deal to him though. Within 10 minutes he was pulling up to pick her up and take her home. She had gotten in the car and immediately had to fight back tears. She didn't want him to see her crying so she faced the window and just stared out the entire ride. He asked her what was wrong. She just told him that she was having a bad day. He asked if there was anything he could do to make it better. She told him no but just knowing that he was concerned was enough. She had gotten a reminder text from her home warranty company that they would be there today to service her air conditioning. She had completely forgotten about that too. Thy said they would call when they were 30 minutes out. She hoped they didn't come during a time frame that she was going be unavailable. When they got to her house she thanked him. He told her that she hoped he felt better and he would hit her up later. She gave him a kiss then went into the house. She really needed to clean up but she was sleepy so she got in bed and went to sleep. She woke up at 3:10 so that she could walk to the school and pick Alton up by 3:30.

Tekerri had culture club after school that day so she wasn't released until 4:30. Alicia would've just taken Alton to play on the playground at the school until she got done but as soon as she got him, the repair company called and said they were 15 minutes out. After her call she got a text from Trevion. *You okay?*

I'm sure I will be. I've been asleep since you dropped me off. I'm walking home from getting Alton from school now.

Why didn't you call me? He chastised her.

Cause I was going to call you for a way to pick up Tekerri at 430 and I didn't want you to have come out twice in an hour. She explained to him.

So do you want me to do that? I'll have to go check back in first.

She told him yes. He was pulling up 15 minutes later at 4:03. The repair man was there when he arrived. Trevion came in and gave her a hug. He looked at her sympathetically knowing that she was having a bad day. They sat down at her kitchen table. She asked him how he was always able to just leave when she needed him. He said he told his NCO that he had to go pick up his daughter from school. She let out a small chuckle. She told him that his NCO must be new. He said it's not his regular NCO so they don't know anything about him. He tried making jokes to cheer up but it just wasn't working. She was just having a day. "You gotta stop moping. I need to see that beautiful smile. I don't like seeing you like this. You are never like this." He told her. She forced back tears. He was making her even more emotional. Just then Alton came running from the back room and immediately ran to Trevion. They started playing and making all kinds of noise. Alicia smiled for the first time all day. She loved how he was with her kids. At 4:25 the repair man was still there. Alicia would've had Trevion go to pick up Tekerri but he wasn't on the list to do so. He didn't speak a word just handed her his car keys. She wrote a check for the repairman and asked him if it was okay if Trevion signed the paperwork if she wasn't back in time. He said it was. She left Alton there with Trevion and went to pick up Tekerri. After they were all done he went back to his 24 hour duty. She called him when she thought he had made it back to work. She just wanted to tell him thanks again.

"Yeah yeah." He said. She let out a loud sigh. "What?" he said.

"You really do have a good heart you know…just fyi."

"I know. That's something you don't have to tell me." He said matter-of-factly.

"Well ok." She said curtly.

He changed the subject. "A back rub would be nice right now."

"For me too. And a foot rub." She told him.

"I don't do feet." He lied. "I want you to send chills down my spine."

"But you do, do feet soooooo." She said to him.

"I don't." He lied again.

"You did mine."

He tried to act like that wasn't true. "When?"

"Many times on my couch. You used to take my sock off and rub my toes all on your arms and shit. Stop acting like you have amnesia." She busted him out.

He started laughing. "Touché." He said.

Alicia had gotten the kids ready for bed then packed their lunches and ironed their clothes for school all while still talking on the phone with Trevion. She was now laying her bed and was going on hour number 3 of being on the phone with him. She heard him getting into his car and asked him what he was doing. He told her that was getting a break so he was going to go by King's house. Five minutes later he asked her what she was doing.

"I'm lying in my bed."

"Oh." He said. "Do you still have the light on in your room?" He asked her.

"Nah not the big light but I have on my lamp." She said. Not even wondering why he was asking her such a weird. She began rubbing her belly as she had one leg lying straight on her bed and the other bent at the knee with the foot resting on the bed.

"Ohhhh. Why you lying there with your leg up like that? You need to put it down." He said.

Alicia stopped moving and looked around her room. "How do you know my leg is up?"

"I'm looking right at you." He said seriously.

Alicia sat up and started getting out of her bed. "No you're not."

"You just got out of your bed and you're walking towards your room door." He told her.

She was expecting him to be standing by the fireplace in her living room or something since he could see her but she couldn't see him. She didn't know how he would have gotten in the house though. Just as she reached the door he knocked on the window that was between her door and the fireplace. She jumped back and screamed and he burst out laughing. Because it was nighttime and she had her light on and he was black as hell, he saw into the room easily and she couldn't see outside. When she realized it was him she yelled. "What the fuck?! You scared the shit out of me!" She smiled and hung up in his face when he started walking around to the front of the house. She went to the front to let him in. He was still laughing. She punched him in his arm pretending to mad. He snatched her up and gave her hug and a kiss on the neck. They went back into the room and he pulled of his boots and uniform jacket and lay in the bed with her. They talked for a couple of hours before he had to go back to work. Even though her day was super fucked up her managed to make her night perfect just by simply being there. The next morning when she woke up she saw that he had texted her at 3:21 and 3:50 in the morning saying get up. She texted back. *You know I was asleep.*

So. How are the kids getting to school? He asked.

Well Noise said yesterday that he would come to take them but I don't want to wake him if you can do it since you are already up anyway.

I gotcha. He told her.

She told him that since Kyle had stayed over their sister's house last night, they didn't have to leave the house until 7:45 this morning instead of 7:30. He pulled up to her house at 7:12. She wasn't even dressed yet. He came in and spoke to the kids. He saw she was running around doing things so he helped Alton to finish getting dressed. He cleaned his face for him then brushed his hair and sprayed his cologne on him. Then he kneeled down in front of him and help put on his shoes before he tied the laces. Although Alicia was moving about doing various things she did notice that and looked on with adoration remembering how he used to do that all the time when they dated back in 2015. When he was finished. Alton skipped happily out of the room. She was standing there putting lotion on her arms when she caught him staring at her. She smiled at him. "What?" she said.

"Your panties match your hair." He said to her referring to the fact that her hair was black with lots of red highlights and her panties were black with red lines. She was standing there with a t-shirt and her panties on and he was getting turned on. She smiled at him seductively and he walked over to her. He peeked his head out the door first to make sure the kids weren't anywhere close by then he came back and grabbed her by the hips with his fingers gripping her butt and pulled her close to him. She wrapped her arms around his neck and they shared a deep kiss. He heard Alton coming through the living room so let her go and stepped back. He winked at her and then went into the living room and played with Alton until she was ready.

Chapter 75

It was Thursday and Alicia was recuperating from a little Spring

Break mini vacation with the kids. They went to an indoor water park in Flint and then to the Discovery Science Place in Tyler. On the drive back her car started acting weird so she hit up various people to see what may have been wrong. She found and auto parts store and was able to get a diagnostic ran to see what the problem was. It read that she needed a new thermostat but luckily she was still good to drive home. Taylor had been calling and texting her every other day since she texted him saying thank you for Alton's birthday gift. He was trying to win her back but she rarely would even respond to him. He offered to buy the thermostat for her and said he would bring it to her the day after she got back, which was today. She agreed and told him he could bring it by Thursday evening. She was also going to try and go through with her plan that she had told the ladies at Talia's house that night. Even though she had no plans of ever being with him, she still wanted to know the truth. They had gotten back around 9 last and she was tired that they all went straight to bed. When she woke up that morning she saw that she had three texts from Trevion. First one at 10:04 pm. *Let me come put this hamma on you.* Then at 11:27pm. *I know you got my message nigga. I guess you with ya boyfriend. I'll just fall back. Nice life.* Then again at 11:55pm. *And don't text me in the morning with no excuses. I don't wanna hear it.*

She didn't understand why he would just go off sometimes without even knowing what was going on. She had realized that she had begun to spend a lot of time with him. She loved spending time with him and she loved being around him. She loved the way they vibe with each other and how much he was there for her. But she had been hearing that he was dealing with other females again and she didn't want to be hurt again. Just as she started to let her guard down with him, here it was the issue of him being community dick again. She had to put some space in between them again if she wanted to keep her heart. She texted him back.

Excuses for what negro?

Nothing.

You're so extra sometimes.

I'm not. He replied.

Ok.

Yeah.

Idk why you say stuff like that to me when ya still fucking ya baby mama. She didn't really believe that but it was a way to put some distance between them.

He didn't respond right then but he called her about four hours later. He asked her to bring him something to eat. She ignored him and told him that she noticed he was trying to disregard what she said. He asked her what she said.

"You saw what I said stop trying to fake."

"I'm not fucking with my baby mama so I didn't feel the need to respond to that." He said calmly.

"You are so full of shit. If you ain't fucking her you are definitely fucking somebody. This is why I can't go all in with you. I can't trust you. I know you out here fucking with other bitches but you won't admit it." She said getting an attitude.

"Are you trying to say that you are done fucking with me?" he asked her.

"Are you going to keep fucking with other bitches?"

"I'm not. Are you done with me?" he asked again.

She asked him again. "Are you going to keep fucking with other bitches?" they went back and forth with that for a few minutes until she finally blew up. "You know what I'm not about to keep playing with you man. You wanna keep fucking with other bitches then do that."

He told her she was tripping then hung up on her. Later that evening Shamelle came by her house to hang out. She was still there when Taylor came over with the part for her car. He was sitting in the living room and they were in the kitchen. Alicia was whispering to

Shamelle trying to tell her everything she had missed. Trevion had started texting her saying 'Who at your fucking house'. A few minutes later he texted her and said 'Don't worry about it I'm about to pull up'. She assumed that he was talking shit because he had staff duty that night. That maybe one of his friends rode by and saw their cars in her driveway. Shamelle had left about an hour after that but at midnight Trevion texted. He sent her the laughing emoji and said just delete my number. I'm done with you. She didn't know what all of that was about. She didn't even respond. Taylor had fallen asleep on her couch which she was happy about. She grabbed his keys of the table and went out to the car with the card in her hand. She quickly opened his armrest and grabbed his wallet looking up to make sure he didn't come out the door. She found his driver's license and looked at the name. Henry Joseph Johnson. She knew it! This nigga had been lying since day one. He looked her in face on more than one occasion and told her his name was Taylor Johnson, no middle name. Boy she was heated. She went back in he tried to pretend like he was asleep. When she sat down on the couch he "woke up" and asked her if she had been outside. She said no. He got angry and told her she was lying because he saw her grab his keys and go. She told him she went to put something his car for him. He asked her why she lied. She replied the same reason he always did. He got super angry and she told him to get the fuck out. A few minutes after he left, he texted her. *Just like u said Taylor no middle name Johnson because you never did believe me in the first place but it's all good.*

Alicia just shook her head. He didn't know if she had seen his license so here he was still trying to flip it to look she had done something wrong. He was still trying to act like he wasn't lying about his name. She laughed. *I put that because you said you don't have a middle name, it doesn't take a rocket scientist to understand that. It's whatever at this point though.* That was all she was going to say to him. There was no point. She didn't want him and he was a liar that got mad when he was called out on his bullshit so that was that. But she did want to know what else he was lying about. She picked up her phone and did a background search on him. What she saw was amazing. Over the next few days he was texting and calling her like everything was normal and all good. She didn't respond nor answer. There was nothing to talk about. He was crazy. He would drive past her house. She would see him around neighborhood when she would be out. She told Talia and Shamelle about it along with name thing and what she found on his background search. They were shocked. They said it was good that Alicia didn't like him or want him in the first place because all of that was just crazy.

Alicia hadn't talked to Trevion in a week. He didn't hit her up and she didn't hit him up. But that night she swallowed her pride. She texted him the emoji eyes.

Wassup.

Nothing Trevion.

You miss me don't you? He meant it more like a statement than a question.

What?

You can read.

I can't comprehend.

Where you at?

Home…why?

Am I invited?

You must miss me. She texted to him.

I'll tell you when I get there.

I'm going to bed. She really was tired and just wanted to sleep.

So I can't come?

I have a very early morning.

So that means I can't come?

Not today. She loved spending time with him but she just had no energy and could barely keep her eyes open.

Bye Alicia.

Whatever Trevion…childish.

He sent the laughing emojis. *Yeah yeah yeah tell that to that nigga that's been at your house.*

You didn't care if a nigga has been at my house when you were trying to come over here. Typical you though, can't get your way when you want it so you resort to being childish…guess some things don't change..it's cool…im sure your little ratchet hoes love that trait about you though. Goodnight. She shot back at him.

A minute later text. *Open the door.*

Nope…I'm not dealing with your childishness tonight.

Open the fucking door mane.

No…that's not how you talk to me.

Please.

You're not even here dude…and my house is a mess.

I'm on the way now. He replied.

I'm going to bed.

I'm otw…See you when I get there.

Don't waste your gas tonight. Nigga! I'm going to bed so I'm not opening the door. She didn't him to come for nothing.

You really finna do this? Okay Alicia. Don't say I didn't put in effort. Night. She hated that he tried to flip that on her like that.

How the fuck did you put in effort? You got an attitude and haven't talked to me in like a week…and ya ass wasn't thinking about me only wanted to come over to what? Fuck? You horny?

I want to see you. He pleaded.

Then why can't you wait for a DAY when I'm not tired or don't have to get up early?

I want to see you NOW.

I'm in bed. She told him honestly.

Ya.

Smh good night man, I'm not about to do this with you. You know what, don't even worry about how I feel...I'm just gonna fall back and let you do you...you good. She was tired of his shit.

Smh.

Chapter 76

Alicia had been going through the day to day motions of trying to keep her emotions in check as far as dealing with Trevion and she had been trying to keep herself from going off on Taylor. He was getting on her nerves calling and texting all day everyday regardless of if she answered him or not. One night as she was getting ready to go to an anniversary party for a new car club, he kept calling her until she answered.

"What's up?" she said when she finally answered the phone after the fourth call.

"Are you busy?"

She rolled her eyes. "Yep."

"Okay, quick question, do you want to be in a relationship?" he asked her.

Alicia had to move the phone from her mouth in order to stifle her laughter. He continued talking. "I want to be in a relationship with you but if you don't then I understand. I just want us to live our lives together and be happy. Do you want this?"

She knew he was crazy but dumb, too? She had already told him multiple times that she didn't like him and that they were never in a relationship to begin with so why did he even bother to ask that question. She decided to see how he would come out of this lie though. "Quick question, what is your full name?"

He was starting to get angry, as usual. "Why you keep asking me that? Cause you looked at my ID?"

"Are you gonna answer the question or nah?" she ignored what he asked.

"You already know my name. When you went out to the car that night you looked at my ID, so you know my name."

"Yep, so why did I have to sneak to your car and look at your ID to know your name?" She asked him in a monotone.

He came up with a dumb lie. "Cause I don't go by that name. I don't like my first name that's why." He thought that was an acceptable answer to why he flat out lied and gave her a completely different and omitted his middle name when she asked more than once. "But hey I understand if you don't want anything else to do with me." When Alicia didn't respond because she had the phone on speaker and had walked away from it while he was talking, he continued. "So what you want to do?" he asked.

"Dude you flat out lied about what your name was. I can respect you not liking your name and saying 'hey I rather you call me this' but nah, you continuously flat out lied about something like that. Your name is Henry Joseph Johnson. You told me not once, not twice, not three times but at least 7 times, including the night that I looked at your ID, that your name was Taylor Johnson, no middle name. And that night we went to Temple you made sure to keep your ID card from me so that I couldn't see your real name and then still continued to lie about what your real name was. That's bogus as fuck." She told him calmly.

He sighed. "You right. Well now you know the truth that I don't like my name and I apologize for not being honest with you. So could you answer the question? Do you not want to see me again? Could you let me know what it's going to be?" He begged.

She was really flabbergasted at the way he tried to downplay that he lied about his name like it was nothing. He didn't lie because he doesn't like his name. He lied because he is a liar. He just made up a fake name for no damn reason. "That isn't the only thing you've lied about and you have absolutely no remorse for lying or your behavior when I've called you out on your multiple lies. That's crazy as fuck." She told him.

He was still trying to plead his case. "I apologize to you for lying and will never do it again no matter what it's about. But like I said, if you want to do you let me know and I will leave you be."

"I've been doing me." She said coldly then hung the phone in his face. He called back 8 times but she didn't answer. She headed out to the party feeling and looking like a million bucks.

She arrived to the party with Talia and the rest of TGL. Shamelle and Mitch were already there. As they were still in the parking lot chatting it up, Alicia caught eyes with Talia. She was mumbling something to her but Alicia couldn't understand what she was saying until the very last minute. She was telling her to turn around and as soon as she did she was looking right into the face of Trevion. He smiled at her then gave her a hug. She laughed and playfully swatted his arm. "You said you weren't coming tonight!" she said to him. He smiled again and winked at her as he turned to walk into the party. When she turned back around all of the members of TGL were staring at her with goofy smiles on their faces as if teasing her. "Y'all leave me alone." she said and laughed. From the parking lot, to the front door, to inside of the party she was hugging and greeting everyone and getting many compliments on how great she looked. She had invited Angel and Deja to come out as well since she had become good friends with Angel and Deja always claimed that she didn't have any female friends to hang out with. Alicia spotted Ravyn inside and went over to speak to her friend. After standing at the bar talking to her for about five minutes she looked over and realized that Nikki was sitting at the bar as well. Alicia just went on about her night but throughout the night she would see Nikki looking over in her direction anytime that she was near Trevion, even if she wasn't actually talking to him. She would catch her taking quick glances when she wasn't near him too. She looked a little sad or uncomfortable being there, she just sat in the same spot all night and drank. TC had pulled Alicia to the side and asked her about Angel. He thought she was good looking and wanted Alicia to put him on. She told him to just go over there and talk to her. Somehow they hit it off that night. After a great party Alicia headed home and Trevion pulled up to her house soon after. She had removed her dress and put on a pair of boy shorts and a t-shirt. He was pretty drunk when he came in. Alicia thought it was funny. She had seen tipsy before but never flat out drunk. He seemed to drink way more now than he did when she first met him almost two years ago. He climbed into bed with her and attempted to cuddle. They may have lay there for about four minutes before he got horny and began kissing on her. He removed her shorts and went down on her and then came back up to slide inside in. She could tell that he wasn't standing fully at attention yet when he tried to slide it in but he started stroking anyway. She wasn't feeling it at that moment. He had gotten too drunk and now he was trying to give her Henny dick. He realized that she wasn't into it so he stopped mid-stroke and lay next to her. They fell asleep. About an hour later he tried again. Same result. Alicia figured he had to be super wasted because they have never had an issue with him getting it up for her. Never. After sleeping for about 2 and a half hours he woke up again, ready try once more. Alicia was willing because he had gotten her aroused and now he needed to finish the job. This time she climbed on top. She began kissing his neck and neck and chest. He moaned in pleasure. She felt his manhood get hard as it started rubbing against her clitoris. She kissed him deeply, parting his lips with her tongue before sliding it into his mouth. He kissed her back and slid his rock hard penis into her vagina at the same time. This time she gasped. That's how she knew he was fully erect now. She began rolling her hips slowly, lifting up slightly to feel his member gliding in and out of her wetness. He liked to talk when they had sex so since she was on top, she started talking to him like he talked to her. She brought her lips to ear then licked his earlobe. "You love me?" she asked him seductively. He moaned again before grabbing her hips and ass and thrusting himself deeper inside of her. "You know I love you or I wouldn't put up with your shit all the time." he said to her breathing heavily. She rode him until she came on his penis then he flipped her on her back and began to stroke her with so much intensity she thought she was going to come again. He finished and they lay there tired, hot, sweaty, and completely satisfied. The next day he took her to pick up her car from having some work done to it. He made sure she got the keys to her car then he gave her a hug and a kiss then left to go to Long Branch Park to play in a football tourney.

Alicia was relaxing at home with the kiddos watching tv when her phone vibrated. It was a text from Taylor. *I made a mistake and I learned from it. I haven't lied to you about anything else. You know where I'm from, you know about my daughter, you know everything about me now.*

Yet I still haven't seen a picture of your daughter and I'm not even sure that you really live where you say you do. You be trying to make stuff different than what is really is. You lie to much dude and you talk in circles. She told him. At this point she didn't really care. She was about to just cut all ties with him cause there was no point in even having a conversation with him.

He was still trying to convince her that he was a decent guy. *I'm sorry okay. I'm not talking in circles and I'm not trying to make anything different. I just want to be with you and I want you to want me. That's it. Can we start over please?*

She shook her head. Time to shoot his ass down so that he will not call or text her anymore. She had to make it clear to him that she wasn't feeling him and that she knew he was bigger liar than just his name. *Lol nope! You can't handle being called out on your bullshit even when you know its bullshit...I don't know what your deal is maybe you have narcissistic personality disorder or you're a pathological liar...not trying to be funny or anything but you've been lying since day one. You good though because like I've been saying I really was not into you and we were not in a relationship.* She had hoped being blunt would with him would make him leave her alone but it didn't.

He continued on but this time the tone of his text changed. He was in his feelings now. *Lol ok you can think whatever you want about me*

I really don't give a damn what you think I know the truth and that's all that matters. Like my big brother say you can't miss nothing you never had. Then he sent her the emoji with the peace sign.

She was just not going to respond but she felt like showing him that she knew more than what he thought she did and she wanted to expose more of his lies. She sent him screenshots of the results of the background search she did on him. There was no question that results were him. It had his full name, date of birth, his phone number and email address, his family members' names, all of his addresses including Alabama, Killeen, and Tennessee. It showed that he had no properties that he owned meaning that he lied about owning a house in Tennessee. It showed that he an eviction filing against him from a Stonebridge Apartments in Alabama and he also had a small claims judgement against him in the amount of $1,018 from a Max Federal Credit Union. Just to make sure the info on the search was correct she had even done a search on herself. Her house showed up as property that she owned. All of her addresses that she has ever lived showed up as well. She was certain that the info was correct and that it was him. She had tried not to even let him know she knew this stuff she was just going to stop dealing with him. But he wouldn't leave her alone and he wanted to catch attitudes when he was the liar here. Oh she needed to blast him. In addition to the screenshots she sent her final text to him. *You're right about that...you never had me so I hope you don't miss me. That would be creepy. Instead of getting an attitude because you're a sick individual you should really work on yourself. Wish you all the best sir...I was never in but now I'm really out...no response needed. There isn't anything else to talk about. Have a great night and God bless you.* She sent him the smiling emoji. No matter what insult he tried to come back with she wasn't going to respond or entertain him. She had played with him enough. The entertainment was over. Her last text was sent at 8:29pm.

He decided to keep texting.

8:31-lol I been out Alicia, you just didn't know.

8:31-Lmao and nothing wrong just don't give a fuck.

8:34-Lmao and your dumbass that's not even me lmao.

8:38-Why your dumbass trying to do a search on me I know what I got and own so you trying to look up shit on me so think what you want.

8:39-That's a picture of my shit in my duplex lmao. It was a picture of the blue charger and a black motorcycle in a one car garage that he already sent her before. She didn't know what that was supposed to prove.

8:39-So think what you want.

8:43-And the Killeen address says 2012 to 2012 and I wasn't even here in 2012 I was in Afghanistan lmao. He was looking dumber by the minute. There were at least two other addresses for Killeen and they were not during the time he was deployed, but yet that was the only one he disputed. She shook her head. An hour had passed and he had stopped texting so she thought he was finally done since she hadn't responded to anything but she was wrong.

12:26-And my life is good. Before I met you it was good and your ex, I'm sure you still fucking him. The next day you had him over lol so I don't hate no man over no pussy cause in Killeen the woman here is like a door knob everybody gets a turn.

12:39- He sent her a link to a YouTube video of a song called For Everybody by Juicy J and Wiz Khalifa.

12:55- He sent her the same link again.

Alicia laughed so hard until her stomach hurt. This negro was truly out of his mind. And to make it even funnier, she still didn't respond.

Chapter 77

Alicia was in her car heading to Austin with Ravyn and Angel, Windii had come along too but she had driven her own car because she had her baby and two friends with her.. It was the weekend of the Texas Relays, an annual track competition with lots of cars and people from all over the state. They usually had a meet up spot where everyone would pull up to and show off their cars and bike and mingle with people from other places. When they pulled up to Capital Plaza it was already almost packed to capacity. It was hard getting into a good parking spot. There were different car and bike clubs from near and far. As soon as Alicia pulled in into the plaza she saw OL2L and of course, Trevion. By the time she had parked he was at her car door. He snatched open the door, grabbed her by the throat, and begin kissing her. She melted into him. She didn't know why but she really liked that aggressive behavior. He held her captive in her car for about five minutes before giving her some room to get out. He was clearly drunk but was in a good mood laughing and dancing all over the place. He wouldn't take 5 steps away from her without coming right back though. He was so playful but people that didn't know how he was or even how he and Alicia was together would have thought he was a real asshole. He kept talking loudly in her face and grabbing on her. He grabbed her by shirt and made her drop her keys on the ground. Her key fob broke. "You really trying me right now Leon!" He walked up to her talking loudly as she was speaking to a couple of guys from a car club out in Dallas. They had come to their car show to benefit breast cancer back in October. Alicia looked at him. "What are you talking about Trevion?"

He grabbed her by the arm. "What the fuck you doing out here with no clothes on? These little ass shorts you got on. Who you dressing like that for?" The guys from the other club stepped back but watched the two of them. Alicia had on some multi-colored gym shorts that showed off her thigh tattoo and a white Michael Kors t-shirt with some long multi-colored socks and the black Jordans' that Taylor had bought for her. She had her hair braided in two pigtails. She wasn't trying to be sexy or anything. It was hot, she just wanted to be comfortable. "Nigga quit making a scene for people think you are serious." She told him as she looked around to see who was watching. "I don't give a fuck what they think." He said loudly. "You shouldn't be out here dressed like that." He scolded her. She rolled her eyes. "Whatever Trevion. You got issues." He grabbed her face. "Gimmie a kiss," He said to her. She kissed him and he walked away smiling like a little ass kid. She shook her and laughed.

She had gone back over to where Ravyn, Angel, and Windii were at. TC had made his way over to talk to Angel. They were both blushing and smiling and like some school kids. She laughed at them too. They spent the next couple of hours mingling with people, they went to eat at CiCi's Pizza in the plaza and Angel brought TC some wings and a drink back. While they were watching the bike show the guys from the Dallas car club came back over to Alicia and started talking to her again. Trevion had left about 15 minutes prior. One of the guys started up a conversation with Alicia. "I'm so confused right now because the last time I checked, I could've sworn you were single." he said to her. Alicia gave him a puzzled look. "I am." She said.

"Oh, that guy isn't your man?" he asked her referring to Trevion. Alicia laughed. "No he's not." The guy laughed too and said, "Oh I was gonna say baby if that's your man you need to leave him. If he does you like that in public ain't no telling how he beat up on you behind closed doors." Alicia fell out laughing. She couldn't believe he thought she was in an abusive relationship. Not that domestic violence was funny but that it was what he thought just from Trevion's aggressive play. The crowd started winding down and Deja and her sister was supposed to meet them at their room. Deja was originally going to share a room with Alicia, Angel, and Ravyn but due to her sister and her two male friends coming down to Austin with her she decided that she wasn't going to stay overnight. She had already paid Alicia her portion for the room at the Hilton so Alicia decided to give her money back to be fair. Once they got to the room and linked up with Deja and her people they all decided to go eat at Papadeaux's, unfortunately the wait was 2 hours so they hit up this smaller, bootleg seafood joint. They were very dissatisfied with not only the food but also the service. However, Deja was sweet on their server and was flirting with young Hispanic guy the whole time.

When they arrived back at the room they smoked a blunt and began to drink. They all showered, including Deja and her sister, and started to get dressed for a night out on Sixth Street. Deja's male friends stayed outside the hotel to give them privacy while they showered and changed clothes. Once they were all finally ready it was already past midnight. The drive to downtown was only about 15 minutes but Alicia took a wrong turn and they ended up on the other side of Sixth Street. That was another 15 minutes wasted. In the car Angel began to voice her opinion about Alicia giving Deja her money back. "I feel like you shouldn't have given her the money back personally. I get that she isn't staying the night but she and her sister spent hours in our room and they both even took showers there. They should chip in something. Ain't no free rides." She said slightly with an attitude. Alicia understood where she was coming from but it wasn't really a big deal to Alicia. Ravyn said she understood both sides. They decided after driving around in circles trying to get back to the other end of Sixth Street to just park where they were and walk back that way. Ravyn paid for the parking area with her card. Once they all started walking, Deja claimed she had to pee really bad so she and Angel left everyone else behind and ran up ahead. They texted and told them what club they had gone into. When the rest of them made it to the club, Deja's sister didn't have any money so Ravyn gave her ten dollars to get into the club. By the time they made it inside Alicia's party mood have vanished. She was tired and annoyed and ready to go. But she put on the happy face and tried to have fun with her ladies. Unfortunately they ended up at the same club OL2L was in and for some reason Nikki and Nella was there with Lady D. The males of OL2L left when Nikki, Nella, and Lady D walked in. Trevion wasn't anywhere to be found. Alicia texted him but got no response. Nikki tried to be seen by Alicia while they were in the club but Alicia paid her no mind. Lady D didn't speak to her, but Nella did and so did King's girlfriend. In the club, Angel was attached to Deja's side. They both seemed to be a little tipsy but in good spirits. After the club as they were all leaving going back out onto Sixth Street, Ravyn and Alicia spotted Nikki and Lady D getting into it with some guys. Ravyn wanted to go tell Nella to back up but Alicia wouldn't let her go. She told her that she had to have her back and make sure she was good and got back home safe so therefore if they want to be in bullshit then that's on them. She didn't know why females would want to be out there trying to fight all these dudes anyway. Fighting period. As they continued to walk they spotted C-No and one of his friends getting some female's phone numbers. Ravyn and C-No had broken up but were still living in the same house due to their lease. Alicia told Angel what she saw and she and Deja decided to be immature and go over and try to check him and the females he was talking to. Alicia, Ravyn, and Deja's sister just walked away. A few minutes later they caught up with them. Every guy that passed by, Deja and Angel stopped them and asked for their numbers. They were looking like little hoes and they were making themselves look thirsty as hell. That's something that Alicia and Ravyn didn't fuck with. They headed back to the hotel and Deja and her crew headed back to Killeen.

When they got back to the room Alicia got a text from Trevion. He said that he had been asleep and that he didn't go out to Sixth Street. She told him that they had just gotten back to their room. Deja had asked earlier if he and his cousin could come to the room and Alicia told them no. Trevion was telling her that he was lying in the bed watching TV and wanted to come to her. She wouldn't let him. They talked until Alicia fell asleep about twenty minutes later. She was a little skeptical of what he may have done after they stopped texting since she knew that Nikki was in Austin too. The next day as they were all heading home from Austin, Trevion texted Alicia. He was letting her know that he had already left and would be back in Killeen before she made. Something was wrong with his car so she agreed to let him borrow hers for the day once she made it back. When she finally made it back and got settled she went and picked him up from King's house. They ran to Wal-Mart first so that she could grab a few things for dinner, then he dropped her back off of at the house. As Alicia was walking out to the garage to close it after Trevion left, she was startled by Noise's girlfriend and her two kids. They had stopped so that the kids could have some playtime.

"Hey I called you earlier and I was passing by and saw your car outside. I thought you were in it but Tre Will told me you were inside." She told Alicia.

Alicia smiled. She came inside and sat in the kitchen while Alicia made dinner. They talked while the kids played. She was telling Alicia about the fight she had with Noise the previous day. She seemed upset still but after venting to Alicia she relaxed more. She told her about what they had bought for the baby yesterday and Alicia reminded her of the upcoming baby shower that she, Talia, and Shamelle were throwing for her. About an hour and a half later, Trevion returned. We he walked in through the kitchen door from the garage, he saw that the ladies were still in conversation so he went into Alicia's bedroom. When he heard the kids in the living room playing, he came out with Alicia's unicorn house slippers on and started playing with the kids. Once the ladies finished up their conversation, Noise's girlfriend left and Trevion came into the kitchen with Alicia. She was standing at the sink washing the dishes that she used to cook with. He walked up behind her and wrapped his arms around her waist, then lay his head on her shoulder. She stopped and looked at him. "Don't worry about what I'm back here doing. You act like you can't concentrate cause I'm back here." He told her. She rolled eyes at him. "Shut up." He let her go then leaned back on the counter next to her. He stared at her for a minute. When she looked up at him he smiled. "You know what?" he said to her. "We really argue like a married couple." Alicia laughed. "I'm serious." He said smiling. "We may as well get married. Then you could come to Germany with me. It's not too late." Alicia didn't know if he was serious or not. "We can't get married." She told him. "And I can't go to Germany with you." He looked at her. "Why not?" he asked. "Just can't. I've got school and my kids have things going on here. I'm not in a rush to get married." She told him.

"So you don't want to marry me?" He asked her.

"I didn't say that."

Trevion was quiet for a minute. "We gon get married when I come back then."

"You're most likely not coming back. And you'll be gone for like 3 years. You will probably meet someone over there and get married."

she told him.

"Nope." He said. "I'm coming back to Fort Hood after I leave Germany. I'm only going to be there for 2 years. Well really like 17 months because I'm going by myself. I'm not taking anyone with me." He explained to her.

Alicia frowned. "But you were gonna take someone with you." She said referring to when she previously heard that Nikki was supposed to go with him. The only way for her to go was to marry him.

"I was." He said simply.

Alicia shook her head. "Yeah I almost forgot that you were engaged to Nikki."

"I wasn't engaged to her." He said.

"You were going to take her to Germany with you. In order to do that, you had to marry her. So if you planned on getting married then that means y'all were engaged." Alicia broke it down to him.

"I wasn't engaged though. I didn't get down on one knee, I didn't propose to her, and I didn't give her a ring." He said matter-of-factly. Alicia just rolled her eyes. She wanted to ask him if Nikki was at his room the night before in Austin but she didn't want to start an argument. She wasn't in the mood to argue. Besides, if he said no she wasn't sure that she would believe him. He played with the kids for a little while longer and chatted up with Alicia somewhere. She dropped him off at King's house with a plate of food a little while later. He texted her before she went to sleep and told her that the food was great and said thank you. She smiled. He was learning manners.

Chapter 78

Alicia had gone over to see Ravyn this afternoon. It was the first week of April. Things were not so bad for her. She was passing all of her classes and the semester was almost over. She was getting along with Trevion pretty well for the most part. Angel and Tc seemed to be hitting it off, well whenever they were able to see each other. Angel would pop up at Ravyn's house to see if TC was over there because his phone was messed up so she couldn't call or text him. While Alicia was at Ravyn's house she had overhead C-No on the phone with someone telling them about Nikki and Nella popping up at the guys' hotel rooms in Austin during the relays. He was saying that Nella's husband was there with another woman and that he cursed her out for showing up to his room uninvited. She heard him pause for a little bit then tell whomever he was speaking to on the phone that Nikki went and knocked on Trevion's room door and when he saw her he immediately dropped his head in exasperation. He asked her why she was there and she said just wanted to see what he was doing. Then she tried to walk in and he stopped her in her tracks and told her she didn't pay for the room so she wasn't welcome inside. He was saying that she just wanted to see what he was doing and then he closed the door in her face. Alicia stifled a laugh. That was kind of funny to her. The next day while Alicia was driving the kids to school she got a text form Trevion.

Oh we're fucking today. I'll be there at 11. He told her

Alicia frowned. *We're doing what?*

Fucking like animals.

She laughed out loud. *Why fucking? And why like animals?*

Because I'm finna load you up. He replied.

You're not slick. You're trying to have a quickie.

I gotta get my baby at 1230. He told her.

I know, that's how I knew you were trying to have quickie.

He responded minutes later. *Let me just get a little bit of it. Let me just stick the head in.*

Alicia laughed until she could barely breathe. *Man get that high school shit out of here.*

Lmao it was worth a try. He told her.

He wasn't able to make it over before time to pick up his son so they agreed that he would come to her later that evening. They had been arguing over stupid stuff that day so when he got to her house that night, he walked in with an attitude and didn't even speak to her. He went straight to her room, took off his shoes and got into bed. When she got into bed he was pretending to be so tired, he didn't even try to cuddle her. She saw that he had an attitude so it made her get one as well. For some reason, whenever they were not talking to each other it was hard for her to fall asleep next to him, no matter how sleepy she was. She lay there for about ten minutes trying to fall asleep while he lay on the other side of her bed ignoring her. She was sleepy af and wanted to get some sleep so she got out of her bed, made her side up, grabbed a pillow, got a small blanket from the hall closet and lay on her couch. Within three minutes she was drifting off to sleep. She had only been asleep for a few minutes when she felt him grab her hand. She woke up to him standing over her and looking down at her with a puppy dog face. "Baby. Why you out here?" He asked her. She sat up a little. "Why you not sleep?" She asked him once her eyes were more in focus. He pulled on her arm to get her off the couch. "Cause you're not next to me." She immediately felt warm all over. She allowed him to guide her by the hand back to her bed. He let her have her side of the bed and then he cuddled up next to her. He kissed her neck and within seconds he was sound asleep. Since they had made up, it was easy for her to fall asleep next to him now. And that she did.

The weekend was here and Alicia was happy to be able to relax with friends. Angel was having a cookout at her house and Alicia had invited all of the girls and her friend Tricky and his friends. They were all enjoying and having a good time and everyone was posting on SnapChat. Alicia posted snaps of everyone but then she posted a snap of herself and Tricky doing a silly dance. She didn't think much of anything that she posted until she called Trevion.

"I wanna go to the movies." she told him.

"Not tonight."

She pouted. "Why not tonight?"

"I'm drinking and I'm finna go get my son."

She questioned him. "So you're staying at the house with you son?"

He had to be an asshole. "Nope I'm staying with them niggas you're with."

She rolled her eyes. "Here we go...What the fuck is your problem like for real? You've been on some asshole fuck nigga type shit and I don't understand why when you know you're leaving in like 3 weeks."

"Gimme Tobbs number." He said ignoring what she said.

"Who?"

"The nigga with the white shirt." He said.

Alicia was getting upset. "So you're just going to disregard what I said?"

"You with ya nigga. That nigga look like me." He said referring to Tricky and the fact that they were both short and dark skin. But that's where the similarities ended.

"You are real ass acting childish as fuck right now. You assuming shit so you can validate bullshit you doing." She spat at him.

He was taken aback. "Oh yeah? That's how you feel?"

She kept going off. "You fucking right that's how I feel. Look how ya ass been acting towards me then gonna say some stupid shit like I'm with my nigga cause I'm at a kickback, meanwhile you out here doing all kinds of bullshit."

"Bet." he said.

"Right, so what the fuck is your problem?" She asked him.

He blurted out to her. "You with them niggas." Sounding jealous.

"I'm at a kickback with females too! Are you with me? Why aren't you with me?"

"You tell me." He said.

She was already drinking and now she was getting mad. "No muthafucka you tell me. I don't know why you're not."

"You better watch who the fuck you're talking to." He warned her.

"No you watch who the fuck you're talking to. You be on some other shit." She said slurring her words a little.

He laughed at her. "You tipsy?"

"Barely. Stop disregarding what I say."

"You want to settle down with me?" He asked her out of the blue.

"You love me?" She asked him.

He countered her. "You love me?"

She sighed. "I'm tired of these attitudes. You're supposed to care about me."

"I do." He said softening his tone a bit.

"Show me." Said her tone changing as well.

"How?" he asked her.

She sighed again. "I don't know honestly. I used to feel it. But we do so much stupid fighting and go days without talking. Really you've been acting like you don't want to be bothered with me all this week."

"I'm just stressed out. I have 100 things going through my mind a day. That's just my way of dealing with it." He told her. This sounded a lot like what he told her when they were talking the first in 2015 when he started changing up on her. She didn't like it.

"You don't have to shut me out though. Everything doesn't have to be so difficult." She told him.

He was silent for a second. "You're right." They talked a few more minutes before hanging up. They had moved the kickback to Tricky's house while she was on the phone and although it was pretty lit, some people had decided to go to the Lil Boosie concert that was going down at Club Tabu that night. Deja had originally said she wasn't going but when she saw that Tricky and his cousin were going to go, she all of a sudden wanted to go to. Angel didn't like that. She made a comment that she felt as though Deja was running behind the niggas. As soon as they said they were going she jumped on the bandwagon. Alicia and Ravyn went back to Angel's house and they all finished drinking and having a girls' night. A little before two Tricky called Alicia and asked if he could bring Deja to Angel's house because she was sloppy drunk and couldn't walk. He didn't know what to do with her. He pulled up about 15 minutes later with her and carried to one of Angel's spare bedrooms and put her in the bed. TC was staying over at Angel's house that night after Ravyn and Alicia had left. The next day Angel called Alicia complaining about Deja coming into her room early that morning and shining her cell phone light into Angel and TC's eyes being nosey trying to see who was in her bed. Then she left without making up the bed that she slept in. Angel was starting to get tired of Deja and her behaviors.

Chapter 79

Alicia was so excited because the weekend of TGL's anniversary was almost here. Her cousin Saucy, who was the secretary for the Louisiana chapter was coming down with Rick to enjoy the turn up. Rick was trying to stay with Alicia at her house for the weekend. After all of this time he was still trying to be with her on that more than friendship level. Alicia did truly love and care for Rick but they one time that they did have sex, from what she remembered, even though he was great at oral sex, his penis was small and unsatisfying. She didn't want it again and made every effort not to do it. Besides, she didn't want to ruin the genuine friendship that they had built over the years. So to her they were better as friends.

During the time that had lapsed since the kickback with Angel and Tricky up until now, Alicia and Trevion had been having so many up and down moments. They would fight and argue and go days without speaking to each other, even if they are in the same public area or at the same event, then somehow they find their way back to each other. He had started being wishy washy, kind of reminded her of when they reached the end the first time they dealt with each other back in 2015. He was leaving soon and all she wanted was to enjoy each other before he was gone for two years. Angel had done another cookout at her house and let TC do the grilling. She was so smitten with him and he seemed to like her too but he also was pulling a whole bunch of disappearing acts on her and really didn't seem too invested in having anything with her. But she still went out of her way to try and see him, including popping up at Ravyn's house all the time thinking he would be there. She gave him her garage door opener after only talking to him for two days so that he could get in when she wasn't home. He never really utilized it though because she got angry him for not keeping his word and she took it back. She would cook for him, make sure if she went out to eat that she brought him something back, made sure he had beer and cigarettes…basically she was trying to show him that she had his back and was there for him. Alicia and Ravyn thought she was doing too much too soon, especially when he wasn't really showing her much effort but all they did was tell her to be careful and take her time. They hoped their advice would make her really look at the whole picture. During that cookout, Trevion showed up with C-No, Swag Billie, and Tru and he and Alicia were not on good terms so he didn't speak to her and she didn't speak to him. She was being childish because she actually wanted him to come but she was just as stubborn as he was and didn't want to be the first to crack. They ignored each other for over an hour until they finally ran into each other on the front porch. A conversation begin, which turned into an argument, which turned into Trevion trying to end the argument by ignoring her fussing at him and asking for a kiss, which turned back into an argument even though she obliged. They started arguing in private in the garage. They argued in front of everyone in the street. Then they would get playful and start showing affection. Then it went right back to arguing. C-No, Swag Billie, and Tru were about to leave but Alicia wasn't finished her conversation with Trevion. His car was messed up so rode with them but Alicia stood in front of Swag Billie's passenger door so that Trevion couldn't get in. Trevion just laughed and told her to move. She wouldn't. He told Swag Billie to go ahead and go. Swag Billie laughed and told them they were crazy before leaving. Alicia liked him, he was a pretty cool guy and he was probably the only guy in OL2L that didn't cheat on his girlfriend and had his on straight. He didn't talk much but that was one of the cool things about him. Trevion acted like he was going to get on the back of C-No's motorcycle but Alicia walked over there too and attempted to keep him from leaving. After a couple of minutes he finally told him to go ahead and go as well. Alicia smiled to herself and was slightly elated because she knew that if he really wanted to go he would've left. He could've easily moved her from in front of the car and motorcycle and he knew she wasn't going to start a physical altercation. He stayed because he cared about her. After Swag and C left, Trevion and Alicia walked down the street away from everyone and went around the corner. They argued some more, this time it was mostly Alicia going off. He had gotten upset with her and told her that he knew she had someone stay at her house one night while he was staff duty. As a matter of fact it was the night that both Taylor and Shamelle were at her house. He said he had come by during his break and after midnight and a white maxima that he had seen there before was there. He held on to that information for like 3 weeks and hadn't said a word to her about it. She felt bad because he saw that and she knew he was putting in effort with her at that time. But on the other hand, she knew all the stuff that he was doing even though she didn't tell him that she knew, not to mention the fact that she didn't even like Taylor. She wanted to him right then and there the whole situation with Taylor and why she was even considering talking to someone else at all. But he was already in his feelings and had shut down during the conversation. He stopped responding to her and stopped answering her questions so she got angry and shut down as well. She wanted to punch him in his mouth but she remembered a conversation she and Angel had with TC a few days prior when he told them the story of when Nikki swung on Trevion and tried to run but he caught her and beat her ass. She didn't mind fighting a female and she didn't mind defending herself if a man hit her first, but she was no dummy and she wasn't about to hit a man first. She just walked away. Went back to the cookout as he started walking the opposite direction. When she got back everyone was asking where he was. And she told them that he walked home. She texted him later that night and to her surprise he was actually responding. He was trying to act like an asshole but somehow she ended up picking him up from King's house once she left the cookout and they went back to her house. As she was putting on her nightgown and he was taking off his shirt and pants to get into bed, he started talking about Taylor. "I can't believe you had that nigga spend the night at your house."

Alicia was going tell him that he didn't even spend the night when he saw his car here but she figured he wouldn't believe her anyway. "You really gonna start another argument right now? You don't even know anything about that situation."

"I don't need to know anything. I know that car and I know exactly who he is. I'm gon beat his muthafucka ass. You tell that next he better ready at all times cause when I see him I'm beating the fuck outta him with no warning." He told her. "Try me if you want to. I don't give a fuck."

Alicia laughed and shook her head. "Okay Trevion. Whatever you say." She told him. He climbed into his side of the bed then looked over at Alicia. "Did he sleep on my side of the bed, too? Was this is his side? Was he sleeping on my pillow?" He asked her. She didn't know if he was serious or not so she just looked at him and shook her head.

"Oh now you ain't got shit to say huh?" He said to her. "Okay, you just better not let me catch that nigga over here." He said before laying down. Alicia snuggled up to his back and wrapped her arm around his waist. He held her hand and they went to sleep. The next morning when they woke up they just lay in the bed talking and goofing around listening to some oldies music on Trevion's phone.

He was laying on his stomach with a pillow under his face. She was laying on his back with her face on his shoulder blade. That was her favorite position with him because she loved his back. He was the only man that she ever lay with like that. He facetimed Swag Billie. "You what up? You good from all that arguing last night?" He teased him. Trevion just smiled then lifted the phone a little so that Billie could see Alicia laying on his back smiling. Billie couldn't really see because Trevion had the brightness on his screen turned down. He asked who it was so Trevion turned the brightness up and Billie started laughing. "Y'all crazy man." He said to them as he and Alicia waved at each other. Trevion laughed "That's bae though." They talked for a little bit and when they got off the phone C-No called Trevion. Trevion had it on speakerphone so Alicia could hear C-No cracking a joke about picking him up on the highway when he walked from Angel's house the night before. He looked at Alicia and said "I told you I really did walk." She really felt bad about letting him walk but he was being stubborn and she assumed that he had called on of the boys to pick him up. Guess he needed that walk to clear his mind. She didn't know. What she did know though, was she happy that he came last night and happy that they were getting along, even though it was short-lived. They kept arguing and both being stubborn and having attitudes. One night he randomly texted her while she was lying in bed watching a movie. *Yo stupid ass must be with yo punk ass boyfriend. I'll kill yo ass nigga. Don't play with me Leon.*

She just stared at her phone for a minute because she really had no idea what the hell he was talking about. She responded back to him. *If you say so.*

K. He texted her. She sent him the thumbs up emoji. Twenty minutes later he texted her again. *What nigga you with?* He asked. She wasn't with anybody but she felt if he could question her then she could question him. *What chick you with?* She asked him not really expecting an answer. *Grace and LaLa.* He told her.

She didn't know who they were. *Good for you.* She replied. He immediately responded. *I want you.*

You don't. She typed. She was waiting for him to respond, to say he was coming over but as the minutes ticked on he didn't. She fell asleep. When she woke up the next morning she saw he texted her back an hour and a half later asking her where she was. Then again an hour after that saying 'bet'. He had an attitude. They didn't talk all that day or night until he went out to Club Ice. She texted him and he told her he would help come help her the next morning set up things for Noise and his girlfriend's baby shower that she was throwing for them. He said he would be there as soon as he could. He was out late and had gotten super drunk. Frannie called Alicia that night while they were out and asked her if she had Trevion's baby. Alicia was confused. "Hell no I don't have his baby. Why would I have his baby? You know good and well Nikki would not let me keep her baby. And why would keep his baby while he was out being a thot?" Alicia said to Frannie. Frannie laughed. "I don't know. He came to me and said 'Where my bae at?' and I was like she is out with her white boyfriend in Austin. And he was like you a lie cause she at home with my baby right now." Alicia shook her head he was so stupid but in a funny way. Frannie continued talking. "Yeah he was out there talking all loud telling everybody how much he love you and I told him he better stop professing his love for you in public all the time with all these eyes and ears cause I don't want to have to beat his baby mama up. She gonna be ready to jump on you cause he still in love with you like it's your fault or something. Then one of the chicks looked at me sideways when I said that." Frannie paused to take a breath. "But anyway, I was just calling to make sure you didn't have his baby, he super drunk though and he just pulled off so can you call him and make sure he gets home safely." They hung up the phone. Alicia checked on Trevion, TC said got on the phone and said he was ok and that they were all leaving. She went sleep. Needless to say that he didn't make it to help her with baby shower, and when he woke up he had to go a club meeting. That was the first time he had ever not been there when she asked if to be.

Chapter 80

Anniversary weekend was here! Rick had made it into town early that Friday evening and he had come over to Ravyn's house to see her and Alicia. When he pulled up both Alicia and Ravyn jumped up to go greet him. They ran but Ravyn reached him first. They all laughed and Alicia wrapped her arms around his neck and gave him the biggest hug. She didn't want to let him go. She was so happy to see her friend. He walked into the garage and dapped up TC and C-No and sat down. They hung out over there for about an hour before they had to go. Saucy had just made it into town and she was staying at Alicia's house so she had to be there to let her inside. Besides she need to get herself situated so that she could be ready for their meet and greet later that night.

The meet and greet was pretty cool, it started out lame and empty but after a couple of hours other clubs begin to show up. Saucy finally got to meet Trevion although she didn't that he and Alicia had a thing going on. They weren't on speaking terms at the moment but Frannie and basically everyone else, was trying to get them back right. Alicia thought it was funny though because they didn't need anyone to get them back right. They handle things their own way. After the meet and greet everyone decided to go turn up at Club Ice. It wasn't super packed but it was a nice size crowd and Alicia liked it like that. They all had drinks in their hand. Alicia saw Trevion talking to Deja's sister and of course her being tipsy made her a little bit jealous even though she was never the jealous type. She walked over to him and whispered in his ear. "Don't get fucked up." She told him slurring her words. He laughed at her knowing she was drunk. "What I do?" He said smiling like a little boy. "You better stay out of bitches' faces bruh." She said looking him in the eyes. He laughed at her again. He liked when she called herself trying to have an attitude and trying to check him. She was such a friendly and sweet person that he liked when that side of her came out, and it usually only came out with him during his shenanigans. "Kiss me." He told her, like he always does when she starts acting like that. Of course, she obliged as usual. TC had knocked someone out in the club because he thought Swag Billie was fighting. It turned into a big scuffle in the middle of the dance floor. Alicia knows protocol for TGL when things like happen so since Angel was only a prospect and didn't know yet, Alicia tried to grab her and pull her out of the way of the guys fighting. Ravyn wasn't anywhere on the dancefloor so Alicia didn't have to worry about her. She was trying to grab Angel but was trying jump into the fight because TC was fighting. Alicia kept telling her to back up and stop trying to jump in because the guys could handle it and the guys from OL2L didn't like to be grabbed when they were about to fight. She didn't listen so Alicia just stepped back out of the way and within seconds, she was surrounded by Rick, Theo, and their "security" SAA TooTall. That's what the males do, when other people are fighting and it has nothing to do with TGL, they make sure the women aren't in harm's way. They protected Alicia like she was a rare diamond. Not that anyone from OL2L was going to purposely hit her or anything, just a precaution because fights in the club get crazy and anything could have accidentally happened. After partying until around 2 am. They all decided to leave. Cops were out full force and Angel was drunk so Theo made sure that TC was going to drive her home. Ravyn, Alicia, and Trevion were all in separate cars going in the same direction for a minute so they began to race each other until Trevion turned off onto a different road to take C-No home. Ravyn and Alicia were headed to Angel's house. Rick called Alicia to make sure she was good. He was trying to come stay at her house but she told him she was staying at Angel's house as an excuse. She didn't want to hurt his feelings but she wasn't trying to go there with him. He said okay but sounded disappointed. He told her to hit him up in the morning then he headed to his cousin's house. Saucy hadn't come to Ice with them, she was tired from her drive. When Ravyn and Alicia made it to Angel's house, she and TC were just pulling up. They all went inside. Angel and TC went straight to her bedroom, Ravyn called dibs on her daughter's bedroom and because she was super drunk and throwing up everywhere they let her have it, and Alicia took the extra bedroom. She went to Angel's bedroom and saw she was in the shower so she decided to annoy TC. "You ain't a real nigga bruh. " She said to him. "A real nigga would strip butt naked and hop in the shower with her." She told him still a little tipsy. TC burst out in laughter. "Bro you are so childish!" He said to Alicia. She started laughing because he always told her that. "For real though! Or better yet, be lying in the bed ass booty naked when she get out, tell her you got a treat for her." Alicia couldn't hold her laughter in when TC looked at her laughing and asked, "Are you ever going to grow up?" They laughed so hard. "Prolly not." She told him with a shrug. She got a text from Trevion. *Where the fuck you at with yo stupid ass?!* He was really childish at times. She responded to him the same way he responded to her. *I'm at Angel house with you stupid ass.*

Well I'm going home. I'm at your house. Goodnight.

She was annoyed. *You didn't tell me you were going to my house. Come to Angel's house.* She texted him the address and he was pulling up on C-No's motorcycle 10 minutes later. He came in and talked to TC, and Angel for a little bit. Ravyn was knocked out already. They all joked around, jumping all over Angel's bed, then Trevion grabbed Alicia and took her to the spare bedroom. The lightheartedness didn't last because they were in the bedroom fighting 30 minutes later. She kicked him a couple of times while they were laying in the bed. He just made her so angry that she got up and went home. She left him lying there in Angel's spare bedroom. HE texted a little while later and told her to tell Angel to close her garage. She didn't respond to him but did text Angel.

The next day they had a car show at Club Ice. It was a huge turnout with over 40 cars, trucks, and bikes to enter. Trevion was there with OL2L of course and Ravyn even entered her car into the show after King's girlfriend helped her clean it out. Alicia was upset that she didn't win anything but she wasn't a judge. Trevion and Alicia didn't speak at all during the show and it was okay with Alicia. She was doing a lot of running around she barely had time to speak to anyone. That morning she had volunteered at a garage sale that the Pink Warrior Angels were having to raise money. They were a non-profit organization that helps women who have been diagnosed with breast cancer. It was a great organization so she didn't mind getting up early after going to bed so late to help them out. She was operating off of only 3 hours of sleep but she just threw on a pair of sunglasses to cover the bags and circles under her eyes. Periodically Rick would come find her just to talk or crack a joke. Really he was just trying to be in her presence. At one point when they were walking between some trucks he reached out and grabbed her butt. She swatted his hand away and asked him not to do it again. She had hoped that no one saw it and told Trevion. Even though they were not a couple she wouldn't disrespect him like that. That night they were holding the main party for anniversary at Club Ice as well. Alicia had a simple black mini dress. The bottom had a layer of lace and the top was sheer with lace accents over the breast area. She was classy yet sexy, very toned down that night. The party was okay. Alicia, Rick and majority of the other members felt it could have been a little bit better but there were other events going on that night so it was understood. Alicia had a couple of drinks at the bar and then a friend from another car club bought her a drink and right after that Angel's friend Cannon had asked her to take a shot with him. Before Alicia knew it she was drunk. Trevion and Alicia were still not speaking. When he was getting ready to leave he was telling everyone bye and he stopped at the front to give Ms.Nisha a hug and to dap Ossie up before leaving. That made Alicia angry. She snatched him by his arm and he stopped in the doorway of the exit. "I know your black ass didn't just think you were about to leave and tell everybody else by but not say shit to me." She said with an attitude. He stepped up to her. "Man shut the fuck up! You always trying to go off on me about something." He said loudly. She got up in his face and held her ground. "No you shut the fuck up don't be talking to me like you done lost your fucking mind!" They started arguing in the door way. She cursed him out again. "Yo little black ass is gonna make me fuck you up for real. I'm fucki-", and before she could finish her sentence he told her to shut the fuck up and give him a kiss and grabbed her and started kissing her right there in the door way. After a minute or two he pulled back, winked at her, and then left. Alicia turned around and looked right into the shocked and smiling faces of Ms. Nisha and Ossie. She had completely forgotten that they were right there. She began blushing. The rest of the night was a blur for Alicia. She remembered that Talia had driven her and Angel to Angel's house. She wasn't sure where her, or Angel's car was. Talia had to pull over on the side of the road so that Alicia could vomit. Then she vomited in the drive through at Taco Bell. Then she vomited a few more times on the floor in Angel's living room as well as in the trashcan that they gave her to use. She was hot and the whole room was spinning. She slid off of the couch onto the floor. She heard Talia saying that she needed to cool down. TC offered to pick her up and carry her to the bedroom but she vomited again and he changed his mind. She told them that she wanted to stay there so Angel brought her a blanket and a pillow. After talking to both Trevion and Rick on the phone as well as her cousin, she lay back and began drifting off to sleep. She didn't know when Talia left or anything else that happened that night. She woke up early the next morning while Angel and TC were still asleep. Shamelle came to pick her up so that she could go get her car from her sister's house. That's where Saucy had driven it to and parked it. Someone else from the club had driven Angel's house around the corner to Ms. Nisha's house so once she got her car she picked up Angel to go get hers. As she was dropping her off they were trying to piece together the events of last night. They had a good laugh at what they could remember because Angel was drunk too. She told Alicia to check her texts when she got home. Alicia did and was kind of confused as to the texts with Trevion. Angel had been texting him while Alicia was drunk and incoherent. She told him to come to her house to fuck Alicia. He said that he wasn't going to come because he didn't want a repeat of the night before with them fighting. Alicia wasn't mad at that because she agreed. She was kind of in her feelings because she didn't even know why Angel would text him that in the first place. When she asked Angel she said because Alicia had told her to text him. Alicia asked Talia if she heard her tell Angel that. Talia said that Alicia did say to text Trevion but she didn't say tell him to come fuck and even she did why would she tell him that when she wasted. Alicia and Angel had a conversation about it and Alicia determined that she didn't mean any harm so she let it go. But Angel had told her something that made her look at her kind of sideways. "So I just wanted to tell you something but I don't know if I'm tripping or not." She said to Alicia. "At the party last night, I was talking to Tre Will and I said I was tired and ready to go home. He looked at me and was like 'are you ready to go home, or you ready to go hooommmee?' and I kind of took that as he was trying to get at me. But I wasn't sure. But I just wanted to tell you in case it was that way."

Alicia was perplexed. That didn't sound like he was trying to get at her. Alicia's first thought was that he was saying that because he knew TC was going to be at her house that night and he was kind of teasing and joking with her about it. Alicia told Angel her take on it.

"As much foul shit as he has done to me one thing I've never questioned and he has never done was try to get at someone that he knows is my friend."

"Yeah I thought maybe I was tripping. You probably right." Angel said to her. That was the end of that conversation. They had a kickball tournament that day at the park. A couple of other car and bike clubs came out. Deja came out with her two kids to play as well as Ravyn and King's girlfriend. Angel had seemed a little down but was trying to be upbeat. Angel was complaining to Alicia and Ravyn about Deja's kids talking about how bad they were and saying that Deja seemed like she had an attitude because they weren't watching her kids. She said she should be over watching her own kids. When Deja's 3 year old daughter was in the truck hitting another child and cursing them out, she immediately went over to discipline her. She didn't spank her or anything but she did fuss at her. The little girl was spoiled and a bad ass cry baby so of course she started screaming bloody murder. Rick and Alicia had planned to go to Pluckers for lunch after the kickball tournament like they did every time he came down but Angel wanted to tag along as well. Alicia and Rick hadn't had any one-on-one friend time since he had been down there but they felt bad for telling her no so they let her come. At Plucker's they were all smitten by their waitress because not only was she friendly, she had a nice body. She was thick. Angel ordered some food to go, she said she was going to eat it later. After they ate and clowned for a little bit, Rick paid for his and Alicia's food and Angel gave the server her debit card to pay for hers while she went to the bathroom. The server came back and said that Angel's card had declined. Alicia would have paid for her food if she needed to but luckily Angel had another card and it went through. Once Alicia picked up her kids and made it home she showered and slept for the rest of the night.

Chapter 81

Alicia met up with Trevion at Lion's park to talk. She wanted to get a lot of stuff off of her chest. She wanted him to know that even she never told him, she has been in love with him since 2015, the feelings didn't go away when they stopped communicating for that year. She wanted him to know that she was aware that he was putting in effort with her but that she was so afraid of history repeating itself that she was consciously and subconsciously doing things to keep him at a distance so that she could protect her heart. One of those things was talking to Taylor. She felt if she didn't only focus on Trevion that she would be able to keep her heart together until he left for Germany. Also, when she told constantly called him a hoe and community dick and kept saying he was fucking with other bitches it more for herself than for him. She wasn't trying to make him feel bad she was telling herself that so that she wouldn't fall in too deep with him and risk being hurt, especially when she knew that he was indeed messing with other females. Also because she had a feeling that Nikki still wanted him and even though he said they were over and he was single since November, she didn't want to chance it. She just wanted to enjoy the rest of his time here and love on him and have him love on her like he had been doing all these months when she was pushing him away. It seemed as though although all they did now was argue. She remembered how Ravyn once told her that she was supposed to be his peace and not be the one that fusses and curses at him at all the time. Then she becomes just like the other bitches. She had every intention on telling him all of that even though she was scared to admit but she was ready. They pulled up at the same time. He was in King's car though. He hopped into her car and smiled at her. The conversation was light and fun. Then she tried to start the serious conversation that she wanted to have with him. She asked him why he always acts likes an ass or like he doesn't care at times. "I do care, but you just always assuming shit and you don't even be right in your assumptions. You always say off the wall shit." He told her.

"Everything I say isn't an assumption. And that doesn't excuse the fact that you act like you do." She replied.

"You know I love you girl. I always have, stop playing." He said to her.

She looked at him and cocked her head to the side. "I can't tell." She said. "We didn't speak for an entire year."

He laughed. "They say if you love something let it go and if it comes back to you then it's meant to be." He grinned like a Cheshire cat. She couldn't help but laugh. King called him just them and Trevion needed to take his car back to him. He asked Alicia to come to King's house so he can drop of the car. Alicia followed him then he got into her car and drove them to a parking lot to finish talking. They talked about a lot but nothing in particular. He told her that all jokes aside he really does care about her. They talked about marriage. He said she should marry him. She just laughed because she didn't know if he was serious or not. He told her he would get her real nice expensive ring. She told him that if she got married she doesn't know if she wants a ring. She wants matching tattoos on the ring fingers. He said he knew she was going to say that and that he wouldn't do that and he wouldn't want to wear a ring on his finger. He would wear it on a necklace. She would never agree to that. The talked about kids. He said he wanted to have a little girl one day. She said she didn't want any more kids but if she did she would want a boy and she would want to name him Atlas. He laughed at her for wanting to name a child that. "You must be trying to tell me that you want to have my baby." He told her.

Alicia frowned up her face. "Why would you assume that?"

"Because you know I make boys and you said you wanted another son. " He said smiling at her.

She burst out laughing. "Man get the fuck out of here!" she said.

"I'm just saying." He laughed, then got serious. "For real though, I do be missing you. I just be having so much going on and so much I'm dealing with on a daily basis. My mind just be everywhere. But I do be missing you and you know I care about you and I love you." He looked at her. "So stop tripping all the time." He said.

Alicia smiled. She didn't even tell him everything that needed to be said. She just enjoyed the next hour with him laughing, talking, fussing, and even on facetime with McCool.

Trevion was leaving in less than two weeks and although they were arguing a lot and not seeing each other as often, Alicia tried was kind of happy because she was preparing herself for him not being around. Everything else in her life was okay for the most part except a few stupid things. Nikki tried to start beef again for no reason at all. She claimed that Alicia had blocked her on Facebook and she was upset about it, talking on Ravyn's status saying that Alicia just blocked after a whole year because she wanted to be relevant and she was thinking about her and that she should have whooped her ass and all kinds of other stuff. Alicia thought it was stupid because she never blocked Nikki, even when all the drama was happening. Nikki was non-factor to her and she didn't bother her at all so blocking her was pointless. After Ravyn posted the screenshot of her not being blocked in the comments section she didn't have anything else to say. The other thing was she didn't know why Nikki and her bad built ass friend Shaw was always talking about beating her ass and calling her scary. Alicia wasn't scared of them or anyone else. She simply just doesn't do all the Facebook beef and arguing on social media, nor does run up on anyone trying to fight. She actually preferred not to fight but that's not to say that won't fight. She would definitely fight if someone touched her or did something to the kids but other than that, she just sat pretty and let whoever say whatever. She was grown and didn't have a thing to prove to anybody. Alicia and Rick were also on the outs and the friendship was declining even further. He was trying to get with Deja and Alicia was too hot about that. She felt like it was trifling as hell on his part to do that knowing that had sex before and that he was still trying to have something going with Alicia even when he was down here for the anniversary. He had called her the day he left and tried to tell her and she told him from the jump she wasn't cool with it.

"So look, I kinda got this little situation with Deja." He told her. "We went to eat today before I left but she asked me if I had anything going on with you and I was like no we just close as fuck." Alicia felt like she already knew where this was going. "What's the situation?" She asked impatiently.

"I really don't know."

"Stop beating around the bush. If you and her are trying to talk then say that." Alicia said getting annoyed.

"I don't think we are trying to do that." He laughed. "I don't know what the fuck it is."

She rolled her eyes. "Man you know but if that's what you want to do, you grown so do you. I definitely don't like that shit but y'all grown so whatever Rick do what you feel."

"I really don't Alicia. And yeah I know I am but I still felt like you should know. What do you not like?" He asked her.

Was this nigga serious? "You already know what I don't like but don't worry about it. You gonna do what you want to do anyway."

"Alicia don't even act like that with me. What's the problem? I don't say anything about nothing you do." Was he really trying to justify this shit? She got upset.

"I don't fuck with your friends Rick! But if you don't see a problem then I guess it ain't one. Fuck how I feel. You good. Shit go ahead and fuck Deja, Talia, Angel, and all the rest of my friends while you're at it." She said angrily.

"That aint the same shit are you serious? You got cool with her the same time I saw her on Facebook and I aint' tried to fuck with none of your friends." He was still trying to explain.

"My nigga you became friends on Facebook at the same time we became cool. Y'all weren't in each other's inboxes, y'all weren't texting or talking on the phone, it wasn't none of that shit. Meanwhile, she and I was. I brought her into my group of friends. We hang out on a damn near every weekend basis. We have group chats together. We are actually friends in real life so what the fuck are you talking about. Yall were not! You literally just met her and only because of me!" She was really going off now.

"You were going to Angel's house every damn night Alicia." That was his rebuttal. He didn't even acknowledge not having any type of friendship with her prior to that weekend.

"I would never so that shit to you." She said. "And we told everybody to come to Angel's house. But I don't even care bruh do what you want, how I felt about it didn't matter when you started trying to holla at her so it shouldn't matter now, right."

He was started to get mad even though he was in the wrong. "Nigga I said something about staying with you and every night you were going to Angel's house. But if you gonna do me like that then I got ya. I could have been like you and not said anything but I did and you trippin over some shit that ain't even nothing."

That was it. "It obviously is something if you felt the need to tell me about it but once again that is my friend but that's the part right there, you don't give a fuck about that. I don't want to see that shit and that shit ain't cool period! But you don't give a fuck so whatever."

"Yeah I told you because we went to eat but still you see me with Ravyn, and Angel and I used to be with Tika so what's the fucking difference. And I'm pretty sure I knew Jacob and ain't say shit about that." He was trying to flip shit now.

She yelled at him. "Nigga I was with Jacob before I ever even knew you! And you clearly said you have a situation with Deja but all of a sudden it ain't shit."

"Don't mean I ain't fucking know him and didn't know y'all was even together. It ain't shit and yea I said situation. I knew what it was with us that's why I ain't say shit about none of your other flings but I can't do a muthafuckin thing." He said in a cold tone.

"You can do whatever the fuck you want to but why do it with my friend? Someone I hang with all the time? If you don't understand that then ain't no point in still talking about it." She said calmly.

He sighed. "I told you because I didn't want it to turn into something and then you mad."

"You told me in case it turned into something then that means you know it's more than what you're saying it is."

"No it's not it's just that I know that y'all are cool or whatever. I do understand but you're only thinking of yourself right now. It's like you don't want me to talk to anybody that you know. I don't even live there." He was trying to be nice in order to change her feelings. It wasn't working. "Me and you took it there that one time, but you have been involved with someone ever since then. You already know it's nothing down here with me so yes I would like to maybe have that like you don't even understand." She didn't say anything so he kept talking. "The whole time that you and whoever were trying to be together or whatever that was, what you think I was doing here? While I'm here and you there you still will be connecting with people and talking to them or whatever. I've had nothing for a long time."

"You know what fuck it Rick. It's obviously more important for you to talk to her than to understand what I'm saying to you." She was getting annoyed.

He was still trying to convince her. "Alicia you not getting what I'm saying, I'm not tryna to talk to her or be her nigga or none of that. I would just like somebody to chill with when I'm there and you're taken." That was the end of that conversation. Alicia was tired of trying to explain to him when he knew he was wrong but was trying to convince her otherwise. He started trying to lie about it saying he didn't like her and was not trying to fuck with her but they made it obvious by tagging each other in posts about wanting to fuck. When she called him out on it and told him again that she didn't like or approve of that shit he was still saying it was nothing. But she knew better. Angel had even told Alicia that Deja had been telling her that she and Rick were talking now on that level. Another friend had told Alicia that Deja said Rick was her man. Deja knew that rick felt some type of way about Trevion and Alicia talking again so she was sitting around on the phone with him during their daily talks telling him everything that she saw happening between the two. She didn't know why though because nobody could make Alicia stop loving or for fucking with Trevion but him and her. She was upset because Rick was showing that he didn't care about their friendship. Not only did he continue to try and fuck with Deja after Alicia had told him that shit wasn't cool, but he kept lying to her like that weren't doing that but yet making obvious on social media and telling her shit about Alicia and past issues. Alicia would have had way more respect for him and would have gotten over the situation quicker if he had been honest and just said that he was still going to fuck with Deja even though Alicia had a problem with it instead of lying like he wasn't. She texted him and told him about himself then it went downhill from there.

Stop acting like that with me.

Stop being untruthful with me and I wouldn't act like that but whatever. She shot back.

He claimed that he hadn't been untruthful but she knew better. She knew him. He told her that he wasn't with Deja or anything and that she was looking too much into shit. She told him he didn't have to explain anything to her.

Alicia whats the damn problem? You being a dick.

She didn't respond right away but later that night she had made the decision she needed to make.

Let's just not even be cool like that nomore dude. Smh.

What? He replied but she didn't answer. He called her and she still didn't answer. *Will you stop fucking ignoring me?*

Nope cause you won't stop ignoring my fucking feelings.

I've never ignored your damn feelings but the first time somebody else come into the picture you wanna act funny. That was his dumb ass response.

She went in on him. *I've repeatedly told you I'm not cool or comfortable with it but you wanna fucking say its not what it is but you damn sure keep making it obvious that it what it is but what the fuck ever man aint no point in talking about it nomore cause you don't give a fuck anyway so if you don't give a fuck then why should I? Do whatever the fuck you you want. I'm I sure know where you gonna be when you come down here so you good…get ya pussy BRO.*

We not in no relationship or nothing so it is what it is.

I DO NOT GIVE A SHIT…you made ya choice so yeah it is what it is. She told him and she meant it.

No you just made your choice. I hope you know what you doing. He warned her.

She just shook her head. She was going to reply then block him. *You don't even give a fuck so why would it matter? All you care about is getting your little dick wet. Whatever my nigga.*

After everything now I don't give a fuck? Ok Alicia. She didn't respond. She added his number to the spam list then went to sleep. That was the end of her most consistent male friendship aside from Noise. She didn't even care at that point because niggas ain't shit.

Chapter 82

Alicia had been feeling a little down over the past few days after ending her friendship with Rick. He was one of her best friends and she couldn't believe that he chose to fuck Deja over keeping their friendship. That wasn't even the part that made her most mad though. What upset her the most, was that he was trying to flip the situation as if he had a right to be mad that she was with Jacob or Trevion. When she was with Jacob before, she didn't even know Rick. She had never even knew him so that had nothing to do with this situation. As far as Trevion was concerned, Rick met Trevion through Alicia when she started dealing with him in 2015, so that wasn't the same situation either. He was trying to make her feel bad but a real friend wouldn't do that and a real friend wouldn't lie. But he always told her to pay attention to people's actions and reactions and stop putting everybody's feelings, needs, and wants before her own. She was finally taking his advice and because he wasn't benefiting him he was mad. Guess it wasn't supposed to apply to him. Alicia didn't care anymore. Fuck the friendship. In dealing with that fall out, stresses of school, spending time with the kids and getting them to their extracurricular activities, and on top of all that Taylor had become a little stalker. He would drive down the street by her house multiple times a day and night, he would end up being right next to her in traffic when she would go pick her brother up from school knowing she took the same route every day at the same time, She would go into a store and he would be sitting there in the next parking lot over just sitting in the car but would act like he didn't see her. He didn't live or work on the side of town she lived on nor did he have to come over that way to get home or to work yet he was always at the store by her house. He was always eating at the Subway by her house. There were a million Subway's in Killeen and a million corner stores. He wanted her to speak to him, to text him, or say something to him but she didn't care about him so why would she? It really didn't even bother her it was just kind of creepy. Angel had been dealing with a lot of stuff lately with her mom being sick, missing her daughter, TC being full of shit, being lonely, being depressed, and drinking a lot. Alicia had been trying to be there for her as much as she could be but it seemed as if Angel just wanted to wallow in depression and self-pity. Alicia would go check on her, she would call and text to see how she was doing, when she would get drunk and couldn't drive or didn't want to be alone Alicia would get out of her bed in the middle of the night to go see about her. She tried going out to eat with her to take her mind off things, she tried cheering her up with laughter, she was even the one who brought Angel into TGL as a prospect and shared her friends with her. She didn't know what else to do to help her so she told Angel she should try talking to Rick because sometimes he had a way of making her look at situations differently. The problem Alicia had with Angel and her situations is that she seemed to not want to change them or get out of them. She seemed like she would rather have a pity party than to try and pick herself up or that she was relying on others to pick her up. Alicia couldn't be on-call and available 24 hours a day every single day for the same situations over and over again, she had kids to take care of and other priorities and responsibilities. But she did love her friend and wanted to help her and be there for her but it was starting to take a toll on her as well. She texted Trevion and told him she needed the duck pond with him today. It was Monday so she knew he would have his son until about 630 that evening. So she was expecting a later time anyway. He was cool with spending time at the duck pond today after Nikki picked up their son. Unfortunately, he had a meeting at 730 so the duck pond was out of the question. He came over to her house a little after 9 after his meeting was over. When he got there Alicia opened the garage for him. He walked in and she was standing there waiting for him. He immediately pulled her into his embrace. He stood there hugging her and rubbing her back as she lay her head on his shoulder and allowed herself to just enjoy him trying to comfort her. "What's wrong?" he asked her knowing she was feeling down. She just shook her head. "I just have a lot going on." she sighed. "I really needed thig hug." He kissed her forehead and they walked into her house. Alicia's mom had just moved back into her house and when he walked into the living room she immediately begin smiling. For some reason her mom loved him. "Is that my little chocolate son?" she said excitedly. He laughed. "Hey mama. How you been?" He stood near the couch where she was sitting. "I been good. How you been? I see you done picked up some weight." she told him jokingly while patting his stomach, that was once a six pack but was now a beer gut. "Where did this come from?" she asked him. He laughed and started rubbing his belly then looked at Alicia. They talked for a few minutes then he and Alicia went to her bedroom. She closed the door and they lay out on the bed watching A Low-Down Dirty Shame, one of Alicia's favorite movies. Alicia was laying on her side in the fetal position and Trevion was lying in front of her on his side with his head and neck on her hip. They talked and watched the movie as he played with her fingers. Alicia loved how she could be feeling so down but just his presence in the simplest way could make her feel better. She used to be that for him. She used to be his peace but so much had happened and she had make the mistake of trying to keep her heart from him for all these months that now she knew she was no longer his peace. She knew he cared for her but she was starting to be more of a fight than the peace she once was. She knew it. But she didn't know what to do about that. She felt that it was too late to go back to that with him leaving so soon. She went to use the bathroom and when she came back he was lying in her spot on his back. She climbed over him and lay on her back with her head resting on his stomach. He was on his phone on Facebook messenger. She saw that it was Angel messaging him. She knew Angel had messaged him on there from time to time, mainly talking about TC and asking him to relay messages to him for her, she didn't really trip on it though because she knew Angel really just wanted friends. But after telling Alicia that she thought he was trying to get at her last week, Alicia didn't think she should still be in his inbox at all for any reason. Alicia knew that he wasn't the one that was hitting her up, he was just responding to her when she messaged him. "Dang dude, you're on my time right now. Tell your little groupies you will talk to the later." Alicia said to Trevion knowing who he was talking to already but wanting to be an ass. He laughed. "Man if you don't shut up. This Angel hitting me up. That's ya homegirl." Alicia rolled her eyes. "What she talking about? TC?" she asked him.

"Mind ya business." He said playfully. "Nah, nothing really. I don't care nothing about what they got going on. She think I'm going to give her advice about their shit but that ain't got nothing to do with me." She decided to take this opportunity to ask him about what Angel had told her last week. She looked at him. "So since we are on the subject of Angel, I have a question." She was trying to put her words together correctly. "At our anniversary party last week, did you say something to Angel about going home with her?" He frowned his face up. "What? What you mean?"

"Well Angel told me last week after our party that you tried to get at her." She told him.

"What the fuck? Man hell nah."

Alicia continued. "She said when she was tired and ready to go home you were like 'are you ready to go home, or you ready to go hooommmee'."

He shook his head. "Man I was talking about her going home with TC. The fuck? She really thought I was trying to get at her?"

"Well that was my first thought when she said it to. Like I didn't see how she took that as you trying to get at her." She told him.

"You really thought I would try your friend?" he shook his head again.

"No I didn't think you would."

"If you didn't think it then you wouldn't have even asked me." He said to her.

"Well I told her that she misunderstood. I really didn't think you tried her."

He just looked at her. "Well I see its time for me to start being an asshole to these hoes."

"Why would you do that? You don't have to be an asshole. She was just making sure that she didn't misinterpret anything." Alicia tried reasoning with him.

"Nah fuck all that. She came out of nowhere like I was trying to get at her. That shit wasn't cool. If she didn't know for sure that I was trying her then she shouldn't have opened her mouth."

Alicia shook her head. "So you don't care about potentially causing a problem in my friendship with her?" she asked him.

He sat up and looked her straight in the eyes. "She didn't care about causing a problem between me and you. Did she?" Alicia didn't argue about it anymore. What else could she say after that? He made a good point so she just left it alone. He wasn't intending on staying over that night but they were enjoying being laid up under each other. He flipped over on his stomach and Alicia lay beside him and rubbed his back until they both fell asleep.

The next day she was on the phone with Ravyn talking about a million different things. Alicia told her about Angel saying Trevion tried to get at her. "What?! Oh no." she said. "Now I know that he has done a lot of fucked up shit and all but I don't believe he tried to get at Angel. I think she just misinterpreted it and ran with it without being sure."

"I thought the same thing. But I asked him about it anyway. Just to be sure."

"Well what did he say?" Ravyn asked. Alicia told her about their conversation. "Damn. Yeah I would be upset too if I were him. And he did make a good point. She didn't care about if that would cause a problem between y'all."

"Right. And the crazy thing is, she was sitting there messaging him on Facebook. Like I kinda thought that was weird since you thought he was trying to get at you. Why are you still in his inbox? But he stopped responding to her after our conversation. I'm going to talk to her and let her know we had that conversation though." Alicia told her.

Ravyn sighed. "Yeah. You should especially so she will be aware that he felt some type of way about her thinking he was trying to get at her. She should know that he will probably be an asshole to her now."

Alicia talked with Angel about it later that day. She said that she figured it was a miscommunication but she didn't want to not say anything to her then it really was something. Alicia could understand that but she felt she should have more clarity before bringing it to her. Angel said now she see why he hasn't been responding to her messages. Alicia just looked at her. She really didn't know why she was even hitting him up. But if he wasn't responding then Alicia didn't feel the need to say anything about it.

Alicia and Trevion had been so up and down the rest of the week that she didn't know how to take anything. They had a conversation one day and he told her that she was way too friendly and that she has always been way too friendly. He believed that she would talk to someone else while he was gone to Germany. She didn't want to fight or argue. She just wanted him to understand. *Look, all this fussing and fighting all the time is stupid. I don't want to keep doing that. I just want good vibes. Can we just enjoy each other for the rest of your time here?* She texted him while she was sitting in Ravyn's kitchen with her and Angel.

He replied quickly. *Of course we can. That's not a problem.*

That makes me happy. She responded.

That's what I'm supposed to do. He texted back and she smiled.

Alicia had been wanting to see the sunset over the lake. She and Trevion had been on a shit stroll so she wanted to do something special with him before he left. She figured the sunset at the lake would be a great memory for them to add to the duck pond and all their goofy times. She drove out to Temple Lake and found the perfect spot. She texted him that day to see if he would be available to spend an hour and a half with her. He said he was. He wanted to know what she was trying to do but she wanted it to be a surprise. When he came to pick her up that day she offered to drive her car but he said he would drive. She had gotten him some wings and a coke from Sonic's because she knew he loved wings. When she got in the car he was smiling and in a good mood. He started driving and asked where they were going. She told him she wasn't going to tell him but to go towards Temple. He looked at her like she was crazy. He started complaining about going all the way to Temple and it immediately fucked up the mood and gave her an attitude. She told him that since he was going to be an ass and complain then don't even worry about it. Just take her back home. He took her home and she got into her car and left. She went to the duck pond by herself then called Ravyn and told her what had happened. Ravyn tried her hardest to comfort her and they just talked on the phone until she felt better. She was happy Ravyn was such a good friend. Later that night Windii brought her baby over to Alicia to babysit so that she could out to Club Ice. When she came to pick her baby up she told Alicia that she saw Trevion at Ice with a female on the back of a motorcycle. Alicia wasn't planning on asking him about it because she was trying not to care. She intended to send a text to Ravyn telling her Windii told her but instead she accidentally sent it to Trevion.

Windii saw Tre Will leaving Ice with a female on the back of a bike smh. She wrote.

Tell that bitch she gone get beat up tonight if she come out. I'm not playing. He responded five hours later.

Alicia rolled her eyes. *Beat up for what though?*

Lying on me.

That's stupid as fuck and you saying you weren't on a bike with a female? She asked.

He responded quickly. *I was and I rode her around the parking lot. That's ok though, whenever I see her, it's going down. I'm tired of hoes lying on my name.*

How is it a lie when you had the chick on the bike? She replied. *And that's stupid. You gonna try to put your hands on little bitty Windii just cause you were with a female?*

I'm not I got somebody for her.

Alicia was getting mad. She would never speak to him again if he had somebody jump on Windii. *That's so lame. What you mad for? You're single so what does it matter if she saw you with a female? You are leaving in a week so what's the point? Why invest time and energy into having someone fight little ass Windii...you got issues. But whatever, hope you used a condom last night. Good day.* She was done with the conversation. For him to be as smart as he is he was so stupid and childish and even ignorant sometimes.

The bitch shouldn't be lying on me. I will enjoy the rest of my day. Alicia didn't bother responding.

Chapter 83

The last Saturday in April and one week until Trevion leaves. Alicia was feeling all kinds of things good and bad. She had to go to an even tonight at Club O'bok with TGL. Talia decided to come out with them as well. Alicia, Ravyn, Talia, and Angel had gotten cute and met up at the club. Of course some of OL2L guys were there including Trevion. She hadn't really talked to him since yesterday after their disaster at trying to surprise him. She had been told that he felt bad about how he acted and that he knew he was wrong but he still hadn't hit her up to apologize so she didn't say shit to him either. They were all drinking and having a good time. Basically they were just pre-gaming for Club Tabu. Alicia heard one of her favorite songs come on. *I'm just stunting on my ex bitch...Hold up, I'm just*

flexing on my ex bitch...fuck a wedding a ring I bought a necklace.
Alicia and the ladies began to really turn up. She looked over and
saw Trevion with his back turned to her talking to Theo and the
president of another motorsports club. She didn't know why or what
made her feel like doing it, but the alcohol had her feeling bold and
the song was calling her to be petty. She walked over to where
Trevion was and began dancing in front of him and flipping her hair
in his face. She danced a complete circle around him singing the
words to the song Stuntin' on my Ex. She heard the ladies hyping her
up and clapping. They were hyped at her little performance. Trevion
just stood there laughing. She had got him good and he thought it
was cute. When she looked at Theo, he laughed and told her to stop
it. As she started walking back to the ladies, she saw the other
president cracking up with laughter. She didn't know who else saw
her pettiness but her ladies were still hype when she made it back to
them. "Yoooo bruh! I was not expecting that!" Talia said to her
when she came back over there. Ravyn agreed. "Me neither but that
shit was everything bitch! You did that. I was like yaaaassssss
bitch!" She was smiling from ear to ear. Angel chimed in. "Girl that
was epic! I'm trying to be like you! That just gave me life!" Alicia
just laughed. They were so silly. Alicia was looking good. She had
on a long sleeve, mesh dress with a gold sleeveless body suit
underneath it. It accentuated her curves so nicely and although it was
super sexy, it was also very classy. They left to go to Tabu and the
ladies were on the dancefloor by the stage. They were still drinking
when Deja and her friends arrived. They all said hello but after a
while, Alicia and Talia went upstairs. They preferred to be able to
see everything from the top. They were dancing and enjoying
themselves and looking down at Ravyn dancing to every song that
came on. She got like that when she drank. Angel seemed a little
down. She wasn't dancing like she normally did. She was just sitting
on the stage looking kind of sad. She was occasionally lean over and
talk to Deja and they would laugh but that was pretty much it.
Trevion, Swag Billie, C-No, and few of the other OL2L guys were in
the middle of the dancefloor. TC wasn't with them. He wasn't really
that into clubs. Alicia saw a few different females talking to Trevion.
He looked like they were females that he already knew. She had seen
them before but couldn't place where. She paid particular attention to
one female that had on an army camouflage jacket. She seemed to

really be trying to get at him. She was all up in his face and trying to grab onto him and talk in his face. He wasn't really paying her much attention though. Alicia didn't know if it was because he wasn't feeling her or if it was because he knew she was somewhere in there and Angel and Deja were only a few feet away from him. She didn't trip she let him have his fun. As the night went on she all of the other ladies came up to where Talia and Alicia were at. They all partied up there until Alicia looked down and saw Trevion talking to a female. It looked she was putting her hand down his pants and he was just standing there smiling and talking to her. Alicia immediately got upset. Deja saw that she was mad and asked her was she good. She told her yeah but she was about to go down there and get on Trevion. Deja told her she would go with her if she wanted to fight the girl. Alicia looked at her like she was crazy. She wasn't about to go fight that girl. She didn't fight over men, especially ones that weren't even hers. She wasn't even going to say anything to the female she was going to have words with him. Alicia walked down stairs to the dancefloor with Deja on her heels. She went up to Trevion and grabbed his arm to pull him so she could talk in his ear. He leaned his ear towards her mouth to hear her. "You better stop fucking trying me with all these bitches in your face...I'm not playing with you! Got bitches putting their hands down your pants and shit!" He looked at her like she was crazy. "Man what the fuck you talking about? That was Billie girlfriend she was putting her phone in my pocket!" he said and pulled her phone out to show her. "That's like my damn sister. You better chill the fuck out." He said to her. "I don't care about all that, you doing too much and this other bitch keep coming over to you." She fussed at him as she started walking away. "Man shut the fuck up with yo stupid ass." He said to her. She turned around "No you shut the fuck up!" She stayed on the dancefloor with her ladies. Trevion stayed with his friends. Alicia was about to walk off the floor to go get Talia when C-No stopped her as she was leaving. He said something about caring about Ravyn and the fact they are still living in the same house and not disrespecting her so she shouldn't be disrespecting him. She didn't understand all of what he said but he asked her to get Ravyn. She went back onto the floor where Ravyn was at dancing with some guy. Before she could get to her Trevion and another guy from OL2L had snatched her up and away from the guy. They told her to chill out before she be the cause of the guy getting his ass beat. Alicia shook her head she went and got Talia and they came back to the dancefloor. When she went over to where the other girls where at, she saw Ravyn and C-No hugged up and dancing together. She thought it was so cute. She knew they still had love for each other and she wanted them to work out so bad. Out of the corner of her, Alicia saw the camouflage jacket chick trying to put her arms around Trevion. He was trying to step away from her but he was laughing. Alicia went over to him. "I'm not gonna keep telling you to keep these hoes out ya face!" He started laughing. "I don't even know her! That's Deja's friend. That's your friend's friend." Alicia rolled her eyes. "Shit I don't know her either. But she keep grabbing you and hugging you and shit." she said to him.

"What you want me to do? I don't know her." he said.

"Tell her to back the fuck up! Push her ass off you." She suggested.

He smiled at Alicia, he liked when she acted jealous. "Baby." he said to her then puckered his lips. "Gimmie a kiss." Alicia leaned in and kissed him on his mouth. Just as she was separating her lips from his, camouflage jacket girl peered over his shoulder at Alicia. "Oooohhhh so you bae?" she asked her. Then she put up her hand to high five Alicia. Alicia was confused as fuck but it was now obvious that the girl was drunk. She just laughed and gave her a little high five. Deja came over and grabbed her friend saying not to pay her any attention because she was drunk. Angel was standing next to Alicia during the whole ordeal. She looked like she was ready to jump into action in case something popped off. Luckily nothing did. They decided to leave a little bit after that. Angel and Ravyn went home but Alicia, Talia, and Deja decided to go eat at IHOP. After eating they all went their separate ways. Trevion came over to Alicia's house when she made it home. She showered and put on a t-shirt. She climbed into her bed next to him. "Come here." He said and pulled her closer to him. They were face to face. Alicia looked him in his eyes. "Kiss me." She said to him. He complied. He began kissing her slowly, sensually, and deeply. He lay her on her back then climbed on top of her, between her legs. Alicia took off his shirt and began rubbing her hands up and down his back. He looked down at her, searching her face as if he was trying to plant every facial feature of hers into his memory. He rubbed her face softly, then grabbed the back of her head and kissed her again. This time with even more passion. He was swirling his tongue around in her mouth and biting her bottom lip. He took off her t-shirt and threw it to the floor. He began kissing her neck as he rolled her nipples between his fingers. She arched her back and moaned with pleasure. This man just did something to her, she couldn't help but to melt under his touch. She was ready. He positioned his penis at the opening of her vagina then paused. She squirmed beneath him wanting him inside of her. He entered her slowly. She gasped. He was rock hard. He began with a slow steady rhythm. Kissing her as she moved under him catching his rhythm. He was breathing heavily, his forehead pressed to her forehead and his nose pressed to her nose. "I missed you so much." He said to her still stroking. "I missed you too." She responded honestly. "Why you be trying to flex on me all the time?" He asked her.

"I don't. That be you." she said.

He pushed deeper. "No it be you. You get mad and won't talk to me. Trying to stunt on me like you did tonight." he went deeper again. Her breath got caught in her throat. She didn't respond to him. He kept talking. "You just be using me for dick. That's all you want from me is my dick."

Alicia spread her legs wider and gripped his lower back, pushing him deeper into her. No I don't. I don't care about your dick. I care about you." She said to him as she felt herself on the verge of an orgasm. He sensed that she was about to come so he sped up just a little and gripped her ass to pull her closer to him. He stared at her as she released her juices all over his manhood. She was moaning and loving the feeling of unparalleled pleasure as she was thrown into ecstasy. He caressed the side of her face with the side of his own face while whispering to her. "I missed you so much. I love you." He said. Alicia was still experiencing her orgasm. She wrapped her arms around him and kissed his neck. "I love you too" she whispered. That was the first time she had ever told him that before. But she meant it. That sparked something in him and began to fuck her like he knew he was going to miss her. He lifted her leg up to her shoulder and began thrusting hard inside of her. He smacked her ass so hard that she thought would she have a hand print on her cocoa skin. In and out, in and out. Faster and harder. He pulled his member out then turned her over on her stomach. She positioned herself on her knees with them spread as far apart as she could and balanced herself on her forearms. Then she arched her back and when he entered her from behind, she gasped and buried her face in the pillow. He was hitting every spot he could find and the pain was so pleasurable. He was smacking her ass and pulling her hair, he even grabbed her by the throat when he got too good to him. At first he gave her what he wanted and made sweet love to her. Now she was giving him what he wanted, allowing him to fuck her with no inhibitions. He groaned loudly then came so hard that Alicia thought she felt the house shake. They lay there panting, trying to catch their breath. Alicia had to get up and clean herself up. When she came back to the bed he was laying there half asleep. He felt her climb back into the bed so he reached out for here. She cuddled up in his arms and they went to sleep. Then next morning when they woke up they lay in bed and talked and goofed around for about an hour. When she walked him outside as he was getting ready to leave, he pulled her to him for a hug. He held her for a minute then kissed her cheek and told her that he would talk to her later. She watched him drive away as she thought about last night. It was the sweetest agony.

Epilogue

Alicia spent time with Trevion on the last Monday that he was in the states. They had a funny evening together. They went to get something to eat at McDonald's and her car battery died in the drive through line. They called different people to come help before they knew what was wrong with it. Swag Billie came and an old TGL member sent someone to help as well. They tried everything they could think of it didn't help. After over an hour of sitting in the drive through some lady said they should just check the battery. As soon as they hooked up the cables everything powered on. They laughed so hard at that. Trevion wouldn't let her drive back to King's house. They spent the next 3 hours talking, play fighting, laughing, and loving. She had smoked with Ravyn before she went to Trevion so she was in a good mood. She was sitting in his lap in the passenger seat of her car, looking up at him smiling. She cracked a joke and started laughing. He asked her if she had smoked today. She told him no. He asked if she was lying to him. She told him yes. He started laughing. They talked about a lot that day. He told her how a lot of guys be checking for her. He said that he's had guys come to him and ask if he used to deal with her and if he still deals with her, then they would say they wanted to fuck with her, almost as if they were asking him if it was okay. He told her how she makes him laugh when she tries to check him about bitches in the club. He mentioned her petty stunt at Club O'bok, said it was cute how she came over there dancing around him to the song and swinging her red hair in his face. He said he thought that was funny too. He told her that he really did love her then he asked her if she would really wait for him while he was Germany. She answered him honestly, telling him that if they were actually together she would with no problem and no hesitation. But since they are not and the past month they haven't been getting along, she wasn't going to lie and tell him yes. She told him that she wasn't planning to go out looking for anyone and she wasn't worried about being with anyone but two years is a long time to be in an unsure situation so she wouldn't say that she won't end up talking to someone. He told her that he wasn't trying to be with anyone either that he was just going to be on chill mode. Even though they were getting along and kissing and loving on each other that night, it ended with them arguing. They talked the next day after she sent him about 3 memes every single hour of the day. He told her was going to block her for sending all those memes then unblock her the next day and send her a text talking about good morning beautiful like nothing had ever happened. She laughed so hard because she thought it was cute. The last time she saw him was the Friday that he had his going away party at Club Ice. He was in his feelings because she was talking and laughing with Jacob and because she hugged and old member of OL2L that he didn't know. The he had an attitude because she was dancing.

They talked in the club for a long time that night and she got to meet the girl who put her phone in his pocket at Club Tabu the previous week, she didn't remember her name. The same girl was asking Angel a question about TC and Angel got upset and wanted to fight the girl. Alicia had to calm her down and the other girl's friends had to come get her because she was drunk. Angel almost ruined his whole party for causing a scene because TC wasn't speaking to her or paying her any attention. She was trying hard to get his attention, she even asked another guy to come up there and was all over him in front of TC. That backfired on her and he ended up getting another female's phone number in front of Angel. Angel got upset and pushed the girl in her face and tried to fight to TC while Alicia was outside with Trevion. When Alicia had come back and saw that TC was upset and found out what happened. She tried to get Angel out of there. Angel was still trying to fight him in the parking lot and eventually everything settled down and they all went home. Angel was upset with Alicia the next day when she called to check on her but after she made sure she was okay, Alicia told her that she was wrong for all that went down. She didn't like that. That was the start of the strain of their friendship and it eventually ended due to pettiness and fakeness on Angel's part in the Rick and Deja situation.

Alicia had talked to Trevion until his phone died after his party. He was leaving at 4am Sunday morning and she wasn't going to see him again before he left unless she came to the airport. She asked if he wanted her to, he said it was up to her. That wasn't what she needed to hear so she decided not to go. That Sunday evening she went to Ravyn's house. They sat outside on the curb and she let Alicia pour out everything in her heart and cry. She even cried a little with her. She understood what she was feeling. Alicia put a lot of blame on herself for him leaving the way he did. She felt like it was her fault that they drifted apart this time because of her actions. He was putting in effort and he was trying to show her that he changed for the better but she was still so stuck in the past and hurt and afraid of history repeating itself that she sabotaged them. She wanted him to know that but never had the opportunity to tell him face to face like she wanted to. She cried to Ravyn that night about everything that she kept bottled up inside.

She thought about her life over the years and she realized that she was too soft and to accepted too much. She should have learned from Alton's deadbeat dad that when a person does you dirty, that you don't owe them anything. She needed to learn how to be stronger and allow anyone to constantly treat her badly and not appreciate her. She didn't know what would with Trevion, she didn't care to dwell on it either. She also wasn't going to dwell on why Alton's dad didn't want to be a part of his life. He didn't pay child support, he didn't come to see him, and he didn't even call to check on him. But that was kay because she was taking excellent care of him on her own. She was in a better place mentally and at the end of the day, everything was going to fall into place where it's supposed and when it's supposed to. She had made the choice. She was no longer going to deal with foul people no matter if they were lovers, friends, or even family. She was done being a part of these pretenders' games....